T0155956

Lecture Notes in Computer Science 14412

Founding Editors

Gerhard Goos
Juris Hartmanis

Editorial Board Members

The series Lecture Notes in Computer Science (LNCS), including its subseries Lecture Notes in Artificial Intelligence (LNAI) and Lecture Notes in Bioinformatics (LNBI), has established itself as a medium for the publication of new developments in computer science and information technology research, teaching, and education.

LNCS enjoys close cooperation with the computer science R & D community, the series counts many renowned academics among its volume editors and paper authors, and collaborates with prestigious societies. Its mission is to serve this international community by providing an invaluable service, mainly focused on the publication of conference and workshop proceedings and postproceedings. LNCS commenced publication in 1973.

Francesco Regazzoni · Bodhisatwa Mazumdar ·
Sri Parameswaran

Editors

Security, Privacy, and Applied Cryptography Engineering

13th International Conference, SPACE 2023
Roorkee, India, December 14–17, 2023
Proceedings

 Springer

Editors
Francesco Regazzoni
University of Amsterdam
Amsterdam, The Netherlands

Bodhisatwa Mazumdar
Indian Institute of Technology Indore
Indore, India

Sri Parameswaran
The University of Sydney
Camperdown, NSW, Australia

ISSN 0302-9743   ISSN 1611-3349 (electronic)
Lecture Notes in Computer Science
ISBN 978-3-031-51582-8   ISBN 978-3-031-51583-5 (eBook)
https://doi.org/10.1007/978-3-031-51583-5

This Springer imprint is published by the registered company Springer Nature Switzerland AG
The registered company address is: Gewerbestrasse 11, 6330 Cham, Switzerland

Paper in this product is recyclable.

Preface

The 13th International Conference on Security, Privacy, and Applied Cryptographic Engineering (SPACE 2023), was held during December 14–17, 2023 at Indian Institute of Technology Roorkee, India. This annual event is devoted to various aspects of security, privacy, applied cryptography, and cryptographic engineering. This is a challenging field, requiring expertise from diverse domains, ranging from mathematics and computer science to circuit design.

This year we received 45 submissions from authors in many different countries, mainly from Asia and Europe. The submissions were evaluated based on their significance, novelty, technical quality, and relevance to the SPACE conference. The submissions were each reviewed in a double-blind mode by at least two members of the Program Committee, which consisted of 41 members from all over the world. After an extensive review process, 14 papers were accepted for presentation at the conference, leading to an acceptance rate of 31%.

The program also included four keynote talks and tutorial sessions on various aspects of applied cryptology, security, and privacy delivered by world-renowned researchers: Elena Dubrova, Arpita Patra, Divya Ravi, Subhadeep Banik, Benedikt Gierlichs, and Mainack Mondal. We sincerely thank the invited speakers for accepting our invitations in spite of their busy schedules. In addition, a workshop on post-quantum cryptography was conducted by Debdeep Mukhopadhyay and team from IIT Kharagpur, and Benedikt Gierlichs and team from KU Leuven. Furthermore, a banquet talk at SPACE 2023 was delivered by Siddharth Garg, Institute Associate Professor of ECE at NYU Tandon, where he leads the EnSuRe Research group.

As in previous editions, SPACE 2023 was organized in cooperation with the Indian Institute of Technology Roorkee. We are grateful to general chairs Sugata Gangopadhyay and Debdeep Mukhopadhyay for their willingness to host it physically at IIT Roorkee. There is a long list of volunteers who invested their time and energy to put together the conference. We are grateful to all the members of the Program Committee and their sub-reviewers for all their hard work in the evaluation of the submitted papers. We thank our publisher Springer for agreeing to continue to publish the SPACE proceedings as a volume in the Lecture Notes in Computer Science (LNCS) series. We are grateful to the local Organizing Committee who invested a lot of time and effort in order for the conference to run smoothly. Last, but not least, our sincere thanks go to all the authors who submitted papers to SPACE 2023 and everyone who participated (either in person or virtually).

December 2023

Francesco Regazzoni
Bodhisatwa Mazumdar
Sri Parameswaran

Organization

Program Committee

Subidh Ali	Indian Institute of Technology Bhilai, India
N. Nalla Anandakumar	Continental Automotive, Singapore
Utsav Banerjee	Indian Institute of Science, India
Subhadeep Banik	University of Lugano, Switzerland
Debapriya Basu Roy	IIT Kanpur, India
Jakub Breier	Silicon Austria Labs, Austria
Claude Carlet	University of Paris 8, France
Rajat Subhra Chakraborty	IIT Kharagpur, India
Urbi Chatterjee	IIT Kanpur, India
Anupam Chattopadhyay	Nanyang Technological University, Singapore
Lukasz Chmielewski	Masaryk University, Czechia
Diego F. Aranha	Aarhus University, Denmark
Sugata Gangopadhyay	Indian Institute of Technology Roorkee, India
Maël Gay	University of Stuttgart, Germany
Dirmanto Jap	Nanyang Technological University, Singapore
Jayaprakash Kar	LNM Institute of Information Technology, India
Kerstin Lemke-Rust	Bonn-Rhein-Sieg University of Applied Sciences, Germany
Bodhisatwa Mazumdar	Indian Institute of Technology Indore, India
Silvia Mella	Radboud University, The Netherlands
Marine Minier	CITI INSA-Lyon, France
Mainack Mondal	Indian Institute of Technology, Kharagpur, India
Debdeep Mukhopadhyay	IIT Kharagpur, India
Ruben Niederhagen	Academia Sinica, Taiwan, and University of Southern Denmark, Denmark
Kostas Papagiannopoulos	Radboud University, The Netherlands
Sri Parameswaran	University of Sydney, Australia
Sikhar Patranabis	IBM Research India, India
Guilherme Perin	TU Delft, The Netherlands
Md Masoom Rabbani	KU Leuven, Belgium
Chester Rebeiro	Indian Institute of Technology Madras, India
Francesco Regazzoni	University of Amsterdam, The Netherlands and Università della Svizzera italiana, Switzerland
Ulrich Rührmair	Ruhr University Bochum, Germany
Reihaneh Safavi-Naini	University of Calgary, Canada

Dhiman Saha	de.ci.phe.red Lab, Indian Institute of Technology Bhilai, India
Kazuo Sakiyama	University of Electro-Communications, Japan
Somitra Sanadhya	IIT Jodhpur, India
Vishal Saraswat	Bosch Global Software Technologies, India
Peter Schwabe	Radboud University, The Netherlands
Sujoy Sinha Roy	IIT Kharagpur, India
Marc Stöttinger	RheinMain University of Applied Science, Germany
Bohan Yang	Tsinghua University, China
Amr Youssef	Concordia University, Canada
Nusa Zidaric	Leiden University, The Netherlands

Additional Reviewers

Aikata, Aikata	Lahr, Norman
Badola, Ritwik	Mandal, Suraj
Chen, Xiangren	Petri, Richard
Das, Bijoy	Picek, Stjepan
Das, Reetwik	Raya, Ali
Hünseler, Marco	Zhang, Tao
Kumar, Vikas	Zhao, Cankun

Contents

Results on the Key Space of Group-Ring NTRU: The Case of the Dihedral Group

Ali Raya[1]($\boxtimes$)(iD), Vikas Kumar[2](iD), Sugata Gangopadhyay[1],
and Aditi Kar Gangopadhyay[2]

[1] Department of Computer Science and Engineering, IITR, Roorkee, Uttarakhand,
India
{ali_r,sugata.gangopadhyay}@cs.iitr.ac.in
[2] Department of Mathematics, IITR, Roorkee, Uttarakhand, India
{v_kumar,aditi.gangopadhyay}@ma.iitr.ac.in

Abstract. NTRU-like schemes are among the most studied lattice-based cryptosystems. Since the first scheme was introduced, many variants of NTRU have been developed in the literature. These variants involve a high degree of freedom in designing the cryptosystem aspects, from sampling the polynomials (representing the private key) to the underlying ring used to build the structure. As a generalization of NTRU, Group-ring NTRU describes how to create different variants of NTRU by employing other groups. While most designs in literature are built over a commutative group-ring, a non-commutative group can also be used. Some groups can result in more efficient implementations or better resistance against some attacks. However, introducing new groups triggers fundamental questions related to the key space, encryption, decryption failures, and correctness of the new scheme. This paper uses the non-commutative dihedral group to explore the key space for a group-ring NTRU. Our work investigates whether elements sampled according to specific properties in the reference NTRU implementations can still be used as a key space in the case of the dihedral group. We show that the key space is suitable for building a non-commutative group-ring NTRU based on the dihedral group. Experimental results are provided for polynomials with different properties and compared to the results of reference implementations of NTRU over well-defined parameter sets.

Keywords: Post-quantum cryptography · NTRU · Group-ring
NTRU · Dihedral group

1 Introduction

Many candidates have been proposed as post-quantum schemes to secure information in the quantum era. The introduced schemes are defined over mathematical problems that are believed to be hard to solve by a quantum or classical machine. Lattice-based cryptography is one of the promising families in building

F. Regazzoni et al. (Eds.): SPACE 2023, LNCS 14412, pp. 1–19, 2024.
https://doi.org/10.1007/978-3-031-51583-5_1

quantum-secure cryptosystems. Most National Institute of Standards and Technology (NIST) competition submissions belong to this family [2,3,8,18]. NTRU candidate is a lattice-based scheme that has undergone a long history of cryptanalysis. Although NIST has not selected NTRU for standardization, NTRU has been marked as an alternate for standardization in case the intellectual property (IP) of Kyber, another lattice-based candidate, is not resolved [1]. In 1996, Hoffstein, Pipher, and Silverman introduced the first variant of NTRU [12] as a public key cryptosystem based on a ring of convolutional polynomials.

Since that time, many versions of NTRU have been developed. The security of these systems relies on the hardness of factoring a given polynomial in the ring (representing the public key) into a quotient of two polynomials (representing the private key). Recovering the key of NTRU-based systems can be reduced to solving some problems in a special sort of lattice (NTRU-lattice), and in this regard, NTRU is related to lattice-based cryptography.

The polynomials representing the private key f, g are sampled with certain properties (usually with small coefficients). Reviewing the literature, we can see that the private polynomials have been sampled uniformly in different ways, from binary polynomials [13] to ternary polynomials [9] with a certain number of non-zero coefficients. Other works like NTRU-HPS [4] samples f to be any ternary polynomial, while NTRU-HRSS [4] needs f to be a polynomial that follows the *"non-negative correlation"* property. Other implementations based on NTRU like BLISS [7] have sampled the private key from a set of polynomials with certain number of coefficients in $\{+1, -1\}$, other coefficients in $\{+2, -2\}$ and the remaining coefficients in $\{0\}$, many more variants [10,22] have also sampled the key from a space different from binary or ternary polynomials to increase the entropy of the key and therefore provide better resistance against some attacks. The majority of NTRU-like schemes in literature and NIST's competition are based on commutative rings of polynomials like $\mathcal{R} = \mathbb{Z}[x]/(x^N - 1)$ or $\mathcal{R} = \mathbb{Z}[x]/(x^{2^n} + 1)$. However, some other NTRU-like schemes have been proposed by replacing or modifying the structure of $\mathcal{R}$, which may result even in non-commutative rings. The new rings can empower faster computations and result in smaller keys [15] or achieve more resistance against some lattice attacks [19,23]. Yasuda et al. [24] provided a general structure to represent NTRU-like schemes called Group-Ring NTRU. Using the group-ring $\mathbb{Z}\mathcal{G}$, we can build an NTRU-like scheme for different finite groups $\mathcal{G}$. The standard NTRU built over the commutative rings of polynomials can be thought of as a group-ring NTRU based on the cyclic group of order N. Similarly, different instantiations of NTRU can be built by adapting other groups. This work looks at the group-ring NTRU based on the dihedral group. Building the dihedral group-ring NTRU raises several questions related to the adaptions needed to build the cryptosystem compared to reference implementations. The first natural question is whether the key space used in the existing schemes can still be used in the group-ring scheme based on the dihedral group. This paper explores this problem by providing experimental results on the key space of dihedral group-ring NTRU. The experiment tries to figure out whether the polynomials sampled as private keys in the cyclic group-ring

NTRU are also invertible in the new setting of the dihedral group implementation (and, therefore, can serve as keys). Different polynomials sampled with different properties are checked and compared to the reference implementations of NTRU.

2 Motivation

Noncommutative group algebra can be another direction to provide better security against attacks on lattice-based cryptosystems. When Coppersmith and Shamir established their famous lattice attack against NTRU [6], they highlighted the importance of considering a noncommutative structure to build future variants of NTRU. Furthermore, J. Kim and C. Lee [17] recently proposed a polynomial time algorithm to break NTRU with multiple keys that break NTRU learning problem [21, 4.4.4] and not the original problem of NTRU. A refined analysis of their algorithm shows that the entire assumption worked due to the underlying commutative group-ring of the standard NTRU.

Introducing a noncommutative structure usually comes with high costs related to the practical implementation of a cryptosystem. The dihedral group, as a noncommutative group, is closely related by definition to the cyclic group and, therefore, can easily inherit many of the implementations and tricks that have been constructed through the lengthy process of optimization and cryptanalysis of the commutative schemes based on the cyclic group. Naturally, one attempt has been considered to build a variant of NTRU based on the dihedral group [23] that has been broken soon by [5]. Group-Ring NTRU (GR-NTRU) is a different framework that enables building a noncommutative NTRU, which is not vulnerable to the attack introduced in [5]. Our work considers GR-NTRU based on the dihedral group and focuses on checking whether this variant can be useful to build a noncommutative variant of NTRU by exploring the key space of the elements sampled similarly to those used in standard and celebrated variants of commutative NTRU based on the cyclic group.

3 Organization of Our Paper

Section 4 describes the notations used throughout this paper. Section 5 provides the preliminaries of group-rings. Section 6 describes general steps to build an NTRU-like cryptosystem and sketches the properties of the key elements for some of the prominent NTRU-based schemes in the literature. Section 7 introduces the group-ring NTRU and describes the matrix representation of elements in group-rings, highlighting how this representation can be used to check the invertibility (and therefore determine key space). Section 8 gives the experimental results by mentioning the sampling procedures designed to sample elements from the space and then showing the results compared to the well-defined parameter sets of the prominent NTRU schemes. Finally, discussions and conclusions are drawn.

4   Notations

- For a positive integer n, $\mathbb{Z}_n = \{0, 1, \ldots, n-1\}$ is the ring of integers modulo n.
- For $x \in \mathbb{Z}_n$, $-x$ denotes the additive inverse of x modulo n given by $n - x$.
- $M_n(R)$ is the ring of $n \times n$ matrices with entries from the ring R.
- Symbol $\star$ denotes the multiplication between two elements of the underlying structure.
- $\#A$ denotes the cardinality of set A.
- $\lfloor x \rfloor$ denotes the floor function that takes a real number x to the greatest integer less than or equal to x, and $\lceil x \rceil$ denotes the ceiling function that maps x to the least integer greater than or equal to x.
- $a \leftarrow_\$ A$ means element a is sampled uniformly at random from the set A.
- A circulant matrix is a square matrix whose rows have the same elements, and each row vector is rotated one position with respect to the previous row. If rotation happens toward the right, we call the matrix *right circulant*; otherwise, we call it *left circulant*.

5   Group-Rings

Let R be a ring and $\mathcal{G}$ be a group with identity element e. Consider the set of formal sums

$$RG = \left\{ \sum_{g \in \mathcal{G}} a_g[g] : a_g \in R, a_g = 0 \text{ for all except for finitely many } g \in \mathcal{G} \right\}. \quad (1)$$

Consider two elements $\alpha = \sum_{g \in \mathcal{G}} a_g[g]$ and $\beta = \sum_{g \in \mathcal{G}} b_g[g]$ in RG. We have, $\alpha = \beta$ if and only if $a_g = b_g$ for all $g \in \mathcal{G}$.

Define the sum of α and β as:

$$\alpha + \beta = \sum_{g \in \mathcal{G}} a_g[g] + \sum_{g \in \mathcal{G}} b_g[g] = \sum_{g \in \mathcal{G}} (a_g + b_g)[g] \quad (2)$$

The product is defined as the convolutional product:

$$\alpha \star \beta = \sum_{g \in \mathcal{G}} a_g[g] \star \sum_{g \in \mathcal{G}} b_g[g] = \sum_{g \in \mathcal{G}} c_g[g] \quad (3)$$

where

$$c_g = \sum_{hk=g} a_h b_k \quad (4)$$

Definition 1. *([20, Chapter 3]) The set RG forms a ring with respect to the operations defined in (2) and (3), and we say that RG is the group-ring of $\mathcal{G}$ over R.*

If R has unity 1_R, then $R\mathcal{G}$ is a ring with unity $1_{R\mathcal{G}} = \sum_{g \in \mathcal{G}} a_g[g]$, where $a_e = 1_R$ and $a_g = 0$ for $g \neq e$. We can make $R\mathcal{G}$ an R-module by defining the scalar product of elements of $R\mathcal{G}$ with elements $\lambda \in R$ as follows:

$$\lambda \alpha = \lambda \left(\sum_{g \in \mathcal{G}} a_g[g] \right) = \sum_{g \in \mathcal{G}} (\lambda a_g)[g] \tag{5}$$

Moreover, if R is commutative, then $R\mathcal{G}$ is an R-algebra.

6 NTRU

The initial NTRU scheme is framed over the factor ring of a polynomial ring. Let us give a simple description of the NTRU cryptosystem [11].

6.1 Parameters Selection

Let N, p, q, d be positive integers with N, p prime, $p \ll q$, $\gcd(N, q) = \gcd(p, q) = 1$, and $q > (6d + 1)p$. Let $\mathcal{R} = \mathbb{Z}[x]/(x^N - 1)$, $\mathcal{R}_q = \mathbb{Z}_q[x]/(x^N - 1)$, and $\mathcal{R}_p = \mathbb{Z}_p[x]/(x^N - 1)$.

For positive integers d_1, d_2,

$$\mathcal{T}(d_1, d_2) = \left\{ f \in \mathcal{R} \,\middle|\, \begin{array}{l} f \text{ has } d_1 \text{ coefficients equal to 1} \\ f \text{ has } d_2 \text{ coefficients equal to -1} \\ \text{rest coefficients are 0} \end{array} \right\}$$

We call polynomials from $\mathcal{T}(d_1, d_2)$ to be ternary polynomials. Suppose $f(x) \in \mathcal{R}_q$, then the centered lift of $f(x)$ is the unique polynomial $f'(x) \in \mathcal{R}$ whose coefficients are in the interval $\left(-\frac{q}{2}, \frac{q}{2} \right]$ and $f'(x) \pmod{q} = f(x)$.

Message space consists of elements from $\mathcal{R}$ whose coefficients are between $-\frac{p}{2}$ and $\frac{p}{2}$. In other words, a message is an element in $\mathcal{R}$ that is the centered lift of some element in $\mathcal{R}_p$.

6.2 Key Generation

(i) Choose $f \in \mathcal{T}(d + 1, d)$ such that there exist $f_q \in \mathcal{R}_q$, $f_p \in \mathcal{R}_p$ satisfying $f \star f_q \equiv 1 \pmod{q}$ and $f \star f_p \equiv 1 \pmod{p}$.
(ii) Choose another element $g \in \mathcal{T}(d, d)$.
(iii) construct $h \in \mathcal{R}_q$ such that $f \star h \equiv g \pmod{q}$.
(iv) declare h, p, q to be public key.
(v) f and f_p are private keys.

6.3 Encryption

To encrypt a message m, we first randomly choose $\phi \in \mathcal{T}(d, d)$. Then, the ciphertext is computed as follows:

$$c \equiv ph \star \phi + m \pmod{q}.$$

6.4 Decryption

First, compute $a \equiv f \star c \pmod{q}$. Then, choose the coefficients of a in the interval $\left(-\frac{q}{2}, \frac{q}{2}\right]$. Now, m can be recovered by computing $f_p \star a \pmod{p}$ and centerlifting it.

6.5 Correctness

We have $a \equiv pg \star \phi + f \star m \pmod{q}$. Since f, g, and ϕ are ternary and coefficients of m lie between $-\frac{p}{2}$ to $\frac{p}{2}$. Therefore, the largest coefficient of $g \star \phi$ can be $2d$, and the largest coefficient of $f \star m$ can be $(2d + 1)\frac{p}{2}$. Consequently, the largest coefficient of $pg \star \phi + f \star m$ is at most $(6d+1)\frac{p}{2}$. Thus, if $q > (6d+1)p$, computing $a \equiv f \star c \pmod{q}$ and then centerlifting it gives exactly the element $pg \star \phi + f \star m$. Now, we can multiply this element with f_p and reduce coefficients modulo p to recover an element in $\mathcal{R}_p$ whose centered lift gives us the message m.

6.6 Prominent NTRU-Based Cryptosystems

The key generation of NTRU-like cryptosystems involves sampling polynomials with specific properties and finding the inverse of some of these polynomials in order to calculate and publish the public key.

In Sect. 6, we have provided the specification for one initial and fundamental variant of NTRU. We can see that the key generation in the initial NTRU is probabilistic, whose success depends on the invertibility of f, where f is a polynomial of degree at most $N - 1$. So, to make the process deterministic, various versions of NTRU are built over the same framework with few modifications to the key generation process. However, the common step in the key generation of all these schemes is to generate polynomials uniformly at random in the ring $\mathcal{R}$ with some restrictions on coefficients and check their invertibility over different quotient rings. This section briefly presents the structure of the polynomials used in different schemes, whose invertibility plays a major role in the key generation.

(i) We have already seen that the NTRU system described in Sect. 6 samples a polynomial $f \in \mathcal{T}(d + 1, d)$: ternary polynomial with $d + 1$ coefficients equal $+1$, d coefficients equal -1 and other coefficients equal 0, we refer to this property as (**P1**). The space size with property (P1) is $\#\mathcal{T}(d+1, d) = \binom{N}{d}\binom{N-d}{d+1}$.

(ii) **NTRU-HPS** [4] involves inverting a polynomial $f \in \mathcal{T}$: any randomly sampled ternary polynomial, we refer to this property as (**P2**). The space size with property (P2) is $\#\mathcal{T} = 3^N$.

(iii) **NTRU-HRSS** [4] uses a polynomial $f \in \mathcal{T}_+$: ternary polynomial that satisfies the non-negative correlation property. A ternary polynomial $f = \sum_i f_i x^i$ has the non-negative correlation property if $\sum_i f_i f_{i+1} \geq 0$. We refer to this property as (**P3**). Since flipping the sign of even indexed coefficients of a non-negatively correlated polynomial gives a non-positively related polynomial. Therefore, the space size with property (P3) is $\#\mathcal{T}_+ \approx \frac{3^N}{2}$.

(iv) **BLISS** [7] given two real values called densities δ_1 and $\delta_2 \in [0, 1)$, the polynomial f is sampled from $\mathcal{P}(w_1, w_2)$: polynomial with w_1 coefficients in $\{+1, -1\}$, w_2 coefficients in $\{+2, -2\}$, and all other coefficients to be 0, where $w_1 = \lceil \delta_1 N \rceil$ and $w_2 = \lceil \delta_2 N \rceil$. We refer to this property as **(P4)**. The space size with property (P4) is $\#\mathcal{P}(w_1, w_2) = \binom{N}{w_1}\binom{N-w_1}{w_2}2^{w_1+w_2}$.

(v) **NTRUEncrypt** [10] deals with inverting a polynomial $f = 1 + 3F$ where $F \in \mathcal{P}_N(d_1, d_2, d_3) = \{\mathcal{A}_1 \star \mathcal{A}_2 + \mathcal{A}_3 : \mathcal{A}_i \in \mathcal{T}(d_i, d_i)\}$. We refer to this property as **(P5)**. The space size with property (P5) is $\#\mathcal{P}_N(d_1, d_2, d_3) = \binom{N}{d_1}\binom{N-d_1}{d_1}\binom{N}{d_2}\binom{N-d_2}{d_2}\binom{N}{d_3}\binom{N-d_3}{d_3}$.

7 Group-Ring NTRU

It is straightforward to observe that the NTRU scheme in Sect. 6 can be reformulated over the group-ring:

$$\mathcal{R}_{(q, C_N)} = \mathbb{Z}_q C_N \left(\cong \mathbb{Z}_q[x]/(x^N - 1) \right) \tag{6}$$

where C_N is a cyclic group of order N.

In [24], following the same idea, Yasuda et al. have proposed variants of NTRU by replacing the group C_N with other groups $\mathcal{G}$ and working over the group-ring $\mathcal{R}_{(q, \mathcal{G})} = \mathbb{Z}_q \mathcal{G}$. They call this new version of NTRU Group-ring NTRU. Group-ring NTRU can form a general framework to build different variants of NTRU-like systems where parameter selection, key generation, encryption, and decryption are almost similar to the original NTRU except that the operations are now performed over the Group-ring $\mathcal{R}_{(q, \mathcal{G})}$ instead of $\mathcal{R}_{(q, C_N)}$.

Our work will focus on the group-ring NTRU built over the group-ring of the dihedral group D_N, defined in 10, over $\mathbb{Z}_q$:

$$\mathcal{R}_{(q, D_N)} = \mathbb{Z}_q D_N \left(\cong \frac{\mathbb{Z}_q[x, y]}{\langle x^N - 1, y^2 - 1, yx - x^{N-1}y \rangle} \right) \tag{7}$$

Considering the technical details of implementing group-ring NTRU, we need to figure out how to find inverses of elements in the new group-ring. These elements play an essential role in generating the key in the NTRU-like systems. In the case of reference implementations over $\mathbb{Z}_q C_N$, there are fast algorithms in literature to find the inverses of elements [16]. However, for group-ring $\mathbb{Z}_q D_N$, to the best of our knowledge, no algorithm can find the inverse efficiently. For this purpose, we will rely on the method discussed in the following subsection that describes the matrix representation of elements in group-rings and how that can be used to find inverses, especially in the case of the dihedral group.

7.1 Matrix Representation of Group-Ring Elements

In [14], T. Hurley establishes an isomorphism between a group-ring $R\mathcal{G}$ and a certain subring of $n \times n$ matrices over R. This relation is of immense use in determining the invertibility of group-ring elements by checking the invertibility of matrices, which is a well-studied concept.

For a finite group $\mathcal{G} = \{g_1, g_2, \ldots, g_n\}$, define the matrix of group as

$$
\mathcal{M}_{\mathcal{G}} = \begin{pmatrix}
g_1^{-1}g_1 & g_1^{-1}g_2 & \cdots\cdots & g_1^{-1}g_n \\
g_2^{-1}g_1 & g_2^{-1}g_2 & \cdots\cdots & g_2^{-1}g_n \\
\vdots & \vdots & \ddots & \vdots \\
g_n^{-1}g_1 & g_n^{-1}g_2 & \cdots\cdots & g_n^{-1}g_n
\end{pmatrix}
\tag{8}
$$

We now construct the $R\mathcal{G}$-matrix of an element $\alpha = (\alpha_{g_1}, \alpha_{g_2}, \ldots, \alpha_{g_n}) \in R\mathcal{G}$ as follows:

$$
\mathcal{M}_{R\mathcal{G}}(\alpha) = \begin{pmatrix}
\alpha_{g_1^{-1}g_1} & \alpha_{g_1^{-1}g_2} & \cdots\cdots & \alpha_{g_1^{-1}g_n} \\
\alpha_{g_2^{-1}y_1} & \alpha_{g_2^{-1}g_2} & \cdots\cdots & \alpha_{g_2^{-1}g_n} \\
\vdots & \vdots & \ddots & \vdots \\
\alpha_{g_n^{-1}g_1} & \alpha_{g_n^{-1}g_2} & \cdots\cdots & \alpha_{g_n^{-1}g_n}
\end{pmatrix}
\tag{9}
$$

The set $\mathcal{M}_{R\mathcal{G}} = \{\mathcal{M}_{R\mathcal{G}}(\alpha) : \alpha \in R\mathcal{G}\}$ is the subring of the ring of $n \times n$ matrices over R, denoted by $\mathcal{M}_n(R)$. We will say a matrix $A \in \mathcal{M}_n(R)$ is an $R\mathcal{G}$-matrix if there is an $\alpha \in R\mathcal{G}$ such that $A = \mathcal{M}_{R\mathcal{G}}(\alpha)$.

Theorem 1. ([14, Theorem 1]) The mapping $\tau : R\mathcal{G} \to \mathcal{M}_{R\mathcal{G}} \subset \mathcal{M}_n(R)$ defined as $\tau(\alpha) = \mathcal{M}_{R\mathcal{G}}(\alpha)$ is a bijective ring homomorphism, i.e., $\tau(\alpha + \beta) = \tau(\alpha) + \tau(\beta)$, and $\tau(\alpha \star \beta) = \tau(\alpha) \cdot \tau(\beta) = \mathcal{M}_{R\mathcal{G}}(\alpha) \cdot \mathcal{M}_{R\mathcal{G}}(\beta)$, where $\cdot$ denote the usual matrix multiplication. Furthermore, τ is a module R-homomorphism, i.e., $\tau(\lambda\alpha) = \lambda\tau(\alpha) = \lambda\mathcal{M}_{R\mathcal{G}}(\alpha)$, for $\lambda \in R$.

Theorem 2. ([14, Theorem 2]) Let R be a ring with unity and $\mathcal{G}$ be a finite group. Then, $\alpha \in R\mathcal{G}$ is unit if and only if $\mathcal{M}_{R\mathcal{G}}(\alpha)$ is invertible in $\mathcal{M}_n(R)$. In that case, inverse of $\mathcal{M}_{R\mathcal{G}}(\alpha)$ is also an $R\mathcal{G}$-matrix.

Corollary 1. ([14, corollary 2]) When R is a commutative ring with unity, α is a unit in $R\mathcal{G}$ if and only if $\det(\tau(\alpha))$ is a unit in R. In case when R is a field, then α is a unit if and only if $\det(\tau(\alpha)) \neq 0$.

7.2   The Case of the Dihedral Group

As discussed above, checking the invertibility of an element in a group-ring based on a finite group of order N is equivalent to checking the invertibility of an $N \times N$ matrix over the underlying ring. Also, the inverse of this matrix gives the inverse of the corresponding element. However, in the case of the dihedral group, there is a faster way to check the invertibility of elements in $\mathbb{Z}_q D_N$. It is important to point out that the following method helps to check the invertibility of elements in $\mathbb{Z}_q D_N$ for all values of q but fails to give the inverse when q is even. As far as the scope of this paper is concerned, we are interested in investigating the size of the key space for the group-ring NTRU based on $\mathcal{R}_{(q,D_N)}$, which involves just checking the invertibility of elements in the concerned group-ring. Thus, the following fast method for checking the invertibility is of great help to us.

The dihedral group D_N of order $2N$ is given by

$$D_N = \langle r, s : r^N = s^2 = 1, rs = sr^{-1} \rangle, \tag{10}$$

i.e., $D_N = \{1, r, \ldots, r^{N-1}, s, \ldots, sr^{N-1}\}$. It can be easily checked that the matrix of D_N and consequently the $R\mathcal{G}$-matrix of any element $\alpha \in RD_N$ is of the form $\mathcal{M}_{RD_N}(\alpha) = \begin{pmatrix} F & G \\ G & F \end{pmatrix}$, where F is a circulant matrix and G is Hankel-type or reverse circulant matrix, both of order N ([14, section 3.3]).

Let $\mathcal{I} = \begin{pmatrix} I_N & I_N \\ I_N & -I_N \end{pmatrix}$ where I_N is an $N \times N$ identity matrix over the ring R. For a ring R with characteristic, not 2, $\mathcal{I}$ is invertible over R or over the field of quotients of R. Conjugating $\mathcal{M}_{RD_N}(\alpha)$ by $\mathcal{I}$, we get

$$\mathcal{I} \begin{pmatrix} F & G \\ G & F \end{pmatrix} \mathcal{I}^{-1} = \begin{pmatrix} F+G & 0_N \\ 0_N & F-G \end{pmatrix} \tag{11}$$

Here, the matrix $\mathcal{I}$ is independent of F and G. Therefore, if R is a commutative ring with unity, then $\alpha \in R\mathcal{G}$ is a unit if and only if $det(F+G)$ and $det(F-G)$ is a unit in R. Consequently, it gives us a faster way to verify the invertibility of any element from $\mathcal{R}_{(q, D_N)}$ by just checking the invertibility of two $N \times N$ matrices instead of checking the invertibility of a $2N \times 2N$ matrix over R.

This method can check invertibility faster. However, for finding the inverse, the faster computations in the group-ring $\mathbb{Z}_q D_N$ can work only for odd values of q. Refer to the Appendix for a detailed discussion.

8   Experimental Results

As we have seen in Sect. 6.6, in the case of working in the quotient ring $\mathcal{R}_{(q, C_N)}$, the majority of the schemes do sampling for polynomials and calculate the inverse of a polynomial f with one of the properties (P1) to (P5). To check the validity of designing an NTRU-like cryptosystem over the group-ring $\mathcal{R}_{(q, D_N)}$, the first question to answer is related to the proportion of the invertible elements which can serve as a key space for the new cryptosystem. For reference, we compare the proportion of invertible elements in $\mathcal{R}_{(q, D_N)}$ with the standard implementation of NTRU-like cryptosystems built over $\mathcal{R}_{(q, C_N)}$ for equivalent parameter sets.

8.1   Sampling

Since the spaces of polynomials/elements that follow the patterns (P1) to (P5) are extremely large for real-world parameters used to design cryptosystems, we need to write sampling procedures that can do random uniform sampling for elements of the space under check. After sampling enough samples (10,000 in our experiment), we can conclude whether the key space (i.e., the invertible elements) is large enough and uniformly distributed over the whole space of elements under examination. Algorithms 1 to 5 mention the sampling procedures written to run our experiment. The implementation of these routines is inspired by the NIST NTRU submission [4].

Briefly, we will mention the intuition behind each sampling procedure. Algorithm 1 samples a polynomial from $\mathcal{T}(d_1, d_2)$. To sample uniformly at random such polynomials, 30 random bits are allocated to generate each coefficient. Let t be the random value generated from the 30-bits allocated to the corresponding coefficient, then d_1 coefficients are set to be $4 \times t + 1$, d_2 coefficients are set to be $4 \times t + 2$, while other coefficients are set to be $4 \times t$. By sorting the obtained values in ascending order and then calculating the residue modulo 4 for each of the coefficients, we get d_1 coefficients equal 1, d_2 coefficients equal 2, and the remaining coefficients equal 0, distributed at random. Finally, by mapping 2 to $-1 \in \mathbb{Z}_q$, we can obtain a ternary polynomial sampled uniformly at random from $\mathcal{T}(d_1, d_2)$.

Algorithm 2 samples from $\mathcal{T}$ by allocating a random byte to each coefficient and then calculating the value of this byte modulo 3. There are $\frac{86}{256}$ chances of getting 0, $\frac{85}{256}$ of getting 1, and $\frac{85}{256}$ of getting 2. By mapping 2 to $-1 \in \mathbb{Z}_q$, we get a ternary polynomial sampled uniformly from $\mathcal{T}$. Algorithm 3 samples from $\mathcal{P}(w_1, w_2)$ simply by calling Algorithm 1 with $(d_1, d_2) = (w_1, w_2)$ and then uniformly at random mapping 1 to ± 1, and -1 to ± 2. Algorithm 4 samples from $\mathcal{T}_+$ by calling Algorithm 2 and checking the correlation of the obtained polynomial. If the returned polynomial is negatively correlated, we change the sign of the even-indexed coefficients to get a non-negatively correlated polynomial. Finally, Algorithm 5 returns polynomial $f = 1 + 3F; F \in \mathcal{P}_N(d_1, d_2, d_3)$ by calling the Algorithm 1 to sample three polynomials $\mathcal{A}_1 \in \mathcal{T}(d_1, d_2), \mathcal{A}_2 \in \mathcal{T}(d_2, d_2)$, and $\mathcal{A}_3 \in \mathcal{T}(d_3, d_3)$, respectively and calculate $F = \mathcal{A}_1 \star \mathcal{A}_2 + \mathcal{A}_3$.

8.2 Parameter Sets

As seen in Sect. 6.6, there are different variants of NTRU-like cryptosystems. The way of defining these variants determines the selection of the parameter sets. The most-studied variants of NTRU in literature and NIST competition are defined over the quotient ring $\mathcal{R}_{(q,C_N)}$, where the value of N is selected to be the group order that satisfies the security levels defined by NIST, and the value of q is selected to ensure the correctness for decryption.

For running the experiment, we will use the parameter sets of NTRU-HPS [4] to check the uniformity of distribution for the key space when the key is sampled from $\mathcal{T}$ or $\mathcal{T}(d+1, d)$. The recommended parameters of NTRU-HPS achieve the security levels equivalent to key search on a block cipher with 128-,192- and 256- bit key for $p = 3$ and (N, q) equals $(509, 2048), (677, 2048)$ and $(821, 4096)$,

---

Algorithm 1: Sample $f \in \mathcal{T}(d_1, d_2)$

Input: n: number of coefficients

d_1: number of coefficients to set as $+1$

d_2: number of coefficients to set as -1

randombytes$[\lfloor (30 * n + 7)/8 \rfloor]$: randomly generated bytes can be written as a bit string $(r_0, r_1, r_2, \ldots, r_{\ell-1})$

// 30 bits are used to generate each single coefficient

Output: $s[n]$: an array of n coefficients represents an element $f \in \mathcal{T}(d_1, d_2)$

1 set $s = [0, 0, \ldots 0]$

2 **for** $i = 0$ to $(d_1 - 1)$ **do**

3    $\lfloor$ $s[i] = 1 + \sum_{j=0}^{29} 2^{2+j} r_{30i+j}$

4 **for** $i = d_1$ to $(d_2 + d_1 - 1)$ **do**

5    $\lfloor$ $s[i] = 2 + \sum_{j=0}^{29} 2^{2+j} r_{30i+j}$

6 **for** $i = (d_1 + d_2)$ to $n - 1$ **do**

7    $\lfloor$ $s[i] = 0 + \sum_{j=0}^{29} 2^{2+j} r_{30i+j}$

8 sort(s)

   for $i = 0$ to $n - 1$ **do**

9   s[i] = s[i] mod 4

     if *(s[i]==2)* **then**

10      $\lfloor$ s[i] = -1 in $\mathbb{Z}_q$

11 **return** s

Algorithm 2: Sample $f \in \mathcal{T}$

Input: n: number of coefficients

$r[n]$: n randomly generated bytes

Output: $s[n]$: an array of n coefficients represents an element $f \in \mathcal{T}$

1 set $s = [0, 0, \ldots 0]$

2 **for** $i = 0$ to $n - 1$ **do**

3    $s[i] = r[i]$ mod 3

   if *(s[i]==2)* **then**

4      $\lfloor$ s[i] = -1 in $\mathbb{Z}_q$

5 **return** s

---

respectively.[1] For keys sampled from $\mathcal{T}_+$, the parameter set of NTRU-HRSS [4] is used to run the experiment. The recommended parameter set for NTRU-HRSS is defined in $\mathcal{R}_{(q, C_N)}$ with $N = 701, q = 8192$, and $p = 3$ to achieve the

---

[1] The security of the parameter sets of NTRU-HPS have been evaluated according to two models (local and non-local model): according to the local model, the parameters achieve the security levels 1,3 and 5, while according to the non-local model, they achieve lower levels of security.

Algorithm 3: Sample $f \in \mathcal{P}(w_1, w_2)$

Input: n: number of coefficients
  $r[\lfloor(30 * n + 7)/8\rfloor]$: randomly generated bytes
  δ_1, δ_2: secret key densities $\in [0, 1)$
Output: $s[n]$: an array of n coefficients represents an element $f \in \mathcal{P}(w_1, w_2)$

1 $w_1 = \lceil \delta_1 n \rceil$
2 $w_2 = \lceil \delta_2 n \rceil$
3 $s \leftarrow$ Sample $f \in \mathcal{T}(w_1, w_2)$ // call Algorithm 1
4 **for** $i = 0$ to $n - 1$ **do**
5   **if** *(s[i] == 1)* **then**
6         $s[i] \leftarrow_\$ \{+1, -1\}$
7   **else if** *(s[i] == -1)* **then**
8         $s[i] \leftarrow_\$ \{+2, -2\}$

9 **return** s

Algorithm 4: Sample $f \in \mathcal{T}_+$

Input: n: number of coefficients
  $r[n]$: randomly generated bytes
Output: $s[n]$: an array of n coefficients represents an element $f \in \mathcal{T}_+$

1 $s \leftarrow$ Sample $f \in \mathcal{T}$ // call Algorithm 2
2 sum $= \sum_{i=0}^{n-2} s[i] * s[i+1]$
3 sign $\leftarrow 1$
4 **if** *(sum<0)* **then**
5   sign $\leftarrow -1$

6 $i \leftarrow 0$
7 **while** *(i < n)* **do**
8      $s[i] = s[i] * sign$
9   i = i+2

10 **return** s

Algorithm 5: Sample $f = 3F + 1; F \in \mathcal{P}_N(d_1, d_2, d_3)$

Input: n: number of coefficients
  $r[3 * \lfloor(30n + 7)/8\rfloor]$: randomly generated bytes
  $d1, d2, d3$: used to sample three polynomials $\mathcal{A}_1, \mathcal{A}_2, \mathcal{A}_3$ respectively
  where $\mathcal{A}_i \in \mathcal{T}(d_i, d_i)$
  // r can be compiled as $r_1||r_2||r_3$ where $length(r_i) = \lfloor(30n + 7)/8\rfloor$
Output: $s[n]$: an array of n coefficients represents an element $f \in \mathcal{P}_N(d_1, d_2, d_3)$

1 $\mathcal{A}_1 \leftarrow$ Sample $f_1 \in \mathcal{T}(d_1, d_1)$ // call Algorithm 1
2 $\mathcal{A}_2 \leftarrow$ Sample $f_2 \in \mathcal{T}(d_2, d_2)$ // call Algorithm 1
3 $\mathcal{A}_3 \leftarrow$ Sample $f_3 \in \mathcal{T}(d_3, d_3)$ // call Algorithm 1
4 $F = \mathcal{A}_1 \star \mathcal{A}_2 + \mathcal{A}_3$ // sum and convolutional product in the group-ring
5 $s = 1 + 3F$
6 **return** s

---

security level 3 (key search on a block cipher of 192-bit key)[2] For keys sampled from $\mathcal{P}(w_1, w_2)$, the parameter sets of BLISS [7] are used. For BLISS, the parameter sets $(N, q, \delta1, \delta2)$ have been chosen to be $(512, 12289, 0.3, 0)$, $(512, 12289, 0.42, 0.03)$ and $(512, 12289, 0.45, 0.06)$ to match the security levels 128-,160-, and 192-bit respectively.

Finally, to check keys sampled as $f = 1 + 3F$, where $F \in \mathcal{P}_N(d_1, d_2, d_3)$, the parameter sets of NTRUEncrypt [10] are used to run the experiment. The recommended parameters (N, q, d_1, d_2, d_3) for NTRUEncrypt have the values: $(439, 2048, 9, 8, 5)$, $(593, 2048, 10, 10, 8)$, and $(743, 2048, 11, 11, 15)$ for the security levels 128-,192-,256- bit respectively.

Since the order of the dihedral group D_N that achieves a certain level of security is two times the order of the cyclic group C_N, to define a cryptosystem in $\mathcal{R}_{(q', D_N)}$ in a similar way to the scheme defined in $\mathcal{R}_{(q, C_N)}$, we need to double the value of q for correctness (i.e., $q' = 2q$).[3]

8.3   Results and Discussion

For each polynomial with one of the properties (P1) to (P5), we do sampling (10,000 samples) from the corresponding polynomial spaces and check the portion of the invertible elements (key space). The results for the group-ring $\mathcal{R}_{(q', D_N)}$ are reported and compared to the results in the group-ring $\mathcal{R}_{(q, C_N)}$ for reference.

Key Space for Polynomials Sampled from $\mathcal{T}(d + 1, d)$: Table 1 shows the results for the polynomials sampled with $d + 1$ coefficients equal 1, d coefficients equal -1, while the values of remaining coefficients are 0. The value of d equals $q/16 - 1$ in the case of $\mathcal{R}_{(q, C_N)}, \mathcal{R}_{(P, C_N)}$ and $q'/16 - 1$ in the case of $\mathcal{R}_{(p, D_N)}, \mathcal{R}_{(q'=2q, D_N)}$, where $q' = 2q$ for correctness reason. We can notice that all the sampled polynomials are invertible when the underlying group is C_N. However, for D_N, all the sampled polynomials are invertible for $\mathcal{R}_{(q'=2q, D_N)}$, but not for $\mathcal{R}_{(p=3, D_N)}$.

Key Space for Polynomials Sampled from $\mathcal{T}$: Table 2 shows the results for the ternary polynomials sampled randomly where each coefficient can be in $\{-1, 0, 1\}$. We can also notice that the percentage of the invertible elements sampled from $\mathcal{T}$ is smaller for $\mathcal{R}_{(p=3, D_N)}$, while for $\mathcal{R}_{(q'=2q, D_N)}$, the percentage is almost similar to $\mathcal{R}_{(q, C_N)}$.

Key Space for Polynomials Sampled from $\mathcal{T}_+$: Table 3 shows the results for the parameter set of NTRU-HRSS that samples polynomials from $\mathcal{T}_+$ (i.e., achieving the non-negative correlation). We can also notice that the percentage of the invertible elements sampled from $\mathcal{T}_+$ is smaller for the modulus $p = 3$ in

---

[2] The parameter set of NTRU-HRSS matches the security level 3 according to the local model and the level 1 according to the non-local model.

[3] The order of the dihedral group D_N is 2N; therefore, the number of coefficients in the sampled element in $\mathcal{R}_{(q, D_N)}$ will be 2N.

the case $\mathcal{R}_{(p=3,D_N)}$, while for the modulus q', the percentage in $\mathcal{R}_{(q'=2q,D_N)}$ is almost similar to $\mathcal{R}_{(q,C_N)}$.

Key Space for Polynomials Sampled from $\mathcal{P}(w_1, w_2)$: Table 4 highlights the results for polynomials sampled randomly from $\mathcal{P}(w_1, w_2)$ according to the parameter sets of BLISS and compares the percentage of the invertible elements for both dihedral and cyclic group as underlying groups in the group-ring NTRU.

We can see that for the first parameter set, the one that samples polynomials with one-third of the coefficients in $\{+1, -1\}$ and others equal 0, none of the samples were found to be invertible in $\mathcal{R}_{(q',D_N)}$. While for the second and third parameter sets, which increase the number of the coefficients in $\{+1, -1\}$ and add some in $\{+2, -2\}$, the percentage of invertible elements and, therefore, the key space increases significantly.

Key Space for Polynomials Sampled as $f = 1 + 3F; F \in \mathcal{P}_N(d_1, d_2, d_3)$: Finally, Table 5 shows the results for the parameter sets of polynomials sampled according to the way of designing the scheme of NTRUEncrypt [10]. Interestingly, all the sampled elements were found to be invertible in $\mathcal{R}_{(q,C_N)}$ as well as in $\mathcal{R}_{(q'=2q,D_N)}$.

We have to highlight some points from the previous results; the mentioned percentages in Tables 1, 2, 3, 4 and 5 refer to the chance of hitting a key when we pick a random sample from the corresponding space. However, the two spaces in $\mathcal{R}_{(p,C_N)}$ and $\mathcal{R}_{(p,D_N)}$ have different sizes. For instance the entire space size of $\mathcal{T}(d+1,d)$ in $\mathcal{R}_{(p,C_N)}$ for the parameter set NTRU-HPS with $(p, q, N) = (3, 2048, 509)$ is $\#\mathcal{T}(128, 127) = \binom{509}{127}\binom{509-127}{128}$, and the key space approximately has the same size. For the same parameter set in $\mathcal{R}_{(p,D_N)}$, the total space size is $\#\mathcal{T}(256, 255) = \binom{1018}{255}\binom{1018-255}{256}$, which is much more than the corresponding space of $\mathcal{R}_{(p,C_N)}$. However, the key space is almost 76% of the total space, which is still huge. Therefore, the key space of $\mathcal{R}_{(p,D_N)}$ is larger than the key space of $\mathcal{R}_{(p,C_N)}$. However, the chance of hitting a key is lower (remember, according to this design of NTRU, the key needs to be an invertible element in both $\mathcal{R}_{(p,D_N)}$, $\mathcal{R}_{(q,D_N)}$). Similarly, for other spaces of $\mathcal{T}, \mathcal{T}_+$, even though the percentage of key elements in $\mathcal{R}_{(p,D_N)}$ is smaller, the absolute size of the key space is larger, i.e., a larger number of invertible elements with lower probability of selecting one of them, compared to $\mathcal{R}_{(p,C_N)}$.

The case is different for the parameter sets of BLISS and NTRUEncrypt. While the first parameter set of BLISS is not suitable for $\mathcal{R}_{(q',D_N)}$, other parameter sets of (BLISS, NTRUEncrypt) provide higher throughput and higher or equal probability of hitting keys. Figure 1 compares the percentage of invertible elements versus the tested parameter sets.

Table 1. Experimental results for polynomials sampled from $\mathcal{T}(d+1, d)$.

security level	(p, q, N)	% of invertible samples			
		$\mathcal{R}_{(p,C_N)}$	$\mathcal{R}_{(q,C_N)}$	$\mathcal{R}_{(p,D_N)}$	$\mathcal{R}_{(q,D_N)}$
128-bit	(3, 2048, 509)	100	100	76	100
192-bit	(3, 2048, 677)	100	100	66	100
256-bit	(3, 4096, 821)	100	100	61	100

Table 2. Experimental results for polynomials sampled from $\mathcal{T}$.

security level	(p, q, N)	% of invertible samples			
		$\mathcal{R}_{(p,C_N)}$	$\mathcal{R}_{(q,C_N)}$	$\mathcal{R}_{(p,D_N)}$	$\mathcal{R}_{(q,D_N)}$
128-bit	(3, 2048, 509)	67	50	45	53
192-bit	(3, 2048, 677)	67	49	46	52
256-bit	(3, 4096, 821)	66	50	46	50

Table 3. Experimental results for polynomials sampled from $\mathcal{T}_+$.

security level	(p, q, N)	% of invertible samples			
		$\mathcal{R}_{(p,C_N)}$	$\mathcal{R}_{(q,C_N)}$	$\mathcal{R}_{(p,D_N)}$	$\mathcal{R}_{(q,D_N)}$
192-bit	(3, 8192, 701)	66	50	43	52

Table 4. Experimental results for polynomials sampled from $\mathcal{P}(w_1, w_2)$.

security level	$(q, N, \delta_1, \delta_2)$	% of invertible samples	
		$\mathcal{R}_{(q,C_N)}$	$\mathcal{R}_{(q,D_N)}$
128-bit	(12289, 512, 0.3, 0)	83.5	0
160-bit	(12289, 512, 0.42, 0.03)	87.5	99
192-bit	(12289, 512, 0.45, 0.06)	96	98

Table 5. Experimental results for polynomials sampled as $f = 1 + 3F; F \in \mathcal{P}_N(d_1, d_2, d_3)$.

security level	$(q, N, \delta_1, \delta_2)$	% of invertible samples	
		$\mathcal{R}_{(q,C_N)}$	$\mathcal{R}_{(q,D_N)}$
128-bit	(2048, 439, 9, 8, 5)	100	100
192-bit	(2048, 593, 10, 10, 8)	100	100
256-bit	(2048, 743, 11, 11, 15)	100	100

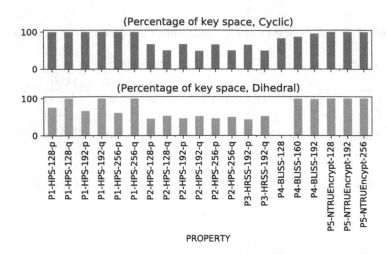

Fig. 1. Percentage of invertible elements (keyspace) vs. parameter sets.

9   Conclusions

Group-ring NTRU, in general, enables the building of different variants of NTRU-like schemes. In this paper, we provide experimental results on the group-ring NTRU based on the dihedral group, $\mathcal{R}_{(q',D_N)}$. We compare these results to the reference implementations of group-ring NTRU based on a cyclic group, $\mathcal{R}_{(q,C_N)}$. We have investigated elements with different properties to see if they can serve as a key space in $\mathcal{R}_{(q',D_N)}$. The results show that the key space is large for all properties (P1) to (P5); therefore, they are suitable for building a group-ring NTRU based on the dihedral group. However, the second and third parameter sets of property (P4) and all the parameter sets of property (P5) seem to be the most promising.

Future work should explore the following:

– Since the matrix inversion method becomes time-consuming for larger dimensions, extending the fast inversion algorithms used in NIST NTRU submission to the new structure in this paper should be considered.
– Designing a full-fledged GR-NTRU over the dihedral group with appropriate parameters.
– Thoroughly estimating the security of the proposed cryptosystem against lattice attacks.

Appendix

Faster Computation of Inverses in $R\mathcal{G} = \mathcal{R}_{(q,D_N)}$ when q is Odd

Let $\alpha \in \mathcal{R}_{(q,D_N)}$ be an unit, where q is odd. Let $\mathcal{M}_{R\mathcal{G}}(\alpha) = \begin{pmatrix} F & G \\ G & F \end{pmatrix}$, and $\mathcal{M}_{R\mathcal{G}}(\alpha^{-1}) = \begin{pmatrix} A & B \\ B & A \end{pmatrix}$, two matrices of dimension $2N \times 2N$. We know that,

$\mathcal{M}_{R\mathcal{G}}(\alpha^{-1}) = \mathcal{M}_{R\mathcal{G}}(\alpha)^{-1}$, i.e., $\begin{pmatrix} A & B \\ B & A \end{pmatrix} = \begin{pmatrix} F & G \\ G & F \end{pmatrix}^{-1}$. Conjugating both sides by

$\mathcal{I} = \begin{pmatrix} I_N & I_N \\ I_N & -I_N \end{pmatrix}$ gives

$$\mathcal{I} \begin{pmatrix} A & B \\ B & A \end{pmatrix} \mathcal{I}^{-1} = \mathcal{I} \begin{pmatrix} F & G \\ G & F \end{pmatrix}^{-1} \mathcal{I}^{-1}$$

$$\begin{pmatrix} A+B & \mathbf{0}_N \\ \mathbf{0}_N & A-B \end{pmatrix} = \left(\mathcal{I} \begin{pmatrix} F & G \\ G & F \end{pmatrix} \mathcal{I}^{-1} \right)^{-1}$$

$$\begin{pmatrix} A+B & \mathbf{0}_N \\ \mathbf{0}_N & A-B \end{pmatrix} = \begin{pmatrix} (F+G)^{-1} & \mathbf{0}_N \\ \mathbf{0}_N & (F-G)^{-1} \end{pmatrix}$$

When q is odd, 2 is a unit in the ring $\mathbb{Z}_q$. Therefore, we get

$$A = \frac{(F+G)^{-1} + (F-G)^{-1}}{2} \text{ and } B = \frac{(F+G)^{-1} - (F-G)^{-1}}{2}$$

Finally, the first row of the matrix $\mathcal{M}_{R\mathcal{G}}(\alpha^{-1})$ is precisely the coefficients of α^{-1}. This method will help in faster computations of inverses in $\mathcal{R}_{(q,D_N)}$ for odd q as we need to invert two $N \times N$ matrices $(F+G), (F-G)$ instead of big matrix of $2N \times 2N$. Figure 2 refers to the time needed to find inverses using the conventional matrix inversion versus the second approach that can find the inverse faster for odd values of q. We can see that the second method gives noticeable better results for larger values of q, N[4].

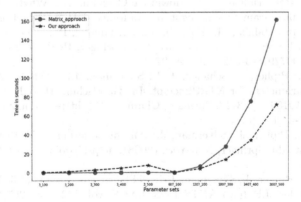

Fig. 2. Matrix approach vs. faster approach of finding inverses for odd values of q.

---

[4] The horizontal axis refers to the tested values of q, N denoted as q _N. We ran the code using Sagemath on Jupyter Notebook on a machine powered by Intel(R) Core(TM) i7-7700 CPU@3.60GHZ, running Windows 10 pro.

References

1. Alagic, G., et al.: Status report on the third round of the NIST post-quantum cryptography standardization process. US Department of Commerce, NIST (2022). https://tsapps.nist.gov/publication/get_pdf.cfm?pub_id=934458
2. Avanzi, R., et al.: Crystals-Kyber algorithm specifications and supporting documentation. NIST PQC Round (2020). https://csrc.nist.gov/Projects/post-quantum-cryptography/post-quantum-cryptography-standardization/round-3-submissions
3. Basso, A., et al.: SABER: Mod-LWR based KEM (round 3 submission). NIST PQC Round (2020). https://csrc.nist.gov/Projects/post-quantum-cryptography/post-quantum-cryptography-standardization/round-3-submissions
4. Chen, C., et al.: NTRU: algorithm specifications and supporting documentation. NIST (2020). https://csrc.nist.gov/Projects/post-quantum-cryptography/post-quantum-cryptography-standardization/round-3-submissions
5. Coppersmith, D.: Attacking non-commutative NTRU. Technical report, IBM research report, April 1997. Report (2006). https://dominoweb.draco.res.ibm.com/d102d0885e971b558525659300727a26.html
6. Coppersmith, D., Shamir, A.: Lattice attacks on NTRU. In: Fumy, W. (ed.) EUROCRYPT 1997. LNCS, vol. 1233, pp. 52–61. Springer, Heidelberg (1997). https://doi.org/10.1007/3-540-69053-0_5
7. Ducas, L., Durmus, A., Lepoint, T., Lyubashevsky, V.: Lattice signatures and bimodal gaussians. In: Canetti, R., Garay, J.A. (eds.) CRYPTO 2013. LNCS, vol. 8042, pp. 40–56. Springer, Heidelberg (2013). https://doi.org/10.1007/978-3-642-40041-4_3
8. Fouque, P.A., et al.: Falcon: fast-fourier lattice-based compact signatures over NTRU. NIST PQC Round (2020). https://csrc.nist.gov/Projects/post-quantum-cryptography/post-quantum-cryptography-standardization/round-3-submissions
9. Hirschhorn, P.S., Hoffstein, J., Howgrave-Graham, N., Whyte, W.: Choosing NTRUEncrypt parameters in light of combined lattice reduction and MITM approaches. In: Abdalla, M., Pointcheval, D., Fouque, P.-A., Vergnaud, D. (eds.) ACNS 2009. LNCS, vol. 5536, pp. 437–455. Springer, Heidelberg (2009). https://doi.org/10.1007/978-3-642-01957-9_27
10. Hoffstein, J., Pipher, J., Schanck, J.M., Silverman, J.H., Whyte, W., Zhang, Z.: Choosing parameters for NTRUEncrypt. In: Handschuh, H. (ed.) CT-RSA 2017. LNCS, vol. 10159, pp. 3–18. Springer, Cham (2017). https://doi.org/10.1007/978-3-319-52153-4_1
11. Hoffstein, J., Pipher, J., Silverman, J.: An Introduction to Mathematical Cryptography, 1st edn. Springer, New York (2008). https://doi.org/10.1007/978-0-387-77993-5
12. Hoffstein, J., Pipher, J., Silverman, J.H.: NTRU: a ring-based public key cryptosystem. In: Buhler, J.P. (ed.) ANTS 1998. LNCS, vol. 1423, pp. 267–288. Springer, Heidelberg (1998). https://doi.org/10.1007/BFb0054868
13. Howgrave-Graham, N., Silverman, J.H., Whyte, W.: Choosing parameter sets for NTRUEncrypt with NAEP and SVES-3. In: Menezes, A. (ed.) CT-RSA 2005. LNCS, vol. 3376, pp. 118–135. Springer, Heidelberg (2005). https://doi.org/10.1007/978-3-540-30574-3_10
14. Hurley, T.: Group rings and rings of matrices. Int. J. Pure Appl. Math. **31**, 319–335 (2006). https://www.researchgate.net/publication/228928727_Group_rings_and_rings_of_matrices

15. Jarvis, K., Nevins, M.: ETRU: NTRU over the Eisenstein integers. Des. Codes Crypt. **74**(1), 219–242 (2015). https://doi.org/10.1007/s10623-013-9850-3
16. Joseph, S.H.: Almost inverses and fast NTRU key creation. NTRU cryptosystems Technical Report (1999). https://ntru.org/f/tr/tr014v1.pdf
17. Kim, J., Lee, C.: A polynomial time algorithm for breaking NTRU encryption with multiple keys. Des. Codes Cryptogr. 1–11 (2023)
18. Lyubashevsky, V., et al.: Crystals-dilithium: algorithm specifications and supporting documentation. NIST PQC Round (2020). https://csrc.nist.gov/Projects/post-quantum-cryptography/post-quantum-cryptography-standardization/round-3-submissions
19. Malekian, E., Zakerolhosseini, A., Mashatan, A.: QTRU: a lattice attack resistant version of NTRU. Cryptology ePrint Archive (2009). https://eprint.iacr.org/2009/386
20. Milies, C., Sehgal, S.: An Introduction to Group Rings (2002). https://doi.org/10.1007/978-94-010-0405-3
21. Peikert, C., et al.: A decade of lattice cryptography. Found. Trends® Theor. Comput. Sci. **10**(4), 283–424 (2016)
22. Stehlé, D., Steinfeld, R.: Making NTRU as secure as worst-case problems over ideal lattices. In: Paterson, K.G. (ed.) EUROCRYPT 2011. LNCS, vol. 6632, pp. 27–47. Springer, Heidelberg (2011). https://doi.org/10.1007/978-3-642-20465-4_4
23. Truman, K.R.: Analysis and extension of non-commutative NTRU, Ph.D. thesis, University of Maryland, College Park (2007)
24. Yasuda, T., Dahan, X., Sakurai, K.: Characterizing NTRU-variants using group ring and evaluating their lattice security. IACR Cryptology ePrint Archive 1170 (2015). https://eprint.iacr.org/2015/1170

Token Open Secure and Post-quantum Updatable Encryption Based on MLWE

Yang Song, Haiying Gao$^{(\boxtimes)}$, Keshuo Sun, and Chao Ma

PLA SSF Information Engineering University, Zhengzhou, China
xdgaohaiying@163.com

Abstract. Updatable encryption (UE) allows a client to outsource ciphertexts to some untrusted server and periodically rotate the encryption key. Recently, a Token Open security model is presented, which is closer to the real attack scenario for UE. The existing post-quantum secure UE schemes are all based on the LWE assumption without engineering implementation. In this paper, we present a new model based on the Token Open security model which reflects the characteristics of UE. Then we construct an updatable encryption scheme based on the MLWE assumption by using the key switching technology and ciphertext masking technology to achieve backward-leak uni-directional key update and uni-directional ciphertext update. We show that the new scheme satisfies our new model. In addition, we present the practical safety analysis of the new scheme by engineering implementation.

Keywords: Updatable Encryption · MLWE assumption · backward-leak uni-directional key update

1 Introduction

1.1 Background

Updatable Encryption. As an emerging network storage technology in the cloud era, cloud storage can make full use of the storage capacity of existing hardware and provide nearly unlimited storage space for users. According to SP800-57 [6] issued by NIST, keys have strict lifetimes and rotating keys regularly is a common requirement in practice. When a user stores encrypted data on a cloud server, the traditional way to rotate the key is to download the old ciphertext, decrypt it with the old key, re-encrypt it with the new key and re-upload the new ciphertext. This way is expensive because it requires lots of computing cost and communication cost of the user. Updatable encryption (UE), first proposed by Boneh et al. [1], provides a better solution for key rotation, in which the period the key is valid is called an epoch. (Denote the index of an epoch with e.) The user uploads the ciphertext encrypted by the UE scheme to the cloud server. If the user needs to update the key, he computes an update token (Δ_{e+1}) via the old key (k_e) and the new key (k_{e+1}) and sends it to the

© The Author(s), under exclusive license to Springer Nature Switzerland AG 2024
F. Regazzoni et al. (Eds.): SPACE 2023, LNCS 14412, pp. 20–47, 2024.
https://doi.org/10.1007/978-3-031-51583-5_2

server. The server uses the update token to update the old ciphertext to the ciphertext encrypted by the new key. Using the UE scheme can greatly reduce the computing cost and communication cost of the user.

Classification of UE Schemes. According to the independence of ciphertext, we categorize UE schemes into two types. One is the ciphertext-dependent scheme. The user needs to pre-store or download the ciphertext or part of the ciphertext from the cloud when generating tokens. The other is the ciphertext-independent scheme. The user does not need ciphertext when generating tokens. This paper focuses on the ciphertext-independent scheme.

According to the randomness of the ciphertext update, we categorize UE schemes into two types. One is the det-update scheme. The ciphertext update algorithm is deterministic so that the same ciphertexts are updated to the same ciphertexts via the token. The other is the rand-update scheme. The ciphertext update algorithm is randomized so that the same ciphertexts are updated to different ciphertexts via the token.

According to the direction of the ciphertext update, we categorize UE schemes into two types. One is the bi-directional ciphertext update scheme. The user can update the ciphertext or downgrade the ciphertext via the token. The other is the uni-directional ciphertext update scheme. The user can update the ciphertext but cannot downgrade the ciphertext via the token.

According to the direction of the key update, we categorize UE schemes into four types. The first is bi-directional key update scheme. The user can derive k_{e+1} (the new key) from k_e (the old key) and Δ_{e+1} (the token), or derive k_e from k_{e+1} and Δ_{e+1}. The second is the forward-leak uni-directional key update scheme (abbreviated as f-uni-directional). The user can only derive k_{e+1} from k_e and Δ_{e+1}. The third is the backward-leak uni-directional key update scheme (abbreviated as b-uni-directional). The user can only derive k_e from k_{e+1} and Δ_{e+1}. The fourth is the no-directional key update scheme. The user cannot derive keys from the token.

1.2   Related Work

In 2013, Boneh et al. [1] first constructed a UE scheme based on a key homomorphic pseudorandom function and a symmetric cryptographic algorithm, named BLMR. Although it is a ciphertext-dependent scheme, its idea guides the design of UE schemes. In 2018, Lehmann and Tackmann [2] constructed a ciphertext-independent scheme based on the ElGamal scheme, named RISE. And they presented two indistinguishable security models, named IND-ENC and IND-UPD. In 2019, Boyd et al. [3] constructed a ciphertext-independent UE scheme based on the DDH assumption, named SHINE, and presented a new indistinguishable security model, named IND-UE.

In 2020, Yao Jiang [4] presented the first post-quantum UE scheme based on the LWE assumption, named LWEUE. She believed that the ideal UE scheme should be no-directional key update and uni-directional ciphertext update. In 2021, Nishimaki [5] firstly constructed a no-directional key update UE scheme based on the indistinguishable obfuscation [11], named UE_{io}. Nishimaki presented a new key update type named backward-leak uni-directional key update setting and constructed the first b-uni-directional key update UE scheme based on the LWE assumption, named RtR. In 2022, Song and Gao [13] presented a new security model, named Token Open security model, which allows the adversary to corrupt all update tokens.

We believe the newly presented security model in [13] is closer to the real attack scenario, because in the practical application of UE, the user and the server should use an open channel to transmit the update token. We improve the study in [13]. In addition, the existing post-quantum UE schemes are all based on the LWE assumption and remain at the theoretical research level. According to the research status and the practical application, we hope to design a ciphertext-independent UE scheme with backward-leak uni-directional key update uni-directional ciphertext update and post-quantum secure property. More importantly, the user and the server can use an open channel to transmit update tokens.

1.3   Our Contribution

Our first work is improving the security model in [13] to the xx-TKOpen-atk security model for UE. By our design, the adversary is allowed to corrupt tokens of all epochs and keys of the past epochs. Then the adversary submits a plaintext and an old ciphertext then obtains a new ciphertext and distinguishes whether the ciphertext is the encryption of the plaintext or the updated ciphertext of the old ciphertext. The new model conforms to the practical application of the UE scheme that the user and the server use an open channel to transmit update tokens.

Our second contribution is proving the relationship between the TKOpen security model and the scheme update setting. We proved if a UE scheme is TKOpen secure, it is a rand-update scheme with b-uni-directional or no-directional key update and uni-directional ciphertext update. And in the TKOpen security model, b-uni-directional key update and no-directional key update are equivalent.

Our third contribution is constructing the first UE scheme based on the MLWE assumption, named MLWEUE. Our update mechanism is a backward-leak uni-directional key update because only the public key part of the key at the next epoch is embedded in the token. Then, we design the ciphertext-masking technique to re-randomize an updated ciphertext. To prove MLWEUE is rand-TKOpen-CPA secure based on the MLWE assumption, we construct the indistinguishable game sequences and embed the MLWE challenge in the challenge epoch of the last game. Therefore, the user and the server can use an open channel to transmit update tokens with post-quantum secure property.

Our fourth work is achieving the practical results of the post-quantum UE scheme firstly. We took the lead in making breakthroughs in the practical application of post-quantum UE scheme. We accomplish the software implementation of MLWEUE by using the NTT technique to speed up the program. MLWEUE can update for 6 times with a decryption error rate of $2^-122.3$ in the ring $R_q = \mathbb{Z}_{64513}[X] / (X^{256} + 1)$. And the strength of MLWE against the prime attack reaches $127/115$ under the classic/quantum model and against the dual attack reaches $126/115$ under the classic/quantum model.

1.4 Organization

In Sect. 2 we introduce preliminaries and syntax. In Sect. 3 we present our new security model TKOpen and prove the relationship between TKOpen security model and scheme update setting. In Sect. 4 we give our new scheme, MLWEUE, including the technique and design ideas behind its construction. In Sect. 5 we prove MLWEUE is rand-TKOpen-CPA secure based on MLWE assumption. In Sect. 6 we present the experimental results of MWLEUE.

2 Preliminaries

2.1 Notations

Polynomial Rings and Vectors. We denote by R the ring $\mathbb{Z}[X] / (X^n + 1)$ and by R_q the ring $\mathbb{Z}_q[X] / (X^n + 1)$, where $n = 2^{n'-1}$ such that $X^n + 1$ is the $2^{n'} - th$ cyclotomic polynomial. Regular font letters denote elements in R or R_q (which includes elements in $\mathbb{Z}$ and $\mathbb{Z}_q$). Bold lower-case letters represent vectors with coefficients in R or R_q. Bold upper-case letters are matrices. For a vector $\mathbf{v}$ (or matrix $\mathbf{A}$), we denote by $\mathbf{v}^T$ (or $\mathbf{A}^T$) its transpose.

Modular Reductions. For an even (resp. odd) positive integer α, we define $r' = r \bmod^{\pm} \alpha$ to be the unique element r' in the range $-\frac{\alpha}{2} < r' \leq \frac{\alpha}{2}$ (resp. $-\frac{\alpha-1}{2} < r' \leq \frac{\alpha-1}{2}$) such that $r' = r \bmod \alpha$. For any positive integer α, we define $r' = r \bmod^{+} \alpha$ to be the unique element r' in the range $0 \leq r' < \alpha$ such that $r' = r \bmod \alpha$. When the exact representation is not important, we simply write $r \bmod \alpha$.

Rounding. For an element $x \in \mathbb{Q}$ we denote by $\langle x \rangle$ rounding of x to the closet integer with ties being rounded up.

Sizes of Elements. For an element $w \in \mathbb{Z}_q$, we write $\|w\|_\infty$ to mean $|w \bmod^{\pm} q|$. For $w = w_0 + w_1 x + ... + w_{n-1} x^{n-1} \in R$, we define $\|w\|_\infty = \max \|w_i\|_\infty$, $\|w\| = \sqrt{\|w_0\|^2 + ... + \|w_{n-1}\|^2}$. For $\mathbf{w} = (w_1, ..., w_k) \in R^k$, we define $\|\mathbf{w}\|_\infty = \max \|w_i\|_\infty$, $\|\mathbf{w}\| = \sqrt{\|w_1\|^2 + ... + \|w_k\|^2}$.

Sets and Distributions. For a set Λ, we write $a \leftarrow \Lambda$ to denote that a is chosen uniformly at random from Λ. For a probability distribution S, we write $s \leftarrow S$ to denote that s is chosen according to the distribution S. Noise in our scheme is sampled from a centered binomial distribution B_β. We define B_β as follows.

Sample $(a_1, ..., a_\beta, b_1, ..., b_\beta) \leftarrow \{0, 1\}^{2\beta}$ and output $\sum_{i=1}^{\beta} (a_i - b_i)$. When we write that a polynomial $f \in R_q$ or a vector of such polynomials is sampled from B_β, we mean that each coefficient is sampled from B_β.

Update Setting. For a UE scheme, we denote xx as the randomness of the ciphertext update, kk as the direction of key update and cc as the direction of ciphertext update, where xx $\in$ {det, rand}, kk $\in$ {no, f-uni, b-uni, bi}, cc $\in$ {uni, bi}.

Let *negl* denote as a negligible function. *PPT* stands for probabilistic polynomial time.

2.2 Syntax of UE

An updatable encryption scheme UE consists of a tuple of *PPT* algorithms described as follows:

(1) Setup algorithm $UE.Setup\,(1^\lambda)$. Input a security parameter λ and output a public parameter pp. (This algorithm is an option for UE).
(2) Key generation algorithm $UE.KG\,(pp)$. Input a public parameter pp and output an epoch key k_e.
(3) Encryption algorithm $UE.Enc\,(k_e, M)$. Input an epoch key k_e and a plaintext M and output a ciphertext C_e.
(4) Decryption algorithm $UE.Dec\,(k_e, C_e)$. Input an epoch key k_e and a ciphertext C_e and output a plaintext M'.
(5) Token generation algorithm $UE.TG\,(k_e, k_{e+1})$. Input two keys of successive epochs k_e and k_{e+1} and output a token Δ_{e+1}.
(6) Update algorithm $UE.Upd\,(\Delta_{e+1}, C_e)$. Input a token Δ_{e+1} and a ciphertext C_e and output an updated ciphertext C_{e+1}.

2.3 MLWE Assumption [12]

Definition 1. *Let* $n = 2^r$, $r \in \mathbb{Z}^+$, $R_q = \mathbb{Z}_q\,[x]\,/\,(x^n + 1)$, $k, l \in \mathbb{Z}^+$, $\mathbf{A} \leftarrow R_q^{k \times l}$, $\mathbf{s} \in R_q^l$ *and* $\mathbf{s} \leftarrow B_\beta^l$. *The adversary* $\mathcal{A}$ *has* $(\mathbf{A}, \mathbf{b}) \in R_q^{k \times l} \times R_q^k$, *and* $\mathcal{A}$ *decides as follows. If* $\mathbf{b} = \mathbf{As} + \mathbf{e}$, *for* $\mathbf{e} \in R_q^k$ *and* $\mathbf{e} \leftarrow B_\beta^k$, $\mathcal{A}$ *outputs 1. If* $\mathbf{b}$ *follows the uniform distribution on* R_q^k, $\mathcal{A}$ *outputs 0. We define that*

$$Adv_{k,l,\beta}^{MLWE}\,(n) = |\Pr\,[\mathcal{A}\,(\mathbf{A}, \mathbf{As} + \mathbf{e} \bmod q) = 1] - \Pr\,[\mathcal{A}\,(\mathbf{A}, \mathbf{u}) = 1]|,$$

where $\mathbf{u} \leftarrow R_q^k$.

MLWE assumption is that, for any *PPT* adversary $\mathcal{A}$, we have $Adv_{k,l,\mathcal{A}}^{MLWE}\,(n) \leq negl\,(n)$.

3 TKOpen Security Model

In the practical application of UE, the user and the server should use an open channel to transmit the update token. Otherwise, the user and the server need to use a secure channel to transmit the update token (that is sharing another encryption scheme), which will bring great inconvenience. Aiming at the above problems, the Token Open security model was presented recently in [13]. However, in the Token Open security model, the adversary submits two plaintexts then obtains an encrypted ciphertext and distinguishes the original plaintext. We improved it to TKOpen security model. In TKOpen, the adversary can corrupt tokens of all epochs and keys of the past epochs. The adversary submits a plaintext and an old ciphertext then obtains a new ciphertext and distinguishes whether the challenge ciphertext is the encryption of the plaintext or the update ciphertext of the old ciphertext. Thus, the TKOpen security model reflects the characteristics of UE.

3.1   xx-TKOpen-atk Experiment

We describe the confidentiality experiment of TKOpen for a UE scheme. The adversary $\mathcal{A}$ and the simulator $\mathcal{B}$ play $Exp_{UE,\mathcal{A}}^{xx-TKOpen-atk-b}(\lambda)$ as follows, where xx $\in$ {det, rand}, atk $\in$ {CPA, CCA}.

(1) $\mathcal{B}$ does *Setup*.
(2) $\mathcal{A}$ can query $\mathcal{O}.Corr$, $\mathcal{O}.Enc$, $(\mathcal{O}.Dec)$ and $\mathcal{O}.Upd$ oracles and get a pair of plaintext and ciphertext $(\bar{M}, \bar{C})$.
(3) $\mathcal{A}$ sends $(\bar{M}, \bar{C})$ to $\mathcal{B}$ for querying $\mathcal{O}.Chall$ and gets a challenge ciphertext $\tilde{C}_{\tilde{e}}$. $\mathcal{B}$ embeds a bit of information b in $\mathcal{O}.Chall$.
(4) $\mathcal{A}$ continues to query $\mathcal{O}.Corr$, $\mathcal{O}.Enc$, $(\mathcal{O}.Dec)$ and $\mathcal{O}.Upd$ oracles.
(5) $\mathcal{A}$ makes a judgment. If $\tilde{C}_{\tilde{e}}$ is encryption of $\bar{M}$, $\mathcal{A}$ outputs a bit $b' = 0$. If $\tilde{C}_{\tilde{e}}$ is an update of $\bar{C}$, $\mathcal{A}$ outputs a bit $b' = 1$.

Only in the xx-TKOpen-CCA confidentiality experiment, the adversary has access to $\mathcal{O}.Dec$.

Definition 2. *A UE scheme is xx-TKOpen-atk secure, if the following holds, where xx $\in$ {det, rand},atk $\in$ {CPA, CCA}. For any PPT adversary $\mathcal{A}$, we have*

$$Adv_{UE,\mathcal{A}}^{xx-TKOpen-atk}(\lambda) =$$

$$\left| \Pr\left[Exp_{UE,\mathcal{A}}^{xx-TKOpen-atk-1} = 1 \right] - \Pr\left[Exp_{UE,\mathcal{A}}^{xx-TKOpen-atk-0} = 1 \right] \right| \leq negl(\lambda).$$

3.2   Oracles

Different from the oracles established in the IND-UE experiment, we design more intuitive and efficient oracles in the TKOpen experiment. The simulator generates all epoch keys and update tokens via *Setup* and randomly chooses a **challenge epoch** $\tilde{e}$. The adversary challenges in the challenge epoch $\tilde{e}$ via $\mathcal{O}.Chall$ and gets a **challenge ciphertext** $\tilde{C}_{\tilde{e}}$. We call the challenge ciphertext and its updated value the **challenge-equal ciphertext**. The adversary can corrupt all epoch keys before the challenge epoch and all update tokens via $\mathcal{O}.Corr$. The adversary can encrypt arbitrary plaintext via $\mathcal{O}.Enc$ and decrypt the non-challenge ciphertexts via $\mathcal{O}.Dec$, but does not allow decrypting the challenge-equal ciphertexts. (The simulator uses set $\tilde{\mathcal{L}}^*$ and set $\tilde{\mathcal{Q}}^*$ to judge and when querying the challenge-equal ciphertexts, it will return $\bot$.) The adversary can update ciphertexts via $\mathcal{O}.Upd$.

Oracles the adversary is allowed to query in the xx-TKOpen-atk experiment are as follows, where xx $\in$ {det, rand}, atk $\in$ {CPA, CCA}.

(1) $Setup\,(1^\lambda)$. Input a security parameter λ.
   Generate $pp := UE.Setup\,(1^\lambda)$. Let $e, c = 0$, $\mathcal{L}, \tilde{\mathcal{L}}, \mathcal{K}, \mathcal{T} = \varnothing$. Choose the challenge epoch randomly $\tilde{e} \leftarrow \{1, ..., n\}$. Generate $k_0, k_1, ..., k_n =$ $UE.KG\,(pp)$, $\Delta_1, ..., \Delta_n = UE.TG\,(k_e, k_{e+1})$.

(2) $\mathcal{O}.Corr\,(inp, \hat{e})$. Input a corruption type inp and a corruption epoch $\hat{e}$.
   If $\hat{e} \leq n$ and $inp = token$, let $\mathcal{T} = \mathcal{T} \bigcup \{\hat{e}\}$ and return $\Delta_{\hat{e}}$. If $\hat{e} \leq \tilde{e} - 1$ and $inp = key$, let $\mathcal{K} = \mathcal{K} \bigcup \{\hat{e}\}$ and return $k_{\hat{e}}$. Otherwise, return $\bot$.

(3) $\mathcal{O}.Enc\,(M, \hat{e})$. Input a plaintext M and a query epoch $\hat{e}$.
   If $\hat{e} \leq \tilde{e}$, let $c := c+1$, compute $C = UE.Enc\,(k_{\hat{e}}, M)$, let $\mathcal{L} = \mathcal{L} \bigcup \{(c, C, \hat{e})\}$ and return a ciphertext C. Otherwise, return $\bot$.

(4) $\mathcal{O}.Dec\,(C, \hat{e})$. Input a ciphertext C and a query epoch $\hat{e}$.
   If xx=det and $(C, \hat{e}) \notin \tilde{\mathcal{L}}^*$, compute $M = UE.Dec\,(k_{\hat{e}}, C)$ return a plaintext M. If xx=rand, compute $M = UE.Dec\,(k_{\hat{e}}, C)$, and if $(M, \hat{e}) \notin \tilde{\mathcal{Q}}^*$, return a plaintext M. Otherwise, return $\bot$.

(5) $\mathcal{O}.Upd\,(C_{\hat{e}}, \hat{e})$. Input a ciphertext $C_{\hat{e}}$ and a query epoch $\hat{e}$.
   If $(j, C_e, \hat{e}; M) \in \mathcal{L}$, compute $C_{\hat{e}+1} = UE.Upd\,(\Delta_{\hat{e}+1}, C_{\hat{e}})$, let $\mathcal{L} = \mathcal{L} \bigcup \{(j, C_{\hat{e}+1}, \hat{e}+1)\}$, and return a new ciphertext $C_{\hat{e}+1}$. If $(C_{\hat{e}}, \hat{e}) \in \tilde{\mathcal{L}}$, compute $\tilde{C}_{\hat{e}+1} = UE.Upd\,(\Delta_{\hat{e}+1}, C)$, let $\tilde{\mathcal{L}} = \tilde{\mathcal{L}} \bigcup \left\{\left(\tilde{C}_{\hat{e}+1}, \hat{e}+1\right)\right\}$, and return a challenge-equal ciphertext $\tilde{C}_{\hat{e}+1}$. Otherwise, return $\bot$.

(6) $\mathcal{O}.Chall\,(\bar{M}, \bar{C})$. Input a plaintext $\bar{M}$ and a ciphertext $\bar{C}$ at the epoch $\tilde{e}-1$.
   If $(\cdot, \bar{C}, \tilde{e}-1; \bar{M}_1) \notin \mathcal{L}$, return $\bot$. If $b = 0$, compute $\tilde{C}_{\tilde{e}} = UE.Enc\,(k_{\tilde{e}}, \bar{M})$. If $b = 1$, compute $\tilde{C}_{\tilde{e}} = UE.Upd\,(\Delta_{\tilde{e}}, \bar{C})$. Let $\tilde{\mathcal{L}} = \tilde{\mathcal{L}} \bigcup \left\{\left(\tilde{C}_{\tilde{e}}, \tilde{e}\right)\right\}$ and $\mathcal{C} = \mathcal{C} \bigcup \{\tilde{e}\}$. Return challenge ciphertext $\tilde{C}_{\tilde{e}}$.

3.3 Sets in TKOpen

The simulator builds a series of sets to record information that the adversary knows when answering the oracles. The simulator uses these sets to check whether the leaked information would cause the adversary to win the game with probability 1. We record these sets in a similar way to [4], but the oracles inside are different.

3.3.1 Sets of Epochs
We use the following sets to track epochs in which the adversary corrupts keys, and tokens, or learns the challenge ciphertext.

$\mathcal{K}$: Set of epochs in which the adversary corrupted the epoch key (from $\mathcal{O}.Corr$).
$\mathcal{T}$: Set of epochs in which the adversary corrupted the update token (from $\mathcal{O}.Corr$).

$\mathcal{C}$: Set of epochs in which the adversary learned a challenge-equal ciphertext (from $\mathcal{O}.Chall$ or $\mathcal{O}.Upd$).

We use $\mathcal{K}^*, \mathcal{T}^*, \mathcal{C}^*$ as the extended sets of $\mathcal{K}, \mathcal{T}, \mathcal{C}$ in which the adversary has learned or inferred information via its known tokens.

Key Leakage. In addition to the set $\mathcal{K}$, the adversary can infer more keys via its known tokens. The size of $\mathcal{K}^*$ is determined by the key update setting of the UE scheme. In the no-directional key update setting, the adversary does not have more information about keys except for this set. In the f-uni-directional key update setting, if the adversary knows the key k_e and the token Δ_{e+1} it can infer the next key k_{e+1}. In the b-uni-directional key update setting, if the adversary knows the key k_{e+1} and the token Δ_{e+1} it can infer the last key k_e. In the bi-directional key update setting, if the adversary knows the key k_e (or k_{e+1}) and the token Δ_{e+1} it can infer the key k_{e+1} (or k_e).

In the kk-directional key update setting, where kk $\in$ {no, f-uni, b-uni, bi}, denote the set $\mathcal{K}^*_{kk}$ as the extended set of $\mathcal{K}$. We compute these sets as follows.

$$\mathcal{K}^*_{kk} = \{e \in \{0, ..., l\} | \, CorrK(e) = true\}.$$
$$true = CorrK(e) \Leftrightarrow$$
$$(e \in \mathcal{K}) \vee \underbrace{(CorrK(e+1) \wedge e+1 \in \mathcal{T})}_{kk \in \{b-uni, bi\}} \vee \underbrace{(CorrK(e-1) \wedge e \in \mathcal{T})}_{kk \in \{f-uni, bi\}}.$$

Token Leakage. In addition to the set $\mathcal{T}$, the adversary can compute more tokens via two consecutive epoch keys.

In the kk-directional key update setting, where kk $\in$ {no, f-uni, b-uni, bi}, denote the set $\mathcal{T}^*_{kk}$ as the extended set of $\mathcal{T}$. We compute these sets as follows.

$$\mathcal{T}^*_{kk} = \{e \in \{0, ..., l\} | \, (e \in \mathcal{T}) \vee (e \in \mathcal{K}^*_{kk} \wedge e-1 \in \mathcal{K}^*_{kk})\}.$$

Challenge-Equal Ciphertext Leakage. In addition to the set $\mathcal{C}$, the adversary can compute more challenge-equal ciphertext via its known tokens. The size of $\mathcal{C}^*$ is determined by the ciphertext update setting of the UE scheme. In the uni-ciphertext update setting, if the adversary knows the ciphertext C_e and the token Δ_{e+1} it can infer the next ciphertext C_{e+1}. In the bi-ciphertext update setting, if the adversary knows the ciphertext C_e (or C_{e+1}) and the token Δ_{e+1} it can infer the ciphertext C_{e+1} (or C_e).

In the kk-directional key update and cc- directional ciphertext update setting, where kk $\in$ {no, f-uni, b-uni, bi}, cc $\in$ {uni, bi}, denote the set $\mathcal{C}^*_{kk,cc}$ as the extended set of $\mathcal{C}$. We compute these sets as follows.

$$\mathcal{C}^*_{kk,cc} = \{e \in \{0, ..., l\} | \, ChallEq(e) = true\}.$$
$$true = ChallEq(e) \Leftrightarrow$$
$$(e \in \mathcal{C}) \vee (ChallEq(e-1) \wedge e \in \mathcal{T}^*_{kk}) \vee \underbrace{(ChallEq(e+1) \wedge e+1 \in \mathcal{T}^*_{kk})}_{cc=bi}.$$

3.3.2   Sets of Information

We use the following sets to track ciphertexts and their updates that can be known to the adversary.

$\mathcal{L}$: Set of non-challenge ciphertexts $(c, C, e; m)$, where query identifier c is a counter incremented with each new $O.Enc$ query. The adversary learned these ciphertexts from $O.Enc$ or $O.Upd$.

$\tilde{\mathcal{L}}$: Set of challenge-equal ciphertexts $\left(\tilde{C}_e, e\right)$. The adversary learned these ciphertexts from $O.Chall$ or $O.Upd$.

In the det-update setting, we use $\mathcal{L}^*, \tilde{\mathcal{L}}^*$ as the extended (ciphertext) sets of $\mathcal{L}, \tilde{\mathcal{L}}$ in which the adversary infers ciphertexts via its known tokens. In particular, in $\mathcal{L}^*$ we only need to record the ciphertext and the epoch, $\mathcal{L}^* = \{(C, e)\}$.

In the randomized-update setting, we use $\mathcal{Q}^*, \tilde{\mathcal{Q}}^*$ as the extended (plaintext) sets of $\mathcal{L}, \tilde{\mathcal{L}}$ in which the adversary infers ciphertexts containing the corresponding plaintext via its known tokens. We compute $\mathcal{Q}^*, \tilde{\mathcal{Q}}^*$ as follows.

$\mathcal{Q}^*$: Set of plaintexts corresponding to non-challenge ciphertexts (M, e). The adversary learned the ciphertexts corresponding to these plaintexts via its known tokens.

$\tilde{\mathcal{Q}}^*$: Set of plaintexts corresponding to challenge-equal ciphertexts $\{(\bar{M}, e), (\bar{M}_1, e)\}$, where $(\bar{M}, \bar{C})$ is the input of $\mathcal{O}.Chall$ and $\bar{M}_1$ is the plaintext corresponding to $\bar{C}$. The adversary learned the ciphertexts corresponding to these plaintexts via its known tokens.

Based on the above discussion, it is easy to draw the following conclusions.

a. $\left(\tilde{C}_e, e\right) \in \tilde{\mathcal{L}} \Leftrightarrow e \in \mathcal{C}$

b. $\left(\tilde{C}_e, e\right) \in \tilde{\mathcal{L}}^* \Leftrightarrow e \in \mathcal{C}^* \Leftrightarrow (\bar{M}, e), (\bar{M}_1, e) \in \tilde{\mathcal{Q}}^*$

3.4   Relationship Between TKOpen and Settings of UE Schemes

According to the discussion in Sect. 1.1, UE schemes have 16 different settings. We show the relationship between the TKOpen security model and the settings of UE schemes.

Lemma 1. *For a UE scheme in (kk,bi) setting, where kk $\in$ {no, f-uni, b-uni, bi} (bi-directional ciphertext update setting), there exists a PPT adversary $\mathcal{A}$ such that*

$$Adv_{UE,\mathcal{A}}^{xx-TKOpen-atk} (\lambda) = \left| \Pr\left[Exp_{UE,\mathcal{A}}^{xx-TKOpen-atk-1} = 1 \right] - \Pr\left[Exp_{UE,\mathcal{A}}^{xx-TKOpen-atk-0} = 1 \right] \right| = 1,$$

where xx $\in$ {det, rand}, atk $\in$ {CPA, CCA}.

Proof. For a UE scheme in bi-directional ciphertext update setting, there exists a PPT downgrade algorithm $UE.Upd^{-1}(\Delta_e, C_{e+1})$: Input a token Δ_{e+1} and a ciphertext C_{e+1} and output a ciphertext C_e.

The adversary $\mathcal{A}$ and simulator $\mathcal{B}$ play $Exp_{UE,\mathcal{A}}^{xx-TKOpen-atk-b}(\lambda)$ as follows, where xx $\in$ {det, rand}, atk $\in$ {CPA, CCA}.

(1) $\mathcal{B}$ does *Setup*.
(2) $\mathcal{A}$ can query $\mathcal{O}.Corr$, $\mathcal{O}.Enc$, ($\mathcal{O}.Dec$) and $\mathcal{O}.Upd$ oracles and get a pair of plaintext and ciphertext $(\bar{M}, \bar{C})$.
(3) $\mathcal{A}$ sends $(\bar{M}, \bar{C})$ to $\mathcal{B}$ for querying $\mathcal{O}.Chall$ and gets a challenge ciphertext $\tilde{C}_{\tilde{e}}$. $\mathcal{B}$ embeds a bit of information b in $\mathcal{O}.Chall$.
(4) $\mathcal{A}$ has corrupted $\Delta_1, \Delta_2, ..., \Delta_n$. $\mathcal{A}$ computes $\tilde{C}_{\tilde{e}-1} = UE.Upd^{-1}(\Delta_{\tilde{e}}, \tilde{C}_{\tilde{e}})$. $\mathcal{A}$ has corrupted $k_0, k_1, ..., k_{\tilde{e}-1}$, so that $\mathcal{A}$ computes $M' = UE.Dec(k_{\tilde{e}-1}, \tilde{C}_{\tilde{e}-1})$.
(5) $\mathcal{A}$ compares M' with $\bar{M}$. If $M' = \bar{M}$, $\mathcal{A}$ outputs a bit $b' = 0$. Else, $\mathcal{A}$ outputs a bit $b' = 1$.

Only in the TKOpen-CCA confidentiality experiment, the adversary has access to $\mathcal{O}.Dec$.

Since $\mathcal{A}$ has corrupted all the epoch keys before $\tilde{e}$ and the UE scheme is bi-directional ciphertext update, the challenge ciphertext can be downgraded. $\mathcal{A}$ decrypts $\tilde{C}_{\tilde{e}-1}$ to get M' via $k_{\tilde{e}-1}$, compares M' with $\bar{M}$, and then wins the game with probability 1.

Lemma 2. *For a UE scheme in (f-uni,cc) setting, cc $\in$ {uni, bi} (forward-leak uni-directional key update setting), there exists a PPT adversary $\mathcal{A}$ such that*

$$Adv_{UE,\mathcal{A}}^{xx-TKOpen-atk}(\lambda)$$
$$= \left| \Pr\left[Exp_{UE,\mathcal{A}}^{xx-TKOpen-atk-1} = 1 \right] - \Pr\left[Exp_{UE,\mathcal{A}}^{xx-TKOpen-atk-0} = 1 \right] \right| = 1,$$

where xx $\in$ {det, rand}, atk $\in$ {CPA, CCA}.

Proof. For a UE scheme in forward-leak uni-directional key update setting, there exists a PPT key derive algorithm $UE.KD(\Delta_{e+1}, k_e)$: Input a token Δ_{e+1} and a key k_e and output a key k_{e+1}.

The adversary $\mathcal{A}$ and simulator $\mathcal{B}$ play $Exp_{UE,\mathcal{A}}^{xx-TKOpen-atk-b}(\lambda)$ as follows, where xx $\in$ {det, rand}, atk $\in$ {CPA, CCA}.

(1) $\mathcal{B}$ does *Setup*.
(2) $\mathcal{A}$ can query $\mathcal{O}.Corr$, $\mathcal{O}.Enc$, ($\mathcal{O}.Dec$) and $\mathcal{O}.Upd$ oracles and get a pair of plaintext and ciphertext $(\bar{M}, \bar{C})$.
(3) $\mathcal{A}$ sends $(\bar{M}, \bar{C})$ to $\mathcal{B}$ for querying $\mathcal{O}.Chall$ and gets a challenge ciphertext $\tilde{C}_{\tilde{e}}$. $\mathcal{B}$ embeds a bit of information b in $\mathcal{O}.Chall$.

(4) $\mathcal{A}$ has corrupted and $k_{\tilde{e}-1}$. computes $k_{\tilde{e}} = UE.KD\left(\Delta_{\tilde{e}}, k_{\tilde{e}-1}\right)$. decrypts $\tilde{C}_{\tilde{e}}$ via $k_{\tilde{e}}$ to get $M' = UE.Dec\left(k_{\tilde{e}}, \tilde{C}_{\tilde{e}}\right)$.

(5) $\mathcal{A}$ compares M' with $\bar{M}$. If $M' = \bar{M}$, $\mathcal{A}$ outputs a bit $b' = 0$. Else, $\mathcal{A}$ outputs a bit $b' = 1$.

Only in the TKOpen-CCA confidentiality experiment, the adversary has access to $\mathcal{O}.Dec$.

Since $\mathcal{A}$ has corrupted all the epoch keys before $\tilde{e}$ and the UE scheme is f-uni-directional key update, $\mathcal{A}$ can compute $k_{\tilde{e}}$. $\mathcal{A}$ decrypts $\tilde{C}_{\tilde{e}}$ to get M' via $k_{\tilde{e}}$, compares M' with $\bar{M}$, and then wins the game with probability 1.

Lemma 3. *For a UE scheme in (bi,cc) setting, cc $\in$ {uni, bi} (bi-directional key update setting), there exists a PPT adversary $\mathcal{A}$ such that*

$$Adv_{UE,\mathcal{A}}^{xx-TKOpen-atk}(\lambda) =$$
$$\left|\Pr\left[Exp_{UE,\mathcal{A}}^{xx-TKOpen-atk-1} = 1\right] - \Pr\left[Exp_{UE,\mathcal{A}}^{xx-TKOpen-atk-0} = 1\right]\right| = 1,$$

where $xx \in$ {det, rand}, atk $\in$ {CPA, CCA}.

Proof. Similar to the proof of Lemma 3.

Lemma 4. *For a UE scheme in det-update setting, there exists a PPT adversary $\mathcal{A}$ such that*

$$Adv_{UE,\mathcal{A}}^{det-TKOpen-atk}(\lambda) =$$
$$\left|\Pr\left[Exp_{UE,\mathcal{A}}^{det-TKOpen-atk-1} = 1\right] - \Pr\left[Exp_{UE,\mathcal{A}}^{det-TKOpen-atk-0} = 1\right]\right| = 1,$$

where atk $\in$ {CPA, CCA}.

Proof. For a UE scheme in det-update setting, the update algorithm is deterministic, so the updated ciphertext $C_{e+1} = UE.Upd\left(\Delta_{e+1}, C_e\right)$ is deterministic.

The adversary $\mathcal{A}$ and simulator $\mathcal{B}$ play $Exp_{UE,\mathcal{A}}^{det-TKOpen-atk-b}(\lambda)$ as follows, where atk $\in$ {CPA, CCA}.

(1) $\mathcal{B}$ does *Setup*.
(2) $\mathcal{A}$ can query $\mathcal{O}.Corr$, $\mathcal{O}.Enc$, ($\mathcal{O}.Dec$) and $\mathcal{O}.Upd$ oracles and get a pair of plaintext and ciphertext $(\bar{M}, \bar{C})$.
(3) $\mathcal{A}$ sends $(\bar{M}, \bar{C})$ to $\mathcal{B}$ for querying $\mathcal{O}.Chall$ and get a challenge ciphertext $\tilde{C}_{\tilde{e}}$. $\mathcal{B}$ embeds a bit of information b in $\mathcal{O}.Chall$.
(4) $\mathcal{A}$ has corrupted $\Delta_{\tilde{e}}$. $\mathcal{A}$ computes $\bar{C}_{\tilde{e}} = UE.Upd\left(\Delta_{\tilde{e}}, \bar{C}\right)$.
(5) $\mathcal{A}$ compares $\bar{C}_{\tilde{e}}$ with $\tilde{C}_{\tilde{e}}$. If $\bar{C}_{\tilde{e}} = \tilde{C}_{\tilde{e}}$, $\mathcal{A}$ outputs a bit $b' = 1$. Else, $\mathcal{A}$ outputs a bit $b' = 0$.

Only in the TKOpen-CCA confidentiality experiment, the adversary has access to $\mathcal{O}.Dec$.

Since $\mathcal{A}$ has corrupted the token of the challenge epoch $\Delta_{\tilde{e}}$, $\mathcal{A}$ can compute $\bar{C}_{\tilde{e}} := UE.Upd\left(\Delta_{\tilde{e}}, \bar{C}\right)$. Since the UE scheme is det-update, the challenge ciphertext $\tilde{C}_{\tilde{e}}$ is deterministic as the updated value of the ciphertext $\bar{C}$. $\mathcal{A}$ compares $\bar{C}_{\tilde{e}}$ with $\tilde{C}_{\tilde{e}}$ and then wins the game with probability 1.

Theorem 1. *A UE scheme is in rand-(b-uni/no, uni) setting if the scheme is TKOpen-atk secure, where atk $\in$ {CPA, CCA}. That is, a UE scheme is in rand-(b-uni/no, uni) setting if the following holds: For any PPT adversary $\mathcal{A}$, we have that $Adv_{UE,\mathcal{A}}^{TKOpen-atk}(\lambda) =$*

$$\left| \Pr\left[Exp_{UE,\mathcal{A}}^{TKOpen-atk-1} = 1 \right] - \Pr\left[Exp_{UE,\mathcal{A}}^{TKOpen-atk-0} = 1 \right] \right| \leq negl(\lambda).$$

Proof. According to Lemma 1, we know that the UE schemes in (kk,bi) setting, kk $\in$ {no, f-uni, b-uni, bi} are not TKOpen-atk secure. According to Lemma 2 and Lemma 3, we know that the UE schemes in (kk, uni) setting, kk $\in$ {f-uni, bi} are not TKOpen-atk secure. According to Lemma 4, we know that the UE schemes in det-update setting are not TKOpen-atk secure.

Based on Theorem 1, we further discuss the relationship between no-directional key update and backward-leak uni-directional key update. Intuitively, no-directional key update is more secure than b-uni-directional key update. But we show that in TKOpen security model, the security of these two key update settings is equivalent, that is, an adversary in b-uni-directional key update setting cannot obtain more information than in no-directional key update setting.

According to the discussion above, we know that if the UE scheme is bidirectional ciphertext update, the adversary can win the TKOpen experiment with probability 1 regardless of the key update setting. Therefore, we only need to show the equivalence between no-directional key update and b-uni-directional key update when the UE scheme is uni-directional ciphertext update.

Proposition 1. *In TKOpen security model, the security of (no,uni) and (b-uni,uni) settings is equivalent.*

Proof. We consider the most information the adversary can learn in the TKOpen security model.

In (no,uni) setting, the adversary can corrupt all epoch keys before and all tokens, but it cannot learn more epoch keys or tokens because of the limitation of no-directional key update. The adversary can learn all challenge-equal after because of uni-directional ciphertext update. Thus, we have that

$$\mathcal{K}_{no}^* = \{0, .., \tilde{e} - 1\}, \mathcal{T}_{no}^* = \{0, ..., n\}, \mathcal{C}_{no,uni}^* = \{\tilde{e}, ..., n\}.$$

In (b-uni,uni) setting, the adversary can corrupt all epoch keys before $\tilde{e}$ and all tokens, but it cannot learn more epoch keys or tokens because of the limitation of backward-leak uni-directional key update. The adversary can learn all challenge-equal after $\tilde{e}$ because of uni-directional ciphertext update. Thus, we have that

$$\mathcal{K}^*_{b-uni} = \{0,..,\tilde{e}-1\}, \mathcal{T}^*_{b-uni} = \{0,...,n\}, \mathcal{C}^*_{b-uni,uni} = \{\tilde{e},...,n\}.$$

Now we know that no-directional key update and backward-leak uni-directional key update reveal the same information to the adversary. Therefore, for the UE scheme in no-directional key update setting, if the adversary can win the TKOpen experiment, then in the UE scheme in backward-leak uni-directional key update setting, the adversary can also win the TKOpen experiment. That is, in TKOpen security model, the security of (no, uni) and (b-uni, uni) settings is equivalent.

4   Description of Scheme

In this section, we first present a PKE scheme based on the MLWE assumption and then construct our MLWEUE based on the PKE scheme. Our scheme is a rand-update UE scheme in backward-leak uni-directional key update and uni-directional ciphertext update settings. We will prove in the next section that this UE scheme satisfies the TKOpen security model.

4.1   MLWE-PKE

Description of MLWE-PKE. We first present a PKE scheme based on the MLWE assumption, and our PKE scheme is similar to Kyber [8].

(1) Setup algorithm $PKE.Setup\,(1^\lambda)$. Input a security parameter λ.
 Choose $\mathbf{A} \leftarrow R_q^{k\times l}$. Output a public parameter $pp := (\mathbf{A}, k, l, q, n, \alpha)$.
(2) Key generation algorithm $PKE.KG\,(pp)$. Input a public parameter pp.
 Choose $\mathbf{s} \leftarrow B_\alpha^l \in R_q^{l\times 1}$ and $\mathbf{e} \leftarrow B_\alpha^k \in R_q^{k\times 1}$. Compute $\mathbf{b} = \mathbf{As} + \mathbf{e} \bmod q \in R_q^{k\times 1}$. Output $(sk, pk) := (\mathbf{s}, \mathbf{b})$.
(3) Encryption algorithm $PKE.Enc\,(pk, m)$. Input a public key pk and a plaintext $m \in R_q$.
 Choose $\mathbf{r} \leftarrow B_\alpha^k$, $\mathbf{e}_1 \leftarrow B_\alpha^{1\times l}$ and $e_2 \leftarrow B_\alpha$. Compute $\mathbf{u} = \mathbf{rA} + \mathbf{e}_1 \in R_q^{1\times l}$ and $v = \mathbf{rb} + e_2 + \langle q/2\rangle \cdot m \in R_q$. Output a ciphertext $c := (\mathbf{u}, v)$.
(4) Decryption algorithm $PKE.Dec\,(sk, c)$. Input a secret key sk and a ciphertext c.

 Parse $c = (\mathbf{u}, v)$. Compute $m' = (v - \mathbf{us})$. Output a plaintext $m := \langle (2/q) \cdot m'\rangle \bmod 2$.

IND-CPA. We present the MLWE-PKE scheme constructed above is IND-CPA under the MLWE assumption in the following theorem and the proof of which is given in Appendix A.

Theorem 2. *The MLWE-PKE scheme is IND-CPA under the MLWE assumption. That is, for any PPT adversary $\mathcal{A}$ there exists an adversary $\mathcal{B}$ against MLWE such that $Adv^{IND-CPA}_{MLWEPKE,\mathcal{A}}(\lambda) \le 3Adv^{MLWE}_{k,l,\mathcal{B}}(\lambda)$.*

4.2 MLWEUE

Now we present the first UE scheme based on the MLWE assumption. Firstly, we introduce the important technique used in construction – the key-switching technique. We use the technique to ensure that the calculation result of the ciphertext and the key remain unchanged while reducing the modulus of the ciphertext, to control the size of the noise after the update.

4.2.1 Key-Switching Technique

We generalize the key-switching technique in [5,10] for our UE scheme, which consists of two functions, which are the binary-decomposition algorithm $BD\left(\cdot\right)$ and the powers-of-2 algorithm $P2\left(\cdot\right)$. It holds that $BD\left(\mathbf{a}\right)\cdot P2\left(\mathbf{s}\right) = \mathbf{a}\cdot\mathbf{s} \in R_q$ for any $\mathbf{a} \in R_q^{1\times l}, \mathbf{s} \in R_q^{l\times 1}$. (Element-to-element multiplication is the **polynomial multiplication** in R_q). Let $\eta = \lceil \lg q \rceil$. We give a detailed description as follows.

(1) Binary-decomposition algorithm $BD\left(\mathbf{a} \in R_q^{1\times l}\right)$.

Input a vector $\mathbf{a} \in R_q^{1\times l}$. Output a vector group $(\mathbf{u}_1, ..., \mathbf{u}_\eta) \in R_q^{1\times l\eta}$, where $\mathbf{u}_k = \left(u_i^{(k)}, ..., u_i^{(k)}\right)$ and $u_i^{(k)}$ is a polynomial in R_q whose coefficients are taken from $\{0,1\}$. Satisfy the equation $\mathbf{a} = 2^0\mathbf{u}_1 + 2^1\mathbf{u}_2 + \cdots + 2^{\eta-1}\mathbf{u}_\eta$. The calculation process of $BD\left(\mathbf{a} \in R_q^{1\times l}\right)$ is as follows.

Step 1. Input $\mathbf{a} = (a_1, ..., a_l) \in R_q^{1\times l}$, where $a_i \in R_q$.

Let the polynomial representation of a_i be $a_i = a_{i,1} + a_{i,2}x + ... + a_{i,n}x^{n-1}$, where $a_{i,j} \in Z_q$.

Then $\mathbf{a} = (a_1, ..., a_l) = ((a_{1,1}, \cdots, a_{1,n}), \cdots, (a_{l,1}, \cdots, a_{l,n})) \in (Z_q^n)^l$.

Step 2. Let the binary decomposition of be $a_{i,j} = 2^0 u_{i,j}^{(1)} + 2^1 u_{i,j}^{(2)} + ... 2^{\eta-1} u_{i,j}^{(\eta)}$, then

$$\mathbf{a}^T = \begin{bmatrix} a_1 \\ ... \\ a_2 \end{bmatrix} = \begin{bmatrix} (a_{1,1}, ..., a_{1,n}) \\ ... \\ (a_{l,1}, ..., a_{l,n}) \end{bmatrix}$$

$$= \begin{bmatrix} \left(\left(2^0 u_{1,1}^{(1)} + 2^1 u_{1,1}^{(2)} + ...2^{\eta-1} u_{1,1}^{(\eta)}\right), ..., \left(2^0 u_{1,n}^{(1)} + 2^1 u_{1,n}^{(2)} + ...2^{\eta-1} u_{1,n}^{(\eta)}\right)\right) \\ ... \\ \left(\left(2^0 u_{l,1}^{(1)} + 2^1 u_{l,1}^{(2)} + ...2^{\eta-1} u_{l,1}^{(\eta)}\right), ..., \left(2^0 u_{l,n}^{(1)} + 2^1 u_{l,n}^{(2)} + ...2^{\eta-1} u_{l,n}^{(\eta)}\right)\right) \end{bmatrix}$$

$$= 2^0 \begin{bmatrix} \left(u_{1,1}^{(1)}, u_{1,2}^{(1)}, ..., u_{1,n}^{(1)}\right) \\ ... \\ \left(u_{l,1}^{(1)}, u_{l,2}^{(1)}, ..., u_{l,n}^{(1)}\right) \end{bmatrix} + 2^1 \begin{bmatrix} \left(u_{1,1}^{(2)}, u_{1,2}^{(2)}, ..., u_{1,n}^{(2)}\right) \\ ... \\ \left(u_{l,1}^{(2)}, u_{l,2}^{(2)}, ..., u_{l,n}^{(2)}\right) \end{bmatrix} + ... + 2^{\eta-1} \begin{bmatrix} \left(u_{1,1}^{(\eta)}, u_{1,2}^{(\eta)}, ..., u_{1,n}^{(\eta)}\right) \\ ... \\ \left(u_{l,1}^{(\eta)}, u_{l,2}^{(\eta)}, ..., u_{l,n}^{(\eta)}\right) \end{bmatrix}$$

Let $u_i^{(k)} = \left(u_{i,1}^{(k)}, u_{i,2}^{(k)}, ..., u_{i,n}^{(k)}\right)$ and $u_i^{(k)}$ is a polynomial in R_q whose coefficients are taken from $\{0,1\}$, then the polynomial representation of $u_i^{(k)}$ is $u_i^{(k)} = u_{i,1}^{(k)} + u_{i,2}^{(k)}x + ... + u_{i,n}^{(k)}x^{n-1}, u_{i,j}^{(k)} \in \{0,1\}, 1 \le k \le \eta, 1 \le i \le l$.

Then we have $\mathbf{a}^T = 2^0 \begin{bmatrix} u_1^{(1)} \\ ... \\ u_l^{(1)} \end{bmatrix} + 2^1 \begin{bmatrix} u_1^{(2)} \\ ... \\ u_l^{(2)} \end{bmatrix} + ... + 2^{\eta-1} \begin{bmatrix} u_1^{(\eta)} \\ ... \\ u_l^{(\eta)} \end{bmatrix} = 2^0 \mathbf{u}_1^T + 2^1\mathbf{u}_2^T + \cdots + 2^{\eta-1}\mathbf{u}_\eta^T$, which is $\mathbf{a} = 2^0\mathbf{u}_1 + 2^1\mathbf{u}_2 + \cdots + 2^{\eta-1}\mathbf{u}_\eta$.

Step 3. Output the vector group$(\mathbf{u}_1, ..., \mathbf{u}_\eta) \in R_q^{1 \times l\eta}$, where $\mathbf{u}_k = \left(u_1^{(k)}, ..., u_i^{(k)}\right)$ and $u_i^{(k)}$ is a polynomial in R_q whose coefficients are taken from $\{0, 1\}$.

(2) Powers-of-2 algorithm $P2\left(\mathbf{s} \in R_q^{l \times 1}\right)$.

Input a vector $\mathbf{s} \in R_q^{l \times 1}$. Output a vector group $\left(\mathbf{s}; 2\mathbf{s}; ...; 2^{\eta-1}\mathbf{s}\right) \in R_q^{l\eta \times 1}$.
The calculation process of $P2\left(\mathbf{s} \in R_q^{l \times 1}\right)$ is as follows.

Compute$\left(1, 2, ..., 2^{\eta-1}\right)^T \quad \otimes \quad \mathbf{s} \quad = \quad \left[\mathbf{s}; 2\mathbf{s}; ...; 2^{\eta-1}\mathbf{s}\right] \quad = $
$\left[(s_1, ..., s_l)^T \bmod q; 2(s_1, ..., s_l)^T \bmod q; ...; 2^{\eta-1}(s_1, ..., s_l)^T \bmod q\right]$,   where
$\otimes$ denotes the standard tensor product.

According to the description above, we have $BD\left(\mathbf{a}\right) \cdot P2\left(\mathbf{s}\right) = (\mathbf{u}_1, ..., \mathbf{u}_\eta) \cdot$
$\left[\mathbf{s}; 2\mathbf{s}; ...; 2^{\eta-1}\mathbf{s}\right] = \left(\mathbf{u}_1 \cdot \mathbf{s} + \mathbf{u}_2 \cdot 2\mathbf{s} + ... + \mathbf{u}_\eta \cdot 2^{\eta-1}\mathbf{s}\right) = \left(\sum_{k=1}^{\eta} 2^{k-1}\mathbf{u}_k \cdot \mathbf{s}\right) = \mathbf{a} \cdot \mathbf{s}$.

4.2.2 Design Ideas

The Construction Method of the Update Token. We show how our UE scheme update token is constructed, and our construction method is inspired by the RtR scheme in [5].

We begin with the simple bi-directional key update. Let $\mathbf{s}_e, \mathbf{s}_{e+1} \in R_q^{l \times 1}$ be two secret keys at epoch e and $e+1$. We use the key-switching technique to get the ciphertext at epoch $e+1$. The token construction and ciphertext update methods are as follows. $\mathbf{M}_{e+1} = \left[\mathbf{A}' \mid \mathbf{A}'\mathbf{s}_{e+1} + \gamma\right] + \left[\mathbf{O} \mid -P2\left(\mathbf{s}_e\right)\right] \in R_q^{l\eta \times (l+1)}$, where $\mathbf{A}' \leftarrow R_q^{l\eta \times l}, \gamma \leftarrow R_q^{l\eta \times 1}$. We use $(\mathbf{u}, v)$ and $\mathbf{M}_{e+1}$ to generate the ciphertext $(\mathbf{u}', v')$ at epoch $e+1$. We compute

$$(\mathbf{u}', v') = (0, v) + BD\left(\mathbf{u}\right)\mathbf{M}_{e+1} = (0, v) + BD\left(\mathbf{u}\right)\left(\left[\mathbf{A}' \mid \mathbf{A}'\mathbf{s}_{e+1} + \gamma\right] + \left[\mathbf{O} \mid -P2\left(\mathbf{s}_e\right)\right]\right)$$
$$= \left(BD\left(\mathbf{u}\right)\mathbf{A}', v - \mathbf{u}\mathbf{s}_e + BD\left(\mathbf{u}\right)\mathbf{A}'\mathbf{s}_{e+1} + BD\left(\mathbf{u}\right)\gamma\right).$$

We use $\mathbf{s}_{e+1}$ to decrypt the ciphertext $(\mathbf{u}', v')$ at epoch $e+1$. We compute

$$v' - \mathbf{u}'\mathbf{s}_{e+1} = v - \mathbf{u}\mathbf{s}_e + BD\left(\mathbf{u}\right)\mathbf{A}'\mathbf{s}_{e+1} + BD\left(\mathbf{u}\right)\gamma - BD\left(\mathbf{u}\right)\mathbf{A}'\mathbf{s}_{e+1}$$
$$= v - \mathbf{u}\mathbf{s}_e + BD\left(\mathbf{u}\right)\gamma.$$

Therefore, if the newly added noise $BD\left(\mathbf{u}\right) \cdot \gamma$ is small enough, the decryption is still correct.

Next, we consider implementing backward-leak uni-directional key update. In fact, we can construct the update token $\mathbf{M}_{e+1}$ without $\mathbf{s}_{e+1}$. Let the public key at epoch $e+1$ be $\mathbf{b}_{e+1}$, where $\mathbf{b}_{e+1} = \mathbf{A}\mathbf{s}_{e+1} + \mathbf{e}_{e+1} \bmod q \in R_q^k$. We choose $\mathbf{R}_{e+1} \leftarrow \{-1, +1\}^{l\eta \times k}, \mathbf{A}^\Delta \leftarrow R_q^{k \times l}$ and $\mathbf{e}^\Delta \leftarrow B_\alpha^k \in R_q^{k \times 1}$. We compute $\mathbf{b}^\Delta \leftarrow \mathbf{A}^\Delta \mathbf{s}_{e+1} + \mathbf{e}^\Delta \bmod q \in R_q^{k \times 1}$. We construct the update token as follows.

$$\mathbf{M}_{e+1} = \mathbf{R}_{e+1} \cdot \left[\mathbf{A} + \mathbf{A}^\Delta \mid \mathbf{b}_{e+1} + \mathbf{b}^\Delta\right] + \left[\mathbf{O} \mid -P2\left(\mathbf{s}_e\right)\right]$$
$$= \left[\mathbf{A}' \mid \mathbf{A}'\mathbf{s}_{e+1} + \gamma'\right] + \left[\mathbf{O} \mid -P2\left(\mathbf{s}_e\right)\right],$$

where $\mathbf{A}' = \mathbf{R}_{e+1} \cdot [\mathbf{A} + \mathbf{A}^{\Delta}] \in R_q^{l\eta \times l}, \gamma' = \mathbf{R}_{e+1} \cdot [\mathbf{e}_{e+1} + \mathbf{e}^{\Delta}] \in R_q^{l\eta \times 1}$.

It is easy to observe that the newly constructed token has the same structure as above. Therefore, we can use $\mathbf{M}_{e+1}$ to update the ciphertext. Thus, even if given the key s_e at epoch e and the token $\mathbf{M}_{e+1}$, we cannot infer s_{e+1} since only the public key part $\mathbf{b}_{e+1}$ (this is pseudorandom by the MLWE assumption) of the key at epoch $e + 1$ is embedded in $\mathbf{M}_{e+1}$. Thus, this update mechanism is a backward-leak uni-directional key update.

Ciphertext-Masking Technique. The update algorithm above is deterministic. We use the ciphertext $(\tilde{\mathbf{u}}, \tilde{v})$ corresponding to the 0 plaintext to mask $(\mathbf{u}', v')$ in the update algorithm to achieve the re-randomization of the updated ciphertext. We call this method the ciphertext masking technique. In this way, we can reduce the time complexity of token generation and the data complexity of transmitting the token.

4.2.3   Description of MLWEUE

We use the PKE scheme in Sect. 4.1 in MLWEUE.

(1) Setup algorithm $MLWEUE.Setup\,(1^{\lambda})$. Input a security parameter λ.
    Choose $\mathbf{A} \leftarrow R_q^{k \times l}$. Output a public parameter $pp := (\mathbf{A}, k, l, q, n, \alpha)$.
(2) Key generation algorithm $MLWEUE.KG\,(pp)$. Input a public parameter pp.
    Generate $(\mathbf{s}_e, \mathbf{b}_e) = PKE.KG\,(pp)$. Output an epoch key $k_e := (sk_e, pk_e) = (\mathbf{s}_e, \mathbf{b}_e)$.
(3) Encryption algorithm $MLWEUE.Enc\,(k_e, m)$. Input an epoch key k_e and a plaintext m.
    Parse $k_e = (\mathbf{s}_e, \mathbf{b}_e)$. Generate $(\mathbf{u}, v) = PKE.Enc\,(\mathbf{b}_e, m)$. Output a ciphertext $C_e := (\mathbf{u}, v) \in R_q^{1 \times l} \times R_q$.
(4) Decryption algorithm $MLWEUE.Dec\,(k_e, C_e)$. Input an epoch key k_e and a ciphertext C_e.
    Parse $k_e = (\mathbf{s}_e, \mathbf{b}_e)$. Compute $m = PKE.Dec\,(\mathbf{s}_e, C_e)$. Output a plaintext m.
(5) Token generation algorithm $MLWEUE.TG\,(k_e, k_{e+1})$. Input two keys of successive epochs k_e and k_{e+1}.
    Parse $k_e = (\mathbf{s}_e, \mathbf{b}_e)$, $k_{e+1} = (\mathbf{s}_{e+1}, \mathbf{b}_{e+1})$. Choose $\mathbf{A}^{\Delta} \leftarrow R_q^{k \times l}$, $\mathbf{e}^{\Delta} \leftarrow B_{\alpha}^k \in R_q^{k \times 1}$. Compute $\mathbf{b}^{\Delta} = \mathbf{A}^{\Delta} \mathbf{s}_{e+1} + \mathbf{e}^{\Delta} \bmod q \in R_q^{k \times 1}$. Compute $\mathbf{M}_{e+1} = \mathbf{R}_{e+1} \cdot [\mathbf{A} + \mathbf{A}^{\Delta} \mid \mathbf{b}_{e+1} + \mathbf{b}^{\Delta}] + [\mathbf{O} \mid -P2\,(\mathbf{s}_e)]$, where $\mathbf{R}_{e+1} \leftarrow \{-1, +1\}^{l\eta \times k}$.
    Output $\Delta_{e+1} := (\mathbf{M}_{e+1}, \mathbf{b}_{e+1})$.
(6) Update algorithm $MLWEUE.Upd\,(\Delta_{e+1}, C_e)$. Input a token Δ_{e+1} and a ciphertext C_e.
    Parse $\Delta_{e+1} = (\mathbf{M}_{e+1}, \mathbf{b}_{e+1})$, $C_e = (\mathbf{u}, v)$. Compute $(\mathbf{u}', v') = BD\,(\mathbf{u})\,\mathbf{M}_{e+1}$. Compute $(\tilde{\mathbf{u}}, \tilde{v}) = PKE.Enc\,(\mathbf{b}_{e+1}, 0) = (\tilde{\mathbf{r}}\mathbf{A} + \tilde{\mathbf{e}}_1, \tilde{\mathbf{r}}\mathbf{b}_{e+1} + \tilde{e}_2)$. Compute $(\bar{\mathbf{u}}, \bar{v}) = (\mathbf{u}' + \tilde{\mathbf{u}}, v + v' + \tilde{v})$. Output $C_{e+1} := (\bar{\mathbf{u}}, \bar{v})$.

4.2.4 Correctness of MLWEUE

Theorem 3. *After MLWEUE updates for T times, the decryption error rate is*

$$\delta = \Pr\left[\|e_2 + \tilde{e}_2 + \mathbf{r}\mathbf{e}_e + \tilde{\mathbf{r}}\mathbf{e}_{e+1} - \mathbf{e}_1 s_e - \tilde{\mathbf{e}}_1 s_{e+1} + BD\left(\mathbf{u}\right)\mathbf{R}_{e+1}\mathbf{e}_{e+1}\right.$$
$$\left. + BD\left(\mathbf{u}\right)\mathbf{R}_{e+1}\mathbf{e}^\Delta\|_\infty \geq \langle q/4 \rangle / T\right].$$

Proof. Let $\mathbf{b}_e$ and $\mathbf{b}_{e+1}$ are the public key at e and $e+1$, where $\mathbf{b}_e = \mathbf{A} s_e + \mathbf{e}_e$ and $\mathbf{b}_{e+1} = \mathbf{A} s_{e+1} + \mathbf{e}_{e+1}$. The update token from e to $e+1$ is generated as $\mathbf{M}_{e+1} = \mathbf{R}_{e+1} \cdot \left[\mathbf{A} + \mathbf{A}^\Delta \middle| \mathbf{b}_{e+1} + \mathbf{b}^\Delta\right] + \left[\mathbf{O} \middle| - P2\left(s_e\right)\right]$, where $\mathbf{R}_{e+1} \leftarrow \{-1, +1\}^{l\eta \times k}$. We consider a ciphertext $C_e = (\mathbf{u}, v)$ and an updated ciphertext $C_{e+1} = (\bar{\mathbf{u}}, \bar{v}) = (\mathbf{u}' + \tilde{\mathbf{u}}, v + v' + \tilde{v})$. We have

$$(\mathbf{u}', v') = BD\left(\mathbf{u}\right)\mathbf{M}_{e+1} = BD\left(\mathbf{u}\right)\mathbf{R}_{e+1} \cdot \left[\mathbf{A} + \mathbf{A}^\Delta \middle| \mathbf{b}_{e+1} + \mathbf{b}^\Delta\right] + \left[\mathbf{O} \middle| - P2\left(s_e\right)\right]$$
$$= BD\left(\mathbf{u}\right)\left(\left[\mathbf{R}_{e+1}\left(\mathbf{A} + \mathbf{A}^\Delta\right) \middle| \mathbf{R}_{e+1}\left(\mathbf{b}_{e+1} + \mathbf{b}^\Delta\right)\right] + \left[\mathbf{O} \middle| - P2\left(s_e\right)\right]\right)$$
$$= \left(BD\left(\mathbf{u}\right)\mathbf{R}_{e+1}\left(\mathbf{A} + \mathbf{A}^\Delta\right), BD\left(\mathbf{u}\right)\mathbf{R}_{e+1}\left(\mathbf{b}_{e+1} + \mathbf{b}^\Delta\right) - \mathbf{u} s_e\right),$$
$$(\tilde{\mathbf{u}}, \tilde{v}) = PKE.Enc\left(\mathbf{b}_{e+1}, 0\right) = \left(\tilde{\mathbf{r}}\mathbf{A} + \tilde{\mathbf{e}}_1, \tilde{\mathbf{r}}\mathbf{b}_{e+1} + \tilde{e}_2\right).$$

In the decryption algorithm $MLWEUE.Dec\left(k_{e+1}, C_{e+1}\right)$, we compute

$$m' = (\bar{v} - \bar{\mathbf{u}} s_{e+1}) = (v + v' + \tilde{v}) - (\mathbf{u}' + \tilde{\mathbf{u}}) s_{e+1}$$
$$= \left(v + BD\left(\mathbf{u}\right)\mathbf{R}_{e+1}\left(\mathbf{b}_{e+1} + \mathbf{b}^\Delta\right) - \mathbf{u} s_e + \tilde{\mathbf{r}}\mathbf{b}_{e+1} + \tilde{e}_2\right)$$
$$\quad - \left(BD\left(\mathbf{u}\right)\mathbf{R}_{e+1}\left(\mathbf{A} + \mathbf{A}^\Delta\right) + \tilde{\mathbf{r}}\mathbf{A} + \tilde{\mathbf{e}}_1\right) s_{e+1}$$
$$= v - \mathbf{u} s_e + BD\left(\mathbf{u}\right)\mathbf{R}_{e+1}\mathbf{e}_{e+1} + BD\left(\mathbf{u}\right)\mathbf{R}_{e+1}\mathbf{e}^\Delta + \tilde{\mathbf{r}}\mathbf{e}_{e+1} + \tilde{e}_2 - \tilde{\mathbf{e}}_1 s_{e+1}$$
$$= \langle q/2 \rangle \cdot m + e_2 + \tilde{e}_2 + \mathbf{r}\mathbf{e}_e + \tilde{\mathbf{r}}\mathbf{e}_{e+1} - \mathbf{e}_1 s_e - \tilde{\mathbf{e}}_1 s_{e+1} + BD\left(\mathbf{u}\right)\mathbf{R}_{e+1}\mathbf{e}_{e+1}$$
$$\quad + BD\left(\mathbf{u}\right)\mathbf{R}_{e+1}\mathbf{e}^\Delta.$$

Let the error $e_2 + \tilde{e}_2 + \mathbf{r}\mathbf{e}_e + \tilde{\mathbf{r}}\mathbf{e}_{e+1} - \mathbf{e}_1 s_e - \tilde{\mathbf{e}}_1 s_{e+1} + BD\left(\mathbf{u}\right)\mathbf{R}_{e+1}\mathbf{e}_{e+1} + BD\left(\mathbf{u}\right)\mathbf{R}_{e+1}\mathbf{e}^\Delta$ be μ. Let the update times be T. According to Theorem 2, if the absolute values of the coefficients of error μ are all less than $q/4$, the ciphertext can be decrypted correctly. If one of the absolute values of the coefficients of error μ is more than $q/4$, there is a decryption error corresponding to the ciphertext after T times update, and the error rate is $\delta = \Pr\left[\|\mu\|_\infty \geq \langle q/4 \rangle / T\right]$.

5 Security Proof

We prove that MLWEUE is backward-leak uni-directional key update and uni-directional ciphertext update and MLWEUE is rand-TKOpen-CPA in this section.

5.1   MLWEUE is (b-uni, uni)

Lemma 5. *If MLWE-PKE is IND-CPA, the MLWEUE adversary cannot derive* k_{e+1} *via* k_e *and* Δ_{e+1}, *that is MLWEUE is backward-leak uni-directional key update.*

Proof. We construct an IND-CPA adversary $\mathcal{B}$ against MLWE-PKE by using an adversary $\mathcal{A}$ that derives k_{e+1} via k_e and Δ_{e+1}.

First, $\mathcal{B}$ plays the IND-CPA experiment, and $\mathcal{B}$ is given pk_{e+1}. $\mathcal{B}$ chooses a pair of plaintext (m_0, m_1) and sends it to the IND-CPA challenger, then gets the challenge ciphertext $c^* = PKE.Enc\,(pk_{e+1}, m_b)$, where $b \leftarrow \{0,1\}$. Next, $\mathcal{B}$ simulators MLWEUE by using the public parameter in MLWE-PKE, generates $(sk_e, pk_e) = MLWEUE.KG\,(pp)$ and $\Delta_{e+1} = MLWEUE.TG\,(sk_e, pk_{e+1})$, and sends $(k_e = (sk_e, pk_e)\,, \Delta_{e+1})$ to $\mathcal{A}$. $\mathcal{A}$ derives and outputs $k_{e+1} = (sk_{e+1}, pk_{e+1})$. Then, $\mathcal{B}$ computes $m' = MLWE - PKE.Dec\,(sk_e, c^*)$ by using sk_e and if $m' = m_{b'}$, it outputs b'. It is easy to see that if $\mathcal{A}$ can derive k_{e+1} via k_e and Δ_{e+1}, $\mathcal{B}$ outputs $b' = b$ to win IND-CPA.

Lemma 6. *If MLWE-PKE is IND-CPA, the MLWEUE adversary cannot derive* c_e *via* c_{e+1} *and* Δ_{e+1}, *that is MLWEUE is uni-directional ciphertext update.*

Proof. We construct an IND-CPA adversary $\mathcal{B}$ against MLWE-PKE by using an adversary $\mathcal{A}$ that derives c_e via c_{e+1} and Δ_{e+1}.

First, $\mathcal{B}$ plays the IND-CPA experiment, and $\mathcal{B}$ is given pk_{e+1}. $\mathcal{B}$ chooses a pair of plaintext $(m_0, m_1)$and sends it to the IND-CPA challenger, then gets the challenge ciphertext $c^* = PKE.Enc\,(pk_{e+1}, m_b)$, where $b \leftarrow \{0,1\}$. Next, $\mathcal{B}$ simulators MLWEUE by using the public parameter in MLWE-PKE, generates $(sk_e, pk_e) = MLWEUE.KG\,(pp)$ and $\Delta_{e+1} = MLWEUE.TG\,(sk_e, pk_{e+1})$. $\mathcal{B}$ sets $c_{e+1} = c^*$ and sends (c_{e+1}, Δ_{e+1}) to $\mathcal{A}$. $\mathcal{A}$ derives and outputs c_e. Then, $\mathcal{B}$ computes $m' = MLWE - PKE.Dec\,(sk_e, c_e)$ by using sk_e and if $m' = m_{b'}$, it outputs b'. It is easy to see that if $\mathcal{A}$ can derive c_e via c_{e+1} and Δ_{e+1}, $\mathcal{B}$ outputs $b' = b$ to win IND-CPA.

Theorem 4. *MLWEUE is (b-uni, uni) under the MLWE assumption.*

Proof. According to Theorem 3, MLWE-PKE is IND-CPA under the MLWE assumption. And according to Lemma 5 and Lemma 6, if MLWE-PKE is IND-CPA, MLWEUE is backward-leak uni-directional key update and uni-directional ciphertext update. Therefore, MLWEUE is (b-uni, uni) under the MLWE assumption.

5.2   MLWEUE is rand-TKOpen-CPA

The security proof of MLWEUE is based on the indistinguishability between a series of games and the MLWE assumption. We define the game sequences as follows.

$Game_0^b$. The first game is the same as $Exp_{UE,\mathcal{A}}^{rand-TKOpen-CPA-b}$.

38   Y. Song et al.

$Game_1^b$. The difference from $Game_0^b$ is that the public key at $\tilde{e}+1$ is replaced with $\mathbf{b}_{\tilde{e}+1}^r \leftarrow R_q^{k \times 1}$.

$Game_2^b$. The difference from $Game_1^b$ is that the token at $\tilde{e}+1$ is replaced with $\Delta_{\tilde{e}+1}^r \leftarrow R_q^{l\eta \times (l+1)}$.

$Game_3^b$. The difference from $Game_2^b$ is that when the adversary queries $\mathcal{O}.Enc\,(M, \tilde{e}+1)$, return $C^r = (\mathbf{u}^r, v^r) \leftarrow R_q^{1 \times l} \times R_q$.

$Game_4^b$. The difference from $Game_3^b$ is that when the adversary queries $\mathcal{O}.Upd\,(C_{\tilde{e}}, \tilde{e})$, return $C_{\tilde{e}+1}^r = (\bar{\mathbf{u}}^r, \bar{v}^r) \leftarrow R_q^{1 \times l} \times R_q$.

We show these games are indistinguishable in the following lemmas, then we embed the MLWE challenge in the challenge epoch of $Game_4^b$ to complete our proof. The proofs of lemmas are given in Appendix B.

Lemma 7. *If the MLWE assumption holds, then $Game_0^b$ and $Game_1^b$ are indistinguishable. That is* $\left| Adv_0^b\,(\lambda) - Adv_1^b\,(\lambda) \right| \le Adv_{k,l,\alpha}^{MLWE}\,(n)$.

Lemma 8. $Game_1^b$ *and* $Game_2^b$ *are indistinguishable. That is* $\left| Adv_1^b\,(\lambda) - Adv_2^b\,(\lambda) \right| = 0$.

Lemma 9. *If the MLWE assumption holds, then $Game_2^b$ and $Game_3^b$ are indistinguishable. That is* $\left| Adv_2^b\,(\lambda) - Adv_3^b\,(\lambda) \right| \le Adv_{k,l,\alpha}^{MLWE}\,(n)$.

Lemma 10. *If the MLWE assumption holds, then $Game_3^b$ and $Game_4^b$ are indistinguishable. That is* $\left| Adv_3^b\,(\lambda) - Adv_4^b\,(\lambda) \right| \le Adv_{k,l,\alpha}^{MLWE}\,(n)$.

Lemma 11. *If there exists a PPT adversary $\mathcal{A}$ that can win the $Game_4^b$ with a non-negligible advantage, there exists a PPT adversary $\mathcal{B}$ that can solve the MLWE problem. That is* $Adv_{Game4}^b\,(\lambda) \le Adv_{k,l,\alpha}^{MLWE}\,(n)$.

Theorem 5. *The MLWEUE scheme constructed above is rand-TKOpen-CPA under the MLWE assumption. That is* $Adv_{MLWEUE,\mathcal{A}}^{rand-TKOpen-CPA-b}\,(\lambda) =$

$$\left| \Pr\left[Exp_{UE,\mathcal{A}}^{rand-TKOpen-CPA-1} = 1 \right] - \Pr\left[Exp_{UE,\mathcal{A}}^{rand-TKOpen-CPA-0} = 1 \right] \right|$$
$$\le 4Adv_{n,q,k,\alpha}^{MLWE}\,(n)\,.$$

Proof. Under the TKOpen security model, the adversary's attack advantage on the MLWEUE scheme is the attack advantage on $Game_0^b$. From the relationship between the game sequences given above, we have $Adv_{MLWEUE,\mathcal{A}}^{rand-TKOpen-CPA-b}\,(\lambda) = Adv_0^b\,(\lambda) = Adv_0^b\,(\lambda) - Adv_1^b\,(\lambda) + Adv_1^b\,(\lambda) - Adv_2^b\,(\lambda) + Adv_2^b\,(\lambda) - Adv_3^b\,(\lambda) + Adv_3^b\,(\lambda) - Adv_4^b\,(\lambda) + Adv_4^b\,(\lambda) \le \left| Adv_0^b\,(\lambda) - Adv_1^b\,(\lambda) \right| + \left| Adv_1^b\,(\lambda) - Adv_2^b\,(\lambda) \right| + \left| Adv_2^b\,(\lambda) - Adv_3^b\,(\lambda) \right| + \left| Adv_3^b\,(\lambda) - Adv_4^b\,(\lambda) \right| + Adv_4^b\,(\lambda)$.

According to Lemma 7, we have $\left| Adv_0^b\,(\lambda) - Adv_1^b\,(\lambda) \right| \le Adv_{k,l,\alpha}^{MLWE}\,(n)$. According to Lemma 8, we have $\left| Adv_1^b\,(\lambda) - Adv_2^b\,(\lambda) \right| = 0$. According to Lemma 9, we have $\left| Adv_1^b\,(\lambda) - Adv_2^b\,(\lambda) \right| = Adv_{k,l,\alpha}^{MLWE}\,(n)$. According to

Lemma 10, we have $\left|Adv_2^b(\lambda) - Adv_3^b(\lambda)\right| = Adv_{k,l,\alpha}^{MLWE}(n)$. According to Lemma 11, we have $Adv_4^b(\lambda) \leq Adv_{k,l,\alpha}^{MLWE}(n)$.

Then we have $Adv_{MLWEUE,\mathcal{A}}^{rand-TKOpen-CPA-b}(\lambda) \leq 4Adv_{n,q,k,\alpha}^{MLWE}(n)$, that MLWEUE is rand-TKOpen-CPA under the MLWE assumption.

6 Experiment

According to Theorem 4, we know that after MLWEUE updates T times, the decryption error rate is $\delta = \Pr\left[\|\mu\|_\infty \geq \langle q/4\rangle/T\right]$. After a large number of experiments, we give the recommended parameter of MLWEUE with a negligible error rate in Table 1.

Table 1. Recommended parameter of MLWEUE.

q	η	n	k	l	α	T	δ
64513	16	256	3	3	2	6	$2^{-122.3}$

Different from the previous theoretical research, we implement MLWEUE through software programming, use the NTT technique to achieve program acceleration, and make new progress in the practical application of UE. We give the clock cycles of each algorithm under the recommended parameter of MLWEUE in Table 2. The test platform is as follows. Operating System: Windows 7. CPU: Inter Core i5-7200U 2.50 GHz. Programming language: C++. Compilation platform: Visual Studio 2019.

Table 2. Clock cycles of each algorithm under the recommended parameter of MLWEUE

Setup	KeyGen	Enc	Dec	TokenGen	Upd
220653	366682	401579	129385	3539053	4059817

Then, we analyze the security of MLWEUE against existing attacks. At present, due to the ideal attack results of prime attack and dual attack [16], they are considered to be the most effective attack method for the analysis of cryptosystems on practical lattices. To evaluate the security strength of the scheme against the original attack and the dual attack under the recommended parameter, we will sequentially exhaust all possible sample numbers m and the b value of the lattice reduction algorithm BKZ-b to represent the prime attack and the dual attack. The optimal computational complexity, let it be 2^{sec}. In Table 3, we give the corresponding (m, b, sec) values.

Table 3. Security strength of MLWEUE scheme against prime attack and dual attack.

Attack model	Prime attack	Dual attack
Classical model	(713, 436, 127)	(694, 434, 126)
Quantum model	(713, 436, 115)	(694, 434, 115)

Appendix A IND-CPA

IND-CPA Security Model of PKE [11]**.** We describe the confidentiality experiment of IND-CPA for a public key encryption scheme Π. The adversary $\mathcal{A}$ and simulator $\mathcal{B}$ play $Exp_{\Pi,\mathcal{A}}^{IND-CPA}(\lambda)$ as follows:

(1) $\mathcal{B}$ does the key generation algorithm, and outputs a public key.
(2) $\mathcal{A}$ can query the encryption oracle and select a pair of plaintexts (m_0, m_1). $\mathcal{A}$ sends (m_0, m_1) to $\mathcal{B}$.
(3) $\mathcal{B}$ chooses a bit $b \leftarrow \{0, 1\}$, encrypts m_b to get the challenge ciphertext c, and returns it to $\mathcal{A}$.
(4) $\mathcal{A}$ continues to query the encryption oracle.
(5) $\mathcal{A}$ outputs a bit b'.

Definition A.1. *A public key encryption scheme is IND-CPA secure if the following holds: For any PPT adversary $\mathcal{A}$, we have*

$$Adv_{\Pi,\mathcal{A}}^{IND-CPA}(\lambda) = \left| \Pr\left[b' = b\right] - \frac{1}{2} \right| \leq negl(\lambda).$$

Theorem 3. *The MLWE-PKE scheme is IND-CPA under MLWE assumption. That is, for any PPT adversary $\mathcal{A}$ there exists an adversary $\mathcal{B}$ against MLWE such that $Adv_{MLWEPKE,\mathcal{A}}^{IND-CPA}(\lambda) \leq 3Adv_{k,l,\mathcal{B}}^{MLWE}(\lambda)$.*

Proof. We construct a series of games to complete the proof.

Game 0. The first game is the same as $Exp_{MLWEPKE,\mathcal{A}}^{IND-CPA}$, then we have that

$$Adv_{MLWEPKE,\mathcal{A}}^{IND-CPA}(\lambda) = \left| \Pr\left[b = b'\right]_{Game0} - \frac{1}{2} \right|.$$

Game 1. The difference from Game 0 is the public key chosen uniformly at random from $R_q^{k \times 1}$. ($\mathbf{b} \leftarrow R_q^{k \times 1}$). It is easy to prove that for any PPT adversary $\mathcal{A}$, there exists an MLWE adversary $\mathcal{B}$ such that

$$\left[\Pr\left[b = b'\right]_{Game0} - \Pr\left[b = b'\right]_{Game1}\right] \leq Adv_{k,l,\mathcal{B}}^{MLWE}(\lambda).$$

Game 2. The difference from Game 1 is the first part of challenge ciphertext chosen uniformly at random from $R_q^{1 \times l}$. ($\mathbf{u} \leftarrow R_q^{1 \times l}$). It is easy to prove that for any PPT adversary $\mathcal{A}$, there exists an MLWE adversary $\mathcal{B}$ such that

$$\left[\Pr\left[b = b'\right]_{Game1} - \Pr\left[b = b'\right]_{Game2}\right] \leq Adv_{k,l,\mathcal{B}}^{MLWE}(\lambda).$$

Game 3. The difference from Game 2 is the second part of the challenge cipher-text chosen uniformly at random from R_q. $(v \leftarrow R_q)$. It is easy to prove that for any PPT adversary $\mathcal{A}$, there exists an MLWE adversary $\mathcal{B}$ such that

$$[\Pr[b = b']_{Game2} - \Pr[b = b']_{Game3}] \leq Adv_{k,l,\mathcal{B}}^{MLWE}(\lambda).$$

In Game 3, the value of the challenge ciphertext is independent of b, thus $\Pr[b = b']_{Game3} = \frac{1}{2}$.

Then we have $Adv_{MLWEPKE,\mathcal{A}}^{IND-CPA}(\lambda) = |\Pr[b = b']_{Game0} - \frac{1}{2}|$

$$= |\Pr[b = b']_{Game0} - \Pr[b = b']_{Game1} + \Pr[b = b']_{Game1} - \Pr[b = b']_{Game2}$$
$$+ \Pr[b = b']_{Game2} - \Pr[b = b']_{Game3} + \Pr[b = b']_{Game3} - 1/2|$$
$$\leq |\Pr[b = b']_{Game0} - \Pr[b = b']_{Game1}| + |\Pr[b = b']_{Game1} - \Pr[b = b']_{Game2}|$$
$$+ |\Pr[b = b']_{Game2} - \Pr[b = b']_{Game3}| + |\Pr[b = b']_{Game3} - 1/2|$$
$$\leq 3 Adv_{k,l,\mathcal{B}}^{MLWE}(\lambda)$$

Appendix B Security Proof

Lemma B.1. *If two random variables ξ and η are independent and distributed uniformly on $\mathbb{Z}_q$, we have that $\xi + \eta$ and $\xi - \eta$ are distributed uniformly on $\mathbb{Z}_q$.*

Proof. ξ and η are independent, then $\forall z \in \mathbb{Z}_q$, we have

$$\Pr[\xi + \eta = z \bmod q] = \sum_{i \in \mathbb{Z}_q} \Pr[\xi = z - i \bmod q \wedge \eta = i \bmod q]$$

$$= \sum_{i \in \mathbb{Z}_q} \Pr[\xi = z - i \bmod q] \times \Pr[\eta = i \bmod q].$$

ξ is distributed uniformly on $\mathbb{Z}_q$, so $\Pr[\xi = z - i \bmod q] = \frac{1}{q}$. Then, we have that $\Pr[\xi + \eta = z \bmod q] = \frac{1}{q} \sum_{i \in \mathbb{Z}_q} \Pr[\eta = i \bmod q] = \frac{1}{q}$, so $\xi + \eta$ is distributed uniformly on $\mathbb{Z}_q$. Similarly, $\xi - \eta$ is distributed uniformly on $\mathbb{Z}_q$.

Proposition B.1. *If $\xi_1, \xi_2, ..., \xi_n$ are independent and distributed uniformly on $\mathbb{Z}_q$, we have that $\sum_{i=1}^{n} k_i \cdot \xi_i, k_i \leftarrow \{-1, +1\}$ is distributed uniformly on $\mathbb{Z}_q$.*

Lemma 7. *If the MLWE assumption holds, then and are indistinguishable. That is $|Adv_0^b(\lambda) - Adv_1^b(\lambda)| \leq Adv_{k,l,\alpha}^{MLWE}(n)$.*

Proof. The difference between $Game_0^b$ and $Game_1^b$ is the public key at $\tilde{e}+1$:

$Game_0^b$: $\mathbf{b}_{\tilde{e}+1} = \mathbf{A}\mathbf{s}_{\tilde{e}+1} + \mathbf{e}_{\tilde{e}+1} \bmod q \in R_q^{k\times 1}$,
    where $\mathbf{A} \leftarrow R_q^{k\times l}$, $\mathbf{s}_{\tilde{e}+1} \leftarrow B_\alpha^l \in R_q^{l\times 1}$, $\mathbf{e}_{\tilde{e}+1} \leftarrow B_\alpha^k \in R_q^{k\times 1}$.
$Game_1^b$: $\mathbf{b}_{\tilde{e}+1}^r \leftarrow R_q^{k\times 1}$.

If the adversary can distinguish two games with a non-negligible advantage, it can solve the MLWE problem. Therefore, $\left| Adv_0^b(\lambda) - Adv_1^b(\lambda) \right| \leq Adv_{n,q,l,\alpha}^{MLWE}(n)$.

Lemma 8. $Game_1^b$ and $Game_2^b$ are indistinguishable. That is $\left| Adv_1^b(\lambda) - Adv_2^b(\lambda) \right| = 0$.

Proof. The difference between $Game_1^b$ and $Game_2^b$ is the public key at $\tilde{e}+1$:
    The difference between $Game_1^b$ and $Game_2^b$ is the token at $\tilde{e}+1$:

$Game_1^b$: $\Delta_{\tilde{e}+1} := \mathbf{M}_{\tilde{e}+1}$, $\mathbf{M}_{\tilde{e}+1} = \mathbf{R}_{\tilde{e}+1} \cdot \left[\mathbf{A}+\mathbf{A}^\Delta \,\middle|\, \mathbf{b}_{\tilde{e}+1}^r + \mathbf{b}^\Delta \right] + \left[\mathbf{O} \,\middle|\, -P2(\mathbf{s}_{\tilde{e}}) \right]$,
    where $\mathbf{R}_{\tilde{e}+1} \leftarrow \{-1, +1\}^{l\eta \times k}$.
$Game_2^b$: $\Delta_{\tilde{e}+1}^r := \mathbf{M}_{\tilde{e}+1}^r$, $\mathbf{M}_{\tilde{e}+1}^r \leftarrow R_q^{l\eta \times (l+1)}$.

Note that the public key at $\tilde{e}+1$ in $Game_1^b$ has been replaced with $\mathbf{b}_{\tilde{e}+1}^r$.

(1) First, we prove that $\mathbf{A}+\mathbf{A}^\Delta$ is uniformly distributed on $R_q^{k\times l}$.

Let $\mathbf{A} = \begin{bmatrix} a_{1,1} & \cdots & a_{1,l} \\ \vdots & \ddots & \vdots \\ a_{k,1} & \cdots & a_{k,l} \end{bmatrix}$, $\mathbf{A}^\Delta = \begin{bmatrix} a_{1,1}^\Delta & \cdots & a_{1,l}^\Delta \\ \vdots & \ddots & \vdots \\ a_{k,1}^\Delta & \cdots & a_{k,l}^\Delta \end{bmatrix}$ and $\mathbf{A}+\mathbf{A}^\Delta =$

$\begin{bmatrix} a_{1,1}^* & \cdots & a_{1,l}^* \\ \vdots & \ddots & \vdots \\ a_{k,1}^* & \cdots & a_{k,l}^* \end{bmatrix}$, then $a_{i,j}^* = a_{i,j} + a_{i,j}^\Delta \in R_q$.

Let $a_{i,j} = a_{i,j(0)} + a_{i,j(1)}x + \ldots + a_{i,j(n-1)}x^{n-1}$, $a_{i,j}^\Delta = a_{i,j(0)}^\Delta + a_{i,j(1)}^\Delta x + \ldots + a_{i,j(n-1)}^\Delta x^{n-1}$ and $a_{i,j}^* = a_{i,j(0)}^* + a_{i,j(1)}^* x + \ldots + a_{i,j(n-1)}^* x^{n-1}$, then $a_{i,j(t)}^* = a_{i,j(t)}^\Delta + a_{i,j(t)} \bmod q, 0 \leq t \leq n-1$.

$\mathbf{A}^\Delta \leftarrow R_q^{k\times l}$, then a_{ij}^Δ is uniformly distributed on R_q, so that $a_{i,j(t)}^\Delta$ is uniformly distributed on $\mathbb{Z}_q$. $\forall z \in \mathbb{Z}_q$, we have that $\Pr\left[a_{i,j(t)}^* = z \bmod q \right] = \Pr\left[a_{i,j(t)}^\Delta + a_{i,j(t)} = z \bmod q \right] = \Pr\left[a_{i,j(t)}^\Delta = z - a_{i,j(t)} \bmod q \right] = 1/q$. Therefore, $a_{i,j(t)}^*$ is uniformly distributed on $\mathbb{Z}_q$, then $a_{i,j}^*$ is uniformly distributed on R_q, so that $\mathbf{A}+\mathbf{A}^\Delta$ is uniformly distributed on $R_q^{k\times l}$.

(2) Next, we prove that $\mathbf{R}_{e+1} \cdot [\mathbf{A}+\mathbf{A}^{\Delta}]$ is uniformly distributed on $R_q^{l\eta \times l}$.

$$\text{Let } \mathbf{R}_{\tilde{e}+1} = \begin{bmatrix} r_{1,1} & \cdots & r_{1,k} \\ \vdots & \ddots & \vdots \\ r_{l\eta,1} & \cdots & r_{l\eta,k} \end{bmatrix}_{l\eta \times k} \in \{-1,+1\}^{l\eta \times k}, \ \mathbf{A}+\mathbf{A}^{\Delta} = \begin{bmatrix} a_{1,1}^{*} & \cdots & a_{1,l}^{*} \\ \vdots & \ddots & \vdots \\ a_{k,1}^{*} & \cdots & a_{k,l}^{*} \end{bmatrix}$$

and $\mathbf{R}_{\tilde{e}+1} \cdot [\mathbf{A}+\mathbf{A}^{\Delta}] = \begin{bmatrix} a_{1,1} & \cdots & a_{1,l} \\ \vdots & \ddots & \vdots \\ a_{l\eta,1} & \cdots & a_{l\eta,l} \end{bmatrix}_{l\eta \times l}$, then $\alpha_{i,j} = \sum_{s=1}^{k} r_{i,s} \cdot a_{s,j}^{*} \in R_q$.

Let $a_{i,j}^{*} = a_{i,j(0)}^{*} + a_{i,j(1)}^{*} x + \ldots + a_{i,j(n-1)}^{*} x^{n-1}$ and $\alpha_{i,j} = \alpha_{i,j(0)} + \alpha_{i,j(1)} x + \ldots + \alpha_{i,j(n-1)} x^{n-1}$, then $\alpha_{i,j(t)} = \sum_{s=1}^{k} r_{i,s} \cdot a_{s,j(t)}^{*} \mod q, 0 \leq t \leq n-1, r_{i,s} \in \{-1,+1\}$. According to (1), we know that $\mathbf{A}+\mathbf{A}^{\Delta}$ is uniformly distributed on $R_q^{k \times l}$, then $a_{1,j(t)}^{*}, a_{2,j(t)}^{*}, \ldots a_{k,j(t)}^{*}$ are k independent random variables uniformly distributed on $\mathbb{Z}_q$. $\mathbf{R}_{\tilde{e}+1} \leftarrow \{-1,+1\}^{l\eta \times k}$, then $r_{i,j} \leftarrow \{-1,+1\}$. According to Lemma B.1 and Proposition B.1, we have that $\alpha_{i,j(t)} = \sum_{s=1}^{k} r_{i,s} \cdot a_{s,j(t)}^{*}$ is uniformly distributed on $\mathbb{Z}_q$, then $\alpha_{i,j}$ is uniformly distributed on R_q, so that $\mathbf{R}_{e+1} \cdot [\mathbf{A}+\mathbf{A}^{\Delta}]$ is uniformly distributed on $R_q^{l\eta \times l}$.

(3) Similar to (1) and (2), $\mathbf{b}_{\tilde{e}+1}^{r} \leftarrow R_q^{k \times 1}$, then $\mathbf{R}_{\tilde{e}+1} \leftarrow \{-1,+1\}^{l\eta \times k}$, so that $\mathbf{R}_{\tilde{e}+1} \cdot [\mathbf{b}_{\tilde{e}+1}^{r} + \mathbf{b}^{\Delta}]$ is uniformly distributed on $R_q^{l\eta \times 1}$. In addition, similar to (1), $\mathbf{R}_{\tilde{e}+1} \cdot [\mathbf{b}_{\tilde{e}+1}^{r} + \mathbf{b}^{\Delta}]$ is uniformly distributed on $R_q^{l\eta \times 1}$, then $\mathbf{R}_{\tilde{e}+1} \cdot [\mathbf{b}_{\tilde{e}+1}^{r} + \mathbf{b}^{\Delta}] - P2(s_e)$ is uniformly distributed on $R_q^{l\eta \times 1}$.

(4) Now we know that $\mathbf{R}_{e+1} \cdot [\mathbf{A}+\mathbf{A}^{\Delta}]$ is uniformly distributed on $R_q^{l\eta \times l}$ and $\mathbf{R}_{\tilde{e}+1} \cdot [\mathbf{b}_{\tilde{e}+1}^{r} + \mathbf{b}^{\Delta}] - P2(s_e)$ is uniformly distributed on $R_q^{l\eta \times 1}$. We have $\mathbf{M}_{\tilde{e}+1} = \mathbf{R}_{\tilde{e}+1} \cdot [\mathbf{A}+\mathbf{A}^{\Delta} | \mathbf{b}_{\tilde{e}+1}^{r} + \mathbf{b}^{\Delta}] + [\mathbf{O} | -P2(s_{\tilde{e}})] = [\mathbf{R}_{\tilde{e}+1} \cdot [\mathbf{A}+\mathbf{A}^{\Delta}] | \mathbf{R}_{\tilde{e}+1} \cdot [\mathbf{b}_{\tilde{e}+1}^{r} + \mathbf{b}^{\Delta}] - P2(s_{\tilde{e}})]$ is uniformly distributed on $R_q^{l\eta \times (l+1)}$.

According to the discussion above, in $Game_1^b$, $\mathbf{M}_{\tilde{e}+1}$ is uniformly distributed on $R_q^{l\eta \times (l+1)}$. In $Game_2^b$, $\mathbf{M}_{\tilde{e}+1}^{r} \leftarrow R_q^{l\eta \times (l+1)}$ is uniformly distributed on $R_q^{l\eta \times (l+1)}$. Therefore, the adversary cannot distinguish between the two games, that is $|Adv_1^b(\lambda) - Adv_2^b(\lambda)| = 0$.

Lemma 9. *If the MLWE assumption holds, then $Game_2^b$ and $Game_3^b$ are indistinguishable. That is $|Adv_2^b(\lambda) - Adv_3^b(\lambda)| \leq Adv_{k,l,\alpha}^{MLWE}(n)$.*

Proof. The difference between $Game_2^b$ and $Game_3^b$ is the returned value when the adversary queries $\mathcal{O}.Enc(M, \tilde{e}+1)$.

$Game_2^b$: When the adversary queries $\mathcal{O}.Enc(M, \tilde{e}+1)$,
   return $C = MLWEUE.Enc(\mathbf{b}_{\tilde{e}+1}^{r}, M)$.
   $C = (\mathbf{rA} + \mathbf{e}_1, \mathbf{rb}_{\tilde{e}+1}^{r} + e_2 + \langle q/2 \rangle \cdot m_0)$, where $\mathbf{A} \leftarrow R_q^{k \times l}$, $\mathbf{r} \leftarrow B_\alpha^k$, $\mathbf{e}_1 \leftarrow B_\alpha^k$, $e_2 \leftarrow B_\alpha$ and $\mathbf{b}_{\tilde{e}+1}^{r} \leftarrow R_q^{k \times 1}$.

$Game_3^b$: When the adversary queries $\mathcal{O}.Enc(M, \tilde{e}+1)$,
   return $C^r := (\mathbf{u}^r, v^r) \leftarrow R_q^{1 \times l} \times R_q$.

If the adversary can distinguish two games with a non-negligible advantage, it can distinguish $\left(\left[\mathbf{A}|\mathbf{b}_{\tilde{e}+1}^{r}\right]^{\mathrm{T}}, \left[\mathbf{r}\left(\mathbf{A}|\mathbf{b}_{\tilde{e}+1}^{r}\right) + (\mathbf{e}_1|e_2)\right]^{\mathrm{T}}\right)$ and $\left(\left[\mathbf{A}|\mathbf{b}_{\tilde{e}+1}^{r}\right]^{\mathrm{T}}, [\mathbf{u}^r|v^r]^{\mathrm{T}}\right)$ with a non-negligible advantage, so it can solve the MLWE problem. Therefore, $\left|Adv_2^b(\lambda) - Adv_3^b(\lambda)\right| \leq Adv_{k,l,\alpha}^{MLWE}(n)$.

Lemma 10. *If the MLWE assumption holds, then $Game_3^b$ and $Game_4^b$ are indistinguishable. That is $\left|Adv_3^b(\lambda) - Adv_4^b(\lambda)\right| \leq Adv_{k,l,\alpha}^{MLWE}(n)$.*

Proof. The difference between $Game_3^b$ and $Game_4^b$ is the returned value when the adversary queries $\mathcal{O}.Upd\left(C_{\tilde{e}}, \tilde{e}\right)$.

$Game_3^b$: When the adversary queries $\mathcal{O}.Upd\left(C_{\tilde{e}}, \tilde{e}\right)$,
     return $C_{\tilde{e}+1} = MLWEUE.Upd\left(\Delta_{\tilde{e}+1}^{r}, C_{\tilde{e}}\right)$.
     $C_{\tilde{e}+1} = (\bar{\mathbf{u}}, \bar{v}) = (\mathbf{u}' + \tilde{\mathbf{u}}, v_{\tilde{e}} + v' + \tilde{v}) = (0, v_{\tilde{e}}) + BD\left(\mathbf{u}_{\tilde{e}}\right)\mathbf{M}_{\tilde{e}+1}^{r} + PKE.Enc\left(\mathbf{b}_{\tilde{e}+1}^{r}, 0\right)$, where $\mathbf{M}_{\tilde{e}+1}^{r} \leftarrow R_q^{l\eta \times (l+1)}$. Let the first l columns of $\mathbf{M}_{\tilde{e}+1}^{r}$ be $\mathbf{M}_{\tilde{e}+1}^{a}$, the last column of $\mathbf{M}_{\tilde{e}+1}^{r}$ be $\mathbf{M}_{\tilde{e}+1}^{b}$, then we have

$$C_{\tilde{e}+1} = \left(\tilde{\mathbf{r}}\mathbf{A} + \tilde{\mathbf{e}}_1 + BD\left(\mathbf{u}_{\tilde{e}}\right)\mathbf{M}_{\tilde{e}+1}^{a}, \tilde{\mathbf{r}}\mathbf{b}_{\tilde{e}+1}^{r} + \tilde{e}_2 + v_{\tilde{e}} + BD\left(\mathbf{u}_{\tilde{e}}\right)\mathbf{M}_{\tilde{e}+1}^{b}\right),$$

where $\mathbf{A} \leftarrow R_q^{k \times l}$, $\tilde{\mathbf{r}}, \tilde{\mathbf{e}}_1 \leftarrow B_\alpha^k$, $\tilde{e}_2 \leftarrow B_\alpha$, $\mathbf{b}_{\tilde{e}+1}^{r} \leftarrow R_q^{k \times 1}$.
$Game_4^b$: When the adversary queries $\mathcal{O}.Upd\left(C_{\tilde{e}}, \tilde{e}\right)$,
     return $C_{\tilde{e}+1}^{r} := (\bar{\mathbf{u}}^r, \bar{v}^r) \leftarrow R_q^{1 \times l} \times R_q$.

If the adversary can distinguish two games with a non-negligible advantage, it can distinguish $\left(\left[\mathbf{A}|\mathbf{b}_{\tilde{e}+1}^{r}\right]^{\mathrm{T}}, \left[\tilde{\mathbf{r}}\left(\mathbf{A}|\mathbf{b}_{\tilde{e}+1}^{r}\right) + (\tilde{\mathbf{e}}_1|\tilde{e}_2)\right]^{\mathrm{T}}\right)$ and $\left(\left[\mathbf{A}|\mathbf{b}_{\tilde{e}+1}^{r}\right]^{\mathrm{T}}, [\bar{\mathbf{u}}^r|\bar{v}^r]^{\mathrm{T}}\right)$ with a non-negligible advantage, so it can solve the MLWE problem. Therefore, $\left|Adv_3^b(\lambda) - Adv_4^b(\lambda)\right| \leq Adv_{k,l,\alpha}^{MLWE}(n)$.

So far, we have proved the indistinguishability of game sequences. Next, we embed the MLWE challenge in the challenge epoch in $Game_4^b$. We construct a simulator $\mathcal{B}$ of the MLWEUE scheme, which is an adversary to the MLWE problem, and responds to queries from the TKOpen adversary $\mathcal{A}$ in $Game_4^b$.

Lemma 11. *If there exists a PPT adversary $\mathcal{A}$ that can win the $Game_4^b$ with a non-negligible advantage, there exists a PPT adversary $\mathcal{B}$ that can solve the MLWE problem. That is $Adv_{Game4}^b(\lambda) \leq Adv_{k,l,\alpha}^{MLWE}(n)$.*

Proof. We construct a simulator of MLWEUE $\mathcal{B}$ against the MLWE problem by using an adversary $\mathcal{A}$ in $Game_4^b$. $\mathcal{B}$ has the MLWE challenge $(\mathbf{A}, \mathbf{b}_{chall})$, it use $\mathbf{b}_{chall}$ as the public key at the challenge epoch $\tilde{e}$, and use a random value to simulate the public key at $\tilde{e}+1$ as Game 1. $\mathcal{B}$ doesn't have the secret key at the challenge epoch, then it cannot generate a real token at $\tilde{e}+1$, so it uses a random value to simulate the token as Game 2. At $\tilde{e}+1$, when $\mathcal{A}$ queries $\mathcal{O}.Enc\,(M, \tilde{e}+1)$, $\mathcal{B}$ returns $C^r := (\mathbf{u}^r, v^r) \leftarrow R_q^{1\times l} \times R_q$ to $\mathcal{A}$ as Game 3, and when $\mathcal{A}$ queries $\mathcal{O}.Upd\,(C_{\tilde{e}}, \tilde{e})$, $\mathcal{B}$ returns $C_{\tilde{e}+1}^r := (\bar{\mathbf{u}}^r, \bar{v}^r) \leftarrow R_q^{1\times l} \times R_q$ to $\mathcal{A}$ as Game 4.

$\mathcal{B}$ modifies the rand-TKOpen-CPA oracles as follows.

$\underline{Setup\,(1^\lambda)}$:
receive the MLWE challenge $(\mathbf{A}, \mathbf{b}_{chall})$
$pp = UE.Setup\,(1^\lambda)$
$\tilde{e} \leftarrow \{1, ..., n\}$
$k_0, ..., k_{\tilde{e}-1}, k_{\tilde{e}+1}, ..., k_n \leftarrow UE.KG\,(pp)$
$pk_{\tilde{e}} := \mathbf{b}_{chall}$(embed challenge)
$pk_{\tilde{e}+1} := \mathbf{b}_{\tilde{e}+1}^r \leftarrow R_q^{k\times 1}$(Game1)
$\Delta_1, ..., \Delta_{\tilde{e}-1} = UE.TG\,(k_i, k_{i+1}), i \in \{0, ..\tilde{e}-2\}$
$\Delta_{\tilde{e}+2}, ..., \Delta_n = UE.TG\,(k_i, k_{i+1}), i \in \{\tilde{e}+1, ..., n-1\}$
$\Delta_{\tilde{e}} = UE.TG\,(sk_{\tilde{e}-1}, pk_{\tilde{e}})$
$\Delta_{\tilde{e}+1} := \Delta_{\tilde{e}+1}^r \leftarrow R_q^{ln\times(l+1)}$(Game2)
$\mathcal{L}, \tilde{\mathcal{L}}, \mathcal{C}, \mathcal{K}, \mathcal{T} = \varnothing$

$\underline{\mathcal{O}.Corr\,(inp, \hat{e})}$:
if $inp = token$ and $\hat{e} \leq n$ then
    $\mathcal{T} = \mathcal{T} \bigcup \{\hat{e}\}$, return $\Delta_{\hat{e}}$
if $inp = key$ and $\hat{e} \leq \tilde{e}-1$ then
    $\mathcal{K} = \mathcal{K} \bigcup \{\hat{e}\}$, return $k_{\hat{e}}$
else
    return $\perp$

$\underline{\mathcal{O}.Enc\,(M, \hat{e})}$
$c = c+1$
if $\hat{e} = \tilde{e}+1$ then
    $C = C^r := (\mathbf{u}^r, v^r) \leftarrow R_q^{1\times l} \times R_q$
    (Game 3)
else

$C = UE.Enc\,(k_{\hat{e}}, M)$
$\mathcal{L} = \mathcal{L} \bigcup \{(c, C, \hat{e}; M)\}$
return C

$\underline{\mathcal{O}.Upd\,(C_{\hat{e}}, \hat{e})}$:
if $(j, C_e, \hat{e}; M) \in \mathcal{L}$ and $\hat{e} = \tilde{e}$ then
    $C_{\hat{e}+1} = C_{\hat{e}+1}^r := (\bar{\mathbf{u}}^r, \bar{v}^r) \leftarrow R_q^{1\times l} \times R_q$
    (Game4)
    $\mathcal{L} = \mathcal{L} \bigcup \{(j, C_{\hat{e}+1}, \hat{e}+1; M)\}$
    return $C_{\hat{e}+1}$
if $(C_{\hat{e}}, \hat{e}) \in \tilde{\mathcal{L}}$ and $\hat{e} = \tilde{e}$ then
    $\tilde{C}_{\hat{e}+1} = C_{\hat{e}+1}^r := (\bar{\mathbf{u}}^r, \bar{v}^r) \leftarrow R_q^{1\times l} \times R_q$
    (Game 4)
    $\mathcal{C} = \mathcal{C} \bigcup \{\hat{e}+1\}$
    $\tilde{\mathcal{L}} = \tilde{\mathcal{L}} \bigcup \{(\tilde{C}_{\hat{e}+1}, \hat{e}+1)\}$
    return $\tilde{C}_{\hat{e}+1}$
if $(j, C_e, \hat{e}; M) \in \mathcal{L}$ and $\hat{e} \neq \tilde{e}$ then
    $C_{\hat{e}+1} = UE.Upd\,(\Delta_{\hat{e}+1}, C_{\hat{e}})$
    $\mathcal{L} = \mathcal{L} \bigcup \{(j, C_{\hat{e}+1}, \hat{e}+1; M)\}$
    return $C_{\hat{e}+1}$
if $(C_{\hat{e}}, \hat{e}) \in \tilde{\mathcal{L}}$ and $\hat{e} \neq \tilde{e}$ then
    $\tilde{C}_{\hat{e}+1} = UE.Upd\,(\Delta_{\hat{e}+1}, C_{\hat{e}})$
    $\mathcal{C} = \mathcal{C} \bigcup \{\hat{e}+1\}$
    $\tilde{\mathcal{L}} = \tilde{\mathcal{L}} \bigcup \{(\tilde{C}_{\hat{e}+1}, \hat{e}+1)\}$
    return $\tilde{C}_{\hat{e}+1}$
else
    return $\perp$

$$\mathcal{O}.Chall\left(\bar{M},\bar{C}\right):$$

if $\left(\cdot,\bar{C},\tilde{e}-1;\bar{M_1}\right)\notin\mathcal{L}$ then

   return $\perp$

if $b=0$ then

$$\tilde{C}_{\tilde{e}}=UE.Enc\left(pk_{\tilde{e}},\bar{M}\right)$$

if $b=1$ then

$$\tilde{C}_{\tilde{e}}=UE.Upd\left(\Delta_{\tilde{e}},\bar{C}\right)$$

$$\tilde{\mathcal{L}}=\tilde{\mathcal{L}}\bigcup\left\{\left(\tilde{C}_{\tilde{e}},\tilde{e}\right)\right\}$$

$$\mathcal{C}=\mathcal{C}\bigcup\{\tilde{e}\}$$

return $\tilde{C}_{\tilde{e}}$

The adversary $\mathcal{A}$ and the simulator $\mathcal{B}$ play $Game_4^b$ as follows:

(1) $\mathcal{B}$ does *Setup*.
(2) $\mathcal{A}$ can query $\mathcal{O}.Corr$, $\mathcal{O}.Enc$ and $\mathcal{O}.Upd$ oracles and get a pair of plaintext and ciphertext $\left(\bar{M},\bar{C}\right)$.
(3) $\mathcal{A}$ sends $\left(\bar{M},\bar{C}\right)$ to $\mathcal{B}$ for querying $\mathcal{O}.Chall$ and get a challenge ciphertext $\tilde{C}_{\tilde{e}}$.
(4) $\mathcal{A}$ continues to query $\mathcal{O}.Corr$, $\mathcal{O}.Enc$ and $\mathcal{O}.Upd$ oracles.
(5) $\mathcal{A}$ makes a judgment. If $\tilde{C}_{\tilde{e}}$ is encryption of $\bar{M}$, $\mathcal{A}$ outputs a bit $b'=0$. If $\tilde{C}_{\tilde{e}}$ is an update of $\bar{C}$, $\mathcal{A}$ outputs a bit $b'=1$.
(6) If $b'=b$, $\mathcal{B}$ outputs 1. Else, $\mathcal{B}$ outputs 0.

In $Game_4^b$, if $\mathcal{A}$ can distinguish the challenge ciphertext with a non-negligible advantage in PPT, then $\mathcal{B}$ can solve the MLWE problem with a non-negligible advantage in PPT. That is $Adv_{Game4}^b\left(\lambda\right)\leq Adv_{k,l,\alpha}^{MLWE}\left(n\right)$.

References

1. Boneh, D., Lewi, K., Montgomery, H., Raghunathan, A.: Key homomorphic PRFs and their applications. In: Canetti, R., Garay, J.A. (eds.) CRYPTO 2013. LNCS, vol. 8042, pp. 410–428. Springer, Heidelberg (2013). https://doi.org/10.1007/978-3-642-40041-4_23
2. Lehmann, A., Tackmann, B.: Updatable encryption with post-compromise security. In: Nielsen, J.B., Rijmen, V. (eds.) EUROCRYPT 2018. LNCS, vol. 10822, pp. 685–716. Springer, Cham (2018). https://doi.org/10.1007/978-3-319-78372-7_22
3. Boyd, C., Davies, G.T., Gjøsteen, K., Jiang, Y.: Fast and secure updatable encryption. In: Micciancio, D., Ristenpart, T. (eds.) CRYPTO 2020. LNCS, vol. 12170, pp. 464–493. Springer, Cham (2020). https://doi.org/10.1007/978-3-030-56784-2_16
4. Jiang, Y.: The direction of updatable encryption does not matter much. In: Moriai, S., Wang, H. (eds.) ASIACRYPT 2020. LNCS, vol. 12493, pp. 529–558. Springer, Cham (2020). https://doi.org/10.1007/978-3-030-64840-4_18
5. Nishimaki, R.: The direction of updatable encryption does matter. In: Hanaoka, G., Shikata, J., Watanabe, Y. (eds.) PKC 2022. LNCS, vol. 13178, pp. 194–224. Springer, Cham (2022). https://doi.org/10.1007/978-3-030-97131-1_7
6. Barker, E.: Recommendation on Key Management SP800-57-Part-1-revised2 08 Mar 2007. NIST (2007). https://csrc.nist.gov/publications/nistpubs/800-57/sp800-57-Part1-revised2_Mar08-2007.pdf
7. Kaltz, J., Lindell, Y.: Introduction to Modern Cryptography: Principles and Protocols. Chapman and Hall, Boca Raton (2008)

8. Bos, J., Ducas, L., Kiltz, E., et al.: CRYSTALS-Kyber: a CCA-secure module-lattice-based KEM. In: 2018 IEEE European Symposium on Security and Privacy (EuroS&P), pp. 353–367. IEEE (2018). https://ieeexplore.ieee.org/abstract/document/8406610/

9. Ducas, L., et al.: CRYSTALS-Dilithium: a lattice-based digital signature scheme. IACR Trans. Cryptographic Hardw. Embed. Syst. 238–268. (2018). https://doi.org/10.13154/tches.v2018.i1.238-268

10. Brakerski, Z., Gentry, C., Vaikuntanathan, V.: (Leveled) fully homomorphic encryption without bootstrapping. ACM Trans. Comput. Theory (TOCT) $6(3)$, 1–36 (2014)

11. Jain, A., Lin, H., Sahai, A.: Indistinguishability obfuscation from well-founded assumptions. In: 53rd Annual ACM SIGACT Symposium on Theory of Computing, STOC 2021. ACM (2021). https://doi.org/10.1145/3406325.3451093

12. Langlois, A., Stehlé, D.: Worst-case to average-case reductions for module lattices. Des. Codes Crypt. $75(3)$, 565–599 (2015). https://doi.org/10.1007/s10623-014-9938-4

13. Song, Y., Gao, H.: Token open security model for updatable encryption. In: 2022 4th International Conference on Data Intelligence and Security (ICDIS), pp. 16–21 (2022). https://doi.org/10.1109/ICDIS55630.2022.00010

14. Song, Y., Gao, H., Wang, S., Ma, C., Sun, K.: Token Open Secure and Practical NTRU-based Updatable Encryption, 26 May 2023, Preprint (Version 2). https://doi.org/10.21203/rs.3.rs-2721947/v2

Zero-Knowledge Proofs for SIDH Variants with Masked Degree or Torsion

Youcef Mokrani$^{(\boxtimes)}$ and David Jao$^{(\boxtimes)}$

Department of Combinatorics and Optimization, University of Waterloo,
Waterloo, ON N2L 3G1, Canada
{ymokrani,djao}@uwaterloo.ca

Abstract. The polynomial attacks on SIDH by Castryck, Decru, Maino, Martindale and Robert have shown that, while the general isogeny problem is still considered unfeasible to break, it is possible to efficiently compute a secret isogeny when given its degree and image on enough torsion points. A natural response from many researchers has been to propose SIDH variants where one or both of these possible extra pieces of information is masked in order to obtain schemes for which a polynomial attack is not currently known. Examples of such schemes include M-SIDH, MD-SIDH and FESTA. Unfortunately, these SIDH variants are still vulnerable to older adaptive attacks against SIDH where the adversary sends public keys whose associated isogeny is either unknown or inexistent. For the original SIDH scheme, one possible defense against these attacks is to use zero-knowledge proofs that a secret isogeny has been honestly computed. However, such proofs do not currently exist for most SIDH variants. In this paper, we present new zero-knowledge proofs for isogenies whose degree or torsion points have been masked. The security of these proofs mainly relies on the hardness of DSSP.

Keywords: Elliptic curves · Supersingular isogenies · Zero-knowledge proofs

1 Introduction

Since polynomial time attacks on SIDH have been discovered [5,13,14], multiple attempts have been made to create SIDH variants that resist these known attacks. It is important to note that these attacks only work on SIDH and not the general isogeny problem, because they require extra information that is leaked by SIDH, namely its degree and its mapping for a large enough set of auxiliary points.

The core idea behind these new variants is to mask the degree or the auxiliary points such that a shared secret can still be generated between honest parties without leaking information that can be used by an attacker to break the scheme. While these new variants are resistant to the currently known attacks on SIDH, there are still vulnerable to older adaptive attacks [10,11] where an attacker

© The Author(s), under exclusive license to Springer Nature Switzerland AG 2024
F. Regazzoni et al. (Eds.): SPACE 2023, LNCS 14412, pp. 48–65, 2024.
https://doi.org/10.1007/978-3-031-51583-5_3

sends invalid public keys in order to gain information about a victim's secret key if a key exchange is attempted.

In the context of SIDH, one way to protect against such attacks is to have the parties prove the validity and knowledge of their secret using a Fiat-Shamir signature based on a zero-knowledge proof for their secret isogeny. However, the new masking techniques of the variants make the old zero-knowledge proofs unusable. Hence there is a need for new proofs. In this paper, we present multiple new zero-knowledge proofs for multiple SIDH variants. The collection of proofs shown here can do any combination of the following:

- Either mask or prove the degree of the secret isogeny.
- Reveal no information about the mapping of torsion points, or prove the honesty of the masked torsion point information when each torsion point is scaled by the same constant (as in M-SIDH [10]) or different ones (as in binSIDH [3] or the diagonal variant of FESTA [4]).

It is worth noting that none of the proofs in this paper requires knowledge of any endomorphism rings, making them compatible with schemes that require these rings to be unknown to all. For security, the zero-knowledge proofs in this paper only require the DSSP assumption as well as a computationally binding and statistically hiding commitment scheme.

In Sects. 2 and 3, we present the theorems, assumptions and notations used in our protocols. The zero-knowledge proofs of this paper are presented in Sects. 4, 5, 6 and 7.

1.1   Related Papers

In cases where the prover has access to the endomorphism ring of the domain curve, they can prove their knowledge of an isogeny between the claimed curves using SQISign [9] or SQISignHD [6]. Since the isogeny revealed in the associated zero-knowledge proof is independent of the secret isogeny, including its degree, it stays zero-knowledge even when the degree of the secret isogeny is part of the secret. However, in the context of using it to prove honest public keys for SIDH variants, this technique cannot be used to prove that the claimed torsion point information is correct. Also, there are protocols where the endomorphism ring has to be kept unknown from all participants, and SQISign cannot be used in these cases.

Fouotsa et al. have already proposed a zero-knowledge proof for M-SIDH [10]. However, this proof relies on a stronger assumption than DSSP. In this paper, we present zero-knowledge proofs which are able to show the same properties while only needing DSSP, at the cost of a slight loss in efficiency.

2   Background Knowledge and Assumptions

The security of the zero-knowledge proofs we are proposing in this paper rely on the following two theorems. The first give us an upper bound on the probability to distinguish the codomain of a random isogeny from a random supersingular curve, while the second gives a similar bound on the probability of distinguishing the parallel isogeny in an SIDH square from a random one.

Theorem 2.1 ([12]). *Let p, ℓ be a prime numbers, e be a positive integer and E_0 be a supersingular elliptic curve of $\mathbb{F}_{p^2}$. Let E be the codomain of a random cyclic isogeny of degree ℓ^e and domain E_0. Let Γ be the set of supersingular elliptic curves over $\mathbb{F}_{p^2}$. For every $E' \in \Gamma$, we have that*

$$\left| \mathbb{P}(E = E') - \frac{1}{|\Gamma|} \right| \leq \left(\frac{2\sqrt{\ell}}{\ell + 1} \right)^e$$

Theorem 2.2 (Corollary of Theorem 11 of [2]**).** *Let p, ℓ be a prime numbers, A be a positive integer not divisible by ℓ, and $\psi : E_0 \rightarrow E_1$ be cyclic isogeny of degree A between two supersingular elliptic curves over $\mathbb{F}_{p^2}$.*

Let ψ be a random cyclic isogeny of degree ℓ^e and ϕ' be the isogeny parallel to ϕ in an SIDH square between ϕ and ψ.

As e grows to infinity, the domain E_2 of ϕ' converges towards a uniformly random curve in Γ and ϕ' converges towards a uniformly random cyclic isogeny of degree A and domain E_2. The convergence rate is exponential.

It is worth noting that Theorems 2.1 and 2.2 can be generalized so that we still obtain exponential convergence towards uniform distributions when ℓ^e is replaced with a positive integer B increasing to infinity. With the above results, given large enough parameter sets, we can assume that the following problem is hard.

Assumption 1 (DSSP) *Let A and B be two large, relatively prime integers. Given a cyclic isogeny $\phi : E_0 \rightarrow E_1$ of degree A, the decisional supersingular product problem is to distinguish between the following two distributions:*

1. $\mathcal{D}_0 = \{(E_2, E_3, \phi')\}$ *such that there exists a cyclic subgroup $G \subseteq E_0[B]$ of order B and $E_2 \cong E_0/G$ and $E_3 \cong E_1/\phi(G)$, and $\phi' : E_2 \rightarrow E_3$ is a degree A cyclic isogeny.*
2. $\mathcal{D}_1 = \{(E_2, E_3, \phi')\}$ *such that E_2 is a random supersingular elliptic curve with the same cardinality as E_0 and E_3 is the codomain of a random cyclic isogeny $\phi' : E_2 \rightarrow E_3$ of degree A.*

We assume that this problem is hard.

We also need to assume the existence of a function with the following security properties.

Assumption 2 ([2]) *We assume the existence of a function H which is a statistically hiding and computationally binding commitment scheme on the set of binary strings. Denote by $\mathcal{H}$ the codomain of H.*

In cases where we use H on arbitrary data, we implicitly assume that this data is encoded in the form of a binary string using a suitable encoding scheme.

3   Additional Definitions and Notations

The protocols presented in this paper use multiple functions and mathematical objects, many of these being used for more than one protocol. In order to avoid repeating these definitions every time, we present them once in this section.

Definition 3.1. *Given a cyclic isogeny* $\phi : E \to F$, GENERATINGPOINT(ϕ) *return a point K generating the kernel of ϕ. Given an elliptic curve point $K \in E$,* ISOGENYFROMKERNEL(K) *returns an isogeny whose kernel is generated by K.*

Definition 3.2. *Given a supersingular elliptic curve E and a positive integer n,* CYCLICISOGENY(E, n) *returns a random cyclic isogeny whose domain is E and degree is n.*

Definition 3.3. *Given two isogenies* $\phi : E \to E_1$ *and* $\psi : E \to E_2$ *of relatively prime degrees,* PARALLELISOGENY(ϕ, ψ) *returns the isogeny parallel to ϕ in the isogeny square generated by ϕ and ψ.*

Definition 3.4. *Given an elliptic curve E and a positive integer n, $E[n]$ is the subgroup formed of the points of order dividing n while $E[[n]]$ is the subset of the points of order exactly n.*

Definition 3.5. *Given an elliptic curve E and a positive integer n, the function* RANDOMBASIS(E, n) *returns a uniformly random basis (P, Q) of $E[n]$.*

Definition 3.6. *Given three elliptic curve points P, Q, R,* DDLOG(P, Q, R) *returns a pair of integers (e, f) such that $[e]P + [f]Q = R$. Note that we only use this function where a solution exists and is unique modulo a known integer. Also note that we only use this function in groups whose order is smooth, making the function efficient.*

Definition 3.7. *Given an isogeny* $\phi : E \to F$, CODOMAIN(ϕ) *returns F.*

Definition 3.8. *Given a positive integer A and two integers (a, b),* INVERPAIR(a, b, A) *returns a pair of integers (a', b') such that $a'b - b'a$ is invertible modulo A. Note that we only use this function in cases where a valid solution exists.*

Definition 3.9. *Given a positive integer A, FacSet(A) is the set of positive factors of A. Given two positive integers A and B, FacSetTwo(A, B) is the set of integers d such that $A \mid D \mid B$.*

Definition 3.10. *Given a possibly non-cyclic isogeny ϕ, Cycliphy(ϕ) return a cyclic isogeny with the same domain and codomain. This can be easily obtained by seeing ϕ as a walk on the isogeny graph and removing the backtracking.*

Definition 3.11. *The function IsoValid(E, F, ϕ) returns* **true** *if ϕ is a valid isogeny from E to F and* **false** *otherwise.*

Definition 3.12. *In this paper, we work on elliptic curves defined over a known field* $\mathbb{F}$. *Also, we consider to elliptic curves with the same j-invariant to be the same. Let* Γ *be the set of supersingular elliptic curves defined over that field.*

Definition 3.13. *During the Verification step of the zero-knowledge proofs in this paper, we use* **accept** *to note that the Verifier accepts and* $\perp$ *to note refusal.*

4   Masking the Degree

Suppose that we want to prove knowledge of an isogeny between two supersingular elliptic curves without revealing its degree. When possible, the most efficient solution would be to use SQISign [9] or SQISignHD [6]. However, these protocols both require the prover to know the endomorphism ring of the starting curve, which limits the possible applications.

In protocols where the degree of an isogeny is part of the secret, a multiple of said degree is usually publicly known. That is the case for both MD-SIDH [10] and terSIDH [3]. In such cases, we can use rejection sampling first introduced in the context of isogenies in SeaSign [8] in order to mask the degree during a normal SIDH proof.

The core idea of MDISOZKP, when trying to prove knowledge of an isogeny $\phi : E_0 \to E_1$, is to start by computing an isogeny $\phi' : E_1 \to E_1'$ of random and potentially large degree with the same prime factors as the degree of ϕ.

We can then remove the backtracking appearing in $\phi'\phi$ in order to obtain the cyclic isogeny $\Phi : E_0 \to E_1'$. The step is necessary to make sure that the adversary does not learn anything about the secret isogeny since the degree of backtracking is a non-trivial factor of the degree of ϕ.

We can then compute an isogeny $\psi_L : E_0 \to E_2$ of degree relatively prime to Φ and compute the SIDH square between the two in order to obtain the isogenies $\Phi' : E_2 \to E_3$ and $\psi_R : E_1' \to E_3$. For the commitment, the prover can publish a hash of E_2 and E_3 and, depending on the challenge, the prover either reveals ψ_L, Φ' or $\psi_R\phi'$.

Since we use rejection sampling, in cases where the challenge asks for Φ' to be revealed, the prover needs to check that the degree respects some additional conditions. Otherwise, the proof is aborted. Later in this section, we prove that the probability of requiring an abort is low enough for a Fiat-Shamir signature to be feasible.

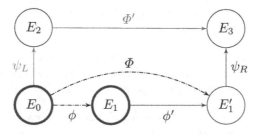

Definition 4.1 (MDISOZKP). *Let* $A = \prod_{i=1}^{s} q_i^{f_i}$ *be a large integer such that the* $q_i s$ *are distinct primes dividing* $p + 1$. *Let* B *be a large positive integer relatively prime to* A. *Let* $\phi : E_0 \to E_1$ *be a secret cyclic isogeny of degree* $A \mid \mathcal{A}$.

n is a positive integer representing the number of times the following proof will be repeated. The challenge is a random $chall \in \{-1, 0, 1\}$.

Commitment	Response
$A' \leftarrow\!\!\$ \ FacSet(\mathcal{A}^{sn})$	**if** $chall = -1$:
$\phi' \leftarrow CyclicIsogeny(E_1, A')$	$\quad$ **return** (E_2, r_2, ψ_L)
$E_1' \leftarrow Codomain(\phi')$	**if** $chall = 0$:
$\Phi \leftarrow Cycliphy(\phi'\phi)$	$\quad$ **return** $(E_3, r_3, \psi_R\phi')$
$K_{\psi_L} \leftarrow\!\!\$ \ E_0[[B]]$	**if** $chall = 1$:
$\psi_L \leftarrow \textsc{IsogenyFromKernel}(K_{\psi_L})$	$\quad$ **if** $\deg(\Phi) \notin FacSetTwo(A, \mathcal{A}^{sn})$: **abort**
$E_2 \leftarrow Codomain(\psi_L)$	$\quad$ **return** $(E_2, E_3, r_2, r_3, \Phi')$
$\Phi' \leftarrow ParallelIsogeny(\Phi, \psi_L)$	

Verification
if $chall = -1$:
$\quad$ **if** $C_2 \neq H(E_2, r_2)$:$\perp$
$\quad$ **if** $\neg IsoValid(E_0, E_2, \psi_L)$:$\perp$
if $chall = 0$:
$\quad$ **if** $C_3 \neq H(E_3, r_3)$:$\perp$
$\quad$ **if** $\neg IsoValid(E_1, E_3, \psi_R\phi')$:$\perp$
if $chall = 1$:
$\quad$ **if** $(C_2, C_3) \neq (H(E_2, r_2), H(E_3, r_3))$:$\perp$
$\quad$ **if** $\neg IsoValid(E_2, E_3, \Phi')$:$\perp$
return true

Other commitment lines:

$K_{\psi_R} \leftarrow \Phi(K_{\psi_L})$

$\psi_R \leftarrow \textsc{IsogenyFromKernel}(K_{\psi_R})$

$E_3 \leftarrow Codomain(\psi_R)$

$r_2, r_3 \leftarrow\!\!\$ \ N$

$C_2 \leftarrow H(E_2, r_2)$

$C_3 \leftarrow H(E_3, r_3)$

return (C_2, C_3)

Theorem 4.2. *Given Assumption 2, MDISOZKP is 3-special sound for the knowledge of an isogeny from* E_0 *to* E_1.

Proof. Since H is computationally binding, the commitments are equivalent to obtaining E_2 and E_3 directly when it comes to soundness. Given valid ψ_L, $\psi_R\phi'$ and Φ' for the same commitment (E_2, E_3), $\psi_R\phi'\hat{\Phi}'\psi_L$ is an isogeny from E_0 to E_1.

Theorem 4.3. *If MDISOZKP does not abort when chall* $= 1$, *then the degree of* Φ' *is a uniformly random element of FacSetTwo$(A, \mathcal{A}^{sn})$.*

Proof. Let $d = \frac{\deg(\phi'\phi)}{\deg(\Phi)}$. For any value of d, $\frac{\deg(\phi)}{d}$ divides $\mathcal{A}$. If we fix the value of d, ϕ' can have any degree dividing $\mathcal{A}^{ns}$. We also have that the degree of ϕ' must divide $\mathcal{A}^{ns}$. Hence, since we are conditioning on the fact that MDISOZKP does not abort and chall $= 1$, for any possible degree of ϕ and value of d, there is a unique degree of ϕ' for every target degree of Φ. This makes the degree of Φ uniform, and since Φ and Φ' have the same degree, the same holds for Φ'.

Theorem 4.4. *Given Assumptions 1 and 2, if MDISOZKP does not abort, then it is honest verifier zero-knowledge.*

Proof. For the proof, we can create a simulator $\mathcal{S}$ for outputting a commitment-challenge-answer triple indistinguishable from that of honest parties. To do so, we describe the simulator for each possible challenge. When chall $= -1$, $\mathcal{S}$ can generate $(K_{\psi_L}, \psi_L, E_2, r_2)$ as would an honest party and generate an honest commitment C_2. Since H is statistically hiding, randomly sampling C_3 from $\mathcal{H}$ is indistinguishable from an honest computation. If chall $= 0$, $\mathcal{S}$ can generate (A', ϕ', E_1') as would an honest party. Since there is a bijection between $E_0[[B]]$ and $E_1'[[B]]$ in addition to the fact that K_{ψ_L} is never revealed, directly sampling K_{ψ_R} is indistinguishable from an honest output. Using this value, $\mathcal{S}$ can generate (ψ_R, E_3, r_3, C_3) as normal and randomly sample C_2. When chall $= -1$, $\mathcal{S}$ can sample a random $A'' \in \text{FacSetTwo}(\mathcal{A}, \mathcal{A}^{sn})$, a random supersingular elliptic curve E_2 and then a random cyclic isogeny Φ' using CyclicIsogeny(E_2, A''). Given Assumption 1, This construction is indistinguishable from an honest one. $\mathcal{S}$ can then compute the other values as normal.

Theorem 4.5. *Given n rounds of MDISOZKP, the probability that no abort happens is at least $\frac{1}{e}$.*

Proof. For fixed ϕ and any value of $d = \frac{\deg(\phi'\phi)}{\deg(\Phi)}$, there is always at least $\prod_{i=1}^{s}(ns - 2)f_i$ possible degrees of ϕ' that do not cause an abort. Hence, the probability of the protocol not aborting in a given round can be lower bounded by

$$\frac{2}{3} + \frac{1}{3}\frac{\prod_{i=1}^{s}(ns-2)f_i}{\prod_{i=1}^{s}(ns+1)f_i} = \frac{2}{3} + \frac{1}{3}\left(\frac{ns-2}{ns+1}\right)^s$$

The probability of having no abort in any round can then be lower bounded by

$$\left(\frac{2}{3} + \frac{1}{3}\left(\frac{ns-2}{ns+1}\right)^s\right)^n = \frac{1}{e} + \frac{2s-1}{2ens} + O\left(\frac{1}{n^2}\right) > \frac{1}{e}$$

5   Masked Torsion

M-SIDH [10] has been proposed as a possible fix for the attacks on SIDH [5,13, 14]. The main difference is that, for a secret isogeny $\phi : E_0 \to E_1$ of degree A between two publicly known supersingular elliptic curve, M-SIDH also reveals $([\alpha]\phi(P_0), [\alpha]\phi(Q_0))$ for an unknown random α where (P_0, Q_0) is a basis of $E_0[B]$.

This protocol creates the need of being to prove knowledge of an isogeny with the above properties without leaking extra information. Basso [1] published a 3-sound zero-knowledge proof that does just that. However, that protocol relies on a stronger assumption than DSSP. A 6-sound variation only relying on DSSP is mentioned in the same paper but is dismissed for being too inefficient.

For the original SIDH protocol, De Feo et al. [7] proposed a 3-sound zero-knowledge proof that relied on the double-DSSP assumption. Such an assumption is too strong, as it can be broken by the same attacks as SIDH. However, we can modify the protocol to only rely on the DSSP assumption at the cost of now being 4-sound. Masking the torsion can be done easily by adding a random scalar in the protocol.

The core idea of MTISOZKP consists in generating two cyclic isogenies $\psi_{L,i}$: $E_0 \to E_{2,i}$ of degree B whose kernel generators form a basis of $E[B]$. These isogenies can be used with ϕ to construct two SIDH squares sharing an edge. In order to not leak information by doing so, we work with the dual of the isogenies of degree B as well as random bases of $E_{2,i}$. Also, we use H in order to force the commitments to be honest without leaking information.

Definition 5.1 (MTISOZKP). *Let A and B be two relatively prime positive integers. Let $\phi : E_0 \to E_1$ be a secret isogeny of degree A such that $\phi(P_0) = P_1$ and $\phi(Q_0) = Q_1$ where P_0 and Q_0 are a basis of the $E_0[B]$. Let $\alpha \leftarrow\!\$ \, (\mathbb{Z}/B\mathbb{Z})^*$ be secret and $(E_0, E_1, P_0, Q_0, [\alpha]P_1, [\alpha]Q_1)$ be public. The challenge is a random $chall \in \{-1, 0, 1, 2\}$.*

Commitment

$(P_1', Q_1') \leftarrow ([\alpha]P_1, [\alpha]Q_1)$
$K_\phi \leftarrow \textsc{GeneratingPoint}(\phi)$
$(K_{\psi_{L,0}}, K_{\psi_{L,1}}) \leftarrow \textsc{RandomBasis}(E_0, B)$
$\beta \leftarrow\!\$ \, (\mathbb{Z}/B\mathbb{Z})^*$
$(U, V) \leftarrow \textsc{RandomBasis}(E_0, A)$
$(e, f) \leftarrow \textsc{DDLOG}(U, V, K_\phi)$
for $i \in \{0, 1\}$:
   $\psi_{L,i} \leftarrow \textsc{IsogenyFromKernel}(K_{\psi_{L,i}})$
   $E_{2,i} \leftarrow \textsc{Codomain}(\psi_{L,i})$
   $(P_{2,i}, Q_{2,i}) \leftarrow \textsc{RandomBasis}(E_{2,i}, B)$
   $K_{\phi_i} \leftarrow \psi_i(K_\phi)$
   $\phi_i \leftarrow \textsc{IsogenyFromKernel}(K_{\phi_i})$
   $\psi_{R,i} \leftarrow \textsc{IsogenyFromKernel}(\phi(K_{\psi_{L,i}}))$
   $E_{3,i} \leftarrow \textsc{Codomain}(\phi_i)$
   $(P_{3,i}, Q_{3,i}) \leftarrow ([\beta]\phi_i(P_{2,i}), [\beta]\phi_i(Q_{2,i}))$
   $K_{\hat{\psi_{L,i}}} \leftarrow \textsc{GeneratingPoint}(\hat{\psi}_{L,i})$
   $(c_i, d_i) \leftarrow \textsc{DDLOG}(P_{2,i}, Q_{2,i}, K_{\hat{\psi_{L,i}}})$
   $(c_i', d_i') \leftarrow \textsc{InverPair}(c_i, d_i, B)$
   $R_{0,i} \leftarrow \hat{\psi}_{L,i}([c_i']P_{2,i} + [d_i']Q_{2,i})$
   $(a_i, b_i) \leftarrow \textsc{DDLOG}(P_0, Q_0, R_{0,i})$
   $U_i' \leftarrow \psi_{L,i}(U)$
   $V_i' \leftarrow \psi_{L,i}(V)$
   $r_{L,i}, r_{R,i}, r_{m,i}, r_{w,i} \leftarrow\!\$ \, N$
   $C_{L,i} \leftarrow H(E_{2,i}, P_{2,i}, Q_{2,i}, r_{L,i})$
   $C_{R,i} \leftarrow H(E_{3,i}, P_{3,i}, Q_{3,i}, r_{R,i})$
   $C_{m,i} \leftarrow H(c_i, d_i, c_i', d_i', a_i, b_i, r_{m,i})$
   $C_{w,i} \leftarrow H(U_i', V_i', r_{w,i})$

Commitment (cont.)

$r_A, r_B, r_E \leftarrow\!\$ \, N$
$\gamma \leftarrow \alpha\beta^{-1}$
$C_A \leftarrow H(\gamma, r_A)$
$C_B \leftarrow H(\beta, r_B)$
$C_E \leftarrow H(e, f, r_E)$
$C_1 \leftarrow (C_{L,0}, C_{R,0}, C_{m,0}, C_{w,0})$
$C_2 \leftarrow (C_{L,1}, C_{R,1}, C_{m,1}, C_{w,1})$
$C_3 \leftarrow (C_A, C_B, C_E)$
return (C_1, C_2, C_3)

Response

$z_{L,0} \leftarrow (E_{2,0}, P_{2,0}, Q_{2,0}, r_{L_0})$
$z_{L,1} \leftarrow (E_{2,1}, P_{2,1}, Q_{2,1}, r_{L_1})$
$z_{R,0} \leftarrow (E_{3,0}, P_{3,0}, Q_{3,0}, r_{R_0})$
$z_{R,1} \leftarrow (E_{3,1}, P_{3,1}, Q_{3,1}, r_{R_1})$
$z_{w,0} \leftarrow (U_0', V_0', r_{w,0})$
$z_{w,1} \leftarrow (U_1', V_1', r_{w,1})$
$z_{m,0} \leftarrow (c_0, d_0, c_1, d_1, c_0', d_0', a_0, b_0, r_{m,0})$
$z_{m,1} \leftarrow (c_1', d_1', a_1, b_1, r_{m,1})$
if $chall = -1$:
   return $(z_{L,0}, z_{L,1}, z_{m,0}, z_{m,1}, z_{w,0}, z_{w,1})$
if $chall = 0$:
   return $(z_{R,0}, z_{R,1}, z_{m,0}, z_{m,1}, (\gamma, r_A))$
if $chall = 1$:
   return $(z_{w,0}, (e, f, r_E), z_{L,0}, z_{R,0}, (\beta, r_B))$
if $chall = 2$:
   return $(z_{w,1}, (e, f, r_E), z_{L,1}, z_{R,1}, (\beta, r_B))$

Verification

---

if $chall = -1$:

  for $i \in \{0, 1\}$:

    if $C_{L,i} \neq H(E_{2,i}, P_{2,i}, Q_{2,i}, r_{L,i})$:$\perp$

    if $(C_{m,i}, C_{w,i}) \neq (H(c_i, d_i, c_i', d_i', a_i, b_i, r_{m,i}), H(U_i', V_i', r_{w,i}))$:$\perp$

    $K_{\psi_{\hat{L},i}} \leftarrow [c_i]P_{2,i} + [d_i]Q_{2,i}$

    if $K_{\psi_{\hat{L},i}} \notin E_{2,i}[[B]]$:$\perp$

    $\psi_{\hat{L},i} \leftarrow \text{IsogenyFromKernel}(K_{\psi_{\hat{L},i}})$

    $E_{0,i}' \leftarrow \text{Codomain}(\psi_{\hat{L},i})$

    if $E_{0,i}' \neq E_0$:$\perp$

    $R_{0,i}' \leftarrow \psi_{\hat{L},i}([c_i']P_{2,i} + [d']Q_{2,i})$

    if $R_{0,i}' \neq [a_i]P_0 + [b_i]Q_0$:$\perp$

    if $(\text{GCD}(a_0 b_1 - a_1 b_0, B), \text{GCD}(c_i' d_i - d_i' c_i, B)) \neq (1, 1)$:$\perp$

  if $(\psi_{\hat{L},0}(U_0'), \psi_{\hat{L},0}(V_0')) \neq (\psi_{\hat{L},1}(U_1'), \psi_{\hat{L},1}(V_1'))$:$\perp$

if $chall = 0$:

  for $i \in \{0, 1\}$:

    if $(C_{R,i}, C_A) \neq (H(E_{3,i}, P_{3,i}, Q_{3,i}, r_{R,i}), H(\gamma, r_A))$:$\perp$

    if $C_{m,i} \neq H(c_i, d_i, c_i', d_i', a_i, b_i, r_{m,i})$:$\perp$

    $K_{\psi_{\hat{R},i}} \leftarrow [c_i]P_{3,i} + [d_i]Q_{3,i}$

    if $K_{\psi_{\hat{R},i}} \notin E_{3,i}[[B]]$:$\perp$

    $\psi_{\hat{R},i} \leftarrow \text{IsogenyFromKernel}(K_{\psi_{\hat{R},i}})$

    $E_{1,i}' \leftarrow \text{Codomain}(\psi_{\hat{R},i})$

    if $E_{1,i}' \neq E_1'$:$\perp$

    $R_{1,i}' \leftarrow \psi_{\hat{R},i}([c_i']P_{3,i} + [d']Q_{3,i})$

    if $[\gamma] R_{1,i}' \neq [a_i]P_1' + [b_i]Q_1'$:$\perp$

    if $(\text{GCD}(a_0 b_1 - a_1 b_0, B), \text{GCD}(c_i' d_i - d_i' c_i, B)) \neq (1, 1)$:$\perp$

else :

  $i \leftarrow chall - 1$:

  $K_{\Phi_i'} \leftarrow [e]U_i' + [f]V_i'$

  if $(C_{L,i}, C_{R,i}) \neq (H(E_{2,i}, P_{2,i}, Q_{2,i}, r_{L,i}), H(E_{3,i}, P_{3,i}, Q_{3,i}, r_{R,i}))$:$\perp$

  if $(C_{w,i}, C_E, C_B) \neq (H(U_i', V_i', r_{w,i}), H(e, f, r_E), H(\beta, r_B))$:$\perp$

  if $K_{\phi_i'} \notin E_{2,i}[[A]]$:$\perp$

  $\phi_i' \leftarrow \text{IsogenyFromKernel}(K_{\phi_i'})$

  $E_{3,i}' \leftarrow \text{Codomain}(\Phi_i')$

  if $(E_{3,i}', [\beta]\phi_i'(P_{2,i}), [\beta]\phi_i'(Q_{2,i})) \neq (E_{3,i}, P_{3,i}, Q_{3,i})$:$\perp$

return true

Theorem 5.2 (Correctness). *If the prover is honest, then the verification algorithm will always return* **true**.

Proof. If chall $= -1$, the properties checked by the verification algorithm were directly computed by the prover. Hence, this case will always be correct.

If chall $\in \{1, 2\}$, the properties checked by the verification algorithm are all respected by an honest $[\beta]\phi_{\text{chall}-1}$. Hence, this case will always be correct.

If chall $= 0$, we are working with almost the same SIDH square as in [7]. The main difference being that $(P_{3,i}, Q_{3,i})$ have an extra β factor and (P_1', Q_1') have an extra α factor. This is dealt by multiplying $\hat{\psi}_{R,i}$ by $[\alpha\beta^{-1}]$.

Theorem 5.3 (Soundness). *Given Assumption 2, MTISOZKP is 4-special sound for the knowledge of a cyclic isogeny of the claimed degree between the claimed curves with the claimed torsion point information.*

Proof. We show that for a fixed commitment, if one obtains valid answers to all 4 possible challenges, then they can compute an isogeny with the claimed properties. Since H is a computationally binding commitment scheme, we can assume that the four answers agree on the committed values.

The goal is to use the possible answers in order to compute and isogeny $\rho :$ $E_0 \to E_1$ of degree A and an integer α such that $(P_1', Q_1') = ([\alpha]\rho(P_0), [\alpha]\rho(Q_0))$.

Looking at the isogeny square for each $i \in \{0, 1\}$, we are given the pair (c_i, d_i) which define the point $K_{\hat{\psi}_{L,i}} = [c_i]P_{2,i} + [d_i]Q_{2,i}$ which in turn defines the isogeny $\hat{\psi}_{L,i} : E_{2,i} \to E_0$ of degree B. We are also given $K_{\phi_i'} = [e]U_i' + [f]V_i'$ which defines an isogeny $\phi_i' : E_{2,i} \to E_{3,i}$ of degree A. We can then complete the $(\hat{\psi}_{L,i}, \phi_i')$-isogeny square to obtain a ρ candidate of degree A that we name $\rho_i : E_0 \to E_1$.

Next, we show that ρ_0 and ρ_1 have the same kernel and are therefore equivalent. It is the case since

$$\ker(\rho_0) = \hat{\psi}_{L,0}(\ker(\phi_0')) = \left\langle \hat{\psi}_{L,0}([e]U_0' + [f]V_0') \right\rangle = \left\langle \hat{\psi}_{L,1}([e]U_1' + [f]V_1') \right\rangle$$
$$= \hat{\psi}_{L,1}(\ker(\phi_1')) = \ker(\rho_1)$$

We also have an α candidate in $\gamma\beta$. All that remains is to show that $\rho = \rho_0 = \rho_1$ has the correct torsion point images.

Recall that we are given pairs (a_i, b_i) such that $R_{0,i} = [a_i]P_0 + [b_i]Q_0$ and the matrix $M := \begin{pmatrix} a_0 & b_0 \\ a_1 & b_1 \end{pmatrix}$ is invertible.

Hence, $\{R_{0,0}, R_{0,1}\}$ is a basis of $E_0[B]$.

Also recall that $R_{0,i} = \hat{\psi}_{L,i}([c_i']P_{2,i} + [d_i']Q_{2,i})$, $R_{1,i} = \hat{\psi}_{R,i}([c_i']P_{3,i} + [d_i']Q_{3,i})$ and $(P_{3,i}, Q_{3,i}) = ([\beta]\phi_i(P_{2,i}), [\beta]\phi_i(Q_{2,i}))$. Since $\rho\psi_{L,i} = \psi_{R,i}\phi_i$, we have that $\rho(R_{0,i}) = [\beta^{-1}]R_{1,i}$. Hence:

$$\begin{pmatrix} R_{0,0} \\ R_{0,1} \end{pmatrix} = M \begin{pmatrix} P_0 \\ Q_0 \end{pmatrix} \implies \begin{pmatrix} \rho(R_{0,0}) \\ \rho(R_{0,1}) \end{pmatrix} = M \begin{pmatrix} \rho(P_0) \\ \rho(Q_0) \end{pmatrix}$$
$$\implies \begin{pmatrix} [\beta^{-1}]R_{1,0} \\ [\beta^{-1}]R_{1,1} \end{pmatrix} = M \begin{pmatrix} \rho(P_0) \\ \rho(Q_0) \end{pmatrix} \implies M^{-1} \begin{pmatrix} [\beta^{-1}]R_{1,0} \\ [\beta^{-1}]R_{1,1} \end{pmatrix} = \begin{pmatrix} \rho(P_0) \\ \rho(Q_0) \end{pmatrix}$$
$$\implies \begin{pmatrix} [\gamma^{-1}\beta^{-1}]P_1' \\ [\gamma^{-1}\beta^{-1}]Q_1' \end{pmatrix} = \begin{pmatrix} \rho(P_0) \\ \rho(Q_0) \end{pmatrix} \implies \begin{pmatrix} P_1' \\ Q_1' \end{pmatrix} = \begin{pmatrix} [\beta\gamma]\rho(P_0) \\ [\beta\gamma]\rho(Q_0) \end{pmatrix}$$

and this completes the proof.

Theorem 5.4 (Zero-knowledge). *Given Assumptions 1 and 2, MTISOZKP is zero-knowledge.*

Proof. We prove it by showing a simulator S outputting valid a commitment-challenge-answer tuple with the same distribution as an honest prover for each possible challenge.

When the challenge is -1, value that is published without being masked by H can be computed honestly. $C_{R,0}$, $C_{R,1}$, C_A, and C_B can be randomly sampled from $\mathcal{H}$ while being indistinguishable from an honest output by Assumption 2.

When the challenge is 0, the simulator can use the homomorphism property of isogenies to work on the right side of the SIDH squares instead of the left. The masked values can once again be sampled randomly.

When the challenge is 1 or 2, the simulator can sample a random ϕ_i and β and compute the rest using these values. The masked values are, again, sampled randomly. Distinguishing this simulator from an honest output is equivalent to solving the DSSP, which we assume to be hard.

6   Double Masked Subgroup

Instead of multiplying both torsion points images by the same constant, bin-SIDH, terSIDH [3] and the diagonal variant of FESTA [4] multiply each point by independent random scalars. This has the consequence of making MTISOZKP hard to adapt in this case, as the correctness of the previous protocol relies on the fact that the isogeny multiplying every point by the same constant commutes with every isogeny. Needing to multiply each basis point by a different scalar looses this commutative property, which means that we must look elsewhere for a zero-knowledge proof.

DMSISOZKP is a zero-knowledge proving that a party known an isogeny $\phi : E_0 \to E_1$ such that $([\alpha_P]\phi(P_0), [\alpha_Q]\phi(Q_0)) = (P_1, Q_1)$ for some unknown values of α_P and α_Q. Similarly to MTISOZKP, DMSISOZKP consist of building an SIDH square and using dual isogenies and hashed commitments to maintain zero-knowledge and soundness. The main difference being that, in DMSISOZKP, the generated isogenies are of degree C and the random basis is of order BC. This is so that we can prove information on the B torsion. While only requiring Assumptions 1 and 2 for its security, DMSISOZKP requires some additional conditions on the field for it to be efficient. We need a field such that isogenies of degree C can be efficiently computed while, at the same time, points of order BC can be efficiently be computed and used in other computations. In practice, this requires the chosen prime to be about 50% larger, as isogenies of degree C must also be hard to attack.

Definition 6.1 (DMSISOZKP). *Let A, B and C be two relatively prime positive integers. Let $\phi : E_0 \to E_1$ be a secret isogeny of degree A such that $(\phi(P_0), \phi(Q_0)) = (P_1, Q_1)$ where (P_1, Q_1) form a basis of $E_0[B]$. Let $\alpha_P, \alpha_Q \leftarrow\$ (\mathbb{Z}/(BC)\mathbb{Z})^*$ be secret and $(E_0, E_1, P_0, Q_0, [\alpha_P]P_1, [\alpha_Q]Q_1)$ be public. The challenge is a random chall $\in \{-1, 0, 1\}$.*

Commitment	Verification

Commitment

$(P_1', Q_1') \leftarrow ([\alpha_P]P_1, [\alpha_Q]Q_1)$

$K_\phi \leftarrow \text{GENERATINGPOINT}(\phi)$

$K_{\psi_L} \leftarrow\!\$ E[[C]]$

$K_{\psi_R} \leftarrow \phi(K_{\psi_L})$

$\psi_L \leftarrow IsogenyFromKernel(K_{\psi_L})$

$\psi_R \leftarrow IsogenyFromKernel(K_{\psi_R})$

$E_2 \leftarrow Codomain(\psi_L)$

$E_3 \leftarrow Codomain(\psi_R)$

$(P_{2,P}, Q_{2,P}) \leftarrow RandomBasis(E_2, BC)$

$(P_{2,Q}, Q_{2,Q}) \leftarrow RandomBasis(E_2, BC)$

$\beta_P, \beta_Q \leftarrow\!\$ (\mathbb{Z}/(BC)\mathbb{Z})^*$

$K_{\phi'} \leftarrow \psi_L(K_\phi)$

$\phi' \leftarrow IsogenyFromKernel(K_{\phi'})$

$(P_{3,P}, Q_{3,P}) \leftarrow ([\beta_P]\phi'(P_{2,P}), [\beta_P]\phi'(Q_{2,P}))$

$(P_{3,Q}, Q_{3,Q}) \leftarrow ([\beta_Q]\phi'(P_{2,Q}), [\beta_Q]\phi'(Q_{2,Q}))$

$K_{\hat\psi_L} \leftarrow GeneratingPoint(\hat\psi_L)$

$(c, d) \leftarrow DDLOG(P_{2,P}, Q_{2,P}, K_{\hat\psi_L})$

$(a_P, b_P) \leftarrow DDLOG(\hat\psi_L(P_{2,P}), \hat\psi_L(Q_{2,P}), P_0)$

$(a_Q, b_Q) \leftarrow DDLOG(\hat\psi_L(P_{2,Q}), \hat\psi_L(Q_{2,Q}), Q_0)$

$\gamma_P \leftarrow \alpha_P \beta_P^{-1}$

$\gamma_Q \leftarrow \alpha_Q \beta_Q^{-1}$

$r_L, r_R, r_m, r_A, r_B \leftarrow\!\$ N$

$C_L \leftarrow H(E_2, P_{2,P}, Q_{2,P}, P_{2,Q}, Q_{2,Q}, r_L)$

$C_R \leftarrow H(E_3, P_{3,P}, Q_{3,P}, P_{3,Q}, Q_{3,Q}, r_R)$

$C_m \leftarrow H(a_P, b_P, a_Q, b_Q, c, d, r_m)$

$C_A \leftarrow H(\gamma_P, \gamma_Q, r_A)$

$C_B \leftarrow H(\beta_P, \beta_Q, r_B)$

return $(C_L, C_R, C_m, C_A, C_B)$

Response

$z_L \leftarrow (E_2, P_{2,P}, Q_{2,P}, P_{2,Q}, Q_{2,Q}, r_L)$

$z_R \leftarrow (E_3, P_{3,P}, Q_{3,P}, P_{3,Q}, Q_{3,Q}, r_R)$

$z_m \leftarrow (a_P, b_P, a_Q, b_Q, c, d, r_m)$

if $chall = -1$:

   return (z_L, z_m)

if $chall = 0$:

   return $(z_R, z_m, \gamma_P, \gamma_Q, r_A)$

if $chall = 1$:

   return $(z_L, z_R, \beta_P, \beta_Q, r_B, K_{\phi'})$

Verification

if $chall = -1$:

  if $C_L \neq H(E_2, P_{2,P}, Q_{2,P}, P_{2,Q}, Q_{2,Q}, r_L)$:$\bot$

  if $C_m \neq H(a_P, b_P, a_Q, b_Q, c, d, r_m)$:$\bot$

  if $\neg IsBasis(P_{2,P}, Q_{2,P}, E_2, BC)$:$\bot$

  if $\neg IsBasis(P_{2,Q}, Q_{2,Q}, E_2, BC)$:$\bot$

  $K_{\hat\psi_L} \leftarrow [c]P_{2,P} + [d]Q_{2,P}$

  if $K_{\hat\psi_L} \notin E_2[[C]]$:$\bot$

  $\hat\psi_L \leftarrow IsogenyFromKernel(K_{\hat\psi_L})$

  $E_0' \leftarrow Codomain(\hat\psi_L)$

  if $E_0' \neq E_0$:$\bot$

  if $P_0 \neq [a_P]\hat\psi_L(P_{2,P}) + [b_P]\hat\psi_L(Q_{2,P})$:$\bot$

  if $Q_0 \neq [a_Q]\hat\psi_L(P_{2,Q}) + [b_Q]\hat\psi_L(Q_{2,Q})$:$\bot$

if $chall = 0$:

  if $C_R \neq H(E_3, P_{3,P}, Q_{3,P}, P_{3,Q}, Q_{3,Q}, r_R)$:$\bot$

  if $C_m \neq H(a_P, b_P, a_Q, b_Q, c, d, r_m)$:$\bot$

  if $C_A \neq H(\gamma_P, \gamma_Q, r_A)$:$\bot$

  if $\neg IsBasis(P_{3,P}, Q_{3,P}, E_3, BC)$:$\bot$

  if $\neg IsBasis(P_{3,Q}, Q_{3,Q}, E_3, BC)$:$\bot$

  $K_{\hat\psi_R} \leftarrow [c]P_{3,P} + [d]Q_{3,P}$

  if $K_{\hat\psi_R} \notin E_3[[C]]$:$\bot$

  $\hat\psi_R \leftarrow IsogenyFromKernel(K_{\hat\psi_R})$

  $E_1' \leftarrow Codomain(\hat\psi_R)$

  if $E_1' \neq E_1$:$\bot$

  if $P_1' \neq [a_P\gamma_P]\hat\psi_R(P_{3,P}) + [b_P\gamma_P]\hat\psi_R(Q_{3,P})$:$\bot$

  if $Q_1' \neq [a_Q\gamma_Q]\hat\psi_R(P_{3,Q}) + [b_Q\gamma_Q]\hat\psi_R(Q_{3,Q})$:$\bot$

if $chall = 1$:

  if $C_L \neq H(E_2, P_{2,P}, Q_{2,P}, P_{2,Q}, Q_{2,Q}, r_L)$:$\bot$

  if $C_R \neq H(E_3, P_{3,P}, Q_{3,P}, P_{3,Q}, Q_{3,Q}, r_R)$:$\bot$

  if $C_B \neq H(\beta_P, \beta_Q, r_B)$:$\bot$

  if $K_{\phi'} \notin E_2[[A]]$.$\bot$

  $\phi' \leftarrow IsogenyFromKernel(K_{\phi'})$

  $E_3' \leftarrow Codomain(\phi')$

  if $E_3' \neq E_3$:$\bot$

  if $P_{3,P} \neq [\beta_P]\phi'(P_{2,P})$:$\bot$

  if $Q_{3,P} \neq [\beta_P]\phi'(Q_{2,P})$:$\bot$

  if $P_{3,Q} \neq [\beta_Q]\phi'(P_{2,Q})$:$\bot$

  if $Q_{3,Q} \neq [\beta_Q]\phi'(Q_{2,Q})$:$\bot$

  accept

Theorem 6.2 (Correctness). *If the prover is honest, then the verification algorithm will always return* **true**.

Proof. If chall $= -1$, the properties checked by the verification algorithm were directly computed by the prover. Hence, this case will always be correct.

If chall $= 1$, the properties checked by the verification algorithm are all respected by honest $[\beta_P]\phi'$ and $[\beta_Q]\phi'$. Hence, this case will always be correct.

If chall $= 0$, we have that $\hat{\psi}_R\phi' = \phi\hat{\psi}_L$ since the four isogenies form an SIDH square. Hence:

$$\begin{aligned}
P_1' &= [\alpha_P]\phi(P_0) \\
&= [\alpha_P]\phi([a_P]\hat{\psi}_L(P_{2,P}) + [b_P]\hat{\psi}_L(Q_{2,P})) \\
&= [a_P\alpha_P]\phi\hat{\psi}_L(P_{2,P}) + [b_P\alpha_P]\phi\hat{\psi}_L(Q_{2,P}) \\
&= [a_P\alpha_P]\hat{\psi}_R\phi'(P_{2,P}) + [b_P\alpha_P]\hat{\psi}_R\phi'(Q_{2,P}) \\
&= [a_P\gamma_P]\hat{\psi}_R(P_{3,P}) + [b_P\gamma_P]\hat{\psi}_R(Q_{3,P})
\end{aligned}$$

which is the equation that was to be checked. The same argument also shows that $Q_1' = [a_Q\gamma_Q]\hat{\psi}_R(P_{3,Q}) + [b_Q\gamma_Q]\hat{\psi}_R(Q_{3,Q})$.

Theorem 6.3 (Zero-knowledge). *Given Assumptions 1 and 2, DMSISOZKP is zero-knowledge.*

Proof. We prove it by showing a simulator outputting valid a commitment-challenge-answer tuple with the same distribution as an honest prover for each possible challenge.

When the challenge is -1, the simulator can compute the revealed values honestly and sample random values for the masked data, which is indistinguishable from random by Assumption 2.

When the challenge is 0, the simulator can use the homomorphism property of isogenies to work on the right side of the SIDH squares instead of the left. The masked values can one again be sampled randomly.

When the challenge is 1, the simulator can sample a random ϕ' and (β_P, β_Q) and compute the rest using these values. The masked values are, again, sampled randomly. Distinguishing this simulator from an honest output is equivalent to solving the DSSP, which we assume to be hard.

Theorem 6.4 (Soundness). *Given Assumption 2, DMSISOZKP is 3-special sound for the knowledge of a cyclic isogeny of the claimed degree between the claimed curves with the claimed torsion point information.*

Proof. We show that for a fixed commitment, if one obtains valid answers to all 3 possible challenges, then they can compute an isogeny with the claimed properties.

Since H is a computationally binding commitment scheme, we can assume that the three answers agree on the committed values.

The goal is to use the possible answers in order to compute and isogeny $\rho : E_0 \to E_1$ of degree A and a pair of integers (α_P, α_P) such that $(P_1', Q_1') = ([\alpha_P]\rho(P_0), [\alpha_Q]\rho(Q_0))$.

We are given the pair (c, d) which define the point $K_{\hat{\psi}_L}$, which in turn defines the isogeny $\hat{\psi}_L : E_2 \to E_0$ of degree C. We are also given the point $K_{\phi'}$ which defines the isogeny $\phi' : E_2 \to E_3$. We can then complete the $(\hat{\psi}_L, \phi')$-isogeny square to obtain our ρ candidate.

We also have a (α_P, α_Q) candidate in $(\gamma_P \beta_P, \gamma_Q \beta_Q)$.

We have that $\rho : E_0 \to E_1$ is of degree A, so we only need to check that it respects the claimed mapping. Since ρ is constructed by completing an SIDH square, we have that $\rho \hat{\psi}_L = \hat{\psi}_R \phi'$. Hence:

$$
\begin{aligned}
\rho(P_0) &= \rho([a_P]\hat{\psi}_L(P_{2,P}) + [b_P]\hat{\psi}_L(Q_{2,P})) \\
&= [a_P]\rho\hat{\psi}_L(P_{2,P}) + [b_P]\rho\hat{\psi}_L(Q_{2,P}) \\
&= [a_P]\hat{\psi}_R\phi'(P_{2,P}) + [b_P]\hat{\psi}_R\phi'(Q_{2,P}) \\
\rho(P_0) &= [\beta_P^{-1}\gamma_P^{-1}]P_1' \\
[\alpha_P]\rho(P_0) &= P_1'
\end{aligned}
$$

The same arguments holds for $[\alpha_Q]\rho(Q_0) = Q_1'$. Therefore, ρ is a valid secret isogeny and this completes the proof.

7   Masked Degree and Double Subgroup

Section 4's technique used to prove knowledge of an isogeny while masking its degree can be combined with any of zero-knowledge proof in this paper in order to prove the desired torsion point information. Since the combination method and security proofs of every case are almost identical, we only explicitly present one of them in this paper.

For applications such as terSIDH [3], we require a zero-knowledge proof that that can prove knowledge of an isogeny with the given subgroup images without leaking information about either the isogeny itself or its degree. In order to do this, we start DMSISOZKP and add the random sampling technique presented in MDISOZKP.

Definition 7.1 (MDTISOZKP). *Let $\mathcal{A} = \prod_{i-1}^{s} q_i^{f_i}$ be a large integer such that the $q_i s$ are distinct primes dividing $p + 1$. Let B and C be large positive integers relatively prime to $\mathcal{A}$. Let $\phi : E_0 \to E_1$ be a secret cyclic isogeny of degree $A \mid \mathcal{A}$ such that $(\phi(P_0), \phi(Q_0)) = (P_1, Q_1)$ where (P_1, Q_1) form a basis of $E_0[B]$. Let $\alpha_P, \alpha_Q \leftarrow\!\$ (\mathbb{Z}/(BC)\mathbb{Z})^*$ be secret and $(E_0, E_1, P_0, Q_0, [\alpha_P]P_1, [\alpha_Q]Q_1)$ be public.*

Let $(P_1', Q_1') := ([\alpha_P]P_1, [\alpha_Q]Q_1)$ and let n be a positive integer representing the number of times the following proof will be repeated. The challenge is a random chall $\in \{-1, 0, 1\}$.

Commitment

$A' \xleftarrow{\$} FacSet(\mathcal{A}^{sn})$

$\phi' \leftarrow CyclicIsogeny(E_1, A')$

$E_1' \leftarrow Codomain(\phi')$

$\Phi \leftarrow Cycliphy(\phi'\phi)$

$A'' \leftarrow deg(\Phi)$

$\xi \leftarrow A''/(A \times A')$

$K_{\psi_L} \xleftarrow{\$} E[[C]]$

$K_{\psi_R} \leftarrow \Phi(K_{\psi_L})$

$\psi_L \leftarrow IsogenyFromKernel(K_{\psi_L})$

$\psi_R \leftarrow IsogenyFromKernel(K_{\psi_R})$

$E_2 \leftarrow Codomain(\psi_L)$

$E_3 \leftarrow Codomain(\psi_R)$

$(P_{2,P}, Q_{2,P}) \leftarrow RandomBasis(E_2, BC)$

$(P_{2,Q}, Q_{2,Q}) \leftarrow RandomBasis(E_2, BC)$

$\beta_P, \beta_Q \xleftarrow{\$} (\mathbb{Z}/(BC)\mathbb{Z})^*$

$\Phi' \leftarrow ParallelIsogeny(\Phi, \psi_L)$

$(P_{3,P}, Q_{3,P}) \leftarrow ([\beta_P]\Phi'(P_{2,P}), [\beta_P]\Phi'(Q_{2,P}))$

$(P_{3,Q}, Q_{3,Q}) \leftarrow ([\beta_Q]\Phi'(P_{2,Q}), [\beta_Q]\Phi'(Q_{2,Q}))$

$K_{\hat{\psi}_L} \leftarrow GeneratingPoint(\hat{\psi}_L)$

$(c, d) \leftarrow DDLOG(P_{2,P}, Q_{2,P}, K_{\hat{\psi}_L})$

$(a_P, b_P) \leftarrow DDLOG(\hat{\psi}_L(P_{2,P}), \hat{\psi}_L(Q_{2,P}), P_0)$

$(a_Q, b_Q) \leftarrow DDLOG(\hat{\psi}_L(P_{2,Q}), \hat{\psi}_L(Q_{2,Q}), Q_0)$

$\gamma_P \leftarrow \alpha_P \beta_P^{-1} \xi^{-1}$

$\gamma_Q \leftarrow \alpha_Q \beta_Q^{-1} \xi^{-1}$

$r_L, r_R, r_m, r_A, r_B \xleftarrow{\$} N$

$C_L \leftarrow H(E_2, P_{2,P}, Q_{2,P}, P_{2,Q}, Q_{2,Q}, r_L)$

$C_R \leftarrow H(E_3, P_{3,P}, Q_{3,P}, P_{3,Q}, Q_{3,Q}, r_R)$

$C_m \leftarrow H(a_P, b_P, a_Q, b_Q, c, d, r_m)$

$C_A \leftarrow H(\gamma_P, \gamma_Q, r_A)$

$C_B \leftarrow H(\beta_P, \beta_Q, r_B)$

return $(C_L, C_R, C_m, C_A, C_B)$

Verification

if $chall = -1$:

  if $C_L \neq H(E_2, P_{2,P}, Q_{2,P}, P_{2,Q}, Q_{2,Q}, r_L)$:$\perp$

  if $C_m \neq H(a_P, b_P, a_Q, b_Q, c, d, r_m)$:$\perp$

  if $\neg IsBasis(P_{2,P}, Q_{2,P}, E_2, BC)$:$\perp$

  if $\neg IsBasis(P_{2,Q}, Q_{2,Q}, E_2, BC)$:$\perp$

  $K_{\hat{\psi}_L} \leftarrow [c]P_{2,P} + [d]Q_{2,P}$

  if $K_{\hat{\psi}_L} \notin E_2[[C]]$:$\perp$

  $\hat{\psi}_L \leftarrow IsogenyFromKernel(K_{\hat{\psi}_L})$

  $E_0' \leftarrow Codomain(\hat{\psi}_L)$

  if $E_0' \neq E_0$:$\perp$

  if $P_0 \neq [a_P]\hat{\psi}_L(P_{2,P}) + [b_P]\hat{\psi}_L(Q_{2,P})$:$\perp$

  if $Q_0 \neq [a_Q]\hat{\psi}_L(P_{2,Q}) + [b_Q]\hat{\psi}_L(Q_{2,Q})$:$\perp$

if $chall = 0$:

  if $C_R \neq H(E_3, P_{3,P}, Q_{3,P}, P_{3,Q}, Q_{3,Q}, r_R)$:$\perp$

  if $C_m \neq H(a_P, b_P, a_Q, b_Q, c, d, r_m)$:$\perp$

  if $C_A \neq H(\gamma_P, \gamma_Q, r_A)$:$\perp$

  if $\neg IsBasis(P_{3,P}, Q_{3,P}, E_3, BC)$:$\perp$

  if $\neg IsBasis(P_{3,Q}, Q_{3,Q}, E_3, BC)$:$\perp$

  $K_{\hat{\psi}_R} \leftarrow [c]P_{3,P} + [d]Q_{3,P}$

  if $K_{\hat{\psi}_R} \notin E_3[[C]]$:$\perp$

  $\hat{\psi}_R \leftarrow IsogenyFromKernel(K_{\hat{\psi}_R})$

  $E_1' \leftarrow Codomain(\hat{\psi}_R)$

  if $\neg IsoValid(E_1, E_1', \phi')$:$\perp$

  if $deg(\phi') \nmid \mathcal{A}^{sn}$:$\perp$

  if $\phi'(P_1') \neq [a_P\gamma_P]\hat{\psi}_R(P_{3,P}) + [b_P\gamma_P]\hat{\psi}_R(Q_{3,P})$:$\perp$

  if $\phi'(Q_1') \neq [a_Q\gamma_Q]\hat{\psi}_R(P_{3,Q}) + [b_Q\gamma_Q]\hat{\psi}_R(Q_{3,Q})$:$\perp$

if $chall = 1$:

  if $C_L \neq H(E_2, P_{2,P}, Q_{2,P}, P_{2,Q}, Q_{2,Q}, r_L)$:$\perp$

  if $C_R \neq H(E_3, P_{3,P}, Q_{3,P}, P_{3,Q}, Q_{3,Q}, r_R)$:$\perp$

  if $C_B \neq H(\beta_P, \beta_Q, r_B)$:$\perp$

  if $\neg IsoValid(E_2, E_3, \Phi')$:$\perp$

  if $deg(\Phi') \notin FacSetTwo(\mathcal{A}, \mathcal{A}^{sn})$:$\perp$

  if $(P_{3,P}, Q_{3,P}) \neq ([\beta_P]\phi'(P_{2,P}), [\beta_P]\phi'(Q_{2,P}))$:$\perp$

  if $(P_{3,Q}, Q_{3,Q}) \neq ([\beta_Q]\phi'(P_{2,Q}), [\beta_Q]\phi'(Q_{2,Q}))$:$\perp$

return true

Response

if $chall = -1$:

  return $(E_2, P_{2,P}, Q_{2,P}, P_{2,Q}, Q_{2,Q}, r_L, a_P, b_P, a_Q, b_Q, c, d, r_m)$

if $chall = 0$:

  return $(E_3, P_{3,P}, Q_{3,P}, P_{3,Q}, Q_{3,Q}, r_R, a_P, b_P, a_Q, b_Q, c, d, r_m, \gamma_P, \gamma_Q, r_A, \phi')$

if $chall = 1$:

  if $A'' \notin FacSetTwo(\mathcal{A}, \mathcal{A}^{sn})$: **abort**

  return $(E_2, P_{2,P}, Q_{2,P}, P_{2,Q}, Q_{2,Q}, r_L, E_3, P_{3,P}, Q_{3,P}, P_{3,Q}, Q_{3,Q}, r_R, \beta_P, \beta_Q, r_B, \Phi')$

Theorem 7.2 (Correctness). *If the prover is honest and does not abort, then the verification algorithm will always return* **true**.

Proof. If chall $= -1$, the properties checked by the verification algorithm were directly computed by the prover. Hence, this case will always be correct.

If chall $= 1$, the properties checked by the verification algorithm are all respected by honest $[\beta_P]\Phi'$ and $[\beta_Q]\Phi'$. Hence, this case will always be correct.

If chall $= 0$, we have that $\hat{\psi}_R\Phi' = \Phi\hat{\psi}_L$ since the four isogenies form an SIDH square. We also have that $\phi\phi' = [\xi]\Phi$. Hence:

$$
\begin{aligned}
\phi'(P_1') &= [\alpha_P]\phi\phi'(P_0) \\
&= [\alpha_P\xi]\Phi(P_0) \\
&= [\alpha_P\xi]\Phi([a_P]\hat{\psi}_L(P_{2,P}) + [b_P]\hat{\psi}_L(Q_{2,P})) \\
&= [a_P\alpha_P\xi]\Phi\hat{\psi}_L(P_{2,P}) + [b_P\alpha_P\xi]\Phi\hat{\psi}_L(Q_{2,P}) \\
&= [a_P\alpha_P\xi]\hat{\psi}_R\Phi'(P_{2,P}) + [b_P\alpha_P\xi]\hat{\psi}_R\Phi'(Q_{2,P}) \\
&= [a_P\gamma_P]\hat{\psi}_R(P_{3,P}) + [b_P\gamma_P]\hat{\psi}_R(Q_{3,P})
\end{aligned}
$$

which is the equation that was to be checked. The same argument also shows that $\phi'(Q_1') = [a_Q\gamma_Q]\hat{\psi}_R(P_{3,Q}) + [b_Q\gamma_Q]\hat{\psi}_R(Q_{3,Q})$.

Before proving the security of MDTISOZKP, it is important to remark that Theorems 4.3 and 4.5 also hold for MDTISOZKP as the proof is identical. Hence, the probability of the scheme not aborting during n rounds is at least $\frac{1}{e}$.

Theorem 7.3 (Zero-knowledge). *Given Assumptions 1 and 2, if the MDTI-SOZKP protocol does not abort, then it is zero-knowledge.*

Proof. We prove it by showing a simulator outputting valid a commitment-challenge-answer tuple with the same distribution as an honest prover for each possible challenge.

When the challenge is -1, the simulator can compute the revealed values honestly and sample random values for the masked data, which is indistinguishable from an honest output by Assumption 2.

When the challenge is 0, the simulator can compute ϕ' honestly. Then, we can use the homomorphism property of isogenies to work on the right side of the SIDH squares instead of the left. The masked values can one again be sampled randomly.

When the challenge is 1, the simulator can sample a random Φ' and (β_P, β_Q) and compute the rest using these values. The masked values are, again, sampled randomly. The degree of Φ' is indistinguishable by Theorem 4.3. Hence, distinguishing this simulator from an honest output is equivalent to solving the DSSP, which we assume to be hard.

Theorem 7.4 (Soundness). *Given Assumption 2, MDTISOZKP is 3-special sound for the knowledge of a cyclic isogeny between the claimed curves with the claimed torsion point information.*

Proof. We show that for a fixed commitment, if one obtains valid answers to all 3 possible challenges, then they can compute an isogeny with the claimed properties.

Since H is a computationally binding commitment scheme, we can assume that the three answers agree on the committed values.

We are given an isogeny $\phi' : E_1 \to E_1'$ of degree A'. Let $P_1'' = \phi'(P_1')$ and $Q_1'' = \phi'(Q_1')$. Given an isogeny $\Phi : E_0 \to E_1'$ such that $\Phi(P_0) = [\delta_P]P_1''$ and $\Phi(Q_0) = [\delta_Q]Q_1''$, $\hat{\phi}'\Phi$ is a valid extractor.

Therefore, the goal is to use the possible answers in order to compute and isogeny $\rho : E_0 \to E_1'$ of degree A'' and a pair of integers (δ_P, δ_P) such that $(P_1'', Q_1'') = ([\delta_P]\rho(P_0), [\delta_Q]\rho(Q_0))$.

We are given the pair (c, d) which define the point $K_{\hat{\psi}_L}$, which in turn defines the isogeny $\hat{\psi}_L : E_2 \to E_0$ of degree C. We are also an the isogeny $\Phi' : E_2 \to E_3$ of degree A''. We can then complete the $(\hat{\psi}_L, \Phi')$-isogeny square to obtain our ρ candidate.

We also have a (δ_P, δ_Q) candidate in $(\gamma_P\beta_P, \gamma_Q\beta_Q)$.

We have that $\rho : E_0 \to E_1'$ is of degree A'', so we only need to check that it respects the claimed mapping. Since ρ is constructed by completing an SIDH square, we have that $\rho\hat{\psi}_L = \hat{\psi}_R\Phi'$. Hence:

$$\rho(P_0) = \rho([a_P]\hat{\psi}_L(P_{2,P}) + [b_P]\hat{\psi}_L(Q_{2,P}))$$
$$= [a_P]\rho\hat{\psi}_L(P_{2,P}) + [b_P]\rho\hat{\psi}_L(Q_{2,P})$$
$$= [a_P]\hat{\psi}_R\Phi'(P_{2,P}) + [b_P]\hat{\psi}_R\Phi'(Q_{2,P})$$
$$= [a_P\beta_P^{-1}]\hat{\psi}_R P_{4,P} + [b_P\beta_P^{-1}]\hat{\psi}_R Q_{3,P}$$
$$\rho(P_0) = [\beta_P^{-1}\gamma_P^{-1}]P_1''$$
$$[\delta_P]\rho(P_0) = P_1''$$

The same arguments hold for $[\delta_Q]\rho(Q_0) = Q_1''$. Therefore, ρ can be used to generate a valid secret isogeny and this completes the proof.

8   Conclusion

Using the schemes in this paper, we can prove knowledge of isogenies with masked torsion-point information while either proving the degree or masking it, as desired.

The fact that the security of our scheme relies mainly on DSSP allows us to obtain statistical zero-knowledge using large enough parameters as a consequence of Theorems 2.1 and 2.2.

For further research, it is worth mentioning that some variants of FESTA use non-diagonal matrices to masked their torsion point information. In those cases, the schemes in this paper do not apply. However, the technique in DMSISOZKP can probably be generalized for non-diagonal, but abelian families of matrices.

Acknowledgments. This research was supported by NSERC Alliance Consortia Quantum Grant ALLRP 578463-2022.

References

1. Basso, A.: A post-quantum round-optimal oblivious PRF from isogenies. Cryptology ePrint Archive, Paper 2023/225 (2023). https://eprint.iacr.org/2023/225
2. Basso, A., et al.: Supersingular curves you can trust. In: Hazay, C., Stam, M. (eds.) EUROCRYPT 2023. LNCS, vol. 14005, pp. 405–437. Springer, Cham (2023). https://doi.org/10.1007/978-3-031-30617-4_14
3. Basso, A., Fouotsa, T.B.: New SIDH countermeasures for a more efficient key exchange. Cryptology ePrint Archive, Paper 2023/791 (2023). https://eprint.iacr.org/2023/791
4. Basso, A., Maino, L., Pope, G.: FESTA: fast encryption from supersingular torsion attacks. Cryptology ePrint Archive, Paper 2023/660 (2023). https://eprint.iacr.org/2023/660
5. Castryck, W., Decru, T.: An efficient key recovery attack on SIDH. In: Hazay, C., Stam, M. (eds.) EUROCRYPT 2023. LNCS, vol. 14008, pp. 423–447. Springer Nature Switzerland, Cham (2023). https://doi.org/10.1007/978-3-031-30589-4_15
6. Dartois, P., Leroux, A., Robert, D., Wesolowski, B.: SQISignHD: new dimensions in cryptography. Cryptology ePrint Archive, Paper 2023/436 (2023). https://eprint.iacr.org/2023/436
7. De Feo, L., Dobson, S., Galbraith, S.D., Zobernig, L.: SIDH proof of knowledge. In: Agrawal, S., Lin, D. (eds.) ASIACRYPT 2022. LNCS, vol. 13792, pp. 310–339. Springer, Cham (2022). https://doi.org/10.1007/978-3-031-22966-4_11
8. De Feo, L., Galbraith, S.D.: SeaSign: compact isogeny signatures from class group actions. In: Ishai, Y., Rijmen, V. (eds.) EUROCRYPT 2019. LNCS, vol. 11478, pp. 759–789. Springer, Cham (2019). https://doi.org/10.1007/978-3-030-17659-4_26
9. De Feo, L., Kohel, D., Leroux, A., Petit, C., Wesolowski, B.: SQISign: compact post-quantum signatures from quaternions and isogenies. In: Moriai, S., Wang, H. (eds.) ASIACRYPT 2020. LNCS, vol. 12491, pp. 64–93. Springer, Cham (2020). https://doi.org/10.1007/978-3-030-64837-4_3
10. Fouotsa, T.B., Moriya, T., Petit, C.: M-SIDH and MD-SIDH: countering SIDH attacks by masking information. Cryptology ePrint Archive, Paper 2023/013 (2023). https://eprint.iacr.org/2023/013
11. Galbraith, S.D., Petit, C., Shani, B., Ti, Y.B.: On the security of supersingular isogeny cryptosystems. In: Cheon, J.H., Takagi, T. (eds.) ASIACRYPT 2016. LNCS, vol. 10031, pp. 63–91. Springer, Heidelberg (2016). https://doi.org/10.1007/978-3-662-53887-6_3
12. Galbraith, S.D., Petit, C., Silva, J.: Identification protocols and signature schemes based on supersingular isogeny problems. J. Cryptol. 33(1), 130–175 (2020)
13. Maino, L., Martindale, C.: An attack on SIDH with arbitrary starting curve. Cryptology ePrint Archive, Paper 2022/1026 (2022). https://eprint.iacr.org/2022/1026
14. Robert, D.: Breaking SIDH in polynomial time. In: Hazay, C., Stam, M. (eds.) EUROCRYPT 2023. LNCS, vol. 14008, pp. 472–503. Springer, Cham (2023). https://doi.org/10.1007/978-3-031-30589-4_17

Post-quantum DNSSEC over UDP via QNAME-Based Fragmentation

Aditya Singh Rawat and Mahabir Prasad Jhanwar[✉]

Department of Computer Science, Ashoka University, Sonipat, India
{aditya.rawat_phd21,mahavir.jhawar}@ashoka.edu.in

Abstract. In a typical network, any DNS message exceeding the recommended size of 1232 bytes would 1) either be fragmented into several UDP/IP packets 2) or require a re-transmission over TCP. Unfortunately, IP fragmentation is considered unreliable and a non-trivial number of nameservers do not support TCP. With the advent of DNSSEC, this size constraint becomes even more pressing since DNS messages now additionally carry digital signatures (and in some cases, public keys as well). While signatures of classical schemes such as RSA and ECDSA are sufficiently small to avoid size concerns, their much larger post-quantum counterparts easily cause the DNSSEC message size to exceed 1232 bytes.

Multiple fragmentation schemes at the application (DNS) layer have been proposed, with ARRF (CoRR'22) being the most recent, to address the problem of transmitting large DNS messages. In this paper, we propose a new DNS layer fragmentation solution for integrating post-quantum cryptography in DNSSEC over UDP. Our scheme, called QNAME-Based Fragmentation (QBF), can reconstruct the entire DNS message in just 1 round trip while using only standard DNS resource records. Our experiments show that in a simulated network of 10 ms latency, with an EDNS(0) buffer size of 1232 and Falcon-512 as the zone signing algorithm, a QBF-aware resolver and nameserver setup can resolve Type A DNSSEC queries in 43 ± 1 ms, beating both standard DNS with TCP fallback (83 ± 1 ms) and parallel ARRF (63 ± 1 ms).

Keywords: Secure Networking Protocols · Post-quantum Cryptography Implementations · DNSSEC

1 Introduction

A rapid advancement in quantum computing has motivated the need to replace the classical cryptographic algorithms based on the believed hardness of integer factorization and discrete logarithms. Currently, many applications rely on these algorithms to 1) ensure message confidentiality and integrity, and 2) authenticate the communicating parties. DNS Security Extensions (DNSSEC) [14], being one such application, provides authenticity and integrity for messages exchanged in

Aditya Singh Rawat was supported by a research grant from MPhasis F1 Foundation.

F. Regazzoni et al. (Eds.): SPACE 2023, LNCS 14412, pp. 66–85, 2024.
https://doi.org/10.1007/978-3-031-51583-5_4

the Domain Name System (DNS). In its main capacity, DNS helps computers to translate human readable domain names like example.com to machine readable IP addresses like 128.45.90.21. Without DNSSEC, the recipients of a DNS response cannot verify the integrity of the IP address contained in it, and thus risk being misdirected to a malicious website. Presently, around 20% of the Internet users rely on DNSSEC and the adoption thereof is consistently on the rise [3]. Unfortunately DNSSEC, owing to its use of classical public-key cryptography, can be rendered completely ineffective by the upcoming quantum computers.

Since 2016, the National Institute of Standards and Technology (NIST) is running an open Post-Quantum Cryptography standardization process [12] to standardize quantum-resistant key encapsulation mechanisms (KEMs) and digital signatures. In July 2022, NIST finally selected Kyber [4] as KEM, and Dilithium [9], Falcon [13], and SPHINCS+ [2] as digital signatures. While these primitives provide the same core functionalities as their classical counterparts, they feature strikingly different size and performance characteristics. Table 1 compares the public key and the signature sizes of the future NIST post-quantum signature schemes with those of the classical algorithms currently deployed in DNSSEC [20]: RSA-2048-SHA256 belonging to the most popular algorithm family in DNSSEC [19] and ECDSA-P256-SHA256, an elliptic curve algorithm, widely deployed because of its small signatures.

Table 1. A comparison of signature and public key sizes of various NIST post-quantum signature schemes with those of their classical counterparts

Signature Algorithm	Signature Size	Public Key Size
ECDSA-P256-SHA256	64	64
RSA-2048-SHA256	256	260
Falcon-512	690	897
Dilithium2	2420	1312
SPHINCS+-SHA256-128S	7856	32

This increase in sizes of signatures and public keys (and consequently of DNS messages) has major implications for DNSSEC [8]. Owing to its use of a UDP transport, a DNS message exceeding 1232 bytes in size usually triggers IP fragmentation on most network links [1,11]. This upper bound of 1232 has been derived as follows: 1280 (IPv6 MTU) - 40 (IPv6 Header) - 8 (UDP Header). It is evident that DNSSEC messages carrying post-quantum data will easily exceed 1232 bytes in size, and thus be fragmented by the network. Unfortunately, IP fragmentation is considered to be both unreliable (fragments may never arrive) and insecure (fragments can be spoofed). Moreover, Van den Broek et al. [18] have noted that up to 10% of the resolvers fail to handle fragments correctly.

The other alternative of sending large DNS messages without resorting to fragmentation is via TCP. When a DNS response exceeds the requester's advertised EDNS(0) buffer size (here, 1232), a truncated DNS message (with TC flag set in header) is sent. Subsequently, the requester discards the received response (resulting in a wasted trip) and re-tries the query over TCP. Unfortunately, up to 11% of nameservers in [11] [19] have been shown to lack support for TCP. Moreover, Mao et al. [10] found that up to 4.8% of the resolvers do not fallback to TCP when requested by authoritative nameservers. Even in the case of an available TCP support, the connection might fail to get established because of intruding middle boxes [11]. Using a TCP transport also increases resolution times because of the 3-way TCP handshake.

Related Work

Many proposals have been put forward which address the two aforementioned issues of IP fragmentation and TCP non-availability by fragmenting at the application (DNS) layer. The implication of this approach is that the DNS servers are now responsible for fragmenting and re-assembling DNS messages rather than the network layer.

The works of Sivaraman et al. [15] and Song et al. [16], fragmented the entire DNS message as a unit and sent each fragment sequentially. Unfortunately, both of these schemes failed to get standardized because they sent multiple packets in response to a single request. Many firewalls are configured to accept only one DNS response packet per query. In such a case, there is also a potential risk of ICMP flooding since the dropped packets will generate multiple ICMP 'destination unreachable' messages.

A very recent work of Goertzen et al. [6], known as ARRF, fragmented DNS resource records and addressed the principal shortcoming of earlier approaches by sending additional messages only upon *request*. Since each additional response has its own query, concerns about intruding firewalls and ICMP flooding are mitigated. We review the ARRF design in Sect. 2.3.

Unfortunately, ARRF suffers from two major limitations as acknowledged by its authors in [6]. Firstly, ARRF introduces a new type of DNS resource record called 'Resource Record Fragment (RRFRAG)', which, being non-standard, has the potential to be rejected by certain middle boxes handling DNS messages. Secondly, ARRF is vulnerable to memory exhaustion attacks. Moreover, ARRF needs a minimum of two round trips to reconstruct the full DNS message.

Our Contributions

In this work, we propose a DNS fragmentation solution called QNAME-Based Fragmentation (QBF). Similar to previous approaches, QBF also performs fragmentation at the application layer, thus eliminating concerns of IP fragmentation and lack of TCP support. Additionally, QBF is **request-based** like ARRF in that each additional DNS response has its own associated DNS query. Hence, messages sent by QBF are not susceptible to the issues of firewall filtering or ICMP flooding. In contrast to ARRF [6] however, QBF offers the following benefits:

- **Full Backward Compatibility**: Unlike ARRF [6] which uses a non-standard resource record called RRFRAG, QBF uses only standard DNS resource records while also respecting their wire format. Thus, QBF messages are not susceptible to getting blocked by strict middle boxes which inspect the resource records of a DNS message.
- **Security against Memory Exhaustion Attacks**: Owing to its design, ARRF [6] exposes an attack surface in which an adversary can deplete the memory of a resolver by inserting many malicious RRFRAGs in the initial response. However, QBF is not vulnerable to such attacks since it does not use RRFRAGs.
- **1-RTT Resolution**: ARRF is bottle-necked by a minimum of 2 round trips for reassembling the full DNS message. On the other hand, QBF can reconstruct the complete DNS message in just 1 round trip.

Our implementation of QBF is a light-weight daemon that runs on top of the DNS software (such as BIND9) of nameservers and resolvers. It fragments/reassembles large DNS messages (as and when needed) and requires **no** modifications to be made to the underlying DNS software or zone files.

2 Preliminaries

Notations: RR is shorthand for resource record. || represents concatenation. X → Y denotes member Y of an abstract structure X. RTT stands for round trip time. (A)NS is short for (authoritative) nameserver.

2.1 The Domain Name System

In this section, we briefly review the complete Domain Name System (DNS) lookup process as well as the DNS message wire format. The DNS, being a mission critical service for the Internet, facilitates the navigation thereof by translating human-readable domain names into machine understandable IP addresses. Suppose a DNS client (technically called a 'stub resolver') contacts the local DNS server to determine the IP address for the domain name example.com. The local DNS server first contacts one of the root servers, which returns the IP addresses of TLD servers for the top-level domain .com. The local DNS server then contacts one of these TLD servers, which in turn returns the IP addresses of the authoritative servers for example.com. Finally, it contacts one of the authoritative servers for example.com, which in turn returns the exact IP address of example.com. Once the resolved IP address is obtained, the local DNS server returns the IP address to the client and also stores it in its cache for future use.

The top level format of a generic DNS message is divided into 5 sections: Header, Question, Answer, Authority, and Additional. The Header section is always present and includes fields that specify which of the remaining sections are present, whether the message is a query or a response, a standard query or some other opcode, etc. Table 2 presents the wire format of DNS Header.

The Question section contains the query made by a resolver to a nameserver in order to obtain information about a specific domain name or resource record. Each question entry consists of the following fields: QNAME (Contains the domain name that the resolver is querying about. It is encoded in the standard DNS name notation. For example, test.example is encoded as [4]test[7]example[0]), QTYPE (specifies the type of DNS *resource record* (RR)), and QCLASS (specifies the class of the query, set to IN in most cases). The last three sections have the same format: a possibly empty list of concatenated DNS RRs.

The DNS resource records (RRs) are data entries within a DNS database that provide various types of information about a domain name and its associated data. These records are used to facilitate the translation of a domain name to an IP address. The A, NS, and MX are some of the commonly used DNS records. Each resource record has the following top level sections: NAME (specifies the domain name to which the RR belongs), TYPE (indicates the type of RR), CLASS (specifies the class of data), TTL (time to live), RDLENGTH (specifies the length, in bytes, of the RR's RDATA field), and RDATA (contains the actual data associated with the RR). If NAME = example.com and TYPE=A, then RDATA contains the 32-bit IPv4 address of the example.com domain. If NAME = example.com and TYPE=NS, then RDATA contains the domain names of the authoritative name servers (ANS) for the example.com domain. The Answer section contains RRs that answer the question; the Authority section contains RRs that point toward an authoritative nameserver; the Additional section contains RRs which relate to the query, but are not strictly answers for the question.

Table 2. DNS Message Header Format

Header
ID
QR | Opcode | AA | TC
RD | RA | Z | RCODE
QDCOUNT
ANCOUNT
NSCOUNT
ARCOUNT

The fields relevant to the present discussion are: ID, used by requester to match a DNS response to its query; QR, indicates whether message is a query (0) or a response (1); TC, indicates whether message is truncated (1) or not (0); and RCODE denotes the response code - 0 indicates no error, 1 (FORMERR) indicates that query was malformed, and 3 (NXDOMAIN) indicates that domain name does not exist.

DNS Message Size. DNS messages are sent over the internet using a series of layers. Initially, they are placed into UDP packets, which in turn are placed inside IP packets. These IP packets become the payload of frames at the link layer. However, there is a limit to the payload size of these frames based on the Maximum Transmission Unit (MTU) of the link they are traveling over. If a frame's payload is too large for the link's MTU, routers must break it into

smaller IP packets, resulting in fragmentation of DNS messages. These fragmented IP packets travel independently to their destination. Since DNS relies
on UDP, which does not guarantee a reliable communication like TCP, any loss
of fragmented IP packets can cause transmission failures. Even when fragmentation does work, it may not be secure. It is theoretically possible to spoof parts
of a fragmented DNS message, without an easy detection at the receiving end.
To address these issues, there are two solutions: a) configure servers to limit
the size of DNS messages sent over UDP to ensure they do not trigger fragmentation on typical network links; b) ensure that DNS servers can switch from
UDP to TCP when a DNS response is too large to fit within the limited buffer
size of UDP. Initially, DNS messages were limited to 512 bytes, a size that pre-
vented IP fragmentation. Most standard network links have MTUs large enough
to accommodate these DNS messages (considering an 8-byte UDP header and
a 40-byte IPv6 header, resulting in a maximum payload size of 560 bytes for
link layer frames). However, with the introduction of the Extension Mechanisms
for DNS (EDNS(0)) (see next paragraph), this limit theoretically increased to
64 kilobytes. Using EDNS(0), one can increase the size of DNS messages up to
any 'k' bytes, provided the MTU of the network link is greater than 'k + 8 +
40' bytes. Therefore, the optimum DNS message size to avoid IP fragmentation
while minimizing the use of TCP will depend on the MTU of all the physical
network links connecting two network endpoints. Unfortunately, there is not yet
a standard mechanism for DNS server implementors to access this information.
Until such a standard exists, it is usually recommended that the EDNS buffer
size should, by default, be set to a value small enough to avoid fragmentation
on the majority of network links in use today. An EDNS buffer size of 1232
bytes will avoid fragmentation on nearly all current networks. This is based on
an MTU of 1280, which is required by the IPv6 specification, minus 48 bytes for
the IPv6 and UDP headers. Therefore, the currently recommended DNS message
size over UDP is 1232 bytes.

EDNS(0). Extension Mechanisms for DNS (EDNS(0)) [5] facilitates the transfer of DNS messages larger than the traditional size of 512 bytes. For this purpose, EDNS(0) introduces a pseudo-RR called OPT (short for Options) in the
additional section of the DNS message. Note that unlike traditional RRs, pseudo-
RRs do not actually exist in the zone files and are created on the fly. In queries,
a requester specifies the maximum UDP payload size it is capable of handling
(known as EDNS(0) buffer size) in OPT → CLASS. In addition to this, the
requester also indicates its support for DNSSEC by setting the DO (DNSSEC
OK) bit to 1 in OPT → TTL. OPT also contains DNS cookies which provide a
limited security against certain off-path attacks such as denial of service, cache
poisoning, and answer forgery.

2.2 The DNS Security Extensions

DNS Security Extensions (DNSSEC) enhances the security of the DNS by ensuring the authenticity and integrity of DNS data. It introduces new types of DNS

resource records, such as Resource Record Signature (RRSIG), DNS Public Key (DNSKEY), and Delegation Signer (DS). In regular DNS, when a resolver gets a DNS record from a server, it wants assurances that the record came from the right server and has not been tampered with during transmission. With DNSSEC, a server uses a cryptographic signature to sign the DNS records it provides (digital signature is applied to a group of DNS resource records, referred to as an RRset, that have the same NAME, CLASS, and TYPE). This signature is created using a secret key owned by the server. The server then creates an RRSIG record, which contains the signature, details about the signing method used, and timing information (like expiration date) for the signed DNS record. It also includes a key identifier, which is a unique identifier for the public key needed to verify the signature. The public key is made available in the DNS zone through DNSKEY records. These DNSKEY records are also cryptographically signed in a multi-layered approach, building a chain of trust. When a DNS resolver receives a DNS response with RRSIG records, it uses the associated DNSKEY records to verify the RRSIG's digital signature. If the signature matches, the resolver accepts the DNS record as authentic and untampered.

We quickly go over the key points about how the new DNS resource records (RRSIG, DNSKEY, and DS) are formatted. The various fields of the RDATA section of a DNS RRSIG resource record is given in Table 3.

Table 3. DNS RR of Type RRSIG

DNS RR of Type RRSIG					
Name	Type = RRSIG	Class	TTL		RDLENGTH
	RRSIG RR Wire Format				
RDATA	Type Covered				
	Algorithm	Identifies the signature algorithm			
	Labels				
	Original TTL				
	Signature Expiration				
	Signature Inception				
	Key Tag	Provides a mechanism for selecting a public key efficiently			
	Signer's Name				
	Signature	Contains the signature value computed on RRSIG → RDATA (excluding the signature field) and an RRset containing a collection of resource records RR(i)s. signature = sign(RRSIG → RDATA‖RR(1)‖RR(2)‖ ...)			

A DNSKEY record stores a public key. The wire format of DNSKEY → RDATA is shown in Table 4. In DNSSEC, each DNS zone employs two types of keys: the Zone Signing Key (ZSK) and the Key Signing Key (KSK). The ZSK is responsible for signing the DNS resource records (RRs) within the zone. These records contain information about specific domain names, such as A records. On the other hand, the KSK's primary role is to sign the DNSKEY records. These DNSKEY records contain the public keys used for verifying the zone's data.

The DS record (see Table 5 for its format) plays a vital role in establishing a chain of trust between parent and child DNS zones. For example, it is

Table 4. DNS RR of Type DNSKEY

DNS RR of Type DNSKEY					
Name	Type = DNSKEY		Class	TTL	RDLENGTH
	DNSKEY RR wire format				
RDATA	Flags	Specifies whether the key is a Zone Signing Key (ZSK) or a Key Signing Key (KSK)			
	Protocol				
	Algorithm	Specifies the signature algorithm used to generate the public key			
	Public Key	Contains the actual public key			

used when a top-level domain server acts as the parent, and an authoritative nameserver serves as the child zone. When a resolver verifies an RRSIG record using a corresponding DNSKEY record from a server, it must ensure the authenticity of the server's ZSK contained within the DNSKEY record. The DNSKEY record is signed using the server's KSK. Therefore, the resolver must also verify the authenticity of the server's KSK. To facilitate this, the server generates a cryptographic hash of its public KSK and shares it with its parent servers in a DS record. When a resolver is directed to a server by its parent server, the parent server provides the DS record containing the hash of the child server's public KSK. Importantly, the parent server signs this DS record using its own ZSK when sharing it with a resolver. As a result, when the resolver receives RRSIG and DNSKEY responses from the child server, it employs the information received from the parent server to authenticate the child server's DNSKEY record. This establishes a secure chain of trust, which is essential for DNSSEC to ensure the integrity and authenticity of DNS data across hierarchical levels.

Table 5. DNS RR of Type DS

DNS RR of Type DS					
Name	Type = DS		Class	TTL	RDLENGTH
	DS RR Wire Format				
RDATA	Key Tag				
	Algorithm				
	Digest Type				
	Digest	digest = hash(DNSKEY Owner Name‖DNSKEY RR)			

2.3   ARRF [6]

DNSSEC works seamlessly when the size of the DNS message does not exceed the recommended UDP limit. However, post-quantum signature schemes have larger public key and signature sizes that cannot fit within these limits. To handle post-quantum cryptography in DNSSEC without relying on IP fragmentation or TCP fallback, a recent solution called ARRF was introduced by Goertzen et al.

[6]. This approach avoids IP fragmentation and instead conducts fragmentation at the application layer using a daemon running on top of the DNS software of resolvers and DNS servers. ARRF introduces a new type of DNS resource record called 'Resource Record Fragment (RRFRAG),' similar to the existing pseudo-resource record OPT. RRFRAGs are not explicitly part of DNS zones; they are created when needed and use the standard DNS resource record wire format with some fields repurposed (see Table 6).

Table 6. DNS RR of Type RRFRAG: a) NAME must always be root (.); b) TYPE identifies RRFRAG type; c) Class contains RRID identifying the particular DNS resource record that is being fragmented; d) TTL contains CURIDX specifying the current index in the byte array of the original resource record which is being fragmented; e) RDLENGTH contains FRAGSIZE specifying the total number of bytes contained in RDATA; f) RDATA has two parts: 1) RRSIZE: two bytes specifying the size of the original non-fragmented resource record; and 2) FRAGDATA: the raw bytes of the fragment of the original resource record.

DNS RR of Type RRFRAG					
Name = "."	Type = RRFRAG	Class ≡ RRID	TTL ≡ CURIDX	RDLENGTH FRAGSIZE	≡
	RRFRAG →RDATA Wire Format				
RDATA	RRSIZE				
	FRAGDATA				

When a DNS response is too large to fit within the advertised UDP size, RRFRAGs are used to split the data across multiple queries, ensuring that each response's size remains below the threshold. RRFRAGs replace resource records in place, maintaining the original message format. However, the OPT resource record, containing important metadata like the DNS cookie, is not fragmented.

The initial response containing at least one RRFRAG acts as a 'map' of the non-fragmented message. Requesters use this map to determine how to reassemble the original large DNS message. They can identify missing fragments and send new queries for those missing RRFRAGs. To specify which fragment they want, the size of those fragments, and their starting positions, requesters add RRFRAGs for each distinct RRID in the query's additional section. When responders receive queries with RRFRAGs, they construct a standard DNS response by inserting the corresponding RRFRAGs into the answers section. The FRAGDATA being sent is a copy of the desired resource record's bytes, starting at CURIDX and ending at CURIDX+FRAGSIZE. This request/response cycle continues until the requester successfully reassembles the original large, non-fragmented message. Also, after receiving the initial response with the map, requesters can make subsequent RRFRAG requests in parallel.

Unfortunately, ARRF suffers from two major limitations as acknowledged by its authors in [6]. Firstly, RRFRAG is a non-standard DNS resource record type which can potentially cause middle boxes to reject the DNS message. Secondly, ARRF is vulnerable to memory exhaustion attacks. An on-path adversary can insert many RRFRAGs in the initial response with very large RRSIZEs. Since DNSSEC validation cannot take place until the full DNS message is reconstructed, the requester has no choice but to allocate memory for storing intermediate fragments. ARRF also needs a minimum of two round trips to reconstruct the full DNS message. This is because the resolver requires RRIDs for fetching additional fragments. However, it only learns the RRIDs after receiving the initial response.

3   QBF: QNAME-Based Fragmentation

In this section, we present our solution for retro-fitting post-quantum cryptography in DNSSEC/UDP. Our scheme, called QNAME-Based Fragmentation (QBF), fragments and reassembles large DNS messages using a daemon running on top of the DNS software (here, BIND9) of resolvers and nameservers. The daemon intercepts and modifies (if necessary) all the incoming and outgoing DNS packets. It is also able to construct and send a DNS query of its own. Unlike the previous schemes, which fragmented the entire DNS message [15,16] or DNS resource records [6], the QBF daemon *only* fragments the following data: 1) Raw signature bytes stored in the field RRSIG → RDATA → Signature, and 2) Raw public key bytes stored in the field DNSKEY → RDATA → Public Key. Thus, QBF fragments *resemble the original DNS response* except insofar as they carry partial signatures or public keys. To fetch an additional fragment, the requester daemon constructs a new DNS query and provides information about the desired fragment in QUESTION → QNAME.

QBF can be configured with the following operational modes: 1) Sequential: Wait to receive a requested fragment before sending another request; 2) Parallel 2-RTT: Request and receive the first fragment. Then request and receive all other fragments in parallel; and 3) Parallel 1-RTT: Request and receive all fragments in parallel. We now proceed to delineate QBF in the following subsections.

QBF Fragmentation: Wire Format

When a DNSSEC response exceeds the requester's advertised EDNS(0) buffer size, the responder daemon puts partial signature or public key bytes while keeping the rest of the message intact. We illustrate this by means of the following example scenario. A requester sends a DNSSEC query asking for a Type A DNS resource record containing the IPv4 address of a domain test.example. Assume that the requester specifies a maximum EDNS(0) buffer size of y bytes (e.g. $y = 1232$ bytes, the recommended DNS message size over UDP) in OPT → CLASS. On the responder side, the generated DNS response shown in Table 7 (Left). Assume that the size of this response is z bytes. The answer section contains one Type A RR holding the IPv4 address 1.2.3.4 for test.example and one RRSIG holding a signature over the former Type A RR. The rest of the sections are empty (except for OPT in the additional section). The responder daemon observes that the response exceeds the requester's UDP payload limit by 2 bytes (i.e.,

$z = y+2$). Hence, it removes 2 bytes from RRSIG → RDATA → Signature (i.e., if RRSIG → RDLENGTH is x bytes, then after removing 2 bytes from the Signature, it becomes $x-2$) and sets the HEADER → TC flag to 1. The DNS response, referred to as 'Fragment 1,' is displayed in Table 7 (Middle). Simultaneously, the responder daemon prepares another DNS response, known as 'Fragment 2,' containing the remaining 2 bytes of the signature. At this juncture, the responder stores Fragment 2 in its cache. When the requester subsequently queries the additional fragment, the daemon retrieves it from its cache and transmits it back. Further details regarding the format of additional fragments are elaborated upon in the subsequent discussion. Note that the OPT record (which may hold important DNS cookies) remains intact after fragmentation.

Table 7. Wire format: Original response (Left), Fragment 1 (Middle), Fragment 2 (Right)

Original Response	Fragment 1	Fragment 2
Header Section	**Header Section**	
Question Section	**Question Section**	
QNAME = test.example	QNAME = test.example	**Header Section**
QTYPE = A	QTYPE = A	**Question Section**
QCLASS	QCLASS	QNAME = ?2?test.example
Answer Section	**Answer Section**	QTYPE = A
NAME	NAME	QCLASS
TYPE=A	TYPE=A	**Answer Section**
⋮	⋮	NAME
RDLENGTH=4	RDLENGTH=4	TYPE= RRSIG
RDATA=1.2.3.4	RDATA=1.2.3.4	⋮
NAME	NAME	RDLENGTH = $x-2$
TYPE= RRSIG	TYPE= RRSIG	RDATA
⋮	⋮	Type Covered
RDLENGTH = x	RDLENGTH = $x-2$	Algorithm
RDATA	RDATA	⋮
Type Covered	Type Covered	Signer's Name
Algorithm	Algorithm	Signature=0x5c6d
⋮	⋮	**Authority Section**
Signer's Name	Signer's Name	**Additional Section**
Signature=0x3a4b5c6d	Signature=0x3a4b	RR : OPT
Authority Section	**Authority Section**	
Additional Section	**Additional Section**	
RR : OPT	RR : OPT	

Note that when a generated DNS response contains multiple RRSIG records, the QBF fragmenter removes an equal number of raw signature bytes from each RRSIG. A similar logic is applied in case of multiple DNSKEY records.

QBF Assembly: Additional Fragment Requests

After receiving Fragment 1, a requester daemon requests for additional fragments by constructing a new DNS query and setting QUESTION → QNAME in the following format:

$$\langle \text{DELIMITER} \rangle \langle \text{fragnum} \rangle \langle \text{DELIMITER} \rangle \langle \text{domain} \rangle$$

The DELIMITER is a non-valid domain name character such as ?, #, *, etc. The first delimiter indicates to the responder daemon that the DNS query is for a fragment. The second delimiter is used to mark the end of fragnum field since domain names can also start with a number. We use ? as DELIMITER in all our examples in this paper. The fragnum is the desired fragment number and must be >1 since Fragment 1 is received as response to the original DNS query. The domain is the domain name for which the fragment is required.

Thus, in the ongoing example, to retrieve 'Fragment 2,' the requester daemon initiates a new DNS query with the QUESTION → QNAME field set to ?2?test.example (or in general, set to ?i?test.example for fetching the ith fragment). The resulting DNS response is shown in Table 7 (Right). This specific DNS response, referred to as 'Fragment 2,' was originally prepared by the responder daemon during the fragmentation process and subsequently cached.

Note that the responder daemon sets HEADER → TC flag in all the fragments for maintaining backward compatibility. Furthermore, for all fragnum > 1, the responder daemon removes all RRs except RRSIG, DNSKEY and OPT. This is an efficiency measure to reclaim the space taken by the redundant RRs that were already sent in Fragment 1.

If a requester daemon sends a fragment query that cannot be answered (for example, a fragment with number fragnum is desired, but the entire message requires only (fragnum − 1) fragments), the responder daemon returns an error response with HEADER → RCODE set to FORMERR (indicating a problem with the format of the DNS query).

3.1 QBF Execution Modes

We now describe the functioning of the QBF daemon in both the Parallel 2-RTT (round-trip time) and Parallel 1-RTT modes. The discussion of the sequential mode is omitted since it closely resembles Parallel 2-RTT, with the sole difference being that the requester awaits a response before dispatching another request.

We begin with Parallel 2-RTT, as it lays the foundation for comprehending Parallel 1-RTT. These execution modes explain how a DNSSEC query initiated at a resolver is managed by the client-side QBF daemon deployed on the resolver and the server-side QBF daemon running on a DNS server. In this context, we assume the DNS server to be an Authoritative Name Server (ANS).

Parallel 2-RTT. Consider a scenario in which the resolver has initiated a DNSSEC query, requesting a Type A DNS resource record with QUESTION →

QNAME set to `test.example`. The resolver, operating under the constraint of processing DNS responses of a recommended size - specifically, a maximum of 1232 bytes - configures the EDNS(0) buffer size to 1232 within the OPT → CLASS field. In the following section, we describe how QBF operates in its Parallel 2-RTT mode to resolve the aforementioned query. The execution in Parallel 2-RTT proceeds as follows (Fig. 1 gives a schematic view of the QBF daemon operating in Parallel 2-RTT mode):

1. The resolver QBF daemon forwards the outgoing DNSSEC query as it is.
2. Upon receiving the DNSSEC query, the QBF daemon on the nameserver sets OPT → CLASS to a large value (here 65507, the maximum UDP payload size over IPv4) before forwarding the query to BIND9, the DNS server software running at ANS. This value should be large enough so as to allow the retrieval of the full DNS response from BIND9 without truncation.
3. The nameserver daemon observes that the size of the full response exceeds 1232 bytes. Hence, it removes the necessary number of bytes from RRSIG → RDATA → Signature and marks the response as truncated before sending it to the resolver as Fragment 1. Note that from the complete BIND9 response, the nameserver QBF daemon also prepares and caches all other fragments for a time interval (say, 5 s) within which it expects the resolver daemon to reach out for them. In case, the nameserver daemon does not receive any fragment requests from the resolver daemon within the time duration, it removes the fragments from its cache.
4. On intercepting the first fragment, the resolver QBF daemon calculates the required number of additional fragments as follows:
   (a) It retrieves the signing algorithm from RRSIG → RDATA → Algorithm and infers the size of a full signature (say, 690 bytes in case of Falcon).
   (b) It computes the size of the original DNS response by counting RRSIG → RDATA → Signature as having full size (690) instead of the partial size.
   (c) Subsequently, it calculates the number of additional fragments required based on the EDNS(0) buffer limit.
5. The resolver QBF daemon constructs the required number of extra fragment queries (2 in this case, see Fig. 1) in the format described in Sect. 3 and sends them in parallel.
6. On the nameserver side, the QBF daemon responds to the fragment queries from its cache.
7. On receiving all the fragments, the resolver QBF daemon appends RRSIG → RDATA → Signature from Fragment 2 and 3 (in sequence) to the corresponding place in Fragment 1. It then forwards the complete DNSSEC message to BIND9 for validation.

A similar procedure is followed for a response containing DNSKEY records. In that case, the relevant sections are DNSKEY → RDATA → Algorithm/Public Key.

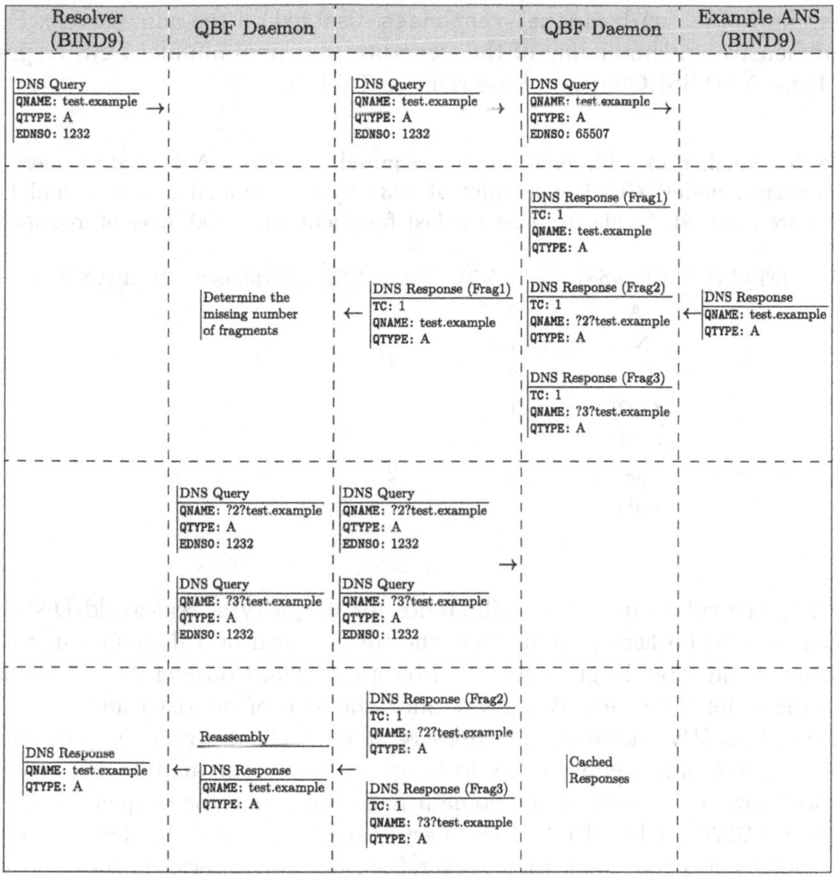

Resolver (BIND9)	QBF Daemon		QBF Daemon	Example ANS (BIND9)

DNS Query / QNAME: test.example / QTYPE: A / EDNS0: 1232 →
DNS Query / QNAME: test.example / QTYPE: A / EDNS0: 1232 →
DNS Query / QNAME: test.example / QTYPE: A / EDNS0: 65507 →

DNS Response (Frag1) / TC: 1 / QNAME: test.example / QTYPE: A

Determine the missing number of fragments ←
DNS Response (Frag1) / TC: 1 / QNAME: test.example / QTYPE: A
DNS Response (Frag2) / TC: 1 / QNAME: ?2?test.example / QTYPE: A ←
DNS Response / QNAME: test.example / QTYPE: A ←

DNS Response (Frag3) / TC: 1 / QNAME: ?3?test.example / QTYPE: A

DNS Query / QNAME: ?2?test.example / QTYPE: A / EDNS0: 1232
DNS Query / QNAME: ?2?test.example / QTYPE: A / EDNS0: 1232
→
DNS Query / QNAME: ?3?test.example / QTYPE: A / EDNS0: 1232
DNS Query / QNAME: ?3?test.example / QTYPE: A / EDNS0: 1232

DNS Response (Frag2) / TC: 1 / QNAME: ?2?test.example / QTYPE: A

DNS Response / QNAME: test.example / QTYPE: A ← Reassembly ← DNS Response / QNAME: test.example / QTYPE: A
Cached Responses

DNS Response (Frag3) / TC: 1 / QNAME: ?3?test.example / QTYPE: A

Fig. 1. QBF in Parallel 2-RTT mode

Parallel 1-RTT. It is important to note that the resolver's QBF daemon has the flexibility to send additional fragment requests in parallel with the original query. The primary variable to consider is the precise number of these supplementary queries to dispatch. Should the daemon send more queries than necessary, it will simply receive a FORMERR response for each surplus query. Conversely, if the daemon sends an inadequate number of queries, it can always calculate the exact count of fragments based on the information provided in the first fragment (as elaborated in Sect. 3.1) and subsequently retrieve any remaining fragments.

Assuming that the daemon possesses knowledge of the nameserver's signing algorithm, possibly from prior interactions, it becomes feasible to estimate an upper-bound on the number of fragments. This estimation can be based on factors such as QUESTION → QTYPE and the EDNS(0) UDP limit. In Table 8 below, we present the calculated number of extra queries needed in the running example of a Type A DNSSEC query for test.example, for all NIST recommended post-quantum signature algorithms. It is worth noting that this represents a worst-case scenario (i.e., with `minimal-responses` disabled on the nameserver). For a comprehensive understanding of the structure of a non-minimal DNS response to a Type A DNSSEC query, please refer to Table 9.

Table 8. Number of additional queries required for Type A DNSSEC query for `test.example` under a UDP constraint of 1232 bytes. Minimal responses and DNS cookies are disabled. * indicates that the last fragment has <100 bytes of free space.

QTYPE	RR Type	No. of RRs	Falcon-512	Dilithium-2	SPHINCS+
	A	2			
A	NS	1	1*	6	22
	RRSIG	3			
	OPT	1			
	RRSIG	2			
DNSKEY	DNSKEY	2	2*	6	14
	OPT	1			

While the values in Table 8 will suffice for majority of real-world DNSSEC queries, it is to be kept in mind that the total length of a domain name (i.e., label bytes and label length bytes) can be up to 255. Considerations also have to be made for Type AAAA queries since the size of an IPv6 address is 4× the size of an IPv4 address. Additionally, a joint client-server DNS cookie in OPT → RDATA can occupy up to 40 bytes of space. Fortunately, the resolver a priori knows the length of the domain name and the type of query from the QNAME and QTYPE fields of the DNS query respectively, and the decision to use DNS cookies also rests with the resolver (i.e., a server inserts its cookie only if the client has provided its own). Thus, the resolver daemon should account for longer than average domain names, Type AAAA IPv6 queries and usage of DNS cookies when determining the number of additional queries. If deemed necessary, it should increment the numbers marked with * in Table 8 by 1.

Figure 2 gives a schematic view of the QBF daemon operating in Parallel 1-RTT Mode. Ideally, the resolver daemon should send the additional queries after a slight delay from the original one so as to give sufficient time to the responder daemon for preparing the fragment cache. Alternatively, the responder daemon should forward only the original query to the BIND9 software and prepare the cache from the resulting response as shown in Fig. 2.

3.2 Backward Compatibility

We now discuss what happens when one of the end points implements QBF while the other one does not.

– QBF-unaware Requester | QBF-aware Responder: On receiving the first fragment, the requester will detect that the HEADER → TC flag is set. It will then discard this response and retry over TCP.

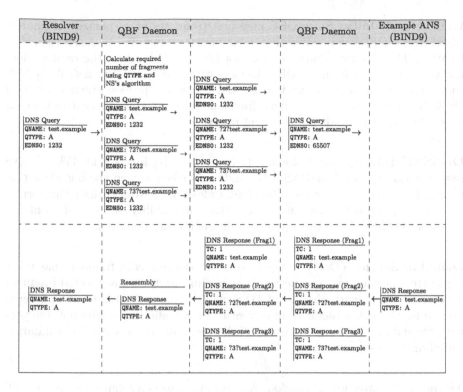

Fig. 2. QBF in Parallel 1-RTT mode

– QBF-aware Requester | QBF-unaware Responder: If the requester daemon
sends queries in Parallel 1-RTT mode, it will receive the first response with
TC flag set and the rest of the responses with HEADER → RCODE set to
NXDOMAIN (stands for 'Non-Existent Domain'). It will then infer that the
responder does not support QBF and repeat the query over TCP. In case
the requester daemon is running in Sequential or Parallel 2-RTT mode, it
will receive the first response with TC flag set. However, responses truncated
by the DNS software only contain the Header section, the Question section
and OPT record in additional section (i.e., the response is identical to the
query but with TC set). On detecting this, the daemon will conclude that the
responder is QBF-unaware and fall back to TCP.

3.3 Security Considerations

DNS Cache Poisoning. Since the QBF daemon forwards only the complete
DNS response to the resolver for DNNSEC validation, DNS cache poisoning is
not a concern assuming a secure algorithm is used for signing.

UDP Unreliablity. Since QBF messages (requests or responses) ultimately travel over UDP, it is possible that some messages may fail to reach their destination. The two immediate solutions for this would be: 1) If the resolver does not get a response from its QBF daemon within 800 ms (the default BIND9 timeout), it sends a fresh query again and the whole process starts over; 2) If the QBF daemon does not receive a fragment response within a shorter timeout (say, 100 ms), it re-sends the fragment query.

DNSSEC Downgrade Attacks. Heftrig et al. [7] found that 45% of DNS resolvers do not perform DNSSEC validation when a new signing algorithm is used in the DNS responses. Therefore, unless IETF standardizes the correct behaviour of resolvers in such a scenario, this vulnerability can possibly continue to affect DNSSEC when post-quantum algorithms are deployed.

Denial of Service (DoS). *Off-path attacks:* Because each fragment has to be explicitly requested for, a requester daemon can reject any unexpected fragment it receives. Thus, with the aid of DNS cookies, off-path attacks are rendered infeasible. *On-path attacks:* If an adversary or a malicious middle-box tampers with the data in the resource records, it'll eventually cause DNSSEC validation to fail on the resolver.

Memory Exhaustion Attacks. An on-path adversary cannot cause a QBF requester daemon to allocate an arbitrarily large amount of memory for fragments. Recall that Fragment 1 is identical to the original DNS response except that it carries only partial raw signature or public key bytes. If parallel 2-RTT or sequential mode is being used, the only way an on-path adversary can cause the requester daemon to over-compute the number of additional fragments is 1) by changing RDATA → Algorithm or 2) by inserting many resource records containing fewer raw signature or public key bytes. In the first attack, the adversary is limited to changing the algorithm to the one with the largest signature or public key footprint (For example, SPHINCS+ which has 7856 bytes of signature). On the other hand, the resolver daemon can easily detect the second type of attack based on the response it is expecting for a particular QTYPE. For example, even in the worst-case, a Type A/AAAA DNS response cannot have more than 3 RRSIGs as shown in Table 9. Note that in Parallel 1-RTT, the number of fragments (and hence, the memory allocated) is fixed as discussed in Sect. 3.1.

4   Evaluation

In this section, we provide implementation details of QBF and compare its DNS resolution performance with standard DNS with TCP fallback and parallel ARRF [6]. The source code of our implementation is available at: https://github.com/aditya-asr/qbf_src.

4.1 Setup

We use the source code of ARRF [6] as base to build QBF. The DNS software is BIND 9.17.12 which uses OpenSSL 1.1.1 and liboqs 0.7.2 [17] for cryptographic operations. The daemon is written in C and uses libnetfilter-queue 1.0.5-2 for intercepting all incoming and outgoing packets. Docker 4.22 is used for constructing the network scenario (described below). To simulate network latency and bandwidth, we use Linux's tc utility. DNS lookups are performed using dig. All experiments are run on a Macbook Air M1 with 8 GB of RAM.

We design a DNS network with the following four participants: 1) A client 2) A resolver 3) A root NS 4) An example ANS. Each participant is running as a private Ubuntu 22.04 Docker container having a networking constraint of 50 Mbps bandwidth and 10 ms latency. The resolver is configured with send-cookie no; in its named.conf. For simplicity, each zone is signed with a single algorithm and has one (ZSK, KSK) pair. The zone file of ANS contains 10 A RRs each with a unique domain name and an associated RRSIG. The ANS is configured with minimal-responses no; in its named.conf file to simulate the worst-case scenario. Table 9 illustrates the format of non-minimal DNSSEC responses generated by the ANS's BIND9 software.

Table 9. Structure of non-minimal DNS responses to a Type A DNSSEC query (left) and to a Type DNSKEY DNSSEC query (right)

Header Section		Header Section
Question Section		Question Section
Answer Section		Answer Section
TYPE A RR		DNSKEY
RRSIG		DNSKEY
Authority Section		RRSIG
TYPE NS RR		RRSIG
RRSIG		Authority Section
Additional Section		Additional Section
TYPE A RR		OPT
RRSIG		
OPT		

4.2 Experiment and Results

In this experiment, we measure the average resolution time of Type A DNSSEC queries when the resolver already has DNSKEY and NS records of the nameservers. In such a case, the resolver directly contacts the ANS with Type A queries. The results of this experiment for the three NIST recommended signature algorithms[1]: Falcon-512 at security level 1, Dilithium2 at security level 2, and SPHINCS+ at security level 1 are tabulated in Table 10 below.

---
[1] Higher security levels are currently not supported by the OQS-BIND9 fork.

Table 10. Average resolution time (± 1 ms) of 10 Type A DNSSEC queries in a 10 ms latency and 50 Mbps network setting. * indicates a TCP fallback. The parallel variants of both ARRF and QBF show high scalability under growing signature sizes because of sending the fragment requests in parallel.

Algorithm	Standard DNS	Parallel ARRF	QBF 2-RTT	QBF 1-RTT
ECDSA-P256-SHA256	42	-	-	-
RSA-2048-SHA256	42	-	-	-
Falcon-512	83*	63	63	43
Dilithium2	83*	64	64	44
SPHINCS+-SHA256-128S	85*	65	66	46

All parallel variants of QBF yield substantially lower resolution times than standard DNS for post-quantum DNSSEC queries. More concretely, QBF in 1-RTT and 2-RTT mode is approximately 50% and 25% faster than standard DNS respectively. This is because DNS, as standardized, incurs the penalty of 1) the (initial) wasted trip over UDP and 2) the ensuing 3-way TCP handshake.

On the other hand, QBF in 1-RTT mode shows an improvement of about 30% over parallel ARRF because of requiring only 1 round trip compared to two of the latter.

5   Conclusion

In this work, we introduced QNAME-Based Fragmentation (QBF): a fully backward-compatible solution for seamlessly integrating post-quantum cryptography into DNSSEC over UDP. QBF achieves its objective using *only* standard DNS resource records and requires just a *single* round trip to reconstruct the full DNS message. We have developed the QBF daemon, designed to operate atop existing DNS software of both resolvers and nameservers. This daemon efficiently manages the fragmentation and reassembly of large DNS messages without necessitating any modifications to DNS software or zone files. To assess its performance, we conducted a comprehensive comparison of QBF's DNS resolution capabilities against those of standard DNS employing TCP fallback and parallel ARRF [6].

References

1. DNS Flag Day 2020. https://www.dnsflagday.net/2020/. Accessed 14 June 2023
2. Bernstein, D.J., Hülsing, A., Kölbl, S., Niederhagen, R., Rijneveld, J., Schwabe, P.: The SPHINCS$^+$ signature framework. In: CCS, pp. 2129–2146. ACM (2019)
3. Bindel, N., Herath, U., McKague, M., Stebila, D.: Transitioning to a quantum-resistant public key infrastructure. In: Lange, T., Takagi, T. (eds.) PQCrypto 2017. LNCS, vol. 10346, pp. 384–405. Springer, Cham (2017). https://doi.org/10.1007/978-3-319-59879-6_22
4. Bos, J.: Crystals - Kyber: a CCA-secure module-lattice-based KEM. In: 2018 IEEE European Symposium on Security and Privacy (EuroS&P), pp. 353–367 (2018)

5. da Silva Damas, J., Graff, M., Vixie, P.A.: Extension Mechanisms for DNS (EDNS(0)). RFC 6891 (2013)
6. Goertzen, J., Stebila, D.: Post-quantum signatures in DNSSEC via request-based fragmentation. In: Johansson, T., Smith-Tone, D. (eds.) PQCrypto 2023. LNCS, vol. 14154, pp. 535–564. Springer, Cham (2023). https://doi.org/10.1007/978-3-031-40003-2_20
7. Heftrig, E., Shulman, H., Waidner, M.: Poster: the unintended consequences of algorithm agility in DNSSEC. In: CCS, pp. 3363–3365. ACM (2022)
8. Kampanakis, P., Lepoint, T.: Vision paper: do we need to change some things? In: Günther, F., Hesse, J. (eds.) SSR 2023. LNCS, vol. 13895, pp. 78–102. Springer, Cham (2023). https://doi.org/10.1007/978-3-031-30731-7_4
9. Lyubashevsky, V., et al.: Crystals dilithium. Technical report, National Institute of Standards and Technology (2022). https://csrc.nist.gov/Projects/post-quantum-cryptography/selected-algorithms-2022
10. Mao, J., Rabinovich, M., Schomp, K.: Assessing support for DNS-over-TCP in the wild. https://doi.org/10.1007/978-3-030-98785-5_22
11. Müller, M., Jong, J., Heesch, M., Overeinder, B., Rijswijk-Deij, R.: Retrofitting post-quantum cryptography in internet protocols: a case study of DNSSEC. ACM SIGCOMM Comput. Commun. Rev. **50**, 49–57 (2020)
12. NIST: Status report on the third round of the NIST post-quantum cryptography standardization process. https://csrc.nist.gov/News/2022/pqc-candidates-to-be-standardized-and-round-4. Accessed 19 Aug 2023
13. Prest, T., et al.: Falcon. Technical report, National Institute of Standards and Technology (2022). https://csrc.nist.gov/Projects/post-quantum-cryptography/selected-algorithms-2022
14. Rose, S., Larson, M., Massey, D., Austein, R., Arends, R.: DNS Security Introduction and Requirements. RFC 4033
15. Sivaraman, M., Kerr, S., Song, L.: DNS message fragments. https://datatracker.ietf.org/doc/draft-muks-dns-message-fragments/00/
16. Song, L., Wang, S.: ATR: additional truncation response for large DNS response. https://datatracker.ietf.org/doc/draft-song-atr-large-resp/03/
17. Stebila, D., Mosca, M.: Post-quantum key exchange for the internet and the open quantum safe project. In: Avanzi, R., Heys, H. (eds.) SAC 2016. LNCS, vol. 10532, pp. 14–37. Springer, Cham (2017). https://doi.org/10.1007/978-3-319-69453-5_2
18. Van Den Broek, G., Van Rijswijk-Deij, R., Sperotto, A., Pras, A.: DNSSEC meets real world: dealing with unreachability caused by fragmentation. IEEE Commun. Mag. **52**(4), 154–160 (2014)
19. van Rijswijk-Deij, R., Jonker, M., Sperotto, A., Pras, A.: A high-performance, scalable infrastructure for large-scale active DNS measurements. IEEE J. Sel. Areas Commun. **34**(6), 1877–1888 (2016)
20. Wouters, P., Sury, O.: Algorithm implementation requirements and usage guidance for DNSSEC. RFC 8624. https://doi.org/10.17487/RFC8624. Accessed 22 Aug 2023

Cryptanalysis of Short and Provable Secure Lattice-Based Signature Scheme

Ramakant Kumar[1]([✉]), Sahadeo Padhye[1], and Swati Rawal[2]

[1] Department of Mathematics, Motilal Nehru National Institute of Technology
Allahabad, Prayagraj 211004, India
ramakantkumar9758@gmail.com, sahadeo@mnnit.ac.in
[2] EY Global, 6 More Londan Place, London SE12AF, UK

Abstract. Fenghe and Zhenhua proposed a short and provable secure
lattice-based signature scheme in the standard model in 2016. Their aim
was to construct a short signature without using any lattice delegation
technique. They claimed that their scheme is strongly unforgeable under
the hardness of the shortest integer solution (SIS) problem. In this article, we highlight a flaw in the signature scheme proposed by Fenghe
and Zhenhua. We show that an adversary can generate a valid message-
signature pair by solving a linear system of equations. We also show that
the design of the scheme leaks some information about the secret key.

Keywords: Lattice-Based Cryptography · Cryptanalysis · Short
Signature · Signature Scheme · Standard Model

1 Introduction

Digital Signature (DS) schemes play an important role in secure communication. Digital signature in a random oracle model (ROM) are more efficient than
schemes in the standard model (SDM), but a random oracle is hard to achieve.
Thus, constructing provably secure DS in the SDM remains an important area of
research. In the literature, some DS schemes are proven secure in SDM. However,
the security of these schemes relies on the hardness of discrete logarithm problem (DLP) and integer factorization problem (IFP). Due to Shor's algorithm [1],
these schemes are not secure against a quantum computer. So, there is a need
for such schemes that are secure against both classical and quantum computers.

Lattice-based cryptography is an important post-quantum candidate. In
2008, Gentry et al. [2] constructed the first lattice-based provable secure DS
scheme using a pre-image sampleable function (PSF). This scheme has been
proven secure in ROM. In 2010, Cash et al. [3] designed a DS using the lattice
delegation technique. They proved their scheme secure in SDM. Also, in 2010,
Boyen [4] proposed a lattice-based DS scheme using a novel delegation tool with
a mixing dimension. This scheme is also secure in SDM. However, the sizes of verification keys and signatures are large in both the schemes [3,4]. In 2014, Ducas

© The Author(s), under exclusive license to Springer Nature Switzerland AG 2024
F. Regazzoni et al. (Eds.): SPACE 2023, LNCS 14412, pp. 86–91, 2024.
https://doi.org/10.1007/978-3-031-51583-5_5

and Micciancio [5] constructed a lattice-based DS scheme secure under SDM. But, they proved their security against non-adaptive chosen message attack.

In 2016, Fenghe and Zhenhua [8] developed a signature scheme for the reduction of verification key size and signature length, and to prove security in the adaptive chosen message attack. They aim to construct a short signature without using any lattice delegation [7]. They proved that their scheme satisfies strong unforgeability, and provides a shorter signature and a smaller verification key. But there are some flaws in the security analysis given by the authors in the scheme [8]. Moreover, the signature generation allows for a forgery attack, which we have pointed out here. The design of the scheme does not hide secret information. We have shown that the scheme's design reveals some information about the Secret key. Before proceeding further, brushing up on the following preliminaries is required.

2   Preliminaries

Definition 1. Lattice. *Let* $\mathbf{B} = \{\mathbf{b}_1, \ldots \mathbf{b}_n\}$ *be a collection of* n *linearly independent vectors. A lattice* $\mathcal{L}$ *is defined by the set* $\mathcal{L} = \{\Sigma_{i=1}^{n} \mathbf{b}_i \alpha_i | \alpha_i \in \mathbb{Z}\}$. *The set* $\{\mathbf{b}_1, \ldots \mathbf{b}_n\}$ *is called the basis of the lattice* $\mathcal{L}(\mathbf{B})$.

Definition 2. *[6] For some positive integers* q, n, m, *and a given matrix* $\mathbf{A} \in \mathbb{Z}_q^{n \times m}$, *we define the following certain families of lattices*

1. $\mathcal{L}^{\perp}(\mathbf{A}) = \{\mathbf{z} \in \mathbb{Z}^m | \mathbf{Az} = 0 \mod q\}$
2. $\mathcal{L}_y^{\perp}(\mathbf{A}) = \{\mathbf{z} \in \mathbb{Z}^m | \mathbf{Az} = \mathbf{y} \mod q\}$

Definition 3. *Gaussian function on* $\mathbb{R}^n$ *with center at* $\mathbf{c}$ *and standard deviation* σ *is defined as* $\rho_{\mathbf{c},\sigma}(\mathbf{z}) = \exp\left(-\frac{\|\mathbf{z} - \mathbf{c}\|^2}{2\sigma^2}\right)$, $\mathbf{z} \in \mathbb{R}^n$.

The discrete Gaussian function over any lattice $\mathcal{L}$ is defined as

$$D_{\mathcal{L},\mathbf{c},\sigma}(\mathbf{z}) = \frac{\rho_{\mathbf{c},\sigma}(\mathbf{z})}{\rho_{\mathbf{c},\sigma}(\mathcal{L})}, \forall \mathbf{z} \in \mathcal{L}.$$

where $\rho_{\mathbf{c},\sigma}(\mathcal{L}) = \Sigma_{\mathbf{z} \in \mathcal{L}} \rho_{\mathbf{c},\sigma}(\mathbf{z})$.

Definition 4. *(**Short Integer Solution Problem** (SIS)) For a given positive integer* q, *a matrix* $\mathbf{A} \in \mathbb{Z}_q^{n \times m}$, *and a real* β, *find a non-zero vector* $\mathbf{v}$ *such that* $\mathbf{Av} = 0 \mod q$ *and* $\|\mathbf{v}\| \leq \beta$.

Fenghe and Zhenhua [8] proposed a short signature scheme using the SIS problem as below.

3   Fenghe and Zhenhua Signature Scheme

Here, we discuss the lattice-based DS scheme given by Fenghe and Zhenhua [8]. Consider a prime number n. Let (m, n, q) denotes the system parameters defined as $m = 6n \log q$, $q = n^3$ and the Gaussian parameter $s = 6(l+1)\omega(\log n)$, where $l < n$ denotes the bit length of the message.

- *S.KeyGen*– Generate the matrix $\mathbf{A} \in \mathbb{Z}_q^{n \times m}$ along with the trapdoor $\mathbf{T} \in \mathbb{Z}_q^{m \times m}$ using *TrapSamp* [2].
  Next, choose $\mathbf{c}_0, \ldots, \mathbf{c}_l$ in $\mathbb{Z}^n$ as random and linearly independent vectors. Then, return the verification key $vk = (\mathbf{A}, \mathbf{c}_0, \ldots \mathbf{c}_l)$ and the signing key $sk = \mathbf{T}$.
- *S.Sign(vk, sk, msg)*– Parse the message $msg = (msg[1], \ldots msg[l]) \in \{0, 1\}^l$ and proceed as follows:
  (i) Compute $\mathbf{u} = \mathbf{c}_0 + \Sigma_{i=1}^l msg[i]\mathbf{c}_i$.
  (ii) Generate $\mathbf{v}$ using PSF algorithm with Gaussian parameter $s \dfrac{1 + \Sigma_{i=1}^l msg[i]}{l+1}$ s.t. $\mathbf{A}\mathbf{v} = \mathbf{u} \mod q$ and $\|\mathbf{v}\| \le s \dfrac{1 + \Sigma_{i=1}^l msg[i]}{l+1} \sqrt{m}$.
  Then, output the signature $\mathbf{v}$ on the message msg
- *S.Verify(v, vk, msg)*– Accept the signature if and only if $\mathbf{A}\mathbf{v} = \mathbf{u} \mod q$ and $\|\mathbf{v}\| \le s \dfrac{1 + \Sigma_{i=1}^l msg[i]}{l+1} \sqrt{m}$.

The security proof given by Fenghe and Zhenhua, which relies on the hardness of the SIS problem, is discussed below.

Theorem 1. *[8] If $\exists$ a successful forger $\mathcal{A}$ who can break the strong unforgeability with probability ϵ with at most q signing queries, then $\exists$ an adversary $\mathcal{C}$ who can solve the SIS problem with probability $(1 - 2^{-\omega(\log n)})\epsilon$.*

Proof. Suppose $\mathcal{C}$ runs $\mathcal{A}$ to obtain the solution of an SIS instance $(\mathbf{A}, n, m, q)$ as follows:

- *Setup*: $\mathcal{C}$ generates the public verification for $\mathcal{A}$, he chooses $\mathbf{e}_i \in \mathbb{Z}_q^m$ satisfying the distribution $D_{s/l+1}$ for $i = 0, \ldots, l$. Then, computes $\mathbf{c}_i = \mathbf{A}\mathbf{e}_i \mod q$.

He sends $(\mathbf{A}, \mathbf{c}_i)$ to $\mathcal{A}$ and stores secrets $\mathbf{e}_i$. For signature queries, he maintains a local storage L to store the responses.

- *SignQuery*: For a l bit message $msg_i = (msg_i[1], msg_i[2], \ldots, msg_i[l])$, first $\mathcal{C}$ checks the local storage, if it is there then returns the stored answer else proceeds as follows:
  • Computes $\mathbf{v}_i = \mathbf{e}_0 + \Sigma_{j=1}^l msg_i[j]\mathbf{e}_j$ as the signature and sends it to $\mathcal{A}$.

Then, $\mathcal{A}$ computes $\mathbf{u} = \mathbf{c}_0 + \Sigma_{j=1}^l msg_i[j]\mathbf{c}_j$ and verifies whether $\mathbf{u} = \mathbf{A}\mathbf{v}_i \mod q$ and $\|\mathbf{v}_i\| \le s \frac{1+\Sigma_{j=1}^l msg_i[j]}{l+1} \sqrt{m}$. Because of the choice of $\mathbf{e}_i's$, both the conditions hold.

At Last, $\mathcal{A}$ outputs the forgery $(msg^\star, \mathbf{v}^\star)$ such that $\mathbf{A}\mathbf{v}^\star \mod q = \mathbf{c}_0 + \Sigma_{j=1}^l msg^\star[j]\mathbf{c}_j$ and $\|\mathbf{v}^\star\| \le s \frac{1+\Sigma_{j=1}^l msg^\star[j]}{l+1} \sqrt{m}$.

$\mathcal{C}$ solves the SIS instance considering the following cases:

Case 1: If $msg^* = msg_i$ for some i, then looks in the local storage to get $\mathbf{v}_i$. If $\mathbf{v}_i \neq \mathbf{v}^*$ then

$$\mathbf{A}(\mathbf{v}_i - \mathbf{v}^*) = 0 \mod q \text{ and}$$
$$\|\mathbf{v}_i - \mathbf{v}^*\| \leq 2\, s \frac{1 + \Sigma_{j=1}^l msg^*[j]}{l+1} \sqrt{m} \leq 2\, s\sqrt{m}.$$

Thus, obtaining a solution to the SIS problem, by pre-image min-entropy [2], $\mathbf{v}_i \neq \mathbf{v}^*$ occurs with a probability $1 - 2^{-\omega(\log n)}$.

Case 2: If $msg^* \neq msg_i$, then $\mathcal{C}$ computes $\mathbf{v} = \mathbf{e}_0 + \Sigma_{j=1}^l msg^*[j]\mathbf{e}_j$, $\therefore \mathbf{Av}$ $\mod q = \mathbf{c}_0 + \Sigma_{j=1}^l msg^*[j]\mathbf{c}_j$ and $\|\mathbf{v}\| \leq s\frac{1+\Sigma_{j=1}^l msg^*[j]}{l+1}\sqrt{m}$.

If $\mathbf{v} \neq \mathbf{v}^*$, then similarly, $\mathcal{C}$ obtains the solution of the SIS problem. From [2] the probability of $\mathbf{v} \neq \mathbf{v}^*$ is $1 - 2^{-\omega(\log n)}$.

Thus, from above, $\mathcal{C}$ obtains the solution of the SIS problem with probability $(1 - 2^{-\omega(\log n)})\epsilon$.

In the next section, we discuss a flaw in the above security model and the design of the scheme. We propose an attack to leak information about the secret key.

4   Cryptanalysis of Fenghe and Zhenhua Scheme

In the security proof given in Theorem 1, the challenger $\mathcal{C}$ chooses $l+1$ secret values $\mathbf{e}_i$'s to answer the signing query of adversary $\mathcal{A}$. To forge the signature, adversary $\mathcal{A}$ queries to the challenger $\mathcal{C}$ and with the help of these queries, he will try to get the secret vectors e_i; i $=0,1,...,l$. Now we show how an adversary can compute these secret vectors e_i's.

Let $msg = (msg[1], msg[2], \ldots, msg[l-1], msg[l]) \in \{0,1\}^l$. Adversary queries on $l+1$ messages $(0,0, \ldots,0,0)$, $(1,0, \ldots,0,0)$, $(1,1, \ldots,0,0)$, $\ldots$, $(1,1, \ldots,1,0)$ and $(1,1, \ldots \ldots,1,1)$ to the challenger $\mathcal{C}$. The challenger $\mathcal{C}$ uses signing oracle and returns the signatures $\mathbf{v}_0 = \mathbf{e}_0$, $\mathbf{v}_1 = \mathbf{e}_0 + \mathbf{e}_1$, $\ldots$, $\mathbf{v}_{l-1} = \mathbf{e}_0 + \mathbf{e}_1 + \ldots + \mathbf{e}_{l-1}$, $\mathbf{v}_l = \mathbf{e}_0 + \mathbf{e}_1 + \ldots + \mathbf{e}_{l-1} + \mathbf{e}_l$ respectively. So the adversary $\mathcal{A}$ has the following system of equations

$$\begin{bmatrix} \mathbf{v}_0 \\ \mathbf{v}_1 \\ \vdots \\ \mathbf{v}_{l-1} \\ \mathbf{v}_l \end{bmatrix} = \begin{bmatrix} 1\,0 \ldots 0\,0 \\ 1\,1 \ldots 0\,0 \\ \vdots\,\vdots \ldots \vdots\,\vdots \\ 1\,1 \ldots 1\,0 \\ 1\,1 \ldots 1\,1 \end{bmatrix} \begin{bmatrix} \mathbf{e}_0 \\ \mathbf{e}_1 \\ \vdots \\ \mathbf{e}_{l-1} \\ \mathbf{e}_l \end{bmatrix}$$

The adversary $\mathcal{A}$ solves this system of equations using forward substitution and gets $\mathbf{e}_0 = \mathbf{v}_0, \mathbf{e}_1 = \mathbf{v}_1 - \mathbf{v}_0, \ldots, \mathbf{e}_{l-1} = \mathbf{v}_{l-1} - \mathbf{v}_{l-2}$ and $\mathbf{e}_l = \mathbf{v}_l - \mathbf{v}_{l-1}$.

In this way, $\mathcal{A}$ gets the secret keys and hence can generate the signatures for the non-queried messages. Hence the Fenghe and Zhenhua scheme is not strongly unforgeable.

Now, we propose an attack that leaks information about the trapdoor $\mathbf{T}$. The value $\mathbf{u}$ in the signature scheme is a linear combination of $l + 1$ linearly independent $\mathbf{c}_i$. Thus, we can obtain $l + 1$ independent $\mathbf{u}_i$'s and their signatures $(\mathbf{u}_i, \mathbf{v}_i)$, for $i = 1, \ldots, (l + 1)$. Taking a linear combination of these $\mathbf{u}_i$'s and $\mathbf{v}_i$'s, we can obtain $(\mathbf{u}', \mathbf{v}')$, which will satisfy the verification equations.

Without loss of generality, let the adversary has signatures on $l + 1$ messages $(0,0, \ldots,0,0)$, $(1,0, \ldots,0,0)$, $(1,1, \ldots,0,0)$, $\ldots$, $(1,1, \ldots,1,0)$ and $(1,1, \ldots,1,1)$. So, $\mathcal{A}$ will have -

$\mathbf{Av}_0 = \mathbf{u}_0 = \mathbf{c}_0 \mod q$, $\mathbf{Av}_1 = \mathbf{u}_1 = \mathbf{c}_0 + \mathbf{c}_1 \mod q$, $\ldots$, $\mathbf{Av}_{l-1} = \mathbf{u}_{l-1} = \mathbf{c}_0 + \mathbf{c}_1 + \ldots + \mathbf{c}_{l-1} \mod q$, and $\mathbf{Av}_l = \mathbf{u}_l = \mathbf{c}_0 + \mathbf{c}_1 + \ldots + \mathbf{c}_{l-1} + \mathbf{c}_l \mod q$.
Now, suppose the adversary wants to find a signature on the message $msg = (msg[1], msg[2], \ldots, msg[l-1], msg[l]) \in \{0,1\}^l$. So, $\mathbf{u} = \mathbf{c}_0 + \sum_{i=1}^{l} msg[i]\mathbf{c}_i$. Now his aim is to compute $\mathbf{v}$ such that $\mathbf{Av} = \mathbf{u} \mod q$ and $||\mathbf{v}|| \leq s\sqrt{m}$.

So, adversary $\mathcal{A}$ solves
$\mathbf{c}_0 + \sum_{i=1}^{l} msg[i]\mathbf{c}_i = \mathbf{c}_0 + \alpha_1(\mathbf{c}_0 + \mathbf{c}_1) + \ldots + \alpha_{l-1}(\mathbf{c}_0 + \mathbf{c}_1 + \ldots + \mathbf{c}_{l-1}) + \alpha_l(\mathbf{c}_0 + \mathbf{c}_1 + \ldots + \mathbf{c}_l)$ for α_i's and gets $\alpha_l = msg[l]$, $\alpha_{l-1} = msg[l-1] - msg[l]$, $\ldots$, $\alpha_2 = msg[2] - msg[3]$, and $\alpha_1 = msg[1] - msg[2]$.

Thus, $\mathcal{A}$ has
$\mathbf{c}_0 + \sum_{i=1}^{l} msg[i]\mathbf{c}_i = \mathbf{c}_0 + (msg[1] - msg[2])(\mathbf{c}_0 + \mathbf{c}_1) + \ldots + (msg[l-1] - msg[l])(\mathbf{c}_0 + \mathbf{c}_1 + \ldots + \mathbf{c}_{l-1}) + msg[l](\mathbf{c}_0 + \mathbf{c}_1 + \ldots + \mathbf{c}_l) = \mathbf{Av}_0 + (msg[1] - msg[2])\mathbf{Av}_1 + \ldots + (msg[l-1] - msg[l])\mathbf{Av}_{l-1} + msg[l]\mathbf{Av}_l \mod q = \mathbf{A}(\mathbf{v}_0 + (msg[1] - msg[2])\mathbf{v}_1 + \ldots + (msg[l-1] - msg[l])\mathbf{v}_{l-1} + msg[l]\mathbf{v}_l) \mod q$.

Thus, $\mathcal{A}$ has
$\mathbf{c}_0 + \sum_{i=1}^{l} msg[i]\mathbf{c}_i = \mathbf{Av} \mod q$, where $\mathbf{v} = \mathbf{v}_0 + (msg[1] - msg[2])\mathbf{v}_1 + \ldots + (msg[l-1] - msg[l])\mathbf{v}_{l-1} + msg[l]\mathbf{v}_l)$ and $||\mathbf{v}|| \leq (l+1)s\sqrt{m}$.

Clearly $\mathbf{v}$ satisfies the first condition of signature verification, i.e., $\mathbf{Av} = \mathbf{u} = \mathbf{c}_0 + \sum_{i=1}^{l} msg[i]\mathbf{c}_i \mod q$, and if it also satisfies the second condition $||\mathbf{v}|| \leq s\sqrt{m}$ then $\mathbf{v}$ is a valid signature on the message msg. If $\mathbf{v}$ does not satisfy the second condition, then $\mathcal{A}$ query on the message msg to the signer. If the signer outputs $\mathbf{v}^*$ as a signature on the message msg then $\mathbf{Av}^* = \mathbf{u} \mod q$ and $||\mathbf{v}^*|| \leq s\sqrt{m}$.
Thus, $\mathbf{A}$ has

$$\mathbf{Av}^* = \mathbf{u} \mod q, \text{and}$$
$$\mathbf{Av} = \mathbf{u} \mod q$$
$$\implies \mathbf{A}(\mathbf{v}^* - \mathbf{v}) = 0 \mod q,$$
$$\text{where } ||\mathbf{v}^* - \mathbf{v}|| \leq (l+2)s\sqrt{m}.$$

In this way, the adversary has found a solution of the SIS problem. It means the design of the scheme leaks information about the secret trapdoor $\mathbf{T}$. In other words, $\mathcal{A}$ obtains a small normed vector in the lattice $\mathcal{L}^{\perp}(\mathbf{A})$, forming a part of the secret trapdoor $\mathbf{T}$.

Toy example - Consider for $l = 3$, we obtain signatures for $msg_0 = (0,0,0)$, $msg_1 = (1,0,0)$, and $msg_2 = (0,0,1)$, then we have $(\mathbf{u_0} = \mathbf{c_0}, \mathbf{v_0})$, $(\mathbf{u_1} = \mathbf{c_0} + \mathbf{c_1}, \mathbf{v_1})$, and $(\mathbf{u_2} = \mathbf{c_0} + \mathbf{c_3}, \mathbf{v_2})$. We can generate a signature for $msg' = (1,0,1)$ as follows-
Here, we have $\mathbf{Av_0} = \mathbf{u_0} = \mathbf{c_0} \mod q$, $\mathbf{Av_1} = \mathbf{u_1} = \mathbf{c_0} + \mathbf{c_1} \mod q$, $\mathbf{Av_2} = \mathbf{u_2} = \mathbf{c_0} + \mathbf{c_3} \mod q$ and $||v_i|| \leq s\sqrt{m}$ for $i =$0,1,2. For $msg' = (1,0,1)$, $\mathbf{u'} = \mathbf{c_0} + \mathbf{c_1} + \mathbf{c_3}$. So our aim is to find $\mathbf{v'}$ of small norm, such that $\mathbf{Av'} = \mathbf{u'} = \mathbf{c_0} + \mathbf{c_1} + \mathbf{c_3} \mod q$.

$\mathbf{Av'} = \mathbf{c_0} + \mathbf{c_1} + \mathbf{c_3} \mod q = -\mathbf{c_0} + (\mathbf{c_0} + \mathbf{c_1}) + (\mathbf{c_0} + \mathbf{c_3}) \mod q = -\mathbf{Av_0} + \mathbf{Av_1} + \mathbf{Av_2} \mod q = \mathbf{A}(-\mathbf{v_0} + \mathbf{v_1} + \mathbf{v_2}) \mod q$.
So, $\mathbf{u'} = \mathbf{c_0} + \mathbf{c_1} + \mathbf{c_3}$ and $\mathbf{v'} = -\mathbf{v_0} + \mathbf{v_1} + \mathbf{v_2}$.

5   Conclusion

Fenghe and Zhenhua [8] tried to construct a provable secure short signature scheme in the standard model, but their construction and security analysis has some flaws which lead to the leakage of the secret key. We showed how an adversary can generate a valid forgery and how he can leak information about the secret key.

Acknowledgement. This work is supported under CSIR-JRF (File number 09/1032(0022)/2020-EMR-I).

References

1. Shor, P.W.: Algorithms for quantum computation: discrete logarithms and factoring. In: Proceedings 35th Annual Symposium on Foundations of Computer Science, pp. 124–134 (1994)
2. Gentry, C., Peikert, C., Vaikuntanathan, V.: Trapdoors for hard lattices and new cryptographic constructions. In: Proceedings of the Fortieth Annual ACM Symposium on Theory of Computing, pp. 197–206 (2008)
3. Cash, D., Hofheinz, D., Kiltz, E., Peikert, C.: Bonsai trees, or how to delegate a lattice basis. J. Cryptol. **25**, 601–639 (2012)
4. Boyen, X.: Lattice mixing and vanishing trapdoors: a framework for fully secure short signatures and more. In: Nguyen, P.Q., Pointcheval, D. (eds.) PKC 2010. LNCS, vol. 6056, pp. 499–517. Springer, Heidelberg (2010). https://doi.org/10.1007/978-3-642-13013-7_29
5. Ducas, L., Micciancio, D.: Improved short lattice signatures in the standard model. In: Garay, J.A., Gennaro, R. (eds.) CRYPTO 2014. LNCS, vol. 8616, pp. 335–352. Springer, Heidelberg (2014). https://doi.org/10.1007/978-3-662-44371-2_19
6. Ajtai, M.: Generating hard instances of the short basis problem. In: Wiedermann, J., van Emde Boas, P., Nielsen, M. (eds.) ICALP 1999. LNCS, vol. 1644, pp. 1–9. Springer, Heidelberg (1999). https://doi.org/10.1007/3-540-48523-6_1
7. Agrawal, S., Boneh, D., Boyen, X.: Lattice basis delegation in fixed dimension and shorter-ciphertext hierarchical IBE. In: Rabin, T. (ed.) CRYPTO 2010. LNCS, vol. 6223, pp. 98–115. Springer, Heidelberg (2010). https://doi.org/10.1007/978-3-642-14623-7_6
8. Fenghe, W., Zhenhua, L.: Short and provable secure lattice-based signature scheme in the standard model. Secur. Commun. Netw. **9**(16), 3627–3632 (2016)

Cryptanalysis with Countermeasure on the SIS Based Signature Scheme

Komal Pursharthi$^{(\boxtimes)}$ (iD) and Dheerendra Mishra (iD)

Maulana Azad National Institute of Technology, Bhopal, India
komalpursharthi.56@gmail.com

Abstract. Digital signatures are widely used in various applications, including email security, document authentication, and electronic transactions. They play an essential role in ensuring the non-repudiation and integrity of digital transactions and communication. Motivated by the progress of developments in quantum computers, researchers are dynamically proposing digital signature schemes that can withstand quantum attacks. Recently, Soni et al. presented a digital signature protocol that relies on the difficulty of the shortest integer solution challenge in lattices. This protocol has significantly smaller key and signature sizes than previously proposed lattice-based protocols. The design is also compact, simple and elegant. Hence, it is crucial to analyse the security of this protocol. Thus, we perform cryptanalysis on the Soni et al. scheme, which indicates that the availability of one valid message-signature pair can enable an attacker to extract the signer's secret key. It is a significant flaw as the singing key is not a one-time key and the one-time use of this key will lead to its leakage. To overcome this flaw, we suggest a countermeasure in which the signing key can't be achieved using any number of valid message-signature pairs.

Keywords: Lattice based Cryptography · Shortest Integer Solution Problem · Digital Signature

1 Introduction

Digital signatures are an important topic of evolution and expansion in cybersecurity and cryptography. These signatures are used to verify the authenticity and integrity of digital documents and messages. Moreover, digital signatures are a fundamental component of various evolving technologies like blockchain, cryptocurrencies and many more. Researchers have been working on enhancing the efficiency and security of digital signatures in these contexts. This includes optimizing signature verification algorithms for faster transaction processing and exploring new signature schemes for various applications. Also, experts are involved in improving the usability of digital signatures and promoting their adoption, which leads to user-friendly interfaces, mobile device integration, and legal frameworks.

© The Author(s), under exclusive license to Springer Nature Switzerland AG 2024
F. Regazzoni et al. (Eds.): SPACE 2023, LNCS 14412, pp. 92–100, 2024.
https://doi.org/10.1007/978-3-031-51583-5_6

Security of the current digital signature schemes relies on the difficulty of one of the two hard assumptions; integer factorization and discrete logarithm problem. In 1994, Peter Shor introduced an algorithm [25] to solve these hard problems. It exploits the principles of quantum mechanics to achieve exponential speedup in factorization. As a result, all digital signature schemes constructed on these assumptions would be exhibited as not secure by a highly scalable quantum computer. Development in quantum computing is slow but unwavering: the current quantum computers can control about four hundred qubits while more than several thousand qubits are required to solve the factorization. Some experts predict that highly scalable quantum computers might become available within the next decades [3]. In effect, most current-day cryptography will be broken once high-scale quantum computers become reality.

Motivated by the progress of developments in quantum computers, researchers are indulging themselves in designing digital signature schemes that can withstand quantum attacks. These protocols generally come under the terminology "quantum-safe cryptography" or "post-quantum cryptography". Several encouraging pathways like cryptography on lattices, code-based cryptography, cryptography on the hardness of multivariate polynomials, isogeny of elliptic curves and security of hash functions exist towards the construction of secure asymmetric post-quantum protocols. In particular, the hardness of problems over lattices seems promising towards the development of quantum secure schemes. Lattice-based cryptography offers solid theoretical security proofs, various achievable cryptographic primitives, and an efficiency level that can stand pre-quantum schemes.

Digital signature schemes constructed over the hardness of Shortest Integer Solution (SIS) problem [27] in lattices have gained popularity because of their smaller key sizes, lesser communication rounds and storage requirements and the feature of easy implementation. Recently, Soni et al. [26] proposed a digital signature protocol constructed on the challenge of the SIS problem. Their scheme withstand attacks by a quantum computer and they have proved its security in a well-established model for quantum adversary. Also, signature size of [26] is significantly lesser than well proposed lattice based digital signatures [2,8,14,21] and [28]. As it is an efficient scheme and this field is an evolving field, it is required to analyse the security of Soni et al. before its adoption.

2 Related Work

Whitfield Diffie and Martin Hellman discuss the first idea of digital signature protocol based on trapdoor functions, which they presented in 1976 [17]. The pioneer digital signature algorithm is RSA, proposed in 1978 [23]. RSA is the most prevalent cryptographic protocol in use today and controls secure data transactions across open communication channels. Various applications of digital signature devised after the introduction of RSA [9,22] and [16]. In 1985, ElGamal proposed a signature scheme based on the hardness of discrete logarithm problem [11]. After that, ElGamal was modified from the domain of natural integers to the domain of Gaussian integers and polynomials over finite fields to enhance the security [15]. In 1998, Johnson et al. [18] proposed an elliptic curve digital signature algorithm (ECDSA). It offers higher security with smaller key sizes. ECDSA was also standardized by NIST in 1999. It is popular in Bitcoin, SSL/TLS, and smart cards. EdDSA is a recent signature scheme based on twisted Edwards curves, a particular class of elliptic curves. It was introduced by Bernstein et al. [6] in 2011. EdDSA has several advantages over ECDSA, such as faster performance, smaller signatures, and resistance to side-channel attacks. EdDSA is used in protocols such as Signal, Tor, and SSH. As all these signatures are either constructed on the factoring hardness (RSA) or the difficulty of the discrete log challenge (DSA/ECDSA), the security of these signatures might be seriously weakened in the era of highly scalable quantum computers.

To prevent a collapse of signature protocols, researchers have worked on building secure digital signatures that do not rely on factorization and discrete logarithms and that can be expected to be impervious to attacks performed by quantum computers. In 2009, Chris Peikert introduced Bonsai Trees, which can be applied to construct an efficient, stateless 'hash-and-sign' signature protocol in the standard security model [21]. In 2010, Boyen proposed a technique for adaptive security from hardness on lattices in the standard model [7]. They obtain fully secure signatures that are easy to implement. In 2012, Lubashevsky introduced lattice signatures without trapdoors [20]. The size of the key and signature of this protocol are lesser than in all foregoing schemes of the 'hash-and-sign' signatures. It is also straightforward, needing only a few vector-matrix multiplications and rejection samplings. Followed by this scheme, Guneysu et al. [13] presented an implementable digital signature protocol and showed that this scheme is more optimized than [20] for embedded systems. Moreover, as an improvement of [20], they lowered the signature size by a factor of two. Additionally, they demonstrated the viability of their scheme by executing an extensible and cost-effective signing and verification engine. In 2013, Ducas et al. [10] presented a signature scheme that modifies the rejection sampling algorithm used in [20]. This new rejection sampling technique takes elements from a bimodal Gauss distribution, in effect with a new protocol instantiation results in decreasing the deviation of the obtained signatures by a number that is asymptotically square root in the factor of security. In 2014, Bai and Galbraith [5] introduced a new compression strategy based on learning with errors. They provided a new technique to the compression idea of [20]. This proposal is incredibly satisfactory for protocols whose security is based on worst-case standard computational hard assumptions. Following the scheme [7], Xu et al. [28] demonstrated that the scheme of Boyen does not satisfy strong unforgeability. In 2015, Alkim et al. [4] presented a tightly safe signature protocol with good efficiency from standard lattices. They improved the security of the proposal of [5]. They tightened the reduction of safety and minimized the primary assumptions of security. In 2016, Akleylek et al. [2] presented the pioneer digital signature protocol with remarkable efficiency and provably secure exemplified. It can compete with RSA and ECDSA in performance. In 2018, Gupta and Biswas presented the construction of a lattice-based Elgamal signature protocol on the difficulty of SIS challenge [14]. They showed that their scheme is well protected in the modern computing environment and achieves strong security characteristics and efficient execution. Recently, Soni et al. [26] proposed SIS-based signature scheme with significantly reduced signature and key sizes than [2,21,28] and [14]. The fundamental motivation of [26] is to develop encryption and signature schemes based on lattices with average case hardness that achieves security against existing attacks and future quantum attacks.

3   Preliminaries

This section discusses the core characteristics and definitions of Shortest Integer Solution (SIS) along with the various notations employed in this article.

Notations: $\mathbb{Z}$, $\mathbb{R}$ denotes the set of integers and real numbers respectively. The symbols m and n are any integers and q be a large prime number.

Definition 1 (Lattices). *Let* $\mathbb{R}^m$ *be the m-dimensional Euclidean space. Let* $u_1, \cdots, u_n \in \mathbb{R}^m$ *be a set of linearly independent elements. The lattice* $\mathcal{L}$ *constructed by* $u_1, \cdots, u_n$ *is the set of linear combinations of* $u_1, \cdots, u_n$ *with coefficients in integers [12].*

$$\mathcal{L} = \{b_1 u_1 + b_2 u_2 + \cdots + b_n u_n : b_1, b_2, \cdots, b_n \in \mathbb{Z}\}.$$

- A basis for $\mathcal{L}$ is any set of independent vectors that constructs $\mathcal{L}$. Any two such sets have the same cardinality.
- The integer n is known as rank and m is known as dimension of the lattice.

Definition 2 (q-ary Lattice). $\mathcal{L}$ *is a q-ary lattice if* $q\mathbb{Z}^n \subseteq \mathcal{L} \subseteq \mathbb{Z}^n$ *[12].*

Definition 3 (Shortest Vector Problem). *Given a lattice* $\mathcal{L}(B)$, *find a (nonzero) vector* Bx *(with* $x \in \mathbb{Z}^n$*) such that* $||Bx|| \leq \lambda_1$, *where* $\lambda_1 = min_{x,y \in \mathcal{L}, x \neq y}$ $||x - y|| = min_{x \in \mathcal{L}, x \neq 0} ||x||$ *[19].*

Definition 4 (Shortest Independent Vectors Problem (SIVP)[1]). *Given a lattice* $\mathcal{L}(B)$, *find n linearly independent lattice vectors* $Bx_1, \cdots, Bx_n$ *of length (at most)* $max_i ||Bx_i|| \leq \lambda_n$, *where*

$$\lambda_i = min\{r : dim \ span(\mathcal{B}(r) \bigcap \mathcal{L}) \geq i\} \ and$$
$$\mathcal{B}(r) \ is \ ball \ of \ radius \ r \ centered \ at \ zero.$$

Definition 5 (Shortest Integer Solution Problem). *Let* $A \in \mathbb{Z}_q^{n \times m}$, $q = poly(n)$, $m = \Omega(n \ log \ q)$, *then for given matrix A, finding "short" (low norm) vector x such that* $Ax = 0 \ mod \ q \in \mathbb{Z}_q^n$ *is SIS problem [27].*

4   Soni et al.'s Signature Scheme

Here, we present Soni et al.'s signature protocol [26]. The following collection of matrices are considered in their scheme $\mathcal{B} \subset \mathbb{Z}_q^{m \times n}$, $\mathcal{T} \subset \mathbb{Z}_q^n$, $\mathcal{P}_u \subset \mathbb{Z}_q^m$ and $\mathcal{P} \subseteq \mathbb{Z}_q^n$. Here, $\mathcal{B}$ is the collection of all modular matrices of order $m \times n$, $\mathcal{T}$ is the collection of all n-tuple modular vectors, $\mathcal{P}_u$ is the public key space, $\mathcal{P}$ is the message space. This protocol comprises of four phases described below.

- **Setup Phase:** Choose m,n $\in \mathbb{Z}$, q as large prime such that n $\geq$ m log q, hash H : $\mathbb{Z}_q^m \rightarrow \mathbb{Z}_q^m$ and message space is of dimension $\mathbb{Z}_q^n$.
- **Key Generation**
  - Signer chooses random matrix B $\in \mathcal{B} \subset \mathbb{Z}_q^{m \times n}$ and a vector t $\in \mathcal{T} \subseteq \mathbb{Z}_q^n$.
  - Computes $P_u = t^T . B^T \in \mathcal{P}_u \subseteq \mathbb{Z}_q^{1 \times m}$.
  - Private Key $\rightarrow$ t, Public Key $\rightarrow$ B, P_u.
- **Signing a message** P$\in \mathbb{Z}_q^n$
  - Selects two random vectors r, s $\in \mathbb{Z}_q^m$
  - Computes $G_1 = s^T r \in \mathbb{Z}_q$ and $G_2 = P^T - G_1 t^T$
  - Sends (H(P), (G_1, G_2)) to verifier.
- **Verification of (H(P), (G_1, G_2))**
  - Verifier computes W = $G_1 . P_u$ and verify W $\in \mathbb{Z}_q^{1 \times m}$
  - Computes $P_1^T B^T = (G_2 B^T + W) mod$ q
  - Verifies H$(P_1^T B^T) \overset{?}{=}$ H$(P^T B^T)$
  - If verified, then signature is valid.

5   Cryptanalysis

We analyse a flaw in Soni et al.'s signature scheme [26]. As message-signature pairs are always available in the public domain, any adversary can access these pairs.

Suppose (P,(G_1, G_2)) is a valid message- signature pair. According to above scheme, signer calculates $G_2 = P^T - G_1 t^T$. Now, we can see

$$G_2 = P^T - G_1 t^T$$
$$\implies G_2 - P^T = -G_1 t^T$$

$$\implies -G_2 + P^T = G_1 t^T \tag{1}$$

Since, $G_1 \in \mathbb{Z}_q$. So, with overwhelming probability G_1^{-1} exist as $\mathbb{Z}_q$ is a field. So, from Eq. (1), we can compute the secret value t as $t^T = G_1^{-1}(-G_2 + P^T)$.

Here, we observe that from any available valid message-signature pair, an attacker can calculate the signer's secret key.

This attack can be efficiently performed as it requires only the following efficient operations:

- One transpose of a vector to calculate P^T.
- One addition operation to add two vectors $-G_2$ and P^T.

- One integer inverse in $\mathbb{Z}_q$.
- One multiplication operation between integer modulo q and a vector $(-G_2 + P^T)$.

Hence, with just one valid message-signature pair, we can efficiently extract the signer's secret key and create a valid sign on any message of our choice.

For instance, we can show retrieving the secret key in the toy example of digital signature presented in [26].

Public parameters taken in [26] for signature generation are m $=2$, n$=3$ and q$=11$. Let $B = \begin{bmatrix} 5 & 6 & 1 \\ 1 & 0 & 3 \end{bmatrix}$ and secret key $t = \begin{bmatrix} 4 \\ 9 \\ 3 \end{bmatrix}$ then the public key is $P_u=$

$t^T.B^T=[0\ 2]$. The sender signed the message $P = \begin{bmatrix} 8 \\ 6 \\ 9 \end{bmatrix}$ by using $r = \begin{bmatrix} 2 \\ 3 \end{bmatrix}$ and

$s = \begin{bmatrix} 6 \\ 8 \end{bmatrix}$. The signature according to [26] is

$$(G_1, G_2) = (s^T r, P^T - G_1 t^T) = ([3], [710]).$$

Now, when adversary gets message-signature pair $(P,(G_1, G_2))$, it can extract secret key t from this pair.

As $G_2 = P^T - G_1 t^T \implies G_2 - P^T = -G_1 t^T \implies -G_2 + P^T = G_1 t^T$
$\implies$ -$[\ 7\ 1\ 0] + [8\ 6\ 9] = G_1 t^T \implies [1\ 5\ 9] = 3t^T$

$\implies 3^{-1}[1\ 5\ 9] = t^T = 4[1\ 5\ 9] = [4\ 20\ 36] = [4\ 9\ 3] \implies t = \begin{bmatrix} 4 \\ 9 \\ 3 \end{bmatrix}$.

6 Countermeasure

During our observation, we realised that the attack was occurring due to the inappropriate selection of parameters in the signing and setup phases. Our countermeasure does not include any change in the key generation phase. We work on the improvement of the setup, signing and verification phases as follows:

- **Setup Phase:** Choose m,n $\in \mathbb{Z}$, q as large prime such that n $\geq$ m log q, hash $H : \mathbb{Z}_q^{n \times m} \to \mathbb{Z}_q^m$ and message space is of dimension $\mathbb{Z}_q^{n \times n}$.
- **Signing a message** P$\in \mathbb{Z}_q^{n \times n}$
  - Selects two random vectors r, s such that r$=(0, r_1, r_2, \cdots, r_{n-1}) \in \mathbb{Z}_q^n$ as $(r_1, r_2, \cdots, r_{n-1}) \in \mathbb{Z}_q^{n-1}$ and s$\in \mathbb{Z}_q$.
  - Computes $G_1 = sr^T \in \mathbb{Z}_q^{1 \times n}$ and $G_2 = P - G_1^T t^T$
  - Sends $(H(P), (G_1, G_2))$ to verifier.
- **Verification of $(H(P), (G_1, G_2))$**
  - Verifier computes $W = G_1^T.P_u$ and verify $W \in \mathbb{Z}_q^{n \times m}$
  - Computes $P_1 B^T = (G_2 B^T + W) mod\ q$
  - Verifies $H(P_1 B^T) \overset{?}{=} H(PB^T)$
  - If verified, then signature is valid.

6.1   Correctness

To show that the signature technique is feasible, it is enough to prove that $P_1 B^T$ is congruent to PB^T.

$$
\begin{aligned}
P_1 B^T &= G_2 B^T + W \\
&= (P - G_1^T t^T)\, B^T + G_1^T . P_u \\
&= PB^T - G_1^T t^T B^T + G_1^T . P_u \\
&= PB^T - G_1^T . P_u + G_1^T . P_u \\
&= PB^T .
\end{aligned}
$$

7   Discussion

The established security components of [26] adjuncts in our countermeasure because we have modified only the dimension of message space and hash input. In effect, we can see that now the dimension of G_1 is $1 \times$ n, it is an element of $\mathbb{Z}_q^n$. So, it belongs to $\mathbb{Z}_q \times \mathbb{Z}_q \times \cdots \times \mathbb{Z}_q$ (n times cartesian product) and it is a zero divisor in this structure as $G_1 = sr^T$ will have first component equals to zero as per the selection of r in our construction. For zero divisor, we cannot calculate the multiplicative inverse [24]. Thus, G_1 will not possess a multiplicative inverse in $\mathbb{Z}_q^n$. Hence, adversary will not be able to compute signer's secret key. Moreover, as the key generation part of both techniques is identical, the advantage of smaller key sizes remains, and it resists quantum attacks because of the SIS challenge on lattices. However, it is required in future to explore the proof of security and other efficient countermeasures.

The same number of similar matrix operations as in [26] pertains to the advantage of storage, key sizes and computation overhead in our technique competing with other lattice-based signature schemes. As signature in our countermeasure is (G_1, G_2), where $G_1 \in \mathbb{Z}_q^{1 \times n}$ and $G_2 \in \mathbb{Z}_q^{n \times n}$, so signature size is $n^2 + n$, which is slightly greater than signature size of [26], but signing key is secured now. However, one could explore the possibility of reducing signature size and improving efficiency without diluting the security. The comparison of key and signature sizes is provided in Table 1.

Table 1. Comparison of key and signature sizes

Scheme	Signing Key	Verification Key	Signature
[26]	n	$nm + m$	$1 + n$
Countermeasure	n	$nm + m$	$n^2 + n$

8 Conclusion

This article presented a cryptanalysis on a recently proposed lattice-based digital signature scheme on SIS hardness. The cryptanalysis shows the retrieval of signer's key using one valid message-signature pair. Moreover, we have suggested a technique to overcome the described attack without compromising any established security component of the scheme. As the key generation part of the proposed countermeasure is identical to that of Soni et al., the advantage of smaller key sizes is sustained. However, the signature size has slightly increased in order to secure the signing key. In future, one may reduce the signature size with adequate security.

References

1. Aggarwal, D., Chung, E.: A note on the concrete hardness of the shortest independent vector in lattices. Inf. Process. Lett. **167**, 106065 (2021)
2. Akleylek, S., Bindel, N., Buchmann, J., Krämer, J., Marson, G.A.: An efficient lattice-based signature scheme with provably secure instantiation. In: Pointcheval, D., Nitaj, A., Rachidi, T. (eds.) AFRICACRYPT 2016. LNCS, vol. 9646, pp. 44–60. Springer, Cham (2016). https://doi.org/10.1007/978-3-319-31517-1_3
3. Alagic, G., et al.: Status report on the second round of the NIST post-quantum cryptography standardization process. US Dept. Commer., NIST **2** (2020)
4. Alkim, E., Bindel, N., Buchmann, J., Dagdelen, Ö., Schwabe, P.: TESLA: tightly-secure efficient signatures from standard lattices. IACR Cryptol. ePrint Arch. **2015**, 755 (2015)
5. Bai, S., Galbraith, S.D.: An improved compression technique for signatures based on learning with errors. In: Benaloh, J. (ed.) CT-RSA 2014. LNCS, vol. 8366, pp. 28–47. Springer, Cham (2014). https://doi.org/10.1007/978-3-319-04852-9_2
6. Bernstein, D.J., Duif, N., Lange, T., Schwabe, P., Yang, B.Y.: High-speed high-security signatures. J. Cryptogr. Eng. **2**(2), 77–89 (2012)
7. Boyen, X.: Lattice mixing and vanishing trapdoors: a framework for fully secure short signatures and more. In: Nguyen, P.Q., Pointcheval, D. (eds.) PKC 2010. LNCS, vol. 6056, pp. 499–517. Springer, Heidelberg (2010). https://doi.org/10.1007/978-3-642-13013-7_29
8. Cash, D., Hofheinz, D., Kiltz, E., Peikert, C.: Bonsai trees, or how to delegate a lattice basis. J. Cryptol. **25**, 601–639 (2012)
9. Davies, D.W.: Applying the RSA digital signature to electronic mail. Computer **16**(02), 55–62 (1983)
10. Ducas, L., Durmus, A., Lepoint, T., Lyubashevsky, V.: Lattice signatures and bimodal gaussians. In: Canetti, R., Garay, J.A. (eds.) CRYPTO 2013. LNCS, vol. 8042, pp. 40–56. Springer, Heidelberg (2013). https://doi.org/10.1007/978-3-642-40041-4_3
11. ElGamal, T.: A public key cryptosystem and a signature scheme based on discrete logarithms. IEEE Trans. Inf. Theory **31**(4), 469–472 (1985)
12. Goldwasser, S., Micciancio, D.: Complexity of Lattice Problems: A Cryptographic Perspective, vol. 671. Springer, Cham (2002)
13. Güneysu, T., Lyubashevsky, V., Pöppelmann, T.: Practical lattice-based cryptography: a signature scheme for embedded systems. In: Prouff, E., Schaumont, P. (eds.) CHES 2012. LNCS, vol. 7428, pp. 530–547. Springer, Heidelberg (2012). https://doi.org/10.1007/978-3-642-33027-8_31

14. Gupta, D.S., Biswas, G.: Design of lattice-based ELGamal encryption and signature schemes using sis problem. Trans. Emerg. Telecommun. Technol. **29**(6), e3255 (2018)
15. Haraty, R.A., El-Kassar, A.N., Shebaro, B.M.: A comparative study of ELGamal based digital signature algorithms. J. Comput. Methods Sci. Eng. **6**(s1), S147–S156 (2006)
16. Harn, L.: Batch verifying multiple RSA digital signatures. Electron. Lett. **34**(12), 1219–1220 (1998)
17. Hellman, M.: New directions in cryptography. IEEE Trans. Inf. Theory **22**(6), 644–654 (1976)
18. Johnson, D.B., Menezes, A.J.: Elliptic curve DSA (ECDSA): an enhanced DSA. In: Proceedings of the 7th Conference on USENIX Security Symposium, vol. 7, pp. 13–23 (1998)
19. Khot, S.: Hardness of approximating the shortest vector problem in lattices. J. ACM (JACM) **52**(5), 789–808 (2005)
20. Lyubashevsky, V.: Lattice signatures without trapdoors. In: Pointcheval, D., Johansson, T. (eds.) EUROCRYPT 2012. LNCS, vol. 7237, pp. 738–755. Springer, Heidelberg (2012). https://doi.org/10.1007/978-3-642-29011-4_43
21. Peikert, C.: Bonsai trees (or, arboriculture in lattice-based cryptography). Cryptol. ePrint Arch. (2009)
22. Qiao, G., Lam, K.-Y.: RSA signature algorithm for microcontroller implementation. In: Quisquater, J.-J., Schneier, B. (eds.) CARDIS 1998. LNCS, vol. 1820, pp. 353–356. Springer, Heidelberg (2000). https://doi.org/10.1007/10721064_32
23. Rivest, R.L., Shamir, A., Adleman, L.: A method for obtaining digital signatures and public-key cryptosystems. Commun. ACM **21**(2), 120–126 (1978)
24. Shepherdson, J.: Inverses and zero divisors in matrix rings. Proc. Lond. Math. Soc. **3**(1), 71–85 (1951)
25. Shor, P.W.: Algorithms for quantum computation: discrete logarithms and factoring. In: Proceedings 35th Annual Symposium on Foundations of Computer Science, pp. 124–134. IEEE (1994)
26. Soni, L., Chandra, H., Gupta, D.S., Keval, R.: Quantum-resistant public-key encryption and signature schemes with smaller key sizes. Cluster Comput.,1–13 (2022)
27. Wang, S., Zhu, Y., Ma, D., Feng, R.: Lattice-based key exchange on small integer solution problem. Sci. China Inf. Sci. **57**, 1–12 (2014)
28. Xu, Y., Tian, M., Huang, L., Yang, W., Shen, X.: Improvement of a lattice-based signature scheme. J. Inf. Hiding Multim. Signal Process. **5**(1), 41–46 (2014)

Vulnerability of Dynamic Masking in Test Compression

Yogendra Sao⊙, Debanka Giri⊙, Soham Saha⊙, and Sk Subidh Ali$^{(\boxtimes)}$⊙

Indian Institute of Technology Bhilai, Durg 491001, India
{yogendras,debankagiri,sohamsaha,subidh}@iitbhilai.ac.in

Abstract. Scan-based Design for Testability (DfT) ensures the testability of chips while providing observability and high fault coverage. In the case of security-critical applications, an attacker can misuse the scan-based DfT of a chip as a backdoor and reveal the secret information embedded inside the chip. Even advanced test infrastructures such as X-compactor and X-masking are vulnerable to such an attack. In this work, we perform a detailed security analysis of one of the DfT techniques known as the Embedded Deterministic Test (EDT), which is used in the test compression tool Tessent TestKompress. EDT uses dynamic masking along with an XOR-based compactor to achieve test compression. The existing state-of-the-art attack is shown to be effective against dynamic masking. However, the attack success rate is highly constrained by the scan chain configuration, with a 20.53% success rate in the worst-case scenario. In this paper, we propose an improved attack by leveraging signature analysis. The advantage of our attack is that it's a deterministic attack on dynamic masking, which can retrieve the secret key with a 100% success rate. The attack is independent of the internal scan infrastructure and can work even in the presence of a compactor.

Keywords: AES · Security · Scan Attack · Design for Testability · Scan Chain · Static Masking · Dynamic Masking · Compactor · XOR Compression

1 Introduction

Scan-based DfT is a popular technology that is associated with the field of circuit testing, for examining manufacturing-related defects, providing high testability and high fault coverage. In the test mode, the internal flip-flops of the chip are converted into fully accessible scan cells and connected to a scan chain. An attacker can exploit it to get the intermediate response of a cipher to reveal the secret key of the cipher embedded inside the crypto chip [18]. The attack by which an attacker bypasses the weakness of these scan infrastructures is known as a scan attack.

The traditional scan attacks [18,19] rely on mode switching. Therefore, a mode-reset countermeasure [7] was proposed to prevent scan-based attacks by

F. Regazzoni et al. (Eds.): SPACE 2023, LNCS 14412, pp. 101–116, 2024.
https://doi.org/10.1007/978-3-031-51583-5_7

flushing the data in the round register of Chip-Under-Test (CUT) while switching from normal mode to the test mode. Later on, test-mode-only attack [1] was proposed, which is performed using only the test mode without mode switching. Another kind of countermeasure was proposed in [19] by introducing a mirror key register (MKR), which is used in test mode at the time of testing and contains a dummy key value. However, it does not support online testing.

VIm-Scan [9] authenticates the testing process using a pattern matching through the first M consecutive test vectors each of N bits. The security of VIm-Scan can be increased by increasing the value of M and N at the cost of area overhead. There are other secure and interesting countermeasures based on obfuscation of scan data [2,3] and encryption of scan data [17]. While encryption-based countermeasures are secure, they incur a huge area overhead, whereas the obfuscation techniques with low area overhead are not proven to be secure.

Most of the testing time is consumed for shifting in and out the scan data, to speed up the testing, multiple scan chains are introduced. Furthermore, to reduce the test data, multiple scan chains with decompressor and compactor are used in advanced DfT infrastructure to achieve time and space compaction for reducing test time and cost. Moreover, the compaction is often combined with additional logic, such as X-tolerance, X-masking, etc., to remove the effect of some unknown states (X-states or don't care) from the compacted output.

These advanced DfT structures were considered secure against scan-based attacks [8]. Later on, advanced attacks are shown against these advanced DfT structures [4–6,13,14,16]. The signature-based attack was proposed in [4,13] against X-masking. In [5,6], a Hamming weight-based attack is proposed on different test compression techniques, such as X-tolerance, static masking, and dynamic masking, used in commercial EDA tools provided by popular EDA vendors: Synopsys, Cadence, and Siemens. The attacks proposed in [5,6] are probabilistic, having a lower success rate. Thus, a deterministic attack on static masking has been proposed recently in [16], which is successful whenever at least 6 bits corresponding to each AES word are observable. However, a deterministic attack on dynamic masking is still unexplored.

Embedded deterministic test (EDT) [12] is a widely used advanced DfT technique based on dynamic masking offered by Siemens. An in-depth security analysis of EDT composed of dynamic masking was done in [5], and they suggested the designer to have a lower number of active slices to provide security to their chips. We refine the security analysis of EDT by proposing an improved attack on dynamic masking, which is successful even when at least one of the scan chains is unmasked. Our contributions to this paper are:

1. We perform a security analysis of the Embedded Deterministic Test employed with the dynamic masking.
2. We propose a state-of-the-art attack on dynamic masking with compaction having a 100% success rate.
3. We perform an analysis of our attack against different levels of masking and compaction for different scan architectures to validate our results.

2   Background

2.1   AES

Advanced Encryption Standard (AES) is a symmetric key encryption algorithm, which is available in different key sizes, AES-128, AES-192, and AES-256 having 128, 192, and 256 bit key, respectively. Figure 1 shows the AES operations with n rounds, where n can be 10, 12, 14. Each round is composed of the following four operations, except the last round, which does not have the *MixColumns* operation:

1. *SubBytes:* This is the only non-linear substitution procedure where each byte of the 4×4 state matrix is replaced using an 8-bit substitution box.
2. *ShiftRows:* In this step, each row of the state matrix is shifted to the left where shift operation involves shifting 0, 1, 2, and 3 number of bytes in respect of 4 rows of the input matrix.
3. *MixColumns:* This is a mixing operation, where the state matrix is multiplied with a 4×4 constant matrix.
4. *AddRoundKey:* This is the XOR operation between the state matrix and the round key.

There is a key whitening phase before the above four operations, where the input plaintext is XORed with the AES key.

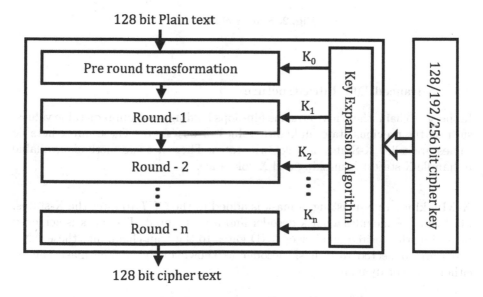

Fig. 1. AES Block Diagram.

2.2   Scan Based DfT

In scan-based DfT, the internal flip-flops of the CUT are converted into fully accessible scan cells (Scan Flip-flops (SFFs) in Fig. 2) and connected in scan chains which can be treated as a configurable shift register. The scan chain infrastructure shown in Fig. 2 has a Test Control (TC) pin connected to a MUX used to control the mode of CUT. The scan in (SI) and Scan out (SO) pins are used to shift in test vectors and shift out the captured responses to and from the scan chain, respectively. As shown in the figure, depending on the test control input line, the input to a scan cell can either be from the round function (in normal mode) or from the previous scan cell (test mode). Scan enables greater access to the chip's internal logic, leading to high test coverage.

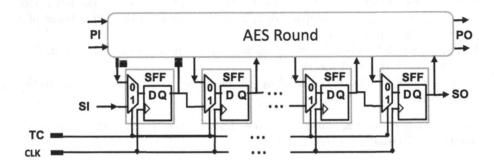

Fig. 2. Scan Architecture.

2.3   Advanced DfT Infrastructure

In the scan chain, there may be some flip-flops holding some unpredictable values, such as the previous state, unknown values of buses, etc. These unpredictable values are called X-States or unknown states. There are two methods available to handle X-states: X-masking and X-tolerance.

X-Masking. In X-masking, a mask is added to the CUT to filter the X-states. Masked CUT includes a mask decoder and a mask input. The mask is achieved by adding the desired number of AND gates to the scan chain, and these AND gates are connected to a mask decoder as shown in Fig. 3. The mask can be either static or dynamic.

- *Static masking:* The static masking always generates a fixed mask value for the entire test with the help of a mask decoder. In order to generate a static mask for a scan chain, the input vector supplied to the mask decoder remains static for the entire test.

– *Dynamic masking:* Dynamic masking always generates different mask values at each clock cycle throughout the test process with the help of a mask decoder. In order to generate a dynamic mask for a scan chain, the input vector supplied to the mask decoder is changed every time for the entire test.

Compaction. Compaction is used to compress the output of the scan chain. In order to achieve the compaction scheme, the output of multiple scan chains is XORed with each other to produce a single output.

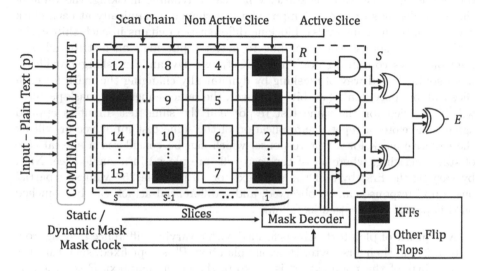

Fig. 3. X-Masking along with the Compactor: P is input plaintext, R is the round output, S is the masked round output, E is the compacted test output, KFFs are the Key Flip Flop containing information related to the target key byte, the number of active scan chains is 3, and the number of active slices is 3, where active scan chain and active slice contains at least one KFF.

3 Proposed Attack Principle

A typical X-masking scheme is shown in Fig. 3. There can be multiple scan chains (scan cells in rows) and multiple slices (scan cells in columns). A flip-flop whose value depends on the targeted key byte (i.e., flip-flops of the round register containing differential information) is known as a Key Flip-flop (KFF) [5,6], and there can be at most 32 KFFs at a time in the scan chain involved in the differential analysis of AES one-round response for a one-byte input difference. A scan chain or a slice with at least one KFF is known as an active scan chain or active slice. There are 3 active scan chains and 3 active slices in Fig. 3. There can be numerous combinations of active scan chains and active slices. To explain our attack analysis and for the sake of simplicity, we consider multiple scan architecture as shown in Table 1 with each of the active slices or active scan chains completely filled with KFFs. Let us consider one of the scenarios of these scan architectures, where all 32 significant bits of the round register (an AES word) are in a single slice with a 32 number of active scan chains. In this case, 32 bits of the round response will be shifted out in just one shift cycle and will be masked with a 32-bit mask value. The mask value will determine which scan chain will be blocked and which one will pass. In the case of static masking, if a scan chain is blocked due to masking, it will remain blocked throughout the test process as the mask value is static. Whereas in dynamic masking, the value of the mask depends on the test input and can change dynamically at each clock cycle (or at regular intervals), blocking different scan chains in each shift cycle.

The test response corresponding to a test input may be distributed over multiple slices containing don't care (X-states). Dynamic masking provides a more sophisticated way of masking by dynamically changing the mask for each slice to block only don't care bits. However, the same sequence of mask patterns will be applied for the same test response if the same test input is applied again. Therefore, a repetitive application of the same test input vector will fix the effective mask for a test response, which can be considered a special case of static masking, where all of the scan cells are placed in a single slice. Now, by varying the first byte of the plaintext for all possible 256 values, a partial one-round response can be observed, and a differential attack can be launched on this partial information as follows:

1. A sequence of plaintext pairs is formed with a varying difference ranging from 0 to 255 in their first byte. Here one plaintext P' is kept fixed, such that the first byte of the plaintext P' is set to 0, the other plaintext P is varied by varying its first byte from 0 to 255 to form a sequence $(0,0), (1,0), (2,0)...,$ $(255,0)$, then differences in their outputs are arranged in the same sequence.
2. Any one of the scan cells is identified for which a difference is observed. Note that there can be only a maximum of 32 such scan cells (bit positions) on which a difference is observed. In the case of masking with compaction, the difference can be observed in the compacted output.
3. The sequence of 1-bit differences in the identified bit position in step (2) can be used as the signature of CUT, which needs to be matched in the signature table(s) containing 256×32 signatures which increases up to 256×255 (generated in Sect. 4) in the presence of compaction, to retrieve the first byte of the key.
4. Similarly, the input difference is applied in the rest of the 15 bytes of the plaintext in step (1), and by repeating step (1) to (3), the other 15 bytes of the key can be retrieved.

4   Attack on Dynamic Masking with Compaction

We consider a CUT with dynamic masking with compaction as shown in Fig. 3 . The detailed attack procedure based on the attack principle (Sect. 3) is explained in this section. Before proceeding to the attack part, we consider the following assumptions similar to [6]:

1. Dynamic masking scheme is applied on an iterative implementation of AES-128 similar to Fig. 3.
2. The attacker has full control over the SI and TC pin, can load the scan chains with any test vector through the SI line and can apply any desired plaintext through the chip's primary inputs (PI).
3. As the value of the mask depends on the test inputs, the attacker can load the same test vector multiple times to apparently fix the mask value for multiple test responses.
4. The scan chain includes the complete 128-bit round register, out of these 128 scan cells, there will be 32 KFFs based on the targeted key byte.

4.1 Basics of Signature-Based Attack

A basic signature attack is a two-phase attack. In the first phase, a signature table is generated based on some observable output difference. For example, one can observe only n-bits of the output difference. In the best case, complete output difference may be observable, which can uniquely identify the key. In the case of partial information, a single output difference may not be sufficient. Therefore, we can apply 256 plaintext pairs with a varying difference in their first byte similar to Sect. 3 and observe 256 partial output differences. These 256 output differences form a signature. Now, in the signature table generation phase, we'll set a key byte value, and apply 256 possible plaintext pairs to observe the output differences to generate one of the signatures. Similarly, we'll generate the entire table for all 256 values of a key byte. In the second phase, we'll apply the same set of 256 plaintext pairs to the CUT and observe the output differences as a signature. Then, we can match this signature in the signature table to get a key byte. This attack works even in the worst case when only 1 bit of the output difference is observable. This makes it suitable against partial scan designs, where the exact bit positions of the round register in the scan cell are unknown.

The proposed attack uses the above signature-based attack, in two phases (online and offline phase). The online phase is the only phase that requires CUT to collect test responses corresponding to 256 desired plaintexts applied to the CUT by varying only one byte of the plaintext. Whereas, offline phase is used to create a signature from CUT responses and match it in the signature table(s) for key recovery. In the rest of the paper, we show how to recover the first byte of the AES key by varying the first byte of plaintexts in the online phase. Similarly, the other 15 bytes of the key can be recovered by targeting the remaining 15 bytes of the plaintexts in the online phase.

4.2 Online Phase: Collecting CUT Responses

The main challenge in dynamic masking is to identify the unmasked bits from CUT responses. If the mask values are changed for each of the CUT responses, it is very difficult to identify the unmasked bits used in the key recovery process. Therefore, a test vector is kept fixed in CUT to fix the mask value for multiple CUT responses as discussed in Sect. 3.

Algorithm 1 shows the sequence of steps followed in the online phase. Initially, 256 different plaintexts are created from a random plaintext P by varying only its first byte for all 256 possible values ($P_i = P$, where $P_i^0 = i$ and $0 \le i \le 255$). These 256 plaintexts are used as the inputs for the Algorithm 1. Before that, a test vector is chosen randomly and stored in a variable TV at the start of the Algorithm 1, and is kept fixed as long as the algorithm runs. In each iteration, the chip is first switched to the test mode ($TC = 1$), and the above-chosen test vector (TV) is shifted into the scan chain (SC) as shown in steps 1 and 1. Then, the chip is switched to normal mode ($TC = 0$), and one of the plaintexts (P_i) is applied through primary input pins PI. The CUT is run for one round of AES to capture its one round masked and compacted response in the scan chain (SC) as shown in steps 1 to 1. $ENC\_CUT()$ in step 1 shows the one-round encryption operation performed by CUT on a given plaintext, where the key used for encryption is the embedded key of the CUT. Finally, the chip is switched to the test mode, and CUT response loaded in the scan chain (SC) is shifted out and stored in a variable E_i corresponding to a plaintext P_i, which is shown in steps 1 and 1. The above steps are repeated for 256 plaintexts in the loop, and at the completion of the loop, 256 CUT responses $E_0, E_1, \ldots, E_{255}$ for each of the 256 plaintexts are obtained as the output of the Algorithm 1, which becomes inputs for the offline analysis. Figure 4 shows how a CUT response is obtained by applying a plaintext with a fixed test vector when CUT is run for one round of AES.

Algorithm 1: Online Phase

Input : $P_i(0 \le i \le 255)$, P_i is the plaintext applied at CUT, where $P_i^j \leftarrow i$ and considering the default value of $j = 0$.
Output: $E_i(0 \le i \le 255)$, where E_i is the one round response from CUT with respect to Plaintext $P_i(0 \le i \le 255)$

$TV \leftarrow Random()$

for $i \leftarrow 0$ **to** 255 **do**

$\quad$ $TC \leftarrow 1$ /*Switching to the test mode*/

$\quad$ $SC \leftarrow TV$ /*Consecutive shift cycles to load the test vector*/

$\quad$ $TC \leftarrow 0$ /*Switching to the normal mode*/

$\quad$ $PI \leftarrow P_i$ /*Apply plaintext through Primary Input*/

$\quad$ $SC \leftarrow ENC\_CUT(PI)$ /*Capture one round response*/

$\quad$ $TC \leftarrow 1$ /*Switching to the test mode*/

$\quad$ $E_i \leftarrow SC$ /*Consecutive shift cycles to Shift out CUT response */

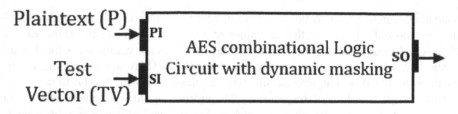

Fig. 4. Online Procedure on CUT

4.3 Offline Phase

The offline phase consists of three steps. In the first step, the required signature tables are built by simulating the first round of AES with predetermined 256 plaintexts, as mentioned in the online phase. In the second step, the same sets of plaintext are applied to the CUT, and the corresponding signature is observed. In the third step, the key byte is recovered by matching the CUT signature with the signature tables.

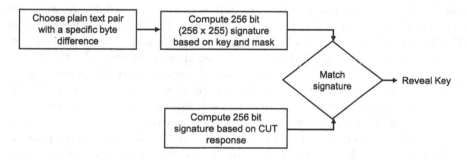

Fig. 5. Offline Procedure

Signature Table Generation. The first step in the offline phase is to build signature tables, where the row of the table will have a unique signature corresponding to each possible key byte value. Let us assume that the signature is corresponding to only one mask, whose value is m.

If we consider the dynamic masking without compaction, anyone unmasked bit from CUT response will be sufficient to reveal the key by matching at most 256×32 signatures. However, if the masked response is further compacted using XOR-tree as shown in Fig. 3, then only the parity of round output will be observable. Thus, the signature obtained using 1-bit parity of CUT responses may not match in 32 signature tables corresponding to each of the individual bit positions of an AES word, as the signature created using 1-bit parity is a combination of 32 signatures from 32 different signature tables corresponding to individual bit

positions. Since there can be a maximum of 32 KFFs in the scan chain, which
can be masked with 2^{32} different values of mask. Hypothetically, there can be
2^{32} possible signature tables corresponding to 2^{32} mask values for a fixed value
of the key. However, experimentally, it is found that there are repetitions of signatures for 2^{32} different masks, and only 2^8 masks applied to the first byte of
round output is sufficient to generate 256 unique signatures, where one of the
signatures is for mask 0, where no output is observed and can not be used to
recover a key. So, using 255 masks (except mask 0), 255 different signature tables
can be generated, each having 256 signatures corresponding to 2^8 possible values
of the key, with a total of 256×255 unique signatures. These signatures can be
matched with the signature created from CUT responses to get the key.

Now, the signature table is generated using Algorithm 2. Initially, all 16 bytes
of the mask M are set to zero. Then, the first loop is run for all 2^8 possible values
of the first byte K^0 of the key K while keeping other bytes of the key constant.
The second loop is for mask M, where the first byte M^0 of mask M is varied
from 1 to 255 running the loop 255 times. The third loop is for plaintexts, where
256 different plaintexts are created by varying their first byte P_i^0 of plaintext P_i,
while the other 15 bytes of the plaintexts are kept constant. Using this newly
created plaintext along with the key K, AES is run for one round using the
function $ENC()$, and the one round output is stored in a variable R, while the
second plaintext P' from plaintext pair is chosen as P_0, effectively selecting R_0 as
R'. The mask M is applied on both R and R' to get S and S' as masked output,
respectively. S and S' are further compressed using a function $PARITY()$ to
get their parities, which are stored in E and E', respectively. By performing an
XOR operation between 1-bit E and E', one bit of the signature is stored in the
signature corresponding to a key byte and a mask value (in the first byte). On
completion of the innermost loop, one complete signature is generated, which is of
size 256 bits. At the completion of the second loop, 255 signatures corresponding
to a fixed value of key byte will be stored in the 255 different signature tables
for 255 values of mask M. And, finally, at the end of the first loop, 256×255
signatures are generated for 255 signature tables, where one of the signatures
represented as $SIG\_TAB_{k,m}$ is the signature for a key byte value k, and a mask
value m in the first byte of mask M keeping other bytes of M as zero.

Signature Generation. The second part of the offline phase is to create a
signature using CUT responses. To generate a signature from CUT responses in
the offline phase, we can directly create a signature using 1-bit CUT responses,
as shown in Algorithm 3. The obtained signature can be stored in the variable
SIG_CUT, which is matched in the signature table to reveal the key.

Key Recovery. Now, SIG_CUT can be matched with 256×255 signatures of
255 signature tables. If a signature $SIG\_TAB_{k,m}$ matches with SIG_CUT, then
the first key byte can be recovered as k, as shown in Algorithm 4. Similarly, other
15 bytes of the key can be obtained by targeting other bytes of the plaintext in
the online phase. Note that the signature tables generated by targeting the first

byte of the key and plaintext are sufficient and reusable and can reveal any of the key bytes using the signature from CUT responses, targeted at any byte of the plaintext in the online phase. The flowchart for the offline phase is shown in Fig. 5, where 256×255 signatures will be generated corresponding to a key byte and mask value.

A complete picture of the attack with an example is shown in Fig. 6, where a signature from CUT responses is matched in the signature table, matching it with one of the signatures corresponding to a key byte $k = 255$.

Algorithm 2: Signature Table Generation

Output: SIG_TAB as a Signature Table of size 256×255
$M^n \leftarrow 0, \forall n \in]0,15[\quad /*M^n$ is the nth byte of $M*/$

for $k \leftarrow 0$ to 255 do
   $K^0 \leftarrow k \quad /*K^j$ is the jth byte of $K*/$
   for $m \leftarrow 1$ to 255 do
      $M^0 \leftarrow m$
      for $i \leftarrow 0$ to 255 do
         $P_i^0 \leftarrow i$
         $R_i \leftarrow ENC(K, P_i)$
         $S \leftarrow R_i \ \& \ M$
         $S' \leftarrow R_0 \ \& \ M$
         $E \leftarrow PARITY(S)$
         $E' \leftarrow PARITY(S')$
         $SIG\_TAB_{k,m}^i \leftarrow E \oplus E'$

Algorithm 3: Generating Signature from compacted CUT Response

Input : $E_i(0 \leq i \leq 255)$, where E_i is the response of CUT with respect to Plaintext $P_i(0 \leq i \leq 255)$;
Output: SIG_CUT
for $i \leftarrow 0$ to 255 do
   $SIG\_CUT^i \leftarrow (E_i \oplus E_0)$

Algorithm 4: Match Signature of CUT in Signature Table

Input : SIG_CUT, SIG_TAB
Output: KEY_BYTE

for $k \leftarrow 0$ to 255 do
    for $m \leftarrow 1$ to 255 do
        if $(SIG\_CUT = SIG\_TAB_{k,m})$ then
            $KEY\_BYTE \leftarrow k$

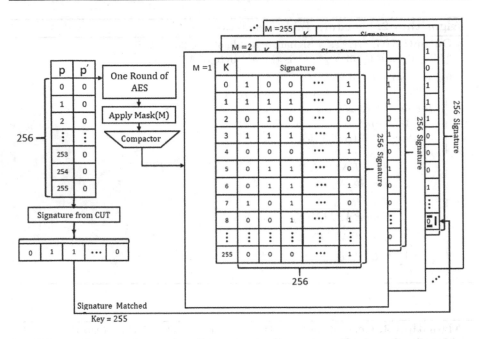

Fig. 6. Attack on dynamic masking with compaction: CUT signature is matched in the signature table, and the recovered key is 255.

5 Security Analysis of Embedded Deterministic Test (EDT)

Dynamic masking with an XOR-based compaction is used in Embedded Deterministic Test (EDT) [10–12], as shown in Fig. 3. Mentor Graphics test compression tool Tessent TestKompress uses EDT [5], where XOR-tree is used for space compaction. The value of the mask depends on the test inputs and can vary frequently as per the mask clock. In the worst case, it can vary at each shift cycle, masking differently for each of the slices.

The main reason for the successful attack is the input-dependent mask, which can be fixed by applying the same test vector multiple times. The proposed attack can be thwarted if the mask values are generated randomly and cannot be controlled by the attacker. Thus, the designer should not depend completely on the EDT logic of dynamic masking and should adopt additional countermeasures to provide security against scan-based attacks. One simple solution is to block primary inputs in test mode; in this case, the attacker would not be able to apply the desired plaintexts through the primary inputs and must apply the plaintexts through the scan input pin SI as a test vector. For differential analysis, it has to apply different plaintexts, therefore changing the mask values. In this case, the proposed attack could be thwarted. To block the primary inputs in test mode, the 128 primary input lines can be controlled using 128 AND gates, where the other input of the AND gate is the output of a NOT gate fed by TC (Test Control) line in 2. In normal mode ($TC = 0$), the one input of AND gates will be 1, and the primary input will pass through it and will not affect the chip's working in normal mode. In the test mode ($TC = 1$), one input of AND gates will be 0, restricting primary inputs in the test mode. It will need only 128 AND gates and one NOT gate, with a total 129 number of additional gates requirement. The other solution could be to link the test vector and the plaintext (from primary input) for mask generation. In this case, the input test vector can be concatenated with the inputs from the primary inputs for mask generation. For a different plaintext, different masks will be generated, and the proposed attack can be thwarted. To implement this, no additional gate will be required for concatenation. However, it may require minor changes in mask generation logic.

6   Results and Comparison

We simulated our proposed attacks on dynamic masking with compaction with the help of C programming language on a system having the configuration of Intel(R) Core(TM) i5-8250U CPU @ 1.60 8 core, 8 GB RAM, loaded with Ubuntu 20.04.2 LTS operating system. The attack was launched for 6 different combinations of active scan chains and active slices as shown in Table 1. We tried to simulate the CUT for the online phase similar to [5], we implemented one round of AES in C. The mask pattern for each of the slices was chosen randomly using the pseudo-random function and is kept fixed assuming a fixed test vector is applied while applying each of the 256 plaintexts. This mask is applied on AES one-round output using bitwise AND operation. The masked output is further compacted with different compression ratios using bitwise XOR operation. For the sake of simplicity, we consider scan chains consisting of only KFFs. One round of compacted masked outputs is collected, corresponding to 256 plaintexts. Then, a signature SIG_CUT was created and matched in the signature table using the methods proposed in Sect. 4, and the first byte of the AES key was recovered correctly. Other 15 bytes of the key were recovered by targeting other bytes of the plaintexts in the online phase.

The attack result is shown in Table 1. Although Fig. 3 shows the worst-case scenario of the compaction, where only parity of the masked output is observable. As the proposed attack requires only a one-bit compacted output of a partial one-round response, in the case of multiple bits after compaction, any one of the bits can be targeted to generate a signature from CUT responses. Different compression ratios can be achieved using multiple slices or by XORing a group of scan chains. This attack is equally applicable in both of the cases, as both the cases are equivalent, either mask some of the KFFs before compaction or ignore compacted outputs from those KFFs. Therefore, the attack results for different compression ratios for different combinations of active scan chains and active slices have a 100% success rate, as shown in Table 1. However, the existing state-of-the-art attack [5,6], where a detailed security analysis of EDT was also performed, is probabilistic in nature and has a worst-case success rate of 20.53% for 32 active scan chains and 16 active slices. The reason behind the low success rate is that the Hamming weight-based attack [5] is not suitable for a partial scan. Suppose a unique Hamming weight 9 is targeted, and one of the bits participating in the Hamming weight calculation is masked. Then, after masking, the resultant Hamming weight will be reduced by one producing Hamming weight 8 [16]. Therefore, the actual plaintext pairs may shift to lower Hamming weights. Since the actual plaintext pair for Hamming weight 9 is shifted to 8, an incorrect plaintext pair from some other Hamming weight may produce Hamming weight 9, and a wrong key will be recovered with an attack failure. Similarly, the distortion of hamming weight distribution due to compaction can be seen in [15]. Therefore, a basic scan attack using Hamming weights on advanced DfT structures [5,6] is probabilistic in nature and has a low success rate for partial scan. Whereas the proposed attack is signature-based and outperforms the partial scan. To recover all 16 bytes of the key, our proposed attack took only 4096 plaintexts and 255 signature tables containing 256×255 signatures with space complexity of $256 \times 255 \times 256 \approx 2^{24}$ bits (using Algorithm 2) to recover all 16 bytes of the key. The time taken for signature table generation was only 94 s. For mask generation, Algorithm 2 needs around $16 \times 256 \times 255 \times 256 \times 7 \approx 2^4 \times 2^8 \times 2^8 \times 2^8 \times 2^3 = 2^{31}$ number of operations.

Table 1. Success for attack on Dynamic Masking with Compaction

Sl. No.	#Active Slices	#Active Scan Chains	Success rate for different compression ratios					
			1:1	2:1	4:1	8:1	16:1	32:1
1	1	32	100%	100%	100%	100%	100%	100%
2	2	16	100%	100%	100%	100%	100%	
3	4	8	100%	100%	100%	100%		
4	8	4	100%	100%	100%			
5	16	2	100%	100%				
6	32	1	100%					

7 Conclusion

In this paper, an attack on dynamic masking with compaction is proposed. Hypothetically, it requires 2^{32} signature tables corresponding to 2^{32} different values of mask. We have experimentally shown that only $2^8 - 1$ masks are sufficient to generate 255 unique signature tables, with an overall requirement of 256×255 signatures. The results show that the attack has a 100% success rate for any combination of active scan chains and active slices, thus making it independent of the internal structure of the scan chain. At the same time, the existing state-of-the-art attack has a 20.53% success rate in its worst case. Based on the attack, we provided a security analysis of EDT employed with dynamic masking, which shows the vulnerability of EDT offered by Siemens against scan-based attacks. The main vulnerability is its input-dependent mask, which can be controlled by an end user by applying a fixed test vector. To thwart the proposed attack, we propose to block the primary inputs in the test mode.

References

1. Ali, S.S., Saeed, S.M., Sinanoglu, O., Karri, R.: Novel test-mode-only scan attack and countermeasure for compression-based scan architectures. IEEE Trans. Comput. Aided Des. Integr. Circuits Syst. **34**(5), 808–821 (2015)
2. Cui, A., Li, M., Qu, G., Li, H.: A guaranteed secure scan design based on test data obfuscation by cryptographic hash. IEEE Trans. Comput.-Aided Des. Integr. Circuits Syst. **39**, 4524–4536 (2020)
3. Cui, A., Luo, Y., Chang, C.H.: Static and dynamic obfuscations of scan data against scan-based side-channel attacks. IEEE Trans. Inf. Forensics Secur. **12**(2), 363–376 (2017)
4. DaRolt, J., Natale, G.D., Flottes, M.L., Rouzeyre, B.: Are advanced DfT structures sufficient for preventing scan-attacks? In: VTS, pp. 246–251. IEEE (2012)
5. Das, A., Ege, B., Ghosh, S., Batina, L., Verbauwhede, I.: Security analysis of industrial test compression schemes. IEEE Trans. Comput. Aided Des. Integr. Circuits Syst. **32**(12), 1966–1977 (2013)
6. Ege, B., Das, A., Ghosh, S., Verbauwhede, I.: Differential scan attack on AES with X-tolerant and X-masked test response compactor. In: DSD, pp. 545–552. IEEE (2012)
7. Hely, D., Bancel, F., Flottes, M.L., Rouzeyre, B.: Test control for secure scan designs. In: ETS, pp. 190–195 (2005)
8. Liu, C., Huang, Y.: Effects of embedded decompression and compaction architectures on side-channel attack resistance. In: VTS, pp. 461–468 (2007)
9. Paul, S., Chakraborty, R.S., Bhunia, S.: VIm-Scan: a low overhead scan design approach for protection of secret key in scan-based secure chips. In: VTS, pp. 455–460. IEEE (2007)
10. Rajski, J., Kassab, M., Mukherjee, N., Tamarapalli, N., Tyszer, J., Qian, J.: Embedded deterministic test for low-cost manufacturing. IEEE Des. Test Comput. **20**(5), 58–66 (2003)
11. Rajski, J., Tyszer, J., Kassab, M., Mukherjee, N.: Embedded deterministic test. IEEE Trans. Comput. Aided Des. Integr. Circuits Syst. **23**(5), 776–792 (2004)
12. Rajski, J., et al.: Embedded deterministic test for low cost manufacturing test. In: ITC, pp. 301–310. IEEE (2002)
13. Rolt, J.D., Natale, G.D., Flottes, M.L., Rouzeyre, B.: A novel differential scan attack on advanced DFT structures. ACM Trans. Des. Autom. Electr. Syst. (TODAES) **18**(4), 58 (2013)

14. Sao, Y., Ali, S.S.: Security analysis of scan obfuscation techniques. IEEE Trans. Inf. Forensics Secur. **18**, 2842–2855 (2023). https://doi.org/10.1109/TIFS.2023. 3265815
15. Sao, Y., Ali, S.S., Ray, D., Singh, S., Biswas, S.: Co-relation scan attack analysis (COSAA) on AES: a comprehensive approach. Microelectron. Reliab. **123**, 114216 (2021)
16. Sao, Y., Pandian, K.S., Ali, S.S.: Revisiting the security of static masking and compaction: discovering new vulnerability and improved scan attack on AES. In: 2020 (AsianHOST), pp. 1–6. IEEE (2020)
17. Vaghani, D., Ahlawat, S., Tudu, J., Fujita, M., Singh, V.: On securing scan design through test vector encryption. In: ISCAS, pp. 1–5. IEEE (2018)
18. Yang, B., Wu, K., Karri, R.: Scan based side channel attack on dedicated hardware implementations of data encryption standard. In: ITC, pp. 339–344. IEEE (2004)
19. Yang, B., Wu, K., Karri, R.: Secure scan: a design-for-test architecture for crypto chips. In: Jr., W.H.J., Martin, G., Kahng, A.B. (eds.) DAC, pp. 135–140. ACM (2005)

An Efficient Generic Insider Secure Signcryption with Non-Interactive Non-Repudiation

Ngarenon Togde(iD) and Augustin P. Sarr(✉)(iD)

Laboratoire ACCA, UFR SAT, Université Gaston Berger, Saint-Louis, Senegal
{ngarenon.togde,augustin-pathe.sarr}@ugb.edu.sn

Abstract. We present a generic construction of an insider secure signcryption scheme with non-interactive non-repudiation. Our construction uses as building blocks a signature scheme, a key encapsulation mechanism (KEM), a keyed hash function, a symmetric encryption scheme, and a pseudo-random function. We show that our construction is insider secure in the dynamic multi-user model, without resorting the random oracle or the key registration model. Our generic scheme provides also non-interactive non-repudiation.

Keywords: generic signcryption · insider security · dynamic multi-user model · non-interactive non-repudiation

1 Introduction

Signcryption schemes provide both the functionalities of signature and encryption schemes. These schemes were proposed for the first time by Zheng [24]. Since Zheng's seminal work, many designs have been proposed, e.g. [2,5,7,8,10,12,18–22]. For the analysis of signcryption schemes, two important lines of separations in the security definitions are: two-party versus multi-party models, and outsider versus insider security models [1,3,4]. Broadly, in a two-party security model, only one sender and one receiver are considered. Whereas in a multi-party model, an attacker can use any public key of its choice. In an outsider model, it is assumed that an attacker cannot access a legitimate sender or receiver long-term secret. In an insider model, an attacker has access to all the secrets except the one "being attacked"; for confidentiality, it is assumed that the attacker knows the sender's static private key, and for unforgeability that the attacker knows the receiver's static private key. The strongest among these models is insider security in the (dynamic) multi-user model.

Some "natural" constructions of signcryption schemes are "encrypt and sign (E&S), "Encrypt then Sign" (EtS) and Sign then Encrypt (StE). Unfortunately, these natural constructions do not yield secure signcryption schemes in the dynamic multi-user insider model [1, Sect. 2.3]. For instance, In an E&S construction, the signature may reveal the encrypted message, confidentiality is not then achieved. In the EtS and StE constructions the difficulty is to maintain the security of the operation performed first. For instance in the EtS construction, for confidentiality, an attacker (a probabilistic polynomial time machine) which knows the sender's static private key can resign and submit the resigned signcrypted text to a decryption oracle. In the StE construction, for

F. Regazzoni et al. (Eds.): SPACE 2023, LNCS 14412, pp. 117–138, 2024.
https://doi.org/10.1007/978-3-031-51583-5_8

unforgeability, an adversary which knows the receiver static private key can decrypt the ciphertext and re-encrypt and submit the resulting signcrypted text as a forgery.

A nice property of signcryption schemes is Non-Interactive Non-Repudiation (NINR), which allows a third party to settle a non-repudiation dispute without engaging a costly protocol. NINR is a main advantage of signcryption schemes compared to one pass key exchange protocols, which often outperform signcryption schemes.

Building high-level secure and efficient cryptographic schemes from low-level primitives is a main focus in modern cryptography. In the case of signcryption schemes, insider security appears to be the right security definition [3]. As far as we are aware, there are only three works, that aim to propose generic insider secure constructions of signcryption schemes in the dynamic multi-user model, [10,19] and [2]. Unfortunately the designs from [19] and [2] are shown to be secure in the registered key model, wherein an attacker has to show that it knows the private keys corresponding to the public keys it uses. This model does not capture some realistic attacks on certificate authorities, e.g. [11,13]. In [10], Chiba *et al.* propose two generic StE type constructions that they show to be insider secure in the dynamic multi-user model, without resorting the random oracle or registered key model. As their constructions are StE, they inherit NINR from the base signature scheme.

In this work, we build a simple and efficient generic EtS signcryption scheme with NINR (SCNINR), termed SN (*S*igncryption with *N*on-interactive non-repudiation). We propose a detailed analysis of our construction, in the insider dynamic multi-user model, without using the random oracle or registered key model.

This paper is organized as follows. In Sect. 2, we present some preliminaries on signcryption schemes and on the building blocks we use in our design. In Sect. 3, we propose our generic SCNINR scheme. In Sect. 4, we propose a detailed security analysis of our construction in the dynamic multi-user model. We compare our design with the previous proposals in Sect. 5.

2   Preliminaries

If S is a set, $a \leftarrow_R S$ means that a is chosen uniformly at random from S; we write $a, b, c, \cdots \leftarrow_R S$ as a shorthand for $a \leftarrow_R S; b \leftarrow_R S$, etc. We denote by $\mathsf{sz}(a)$ the number of bits required to represent a. If S and S' are two sets, $\mathsf{Func}(S, S')$ denotes the set of functions with domain S and range S'.

For a probabilistic algorithm $\mathcal{A}$ with parameters $u_1, \cdots, u_n$ and output $V \in \mathbf{V}$, we write $V \leftarrow_R \mathcal{A}(u_1, \cdots, u_n)$. We denote by $\{\mathcal{A}(u_1, \cdots, u_n)\}$ the set $\{v \in \mathbf{V} : \Pr(V = v) \neq 0\}$. If $x_1, x_2, \cdots, x_k$ are objects belonging to different structures (group, bit-string, etc.) $(x_1, x_2, \cdots, x_k)$ denotes a representation as a bit-string of the tuple such that each element can be unequivocally parsed. For a list L, $\mathsf{Apd}(L, X)$ adds X to L. For a positive integer n, $[n]$ denotes the set $\{1, 2, \cdots, n\}$.

A Symmetric Encryption. A symmetric encryption scheme $\mathcal{E} = (\mathsf{E}, \mathsf{D}, \mathbf{K}(k), \mathbf{M}(k), \mathbf{C}(k))$ is a pair of efficient algorithms (E, D), an encryption and a decryption algorithm, together with a triple of sets $(\mathbf{K}, \mathbf{M}, \mathbf{C})$, which depend on a security parameter k, such that for all $\tau \in \mathbf{K}$ and all $m \in \mathbf{M}$, it holds that $\mathsf{E}(\tau, m) \in \mathbf{C}$ and $m = \mathsf{D}(\tau, \mathsf{E}(\tau, m))$.

Definition 1. *Let* $\mathcal{A} = (\mathcal{A}_1, \mathcal{A}_2)$ *be an adversary against* $\mathcal{E}$ *and let*

$$\Pr(O_{i,i=0,1}) = \Pr\left[\begin{matrix} (m_0, m_1, st) \leftarrow_R \mathcal{A}_1(k); \tau \leftarrow_R \mathbf{K}; c \leftarrow_R \mathsf{E}(\tau, m_i); \\ \hat{b} \leftarrow_R \mathcal{A}_2(k, c, st) \end{matrix} : \hat{b} = 1\right]$$

and $\mathsf{Adv}^{ss}_{\mathcal{A},\mathcal{E}}(k)$ *denote the quantity*

$$\mathsf{Adv}^{ss}_{\mathcal{A},\mathcal{E}}(k) = |\Pr(O_0) - \Pr(O_1)|,$$

where $m_0, m_1 \in \mathbf{M}$ *are distinct messages of equal length. The scheme* $\mathcal{E}$ *is said to be* $(t(k), \varepsilon(k))$*–semantically secure if for all adversaries* $\mathcal{A}$ *running in time* $t(k)$*, it holds that* $\mathsf{Adv}^{ss}_{\mathcal{A},\mathcal{E}}(k) \leqslant \varepsilon(k)$.

We will need also the following definition.

Definition 2. *Let* $\mathcal{E} = (\mathsf{E}, \mathsf{D}, \mathbf{K}(k), \mathbf{M}(k), \mathbf{C}(k))$ *be an encryption scheme. The scheme* $\mathcal{E}$ *is said to be* $(t(k), \varepsilon(k))$*–secure against key clustering attacks if for all adversaries* $\mathcal{A}$ *running in time* $\leqslant t(k)$,

$$\Pr\left[(m, \tau, \tau') \leftarrow_R \mathcal{A}(k) : \tau \neq \tau' \text{ and } \mathsf{E}(\tau, m) = \mathsf{E}(\tau', m)\right] \leqslant \varepsilon(k).$$

Pseudo-Random Function (PRF). A PRF is a deterministic algorithm Prf together with a triple of sets $(\mathbf{K}(k), \mathbf{D}(k), \mathbf{R}(k))$ (which depends on the security parameter k) such that for all $\tau \in \mathbf{K}$ and all $m \in \mathbf{D}$, $\mathsf{Prf}(\tau, m) \in \mathbf{R}$. Notice that for all fixed $\tau \in \mathbf{K}$, $\mathsf{Prf}(\tau, \cdot) \in \mathsf{Func}(\mathbf{D}, \mathbf{R})$.

Definition 3. *Let* Prf *be a pseudo-random function and* $\mathcal{A}$ *be an adversary,*

$$\Pr(O_0) = \Pr\left[\tau \leftarrow_R \mathbf{K}; f \leftarrow \mathsf{Prf}(\tau, \cdot); \hat{b} \leftarrow_R \mathcal{A}^{\mathcal{O}_f(\cdot)}(k) : \hat{b} = 1\right],$$

$$\Pr(O_1) = \Pr\left[f \leftarrow_R \mathsf{Func}(\mathbf{D}, \mathbf{R}); \hat{b} \leftarrow_R \mathcal{A}^{\mathcal{O}_f(\cdot)}(k) : \hat{b} = 1\right],$$

and

$$\mathsf{Adv}_{\mathcal{A},\mathsf{Prf}}(k) = |\Pr(O_0) - \Pr(O_1)|.$$

The PRF Prf *is said to be* $(t(k), \varepsilon(k))$*–secure if for all efficient adversaries* $\mathcal{A}$ *running in time* $\leqslant t$*, it holds that* $\mathsf{Adv}_{\mathcal{A},\mathsf{Prf}}(k) \leqslant \varepsilon(k)$.

Collision Resistant Hash Function. Let $\mathbf{K}(k)$, $\mathbf{M}'(k)$ and $\mathbf{T}(k)$ be sets which depend on a security parameter k and H be a keyed hash function defined over $(\mathbf{K}, \mathbf{M}', \mathbf{T})$, *i. e.* H takes as inputs $\tau_0 \in \mathbf{K}$ and $m \in \mathbf{M}'$ and outputs $t \in \mathbf{T}$; we write $t \leftarrow \mathsf{H}(\tau_0, m)$.

Definition 4. *A keyed hash function* $\mathsf{H} : \mathbf{K} \times \mathbf{M}' \rightarrow \mathbf{T}$ *is said to be* $(t(k), \varepsilon(k))$ *collision resistant if for all efficient adversaries* $\mathcal{A}$ *running in time* $\leqslant t(k)$,

$$\Pr\left[\tau_0 \leftarrow_R \mathbf{K}; (m_0, m_1) \leftarrow_R \mathcal{A}(k, \tau_0) : m_0 \neq m_1 \wedge \mathsf{H}(\tau_0, m_0) = \mathsf{H}(\tau_0, m_1)\right] \leqslant \varepsilon(k).$$

Definition 5. *Let* H : **K** × **M**′ → **T** *be a keyed hash function and* Pfx *be a subset of* {0, 1}*. H is said to be $(t(k), \varepsilon(k))$ resistant to collisions with identical prefix from* Pfx, *if for all efficient adversaries* $\mathcal{A}$ *running in time* ⩽ $t(k)$,

$$\Pr \left[\tau_0 \leftarrow_R \mathbf{K}; (p, m_0, m_1) \leftarrow_R \mathcal{A}(k, \tau_0) : \begin{cases} p \in \mathsf{Pfx}, \\ m_0 \neq m_1 \text{ and} \\ \mathsf{H}(\tau_0, (p, m_0)) = \mathsf{H}(\tau_0, (p, m_1)) \end{cases} \right] \leqslant \varepsilon(k).$$

Notice that resistance to collisions with identical prefix may be a weaker assumption than classical collision resistance. We consider now the following game parameterized by a pseudo-random function Prf.

Game 1 Pre-image with chosen prefix and suffix

---
1) The challenger Chall chooses $\tau_0 \leftarrow_R \mathbf{K}$ and sends τ_0 to $\mathcal{A}$.
2) $\mathcal{A}$ chooses $p_0 \in \mathsf{Pfx}$, $s_0 \in \mathsf{Sfx}$ and $m_0 \in \mathbf{M}$ and sends (p_0, m_0, s_0) to Chall.
3) Chall chooses $(\tau, \tau') \leftarrow_R \mathbf{K}^2$, computes $\tau'' \leftarrow \mathsf{Prf}(\tau, m_0)$ and $\hat{m}_0 \leftarrow \mathsf{H}(\tau_0, (p_0, \tau, \tau', \tau'', s_0))$, and sends $\hat{m}_0$ to $\mathcal{A}$.
4) $\mathcal{A}$ outputs $(\tau^*, \tau'^*) \in \mathbf{K}^2$.
5) $\mathcal{A}$ succeeds if $\hat{m}_0 = \mathsf{H}(\tau_0, (p_0, \tau^*, \tau'^*, \tau''^*, s_0))$ wherein $\tau'''^* \leftarrow \mathsf{Prf}(\tau^*, m_0)$.

Definition 6. *Let* H : **K** × **M**′ → **T** *be a keyed hash function and* Pfx *and* Sfx *be respectively some sets of message prefixes and suffixes. For an adversary* $\mathcal{A}$ *playing Game 1, let* $\mathsf{Succ}_{\mathcal{A},\mathsf{H}}(k)$ *denote the event "$\mathcal{A}$ wins Game 1". H is said to be $(t(k), \varepsilon(k))$ secure against pre-image attacks with chosen prefix from* Pfx *and suffix from* Sfx, *if for all efficient adversaries* $\mathcal{A}$ *running in time* ⩽ $t(k)$, $\Pr(\mathsf{Succ}_{\mathcal{A},\mathsf{H}}(k)) \leqslant \varepsilon(k)$.

The following lemma shows that the pre-image resistance (from Definition 6) follows from identical prefix collision resistance. The proof is given in the appendix.

Lemma 1. *Let* H : **K** × **M**′ → **T** *be a keyed hash function. If* H *is $(t(k), \varepsilon(k))$ secure against collisions with identical prefix from* Pfx, *then it is $(t(k), \varepsilon'(k))$ secure in the sense of Definition 6, where*

$$\varepsilon'(k) \leqslant |\mathbf{T}|/|\mathbf{K}|^2 + \varepsilon(k).$$

Key Encapsulation Mechanism (KEM). A KEM is a four-tuple of efficient algorithms $\mathcal{K} = (\mathsf{Setup}_\mathsf{K}, \mathsf{Gen}_\mathsf{K}, \mathsf{Ecp}, \mathsf{Dcp})$ together with a key space $\mathbf{K}'(k)$ and encapsulated keys space $\mathbf{C}'$, such that:

- $\mathsf{Setup}_\mathsf{K}$ is a probabilistic algorithm which takes as input a security parameter k and outputs a domain parameter dp_K;
- Gen_K is a key pair generator, it takes as input the domain parameter dp_K and outputs a key pair $(sk_\mathsf{K}, pk_\mathsf{K})$;
- Ecp is a probabilistic algorithm which takes as input a public key pk_K and outputs a key $\tau \in \mathbf{K}'$ together with an encapsulated key $c \in \mathbf{C}'$, we write $(\tau, c) \leftarrow_R \mathsf{Ecp}$ (pk_K);
- Dcp takes as inputs a private key sk_K together with an encapsulated key c and outputs $\tau \in \mathbf{K}'$ or and error symbol ⊥.

It is required that for all $k \in \mathbb{N}^*$, all $dp_\mathsf{K} \in \{\mathsf{Setup}_\mathsf{K}(k)\}$, all $(sk_\mathsf{K}, pk_\mathsf{K}) \in \{\mathsf{Gen}_\mathsf{K}(dp_\mathsf{K})\}$, if $(\tau, c) \in \{\mathsf{Ecp}(pk_\mathsf{K})\}$, $\Pr[\mathsf{Dcp}(sk_\mathsf{K}, c) = \tau] = 1$.

Definition 7. *Let $\mathcal{K}$ be a KEM, and $\mathcal{A}$ an adversary against $\mathcal{K}$. Let*

$$\Pr(U_{b,b=0,1}) = \Pr \begin{bmatrix} dp_\mathsf{K} \leftarrow_R \mathsf{Setup}_\mathsf{K}(k); (sk_\mathsf{K}, pk_\mathsf{K}) \leftarrow_R \mathsf{Gen}_\mathsf{K}(dp_\mathsf{K}); \\ (\tau_0, c) \leftarrow_R \mathsf{Ecp}(pk_\mathsf{K}); \tau_1 \leftarrow_R \mathbf{K}'; \\ \hat{b} \leftarrow_R \mathcal{A}^{\mathcal{O}_\mathsf{Dcp}(sk_\mathsf{K}, \cdot)}(k, dp_\mathsf{K}, pk_\mathsf{K}, \tau_b, c) \end{bmatrix} : \hat{b} = 1 \quad (1)$$

wherein the notation $\mathcal{A}^{\mathcal{O}_\mathsf{Dcp}(sk_\mathsf{K}, \cdot)}$ means that $\mathcal{A}$ is given access to a decapsulation oracle $\mathcal{O}_\mathsf{Dcp}(sk_\mathsf{K}, \cdot)$ which, on input $c' \neq c$, outputs $\mathsf{Dcp}(sk_\mathsf{K}, c')$ ($\mathcal{A}$ is not allowed to issue $\mathsf{Dcp}(sk_\mathsf{K}, c)$). Let $\mathsf{Adv}^{\mathsf{cca}}_{\mathcal{A}, \mathcal{K}}(k) = |\Pr(U_0) - \Pr(U_1)|$. $\mathcal{K}$ is said to be $(t(k), \varepsilon(k))$ indistinguishable against chosen-ciphertext attacks (IND-CCA), if for all efficient adversaries $\mathcal{A}$ running in time $\leqslant t(k)$, it holds that $\mathsf{Adv}^{\mathsf{cca}}_{\mathcal{A}, \mathcal{K}}(k) \leqslant \varepsilon(k)$.

Remark 1. In a KEM security experiment, we refer to the challenge (τ_0, c) and (τ_1, c) defined in (1) by $\mathsf{Chall}_{\mathcal{K}_{E_0}}$ and $\mathsf{Chall}_{\mathcal{K}_{E_1}}$, respectively.

Digital Signature. A digital signature scheme is a four-tuple of efficient algorithms $\mathcal{S} = (\mathsf{Setup}_\mathsf{S}, \mathsf{Gen}_\mathsf{S}, \mathsf{Sign}, \mathsf{Vrfy})$ together with a message space $\mathbf{M}_\mathcal{S}$, such that:

- $\mathsf{Setup}_\mathsf{S}$ takes as input a security parameter k and outputs a domain parameter dp_S;
- Gen_S is a probabilistic algorithm which takes as input a domain parameter dp_S and outputs a key pair $(sk_\mathsf{S}, pk_\mathsf{S})$;
- Sign takes as inputs a secret key sk_S and a message $m \in \mathbf{M}_\mathcal{S}$ and outputs a signature $\sigma \in \Sigma$;
- Vrfy is deterministic; it takes as inputs a public key pk_S, a message m, and a signature σ and outputs $d \in \{0, 1\}$; and
- $\mathcal{S}$ is such that for all $k \in \mathbb{N}^*$, all $dp_\mathsf{S} \in \{\mathsf{Setup}_\mathsf{S}(k)\}$, all $(sk_\mathsf{S}, pk_\mathsf{S}) \in \{\mathsf{Gen}_\mathsf{S}(dp_\mathsf{S})\}$, and all $m \in \mathbf{M}_\mathcal{S}$, $\Pr[\mathsf{Vrfy}(pk_\mathsf{S}, m, \mathsf{Sign}(sk_\mathsf{S}, m)) = 1] = 1$.

Game 2 sUF-CMA security game

1) $dp_\mathsf{S} \leftarrow_R \mathsf{Setup}_\mathsf{S}(k); (sk_\mathsf{S}, pk_\mathsf{S}) \leftarrow_R \mathsf{Gen}_\mathsf{S}(dp_\mathsf{S}); \mathsf{L} \leftarrow ()$.
2) For $j = 1, 2, \cdots$, $\mathcal{A}$ submits $m_j \in \mathbf{M}_S$ to the challenger which:
   a) outputs $\sigma_j \leftarrow_R \mathsf{Sign}(sk_\mathsf{S}, m_j)$, and
   b) appends (m_j, σ_j) to L.
3) $\mathcal{A}$ outputs $(m, \sigma) \in \mathbf{M}_S \times \Sigma$.
   - $\mathcal{A}$ succeeds in sUF-CMA if: i) $\mathsf{Vrfy}(pk_\mathsf{S}, m, \sigma) = 1$, and ii) $(m, \sigma) \notin \mathsf{L}$.

Definition 8. *Let $\mathcal{S}$ be a signature scheme; $\mathcal{S}$ is said to be $(t(k), Q_\mathsf{Sign}(k), \varepsilon(k))$ strongly Unforgeable against Chosen Message Attacks if for any adversary $\mathcal{A}$ playing Game 2, if $\mathcal{A}$ runs in time at most $t(k)$ and issues at most $Q_\mathsf{Sign}(k)$ queries to the signing oracle, then it succeeds in the sUF-CMA game with probability $\leqslant \varepsilon(k)$.*

Notice that when $\varepsilon(k)$ does not depend on $Q_\mathsf{Sign}(k)$, we say simply that $\mathcal{S}$ is $(t(k), \varepsilon(k))$–secure. We will need also the following notion, which is not captured in the sUF-CMA security definition, although it seems naturally achieved by many usual signature schemes (which uses a hash function), such as the Full Domain Hash, for instance.

Definition 9. *A signature scheme is said to be* $(t(k), \varepsilon(k))$ *secure against colliding signatures if for all efficient adversaries* $\mathcal{A}$ *running in time* $\leqslant t(k)$,

$$
\Pr\left[
\begin{array}{l}
dp_S \leftarrow_R \mathsf{Setup}_S(k); \\
(pk_S, m_1, m_2, \sigma) \leftarrow_R \mathcal{A}(dp_S)
\end{array}
:
\left\{
\begin{array}{l}
m_1 \neq m_2, \\
\mathsf{Vrfy}(pk_S, m_1, \sigma) = 1, \ and \\
\mathsf{Vrfy}(pk_S, m_2, \sigma) = 1
\end{array}
\right.
\right] \leqslant \varepsilon(k).
$$

2.1 Insider Security for SCNINR

This subsection deals with the syntax of a SCNINR scheme and the insider security definitions in the dynamic Multi-User model [2] (also termed the Flexible Signcryption/ Flexible Unsigncryption Oracle (FSO/FUO) model [5]).

Definition 10. *A* signcryption scheme *is a quintuple of algorithms* $\mathcal{SC} = (\mathsf{Setup}, \mathsf{Gen}_{sd}, \mathsf{Gen}_{rcv}, \mathsf{Sc}, \mathsf{Usc})$ *where:*

a) Setup *takes a security parameter* k *as input, and outputs a public domain parameter* dp;
b) Gen_{sd} *takes as input* dp *and outputs a sender key pair* (sk_{sd}, pk_{sd}), sk_{sd} *is the signcrypting key;*
c) Gen_{rcv} *takes* dp *as input and outputs a receiver key pair* (sk_{rcv}, pk_{rcv});
d) Sc *takes as inputs a sender private key* sk_{sd}, *a receiver public key* pk_{rcv}, *and a message* m, *and outputs a signcryptext* C; *we write* $C \leftarrow_R \mathsf{Sc}(sk_{sd}, pk_{rcv}, m)$;
e) Usc *is a deterministic algorithm. It takes as inputs* dp, *a receiver secret key* sk_{rcv}, *a sender public key* pk_{sd}, *and a signcryptext* C, *and outputs either a valid message* $m \in \mathbf{M}$ *or an error symbol* $\perp \notin \mathbf{M}$.

And, for all $dp \in \{\mathsf{Setup}(k)\}$, *all* $m \in \mathbf{M}$, *all* $(sk_{sd}, pk_{sd}) \in \{\mathsf{Gen}_{sd}(dp)\}$, *and all* $(sk_{rcv}, pk_{rcv}) \in \{\mathsf{Gen}_{rcv}(dp)\}$, $m = \mathsf{Usc}(sk_{rcv}, pk_{sd}, \mathsf{Sc}(sk_{sd}, pk_{rcv}, m))$. *The scheme is said to provide NINR if there are two algorithms* N *and* PV, *a non-repudiation evidence generation and a* pubic verification algorithms, *such that:*

– N *takes as inputs a receiver secret key* sk_{rcv}, *a sender public key* pk_{sd}, *and a signcrypted text* C, *and outputs a* non-repudiation evidence nr *or a failure symbol* $\perp$.
– PV *takes as inputs a signcryptext* C, *a message* m, *a non-repudiation evidence* nr, *a sender public key* pk_{sd}, *and a receiver public key* pk_{rcv}, *and outputs* $d \in \{0, 1\}$.
– *For all* $dp \in \{\mathsf{Setup}(k)\}$, *all* $C \in \{0, 1\}^*$, *all* $(sk_{sd}, pk_{sd}) \in \{\mathsf{Gen}_{sd}(dp)\}$, *and all* $(sk_{rcv}, pk_{rcv}) \in \{\mathsf{Gen}_{rcv}(dp)\}$, *if* $\perp \neq m \leftarrow \mathsf{Usc}(sk_{rcv}, pk_{sd}, C)$ *and* $nr \leftarrow \mathsf{N}(sk_{rcv}, pk_{sd}, C)$ *then* $1 = d \leftarrow \mathsf{PV}(C, m, nr, pk_{sd}, pk_{rcv})$.

Definition 11 (Confidentiality in the $\mathsf{dM-IND-iCCA}$**).** *A SCNINR* $\mathcal{SC}$ *is said to be* $(t(k), q_{\mathsf{Usc}}(k), q_{\mathsf{N}}(k), \varepsilon(k))$ $\mathsf{dM-IND-iCCA}$-secure, *if for all adversaries* $\mathcal{A}$ *playing Game 3, running in time* $\leqslant t(k)$, *and issuing at most respectively* $q_{\mathsf{Usc}}(k)$ *and* $q_{\mathsf{N}}(k)$ *queries to the unsigncryption and non-repudiation evidence generation oracles,* $\mathsf{Adv}_{\mathcal{A}, \mathcal{SC}}^{\mathsf{cca2}}(k) \leqslant \varepsilon(k)$.

Game 3 Insider Confidentiality in the Dynamic Multi–User model (dM–IND–iCCA)

We consider the experiments E_0 and E_1, described hereunder, wherein $\mathcal{A} = (\mathcal{A}_1, \mathcal{A}_2)$ is a two–stage adversary against a SCNINR scheme.

1) The challenger generates $dp \leftarrow_R \mathsf{Setup}(k)$ and $(sk_{\mathsf{rcv}}, pk_{\mathsf{rcv}}) \leftarrow_R \mathsf{Gen}_{\mathsf{rcv}}(dp)$.
2) $\mathcal{A}_1$ is provided with dp and pk_{rcv}, and is given access to:
   (a) an unsigncryption oracle $\mathcal{O}_{\mathsf{Usc}}(\cdot, \cdot)$, which takes as inputs a sender public key pk and a signcrypted text C, and outputs $m \leftarrow \mathsf{Usc}(sk_{\mathsf{rcv}}, pk, C)$, and
   (b) a non–repudiation evidence generation oracle $\mathcal{O}_{\mathsf{N}}(\cdot, \cdot)$ which takes as inputs a sender public key pk and a signcrypted text C and outputs $nr \leftarrow \mathsf{N}(sk_{\mathsf{rcv}}, pk, C)$.
3) $\mathcal{A}_1$ outputs $(m_0, m_1, sk_{\mathsf{sd}}, pk_{\mathsf{sd}}, st) \leftarrow_R \mathcal{A}_1^{\mathcal{O}_{\mathsf{Usc}}(\cdot, \cdot), \mathcal{O}_{\mathsf{N}}(\cdot, \cdot)}(dp, pk_{\mathsf{rcv}})$ where $m_0, m_1 \in \mathbf{M}$, $m_0 \neq m_1$ and $|m_0| = |m_1|$, st is a state, and $(sk_{\mathsf{sd}}, pk_{\mathsf{sd}}) \in \{\mathsf{Gen}_{\mathsf{sd}}(dp)\}$ is the attacked sender key pair.
4) In the experiment $E_{b,b=0,1}$, the challenger computes $C^* \leftarrow_R \mathsf{Sc}(sk_{\mathsf{sd}}, pk_{\mathsf{rcv}}, m_b)$.
5) $\mathcal{A}_2$ outputs $b' \leftarrow_R \mathcal{A}_2^{\mathcal{O}_{\mathsf{Usc}}(\cdot, \cdot), \mathcal{O}_{\mathsf{N}}(\cdot, \cdot)}(C^*, st)$ ($\mathcal{O}_{\mathsf{Usc}}(\cdot, \cdot)$ and $\mathcal{O}_{\mathsf{N}}(\cdot, \cdot)$ are as in step 2).
6) For $E_{b,b=0,1}$, out_b denotes the event: (i) $\mathcal{A}_2$ never issued $\mathcal{O}_{\mathsf{Usc}}(pk_{\mathsf{sd}}, C^*)$ or $\mathcal{O}_{\mathsf{N}}(pk_{\mathsf{sd}}, C^*)$, and (ii) $b' = 1$.

And, $\mathsf{Adv}^{\mathsf{cca2}}_{\mathcal{A},\mathcal{SC}}(k) = | \Pr(\mathsf{out}_0) - \Pr(\mathsf{out}_1) |$ denotes $\mathcal{A}$'s dM–IND–iCCA advantage.

Game 4 Strong Unforgeability in the Dynamic Multi–User model (dM–sUF–iCCA)

$\mathcal{A}$ is a forger against $\mathcal{SC}$.

1) The challenger computes $dp \leftarrow_R \mathsf{Setup}(k)$, $(sk_{\mathsf{sd}}, pk_{\mathsf{sd}}) \leftarrow_R \mathsf{Gen}_{\mathsf{sd}}(dp)$, $\mathsf{L} \leftarrow ()$.
2) $\mathcal{A}$ runs with inputs (dp, pk_{sd}) and is given a flexible signcryption oracle $\mathcal{O}_{\mathsf{Sc}}(\cdot, \cdot)$, which on inputs a valid public receiver key pk and a message m:
   (i) computes $C \leftarrow_R \mathsf{Sc}(sk_{\mathsf{sd}}, pk, m)$,
   (ii) appends (pk, m, C) to L,
   (iii) and outputs C.
3) $\mathcal{A}$ outputs $((sk_{\mathsf{rcv}}, pk_{\mathsf{rcv}}), C^*) \leftarrow_R \mathcal{A}^{\mathcal{O}_{\mathsf{Sc}}(\cdot, \cdot)}(dp, pk_{\mathsf{sd}})$. $\mathcal{A}$ wins the game if:
   (i) $\bot \neq m^* \leftarrow \mathsf{Usc}(sk_{\mathsf{rcv}}, pk_{\mathsf{sd}}, C^*)$, and
   (ii) $(pk_{\mathsf{rcv}}, m^*, C^*) \notin \mathsf{L}$.

We denote by $\mathsf{Adv}^{\mathsf{suf}}_{\mathcal{A},\mathcal{SC}}(k) = \Pr(\mathsf{Succ}^{\mathsf{suf}}_{\mathcal{A}})$ the probability that $\mathcal{A}$ wins the game.

Definition 12 (Unforgeability in the dM–sUF–iCCA **model).** *A SCNINR is said to be $(t(k), q_{\mathsf{Sc}}(k), \varepsilon(k))$ unforgeable in the* dM–sUF–iCCA *model if for all attackers $\mathcal{A}$ playing Game 4, running in time $\leqslant t(k)$, and issuing at most $q_{\mathsf{Sc}}(k)$ signcryption queries, $\mathsf{Adv}^{\mathsf{suf}}_{\mathcal{A},\mathcal{SC}}(k) \leqslant \varepsilon(k)$.*

Game 5 Soundness of non–repudiation

1) The challenger computes $dp \leftarrow_R \mathsf{Setup}(k)$.
2) $\mathcal{A}$ runs with input dp and outputs $(C^*, pk_{\mathsf{sd}}, sk_{\mathsf{rcv}}, pk_{\mathsf{rcv}}, m', nr^*) \leftarrow_R \mathcal{A}(dp)$.
3) $\mathcal{A}$ wins the game if:
   (i) $\bot \neq m \leftarrow \mathsf{Usc}(sk_{\mathsf{rcv}}, pk_{\mathsf{sd}}, C^*)$, and
   (ii) $m \neq m'$ and $1 = d \leftarrow \mathsf{PV}(C^*, m', nr^*, pk_{\mathsf{sd}}, pk_{\mathsf{rcv}})$.

We denote by $\mathsf{Adv}^{\mathsf{snr}}_{\mathcal{A},\mathcal{SC}}(k)$ the probability that $\mathcal{A}$ wins the game.

Definition 13 (Soundness of non-repudiation). *A SCNINR is said to achieve* $(t(k), \varepsilon(k))$*–computational soundness of non-repudiation if for any adversary $\mathcal{A}$ playing Game 5 and running in time* $\leqslant t(k)$*,* $\mathsf{Adv}^{\mathsf{snr}}_{\mathcal{A},\mathcal{SC}}(k) \leqslant \varepsilon(k)$*.*

Game 6 Unforgeability of non–repudiation evidence

$\mathcal{A}$ is an attacker against $\mathcal{SC}$.

1) The challenger computes $dp \leftarrow_R \mathsf{Setup}(k)$, $(sk_{\mathsf{sd}}, pk_{\mathsf{sd}}) \leftarrow_R \mathsf{Gen}_{\mathsf{sd}}(dp)$; and $(sk_{\mathsf{rcv}}, pk_{\mathsf{rcv}}) \leftarrow_R \mathsf{Gen}_{\mathsf{rcv}}(dp)$.

2) $\mathcal{A}$ runs with inputs $(dp, pk_{\mathsf{sd}}, pk_{\mathsf{rcv}})$ and is given access to a signcryption, an unsigncryption, and a non–repudiation evidence generation oracles. It outputs $(C^*, m^*, nr^*) \leftarrow_R \mathcal{A}^{\mathcal{O}_{\mathsf{Sc}}(\cdot, \cdot), \mathcal{O}_{\mathsf{Usc}}(\cdot, \cdot), \mathcal{O}_{\mathsf{N}}(\cdot, \cdot)}(dp, pk_{\mathsf{sd}}, pk_{\mathsf{rcv}})$.

3) $\mathcal{A}$ wins if:

   (i) C^* was generated through the $\mathcal{O}_{\mathsf{Sc}}(\cdot, \cdot)$ oracle on inputs (pk_{rcv}, m) for some m,

   (ii) $1 = d \leftarrow \mathsf{PV}(C^*, m^*, nr^*, pk_{\mathsf{sd}}, pk_{\mathsf{rcv}})$, and

   (iii) $\mathcal{O}_{\mathsf{N}}(pk_{\mathsf{sd}}, C^*)$ was not issued by $\mathcal{A}$.

$\mathsf{Adv}^{\mathsf{unr}}_{\mathcal{A},\mathcal{SC}}(k)$ denotes the probability that $\mathcal{A}$ wins the game.

Definition 14 (Unforgeability of non-repudiation evidence). *A SCNINR is said to achieve* $(t, q_{\mathsf{Sc}}, q_{\mathsf{Usc}}, q_{\mathsf{N}}, \varepsilon)$ *unforgeability of non-repudiation evidence if for all adversaries $\mathcal{A}$ playing Game 6, running in time t, and issuing respectively q_{Sc}, q_{Usc}, and q_{N} queries to the signcryption, unsigncryption, and non-repudiation evidence generation oracles,* $\mathsf{Adv}^{\mathsf{unr}}_{\mathcal{A},\mathcal{SC}}(k) \leqslant \varepsilon$.

3   An Efficient Generic Insider Secure SCNINR

We present our generic SCNINR design termed SN; it uses as building blocks (i) a KEM $\mathcal{K} = (\mathsf{Setup}_\mathsf{K}, \mathsf{Gen}_\mathsf{K}, \mathsf{Ecp}, \mathsf{Dcp})$, (ii) a symmetric encryption scheme $\mathcal{E} = (\mathsf{E}, \mathsf{D}, \mathbf{K}, \mathbf{M}, \mathbf{C})$, (iii) a PRF Prf defined over $(\mathbf{K}, \mathbf{D}, \mathbf{R} = \mathbf{K})$, (iv) a hash function H defined over $(\mathbf{K}, \mathbf{M}', \mathbf{T})$, and (v) a signature scheme $\mathcal{S} = (\mathsf{Setup}_S, \mathsf{Gen}_S, \mathsf{Sign}, \mathsf{Vrfy})$ with message space $\mathbf{M}_S$. We assume that $\mathbf{M} \subset \mathbf{D}$, $\mathbf{\Sigma} \subset \mathbf{D}$, $\mathbf{T} \subset \mathbf{M}_S$, and that for all $(\tau, \tau', \tau'') \in \mathbf{K}^2$, all $c' \in \mathbf{C}'$, all $c \in \mathbf{C}$, all pk_{sd} such that $(sk_{\mathsf{sd}}, pk_{\mathsf{sd}}) \in \{\mathsf{Gen}_S(dp_2)\}$ for some sk_{sd}, and all pk_{rcv} such that $(sk_{\mathsf{rcv}}, pk_{\mathsf{rcv}}) \in \{\mathsf{Gen}_S(dp_1)\}$, $(pk_{\mathsf{sd}}, \tau, \tau', \tau'', c, c', pk_{\mathsf{rcv}}) \in \mathbf{M}'$. We assume that the KEM is such that $\mathbf{K}' = \mathbf{K}^4$ (this can be achieved by using, if needed, an appropriate key derivation function and/or a pseudo-random generator), and that dp_K defines both $\mathbf{K}'$ and $\mathbf{C}'$.

In an encrypt-then-sign design (which aims also at NINR), the signed data cannot be the plain-text m (or publicly depend on it), as otherwise even outsider confidentiality cannot be achieved. Moreover, for insider confidentiality (wherein the attacker knows the sender's private key) it should not be possible to recover the signed data from the sender's private key, as an attacker could resign the data and submit the resulting signcrypted cipher-text for decryption, and then succeed in an insider confidentiality game. To overcome these difficulties, we compute the signed data as a function of the encapsulated key and the plain text m such that it cannot be recovered by an attacker which does not know the receiver's private key. Besides, we append a (PFR based MAC) tag of the signature, to make a "re-signing attack" not feasible. The design we obtain is described hereunder.

The Generic SN Signcryption Scheme

10 Setup(k): The algorithm computes $dp_K \leftarrow_R$ Setup$_K(k)$; $dp_S \leftarrow_R$ Setup$_S(k)$; it defines also $\mathcal{E} = (E, D, K = \{0,1\}^k, M, C)$, a pseudo–random function Prf over (K, M, K), and a hash function H over (K, M', T).

11 $\tau_0 \leftarrow_R K$; $dp \leftarrow (dp_K, dp_S, \mathcal{E}, \text{Prf}, H, \tau_0)$; return dp;

12 Gen$_{sd}(dp)$:

13 Parse dp as $(dp_K, dp_S, \mathcal{E}, \text{Prf}, H, \tau_0)$; $(sk_{sd}, pk_{sd}) \leftarrow_R$ Gen$_S(dp_S)$; return (sk_{sd}, pk_{sd});

14 Gen$_{rcv}(dp)$:

15 Parse dp as $(dp_K, dp_S, \mathcal{E}, \text{Prf}, H, \tau_0)$; $(sk_{rcv}, pk_{rcv}) \leftarrow_R$ Gen$_K(dp_K)$; return (sk_{rcv}, pk_{rcv});

16 Sc(sk_{sd}, pk_{rcv}, m):

17 $((\tau_1, \tau_1', \tau_2, \tau_2'), c_1) \leftarrow_R$ Ecp(pk_{rcv}); $c_2 \leftarrow_R E(\tau_1, m)$; $\tau_3 \leftarrow \text{Prf}(\tau_2, m)$;

18 $\hat{m} \leftarrow H(\tau_0, (pk_{sd}, \tau_2, \tau_2', \tau_3, c_1, c_2, pk_{rcv}))$; $\sigma \leftarrow_R$ Sign($sk_{sd}, \hat{m}$);

19 $t \leftarrow \text{Prf}(\tau_1', \sigma)$; return (t, σ, c_1, c_2);

20 Usc(sk_{rcv}, pk_{sd}, C):

21 Parse C as (t, σ, c_1, c_2); $(\tau_1, \tau_1', \tau_2, \tau_2',) \leftarrow$ Dcp(sk_{rcv}, c_1);

22 $m \leftarrow D(\tau_1, c_2)$; $\tau_3 \leftarrow \text{Prf}(\tau_2, m)$;

23 $\hat{m} \leftarrow H(\tau_0, (pk_{sd}, \tau_2, \tau_2', \tau_3, c_1, c_2, pk_{rcv}))$; $d \leftarrow$ Vrfy($pk_{sd}, \hat{m}, \sigma$); $t' \leftarrow \text{Prf}(\tau_1', \sigma)$;

24 **if** $d = 1$ and $t = t'$ **then** return m; **else** return $\perp$;

25 N(sk_{rcv}, pk_{sd}, C):

26 Parse C as (t, σ, c_1, c_2); $(\tau_1, \tau_1', \tau_2, \tau_2') \leftarrow$ Dcp(sk_{rcv}, c_1);

27 $m \leftarrow D(\tau_1, c_2)$; $\tau_3 \leftarrow \text{Prf}(\tau_2, m)$;

28 $\hat{m} \leftarrow H(\tau_0, (pk_{sd}, \tau_2, \tau_2', \tau_3, c_1, c_2, pk_{rcv}))$; $d \leftarrow$ Vrfy($pk_{sd}, \hat{m}, \sigma$); $t' \leftarrow \text{Prf}(\tau_1', \sigma)$;

29 **if** $d = 1$ and $t = t'$ **then** return $(\tau_1, \tau_1', \tau_2, \tau_2')$; **else** return $\perp$;

30 PV($C, m, nr, pk_{sd}, pk_{rcv}$):

31 Parse C as (t, σ, c_1, c_2) and nr as $(\tau_1, \tau_1', \tau_2, \tau_2')$; $m' \leftarrow D(\tau_1, c_2)$;

32 **if** $m' \neq m$ **then** return 0;

33 $\tau_3 \leftarrow \text{Prf}(\tau_2, m)$; $\hat{m} \leftarrow H(\tau_0, (pk_{sd}, \tau_2, \tau_2', \tau_3, c_1, c_2, pk_{rcv}))$;

34 $d \leftarrow$ Vrfy($pk_{sd}, \hat{m}, \sigma$); $t' \leftarrow \text{Prf}(\tau_1', \sigma)$;

35 **if** $d = 1$ and $t = t'$ **then** return 1; **else** return 0.

For the consistency of the scheme, one can observe that as Dcp(sk_{rcv}, c_1) yields $(\tau_1, \tau_1', \tau_2, \tau_2')$, the receiver can compute $\tau_3 \leftarrow \text{Prf}(\tau_2, m)$ and $\hat{m}$, and then verify whether $1 = \text{Vrfy}(pk_{sd}, \hat{m}, \sigma)$ and $t = \text{Prf}(\tau_1', \sigma)$ to accept or reject m. So, for all $dp \in \{\text{Setup}(k)\}$, all $m \in \mathcal{M}$, all $(sk_{sd}, pk_{sd}) \in \{\text{Gen}_{sd}(dp)\}$, and all $(sk_{rcv}, pk_{rcv}) \in \{\text{Gen}_{rcv}(dp)\}$, $m = \text{Usc}(sk_{rcv}, pk_{sd}, \text{Sc}(sk_{sd}, pk_{rcv}, m))$. Besides, if $nr \leftarrow N(sk_{rcv}, pk_{sd}, \text{Sc}(sk_{sd}, pk_{rcv}, m))$ then $1 = d \leftarrow \text{PV}(C, m, nr, pk_{sd}, pk_{rcv})$. Our construction is a signcryption scheme with non-interactive non-repudiation.

4   Security Analysis of the SN Scheme

We propose in this section a detailed security analysis of our generic construction.

4.1   Insider Confidentiality

Theorem 1. *If the encryption scheme $\mathcal{E}$ is $(t(k), \varepsilon_{\mathsf{ss}}(k))$–semantically secure, the pseudo random function Prf is $(t(k), \varepsilon_{\mathsf{Prf}}(k))$–secure, the key encapsulation mechanism is $(t(k), \varepsilon_{\mathcal{K}}(k))$–secure, and the signature scheme is $(t(k), \varepsilon_{\mathcal{S}}(k))$ resistant against colliding signatures, then the SN signcryption scheme is $(t(k), \varepsilon(k))$–$\mathsf{dM{-}IND{-}iCCA}$ secure, where*

$$\varepsilon(k) \leqslant \varepsilon_{\mathsf{ss}}(k) + 2\left(\varepsilon_{\mathcal{K}}(k) + \varepsilon_{\mathcal{S}}(k) + \varepsilon_{\mathsf{H}}(k) + 2\varepsilon_{\mathsf{Prf}}(k) + (q_{\mathsf{Usc}} + q_{\mathsf{N}})/|\mathbf{K}|\right), \quad (2)$$

wherein q_{Usc} and q_{N} are upper bounds on the number of unsigncryption and non-repudiation evidence generation queries the attacker issues.

Proof. We denote the steps (1) and (2), (3) and (4), and (5) and (6) of Game 3 by PRE-CHALLENGE, CHALLENGE, and POST-CHALLENGE stages respectively. We consider the following simulator to answer $\mathcal{A}$'s queries. The <u>Initialization</u> procedure is executed once at the beginning of the game. The <u>Finalization</u> procedure is also executed once, after $\mathcal{A}$ produces its output, at the end of the game. To keep the description simple, we omit public key validations.

Simulation for the experiments E_0 and $E_0^{(1)}, E_0^{(2)}$, and $E_0^{(3)}$ in the $\mathsf{dM{-}IND{-}iCCA}$ Game

100 <u>Initialization:</u> $dp \leftarrow (dp_{\mathsf{K}}, dp_{\mathsf{S}}, \mathcal{E}, \mathsf{Prf}, \mathsf{H}, \tau_0) \leftarrow_{\mathsf{R}} \mathsf{Setup}(k)$;

E_0	$E_0^{(1)}, E_0^{(2)}, E_0^{(3)}$

101 $\boxed{(sk_{\mathsf{rcv}}, pk_{\mathsf{rcv}}) \leftarrow_{\mathsf{R}} \mathsf{Gen}_{\mathsf{rcv}}(dp);}$ $\boxed{\text{receive } pk_{\mathsf{rcv}} \text{ from the KEM challenger;}}$

102 $\boxed{((\bar{\tau}_1, \bar{\tau}_1', \bar{\tau}_2, \bar{\tau}_2'), \bar{c}_1) \leftarrow_{\mathsf{R}} \mathsf{Ecp}(pk_{\mathsf{rcv}});}$ $\boxed{((\bar{\tau}_1, \bar{\tau}_1', \bar{\tau}_2, \bar{\tau}_2'), \bar{c}_1) \leftarrow_{\mathsf{R}} \mathsf{Chall}_{\mathcal{K}_{E_0}};}$ ($E_0^{(1)}$)

$\boxed{((\bar{\tau}_1, \bar{\tau}_1', \bar{\tau}_2, \bar{\tau}_2'), \bar{c}_1) \leftarrow_{\mathsf{R}} \mathsf{Chall}_{\mathcal{K}_{E_1}};}$ ($E_0^{(2)}, E_0^{(3)}$)

<u>PRE–CHALLENGE PHASE</u> $\mathcal{A}$ is provided with (dp, pk_{rcv}) and is given access to the following oracles.

103 $\mathcal{O}_{\mathsf{Usc}}(pk, C)$: $\mathcal{O}_{\mathsf{N}}(pk, C)$:

104 Parse C as (t, σ, c_1, c_2);   ▶ *Return $\perp$ if the parsing fails*

105 $\boxed{\textbf{if } c_1 = \bar{c}_1 \textbf{ then return } \perp;}$ ($E_0^{(1)}, E_0^{(2)}, E_0^{(3)}$)

106 $\boxed{(\tau_1, \tau_1', \tau_2, \tau_2') \leftarrow \mathsf{Dcp}(sk_{\mathsf{rcv}}, c_1);}$ (E_0) $\boxed{(\tau_1, \tau_1', \tau_2, \tau_2') \leftarrow \mathcal{O}_{\mathsf{Dcp}}(c_1);}$ ($E_0^{(1)}, E_0^{(2)}, E_0^{(3)}$)

107 $m \leftarrow \mathsf{D}(\tau_1, c_2); \tau_3 \leftarrow \mathsf{Prf}(\tau_2, m); \hat{m} \leftarrow \mathsf{H}(\tau_0, (pk, \tau_2, \tau_2', \tau_3, c_1, c_2, pk_{\mathsf{rcv}}))$;

108 $d \leftarrow \mathsf{Vrfy}(pk, \hat{m}, \sigma); t' \leftarrow \mathsf{Prf}(\tau_1', \sigma)$;

109 **if** $d = 1$ and $t = t'$ **then** $\boxed{\text{return } m;}^{\mathcal{O}_{\mathsf{Usc}}}$ $\boxed{\text{return } (\tau_1, \tau_1', \tau_2, \tau_2');}^{\mathcal{O}_{\mathsf{N}}}$ **else** return $\perp$;

CHALLENGE PHASE

110 $(m_0, m_1, sk_{\mathsf{sd}}, pk_{\mathsf{sd}}, st) \leftarrow_{\mathsf{R}} \mathcal{A}_1^{\mathcal{O}_{\mathsf{Usc}, \mathsf{N}}}(dp, pk_{\mathsf{rcv}});$ ▶ $|m_0| = |m_1|$
111 $((\tau_1, \tau_1', \tau_2, \tau_2'), c_1) \leftarrow ((\bar{\tau}_1, \bar{\tau}_1', \bar{\tau}_2, \bar{\tau}_2'), \bar{c}_1);$

$\boxed{E_0, E_0^{(i)}, i = 1, 2, 3}$

112 $\boxed{c_2 \leftarrow_{\mathsf{R}} \mathsf{E}(\tau_1, m_0);}$

$\boxed{E_0, E_0^{(1)}, E_0^{(2)}}$ $\boxed{E_0^{(3)}}$

113 $\boxed{\tau_3 \leftarrow \mathsf{Prf}(\tau_2, m_0);}$ $\boxed{\tau_3 \leftarrow_{\mathsf{R}} \mathbf{K};}$ ▶ $\tau_3 \leftarrow_{\mathsf{R}} \mathbf{K}$ *is equivalent to* $f \leftarrow_{\mathsf{R}} \mathsf{Func}(\mathbf{M}, \mathbf{K}); \tau_3 \leftarrow f(m_0);$

114 $\hat{m} \leftarrow \mathsf{H}(\tau_0, (pk_{\mathsf{sd}}, \tau_2, \tau_2', \tau_3, c_1, c_2, pk_{\mathsf{rcv}})); \quad \sigma \leftarrow \mathsf{Sign}(sk_{\mathsf{sd}}, \hat{m}); \quad t \leftarrow \mathsf{Prf}(\tau_1', \sigma);$
$C^* \leftarrow_{\mathsf{R}} (t, \sigma, c_1, c_2);$

POST–CHALLENGE PHASE
$\mathcal{A}_2$ runs with inputs (C^*, st). It has access to the oracles $\mathcal{O}_{\mathsf{Usc}}(\cdot, \cdot)$, $\mathcal{O}_{\mathsf{N}}(\cdot, \cdot)$,
The simulation aborts if $\mathcal{A}$ issues $\mathcal{O}_{\mathsf{Usc}}(pk_{\mathsf{sd}}, C^*)$ or $\mathcal{O}_{\mathsf{N}}(pk_{\mathsf{sd}}, C^*)$.
115 $\hat{b} \leftarrow_{\mathsf{R}} \mathcal{A}_2^{\mathcal{O}_{\mathsf{Usc}}(\cdot, \cdot), \mathcal{O}_{\mathsf{N}}(\cdot, \cdot)}(C^*, st);$

116 **Finalization: return** $\hat{b}$;

At lines 103 to 109 we describe simultaneously the $\mathcal{O}_{\mathsf{Usc}}(\cdot, \cdot)$ and $\mathcal{O}_{\mathsf{N}}(\cdot, \cdot)$ oracles. When one of the oracles is queried, at line 109, the boxed instruction with corresponding header is executed.

Besides the experiment E_0 in the dM−IND−iCCA security game, we define three other experiments $E_0^{(1)}$, $E_0^{(2)}$, and $E_0^{(3)}$. For each experiment, at a line with boxed codes, only the code with corresponding header is executed. The simulator is efficient in all the experiments. We give a summary of the changes between the experiments hereunder.

1) From E_0 to $E_0^{(1)}$:
    a) in $E_0^{(1)}$, the simulator Sim does not generate $(sk_{\mathsf{rcv}}, pk_{\mathsf{rcv}})$, instead it receives pk_{rcv} from a KEM challenger (see at line 101),
    b) to compute $\mathsf{Dcp}(sk_{\mathsf{rcv}}, c_1)$, the simulator sends c_1 to the KEM challenger and receives $(\tau_1, \tau_1', \tau_2, \tau_2') \leftarrow \mathsf{Dcp}(sk_{\mathsf{rcv}}, c_1)$ from the challenger (see at line 106),
    c) and in the challenge phase, the value of $((\tau_1, \tau_1', \tau_2, \tau_2'), c) \leftarrow_{\mathsf{R}} \mathsf{Ecp}(pk_{\mathsf{rcv}})$ is received from the KEM challenger; we note $((\tau_1, \tau_1', \tau_2, \tau_2'), c) \leftarrow \mathsf{Chall}_{\mathcal{K}_{E_0}}$.
    d) Besides, in the Usc and N oracles, whenever $\mathcal{A}$ provides the simulator with a signcrypted cipher-text $C = (t, \sigma, c_1, c_2)$ with $c_1 = \bar{c}_1$, the simulator considers t as an invalid PRF based MAC and returns $\perp$ (see at line 105).
2) From $E_0^{(1)}$ to $E_0^{(2)}$, the only change is at line 102 of the challenge phase, wherein the KEM challenger provides S with $\mathsf{Chall}_{\mathcal{K}_{E_1}}$ instead of $\mathsf{Chall}_{\mathcal{K}_{E_0}}$.
3) From $E_0^{(2)}$ to $E_0^{(3)}$, the change is in the challenge phase, where τ_3 is computed as $\tau_3 \leftarrow \mathsf{Prf}(\tau_2, m_0)$ in $E_0^{(2)}$, and as $\tau_3 \leftarrow_{\mathsf{R}} \mathbf{K}$ in $E_0^{(3)}$ (see at line 113). Notice that $\tau_3 \leftarrow_{\mathsf{R}} \mathbf{K}$ is equivalent to $f \leftarrow_{\mathsf{R}} \mathsf{Func}(\mathbf{M}, \mathbf{K}); \tau_3 \leftarrow f(m)$.

Let $\Pr(\text{out}_0)$ and $\Pr(\text{out}_0^{(i)})$, for $i \in \{1, 2, 3\}$ denote the probability that $\mathcal{A}$ outputs 1 in the experiments E_0 and $E_0^{(i)}$, respectively. Notice that the <u>FINALIZATION</u> procedure outputs exactly whatever $\mathcal{A}$ returns. Given the difference between E_0 and $E_0^{(1)}$, whenever $\mathcal{A}$ provides the $\mathcal{O}_{\text{Usc}}$ or $\mathcal{O}_\text{N}$ oracles with a valid $C = (t, \sigma, c_1, c_2)$ with $c_1 = \bar{c}_1$ then:

a) If this occurs before the challenge phase, t is a no-message (PRF-based) MAC forgery.
b) If this occurs after the challenge phase (with the restriction $C \neq C^*$), if $(t, \sigma) \neq (t^*, \sigma^*)$, then (t^*, σ^*) is MAC forgery. Otherwise, we necessarily have $(pk, c_1, c_2) \neq (pk_{\text{sd}}, c_1^*, c_2^*)$. And then, if $\hat{m} = \hat{m}^*$, we have a H collision, otherwise we have colliding signatures.

So, using [9, Theorem 6.2, p. 224], it holds that

$$|\Pr(\text{out}_0) - \Pr(\text{out}_0^{(1)})| \leqslant \varepsilon_{\text{Prf}}(k) + (q_{\text{Usc}} + q_\text{N})/|\mathbf{K}| + \varepsilon_\text{H}(k) + \varepsilon_{\mathcal{S}}(k). \quad (3)$$

The difference between $E_0^{(1)}$ and $E_0^{(2)}$ is: in $E_0^{(1)}$ the simulator receives $\text{Chall}_{\mathcal{K}_{E_0}}$ from the KEM challenger, while it receives $\text{Chall}_{\mathcal{K}_{E_1}}$ in $E_0^{(2)}$. As $\mathcal{K}$ is $(t(k), \varepsilon_{\mathcal{K}}(k))$–secure, it follows that

$$|\Pr(\text{out}_0^{(1)}) - \Pr(\text{out}_0^{(2)})| \leqslant \varepsilon_{\mathcal{K}}(k). \quad (4)$$

Also, given that Prf is $(t(k), \varepsilon_{\text{Prf}}(k))$–secure, we have

$$|\Pr(\text{out}_0^{(2)}) - \Pr(\text{out}_0^{(3)})| \leqslant \varepsilon_{\text{Prf}}(k). \quad (5)$$

Now, we consider the experiments $E_1^{(3)}, E_1^{(2)}, E_1^{(1)}$ and E_1 where the only difference between E_1 (resp. $E_1^{(3)}, E_1^{(2)}, E_1^{(1)}$) and E_0 (resp. $E_0^{(3)}, E_0^{(2)}, E_0^{(1)}$) is that the lines 112 and 113 in the challenge phase are modified, to use m_1 instead of m_0, as hereunder:

112 $\boxed{\begin{array}{l} E_1, E_1^{(i)}, i = 1, 2, 3 \\ \hline c_2 \leftarrow_\text{R} \mathsf{E}(\tau_1, m_1); \end{array}}$

113 $\boxed{\begin{array}{l} E_1, E_1^{(1)}, E_1^{(2)} \\ \hline \tau_3 \leftarrow \text{Prf}(\tau_2, m_1); \end{array}}$ $\boxed{\begin{array}{l} E_1^{(3)} \\ \hline \tau_3 \leftarrow_\text{R} \mathbf{K}^2; \end{array}}$

With similar arguments, applied to the experiments E_1 and $E_1^{(i)}$, $i = 1, 2, 3$, we obtain

$$|\Pr(\text{out}_1) - \Pr(\text{out}_1^{(1)})| \leqslant \varepsilon_{\text{Prf}}(k) + (q_{\text{Usc}} + q_\text{N})/|\mathbf{K}| + \varepsilon_\text{H}(k) + \varepsilon_{\mathcal{S}}(k), \quad (6)$$

$$|\Pr(\text{out}_1^{(1)}) - \Pr(\text{out}_1^{(2)})| \leqslant \varepsilon_{\mathcal{K}}(k), \quad (7)$$

and

$$|\Pr(\text{out}_1^{(2)}) - \Pr(\text{out}_1^{(3)})| \leqslant \varepsilon_{\text{Prf}}(k). \quad (8)$$

We consider now, the challenge phases in the experiments $E_b^{(3)}$, $b = 0, 1$, wherein the secret key τ_1 is used only in the encryption $c_2 \leftarrow_\text{R} \mathsf{E}(\tau_1, m_b)$. Recall that in $E_{b,b=0,1}^{(3)}$, $(\tau_1, \tau_1', \tau_2, \tau_2')$ is computed at the KEM challenger as $(\tau_1, \tau_1', \tau_2, \tau_2') \leftarrow_\text{R} \mathbf{K}^3$. Now, we consider the experiments $E_{b,b=0,1}^{(3a)}$, such that the difference between $E_{b,b=0,1}^{(3)}$ and $E_{b,b=0,1}^{(3a)}$ is that in $E_{b,b=0,1}^{(3a)}$ the simulator ignores the value of τ_1 generated by the KEM challenger; it does not compute c_2. Instead, it receives c_2 from a semantic security challenger. The challenger computes c_2 using the instructions: $\tau \leftarrow_R \mathbf{K}; c_2 \leftarrow_R E(\tau, m_b)$. Given the change, it holds that

$$\Pr(\text{out}_b^{(3)}) = \Pr(\text{out}_b^{(3a)}), \text{ for } b = 0, 1 \tag{9}$$

and the difference between $E_0^{(3a)}$ and $E_1^{(3a)}$ is that in $E_0^{(3a)}$ c_2 is computed as $c_2 \leftarrow_R E(\tau, m_0)$ wherein $\tau \leftarrow_R \mathbf{K}$, while in $E_0^{(3a)}$ it is computed as $c_2 \leftarrow_R E(\tau, m_0)$, it then follows that

$$|\Pr(\text{out}_0^{(3)}) - \Pr(\text{out}_1^{(3)})| = |\Pr(\text{out}_0^{(3a)}) - \Pr(\text{out}_1^{(3a)})| \leqslant \varepsilon_{\text{ss}}(k). \tag{10}$$

From the inequalities (3) to (10), we obtain

$$|\Pr(\text{out}_0) - \Pr(\text{out}_1)| \leqslant \varepsilon_{\text{ss}}(k) + 2\left(\varepsilon_{\mathcal{K}}(k) + \varepsilon_{\mathcal{S}}(k) + \varepsilon_{\text{H}}(k) + 2\varepsilon_{\text{Prf}}(k) + (q_{\text{Usc}} + q_{\text{N}})/|\mathbf{K}|\right).$$

$\square$

4.2 Unforgeability of the SN Scheme

Theorem 2. *If the signature scheme is* $(t(k), \varepsilon_S(k))$*–sUF-CMA secure and the hash function* H *is* $(t(k), \varepsilon_H(k))$ *collision resistant, then the* SN *signcryption scheme is* $(t(k), \varepsilon(k))$ dM$-$sUF$-$iCCA*-secure, where* $\varepsilon(k) \leqslant \varepsilon_H(k) + \varepsilon_S(k)$.

Proof. We consider the following simulation to answer $\mathcal{A}$'s queries.

Simulation for the dM$-$sUF$-$iCCA security game
200 <u>Initialization:</u> $dp \leftarrow (dp_K, dp_S, \mathcal{E}, \text{Prf}, \text{H}, \tau_0) \leftarrow_R \text{Setup}(k)$; $L \leftarrow ()$; $L_1 \leftarrow ()$; $L_2 \leftarrow ()$;

E_0	E_1
201 | $(sk_{\text{sd}}, pk_{\text{sd}}) \leftarrow_R \text{Gen}_{\text{sd}}(dp)$; | Get pk_{sd} from the challenger for signature unforgeability; |

202 $\mathcal{O}_{\text{Sc}}(pk, m)$:
203 $((\tau_1, \tau_1', \tau_2, \tau_2'), c_1) \leftarrow_R \text{Ecp}(pk)$; $c_2 \leftarrow_R E(\tau_1, m)$;
204 $\tau_3 \leftarrow \text{Prf}(\tau_2, m)$; $\hat{m} \leftarrow \text{H}(\tau_0, (pk_{\text{sd}}, \tau_2, \tau_2', \tau_3, c_1, c_2, pk))$;

E_0	E_1
205 | $\sigma \leftarrow_R \text{Sign}(sk_{\text{sd}}, \hat{m})$; | Send $\hat{m}$ to the signing oracle and receive σ; |

206 $t \leftarrow \text{Prf}(\tau_1', \sigma)$
207 $\text{Apd}(L, (pk, m, (t, \sigma, c_1, c_2)))$; $\text{Apd}(L_1, (\sigma, \hat{m}))$;
208 $\text{Apd}(L_2, (t, pk_{\text{sd}}, m, \hat{m}, \sigma, \tau_1, \tau_1', \tau_2, \tau_2', \tau_3, c_1, c_2, pk))$;
        return (t, σ, c_1, c_2);

209 <u>Finalization:</u>
210 **if** $\mathcal{A}$ outputs $(sk_{\text{rcv}}, pk_{\text{rcv}}, C^*)$ such that
        (i) $\perp \neq m^* \leftarrow \text{Usc}(sk_{\text{rcv}}, pk_{\text{sd}}, C^*)$ and
        (ii) $(pk_{\text{rcv}}, m^*, C^*) \notin L$

then

211   Parse C^* as $(t^*, \sigma^*, c_1^*, c_2^*)$;

212     $(\tau_1^*, \tau'_1^*, \tau_2^*, \tau'_2^*) \leftarrow \mathsf{Dcp}(sk_{rcv}, c_1^*); \ m^* \leftarrow \mathsf{D}(\tau_1^*, c_2^*); \ \tau_3^* \leftarrow \mathsf{Prf}(\tau_2^*, m^*)$;

213     $\hat{m}^* \leftarrow \mathsf{H}(\tau_0^*, (pk_{sd}, \tau_2^*, \tau'_2^*, \tau_3^*, c_1^*, c_2^*, pk_{rcv}))$;

214   **if** $(\sigma^*, \hat{m}^*) \notin \mathsf{L}_1$ **then**

215   **return** $(\sigma^*, \hat{m}^*)$;   ▶ $(\sigma^*, \hat{m}^*)$ *is a signature forgery;*

216   **else**   ▶ $(\sigma^*, \hat{m}^*) \in \mathsf{L}_1$

217   Find $(t, pk_{sd}, m, \hat{m}, \sigma, \tau_1, \tau'_1, \tau_2, \tau'_2, \tau_3, c_1, c_2, pk) \in \mathsf{L}_2$ such that $(\sigma, \hat{m}) = (\sigma^*, \hat{m}^*)$;

218         $x_1 \leftarrow (pk_{sd}, \tau_2^*, \tau'_2^*, \tau_3^*, c_1^*, c_2^*, pk_{rcv}); \ x_2 \leftarrow (pk_{sd}, \tau_2, \tau'_2, \tau_3, c_1, c_2, pk)$;

219   **if** $(pk, c_1, c_2) \neq (pk_{rcv}, c_1^*, c_2^*)$ **then**

220   **return** (x_1, x_2);   ▶ *This yields a collision,* $x_1 \neq x_2$ *and* $\mathsf{H}(\tau_0, x_1) = \mathsf{H}(\tau_0, x_2)$.

221   **else return** $\bot$;   ▶

$(\sigma^*, \hat{m}^*) \in \mathsf{L}_1$, $pk = pk_{rcv}$, $c_1 = c_1^*$, *and* $c_2 = c_2^*$, *so we have* $(\tau_1, \tau'_1, \tau_2, \tau'_2) = (\tau_1^*, \tau'_1^*, \tau_2^*, \tau'_2^*)$, *then* $m = m^* = \mathsf{D}(\tau_1, c_2)$, *and then* $(pk_{rcv}, m^*, C^* = (t, \sigma^*, c_1^*, c_2^*)) \in \mathsf{L}$; *this cannot occur (see condition (ii) at line 210).*

In experiment E_0 the simulator answers $\mathcal{A}'s$ queries exactly as in an dM−sUF−iCCA security game. In E_1, we modify the simulator such that it receives pk_{sd} from a signature challenger, and whenever $\mathcal{S}$ needs a signature on some $\hat{m}$, it sends it to its signature challenger and receives the corresponding signature (see at line 205). Let $\mathsf{Ev}_{b, b=0,1}$ be the event: "the conditions (i) and (ii) in the FINALIZATION procedure are satisfied in experiment E_b." It is clear that $\Pr(\mathsf{Ev}_0) = \Pr(\mathsf{Ev}_1)$. Let Coll be the event simulator outputs (x_1, x_2) such that $\mathsf{H}(\tau_0, x_1) = \mathsf{H}(\tau_0, x_2)$.

$$\Pr(\mathsf{Ev}_1 \wedge \mathsf{Coll}) \leqslant \Pr(\mathsf{Coll}) \leqslant \varepsilon_{\mathsf{H}}(k).$$

And, if $\mathsf{Ev}_1 \wedge \neg\mathsf{Coll}$ occurs, the simulator outputs a signature forgery, *i. e.*

$$\Pr(\mathsf{Ev}_1 \wedge \neg\mathsf{Coll}) \leqslant \varepsilon_{\mathcal{S}}(k).$$

It follows that $\varepsilon(k) = \Pr(\mathsf{Ev}) \leqslant \varepsilon_{\mathsf{H}}(k) + \varepsilon_{\mathcal{S}}(k)$.   □

4.3   Soundness of Non-Repudiation

Theorem 3. *If the hash function* H *is* $(t(k), \varepsilon_{\mathsf{H}}(k))$–*collision resistant and the signature scheme is* $(t(k), \varepsilon_{\mathcal{S}}(k))$ *secure against colliding signatures, then the* SN *scheme achieves* $(t(k), \varepsilon(k))$ *soundness of non-repudiation, where* $\varepsilon(k) \leqslant \varepsilon_{\mathsf{H}}(k) + \varepsilon_{\mathcal{S}}(k)$.

Proof. We consider the following simulator.

Simulation for Soundness of non–repudiation

300   Initialization: $dp \leftarrow (dp_K, dp_S, \mathcal{E}, \mathsf{Prf}, \mathsf{H}, \tau_0) \leftarrow_R \mathsf{Setup}(k)$;

301   The attacker $\mathcal{A}$ outputs $(C^*, pk_{sd}, sk_{rcv}, pk_{rcv}, m', nr^*) \leftarrow_R \mathcal{A}(dp)$;

302   Finalization:

303   **if** $\mathcal{A}$ outputs $(C^*, pk_{sd}, sk_{rcv}, pk_{rcv}, m', nr^*)$ such that

(i) $\perp \neq m \leftarrow \mathsf{Usc}(sk_{\mathsf{rcv}}, pk_{\mathsf{sd}}, C^*)$, and
(ii) $m \neq m'$ and $1 = d \leftarrow \mathsf{PV}(C^*, m', nr^*, pk_{\mathsf{sd}}, pk_{\mathsf{rcv}})$;
then

304   Parse C^* as $(t^*, \sigma^*, c_1^*, c_2^*)$ and nr^* as $(\tau_1^*, \tau'^*_1, \tau_2^*, \tau'^*_2)$;
305    $nr \leftarrow \mathsf{N}(sk_{\mathsf{rcv}}, pk_{\mathsf{sd}}, C^*)$; parse nr as $(\tau_1, \tau'_1, \tau_2, \tau'_2)$;
306    $\tau_3^* \leftarrow \mathsf{Prf}(\tau_2^*, m')$; $\tau_3 \leftarrow \mathsf{Prf}(\tau_2, m)$;
307    $s_1 \leftarrow (pk_{\mathsf{sd}}, \tau_2^*, \tau'^*_2, \tau_3^*, c_1, c_2, pk_{\mathsf{rcv}})$; $\hat{m}^* \leftarrow \mathsf{H}(\tau_0, s_1)$;
308    $s_2 \leftarrow (pk_{\mathsf{sd}}, \tau_2, \tau'_2, \tau_3, c_1, c_2, pk_{\mathsf{rcv}})$; $\hat{m} \leftarrow \mathsf{H}(\tau_0, s_2)$;   ▸ *As $m \neq m'$ we necessarily have $\tau_1 \neq \tau_1^*$. Also, as $m \neq m'$, $\tau_2 = \tau_2^*$ implies $\tau_3 \neq \tau_3^*$, so it holds that $(\tau_2, \tau_3) \neq (\tau_2^*, \tau_3^*)$;*
309   **if** $\hat{m} = \hat{m}^*$ **then** return (s_1, s_2);   ▸ *A collision is found for H*
310   **else** return $(pk_{\mathsf{sd}}, \hat{m}, \hat{m}^*, \sigma^*)$;   ▸ *Colliding signatures for $\hat{m}$ and $\hat{m}^*$;*
311 **else** return $\perp$;

Clearly, our simulator is efficient and if $\mathcal{A}$ succeeds in the soundness of non-repudiation game, its output $(C^*, pk_{\mathsf{sd}}, sk_{\mathsf{rcv}}, pk_{\mathsf{rcv}}, C^*, m', nr^*)$ is such that the conditions (i) and (ii) at line 303 are satisfied. Then the simulator outputs either (s_1, s_2) such that $s_1 \neq s_2$ and $\mathsf{H}(\tau_0, s_1) = \mathsf{H}(\tau_0, s_2)$, or $(pk_{\mathsf{sd}}, \hat{m}, \hat{m}^*, \sigma^*)$ such that $\hat{m} \neq \hat{m}^*$ and $1 = \mathsf{Vrfy}(pk, \hat{m}, \sigma^*) = \mathsf{Vrfy}(pk, \hat{m}^*, \sigma^*)$. Hence, $\varepsilon(k) \leqslant \varepsilon_{\mathsf{H}}(k) + \varepsilon_{\mathcal{S}}(k)$.   □

4.4   Unforgeability of Non-Repudiation Evidence

Theorem 4. *If the encryption scheme is $(t(k), \varepsilon_{\mathcal{E}}(k))$ resistant to clustering key attacks, the signature scheme is $(t(k), \varepsilon_{\mathcal{S}}(k))$ resistant to colliding signatures, the hash function is $(t(k), \varepsilon_{\mathsf{H}}(k))$ resistant to collisions with identical prefix, and the KEM is $(t(k), \varepsilon_{\mathcal{K}}(k))$ IND-CCA secure, then SN achieves $(t(k), \varepsilon(k))$ unforgeability of non-repudiation evidence with*

$$\varepsilon(k) \leqslant q_{\mathsf{Sc}}(\varepsilon_{\mathsf{Prf}}(k) + (q_{\mathsf{Usc}} + q_{\mathsf{N}} + 1)/|\mathbf{K}| + \varepsilon_{\mathcal{S}}(k) + \varepsilon_{\mathcal{K}}(k) + 2\varepsilon_{\mathsf{H}}(k)) \quad (11)$$

wherein q_{Sc}, q_{Usc}, and q_{N} are upper bounds on the number of times the attacker issues respectively the signcryption, unsigncryption, and non-repudiation evidence generation oracles.

Proof. Let Ev be the event: $\mathcal{A}$ outputs (C^*, m^*, nr^*) such that the conditions

(i) $C^* \leftarrow_{\mathsf{R}} \mathcal{O}_{\mathsf{Sc}}(pk_{\mathsf{rcv}}, m)$ was issued by $\mathcal{A}$, for some $m \in \mathbf{M}$;
(ii) $1 = d \leftarrow \mathsf{PV}(C^*, m^*, nr^*, pk_{\mathsf{sd}}, pk_{\mathsf{rcv}})$;
(iii) $\mathcal{O}_{\mathsf{N}}(pk_{\mathsf{sd}}, C^*)$ was never issued by $\mathcal{A}$.

We consider the following simulation; when abort is set to true, the simulation aborts.

Simulation for Unforgeability of non–repudiation evidence
400 <u>Initialization:</u> $dp \leftarrow (dp_{\mathsf{K}}, dp_{\mathsf{S}}, \mathcal{E}, \mathsf{Prf}, \mathsf{H}, \tau_0) \leftarrow_{\mathsf{R}} \mathsf{Setup}(k)$; $\mathsf{L} \leftarrow ()$; $\mathsf{L}_1 \leftarrow ()$;
401 $(sk_{\mathsf{rcv}}, pk_{\mathsf{rcv}}) \leftarrow_{\mathsf{R}} \mathsf{Gen}_{\mathsf{rcv}}(dp)$; $(sk_{\mathsf{sd}}, pk_{\mathsf{sd}}) \leftarrow_{\mathsf{R}} \mathsf{Gen}_{\mathsf{sd}}(dp)$;
402 $i_0 \leftarrow_{\mathsf{R}} [q_{\mathsf{Sc}}]$; $\mathsf{cnt} \leftarrow 0$; abort $\leftarrow$ false;

E_0
$$((\bar{\tau}_1, \bar{\tau}_1', \bar{\tau}_2, \bar{\tau}_2'), \bar{c}_1) \leftarrow_R \mathsf{Ecp}(pk_{\mathrm{rcv}});$$

E_1
$$((\bar{\tau}_1, \bar{\tau}_1', \bar{\tau}_2, \bar{\tau}_2'), \bar{c}_1) \leftarrow_R \mathsf{Chall}_{\mathcal{K}_{E_0}};$$

E_2, E_3
$$((\bar{\tau}_1, \bar{\tau}_1', \bar{\tau}_2, \bar{\tau}_2'), \bar{c}_1) \leftarrow_R \mathsf{Chall}_{\mathcal{K}_{E_1}};$$

404 $m_0 \leftarrow \bot; \hat{m}_0 \leftarrow \bot; C_0 \leftarrow \bot;$

405 $\mathcal{O}_{\mathsf{Sc}}(pk, m):$

406 $\mathrm{cnt} \leftarrow \mathrm{cnt} + 1;$

407 **if** $\mathrm{cnt} = i_0$ **then**

408   **if** $pk \neq pk_{\mathrm{rcv}}$ **then** abort $\leftarrow$ true;   ▶ *The guess is incorrect.*

E_0, E_1, E_2
$$((\tau_1, \tau_1', \tau_2, \tau_2'), c_1) \leftarrow ((\bar{\tau}_1, \bar{\tau}_1', \bar{\tau}_2, \bar{\tau}_2'), \bar{c}_1);$$

E_3
$$\tau_1 \leftarrow \bar{\tau}_1; \tau_1' \leftarrow \bar{\tau}_1'; c_1 \leftarrow \bar{c}_1;$$

410 $c_2 \leftarrow_R \mathsf{E}(\tau_1, m);$

E_0, E_1, E_2
411 $\tau_3 \leftarrow \mathsf{Prf}(\tau_2, m);$

E_3
Send $(p, m, s) \leftarrow (pk_{\mathrm{sd}}, m, (c_1, c_2, pk_{\mathrm{rcv}}))$ to the pre–image challenger;

E_0, E_1, E_2
412 $\hat{m} \leftarrow \mathsf{H}(\tau_0, (pk_{\mathrm{sd}}, \tau_2, \tau_2', \tau_3, c_1, c_2, pk));$

E_3
Receive $\hat{m}$ from the pre–image challenger;

413 $m_0 \leftarrow m; \hat{m}_0 \leftarrow \hat{m};$

414 **else**

415      $((\tau_1, \tau_1', \tau_2, \tau_2'), c_1) \leftarrow_R \mathsf{Ecp}(pk); c_2 \leftarrow_R \mathsf{E}(\tau_1, m);$

416      $\tau_3 \leftarrow \mathsf{Prf}(\tau_2, m); \hat{m} \leftarrow \mathsf{H}(\tau_0, (pk_{\mathrm{sd}}, \tau_2, \tau_2', \tau_3, c_1, c_2, pk));$

417 $\sigma \leftarrow_R \mathsf{Sign}(sk_{\mathrm{sd}}, \hat{m}); t \leftarrow \mathsf{Prf}(\tau_1', \sigma); \mathsf{Apd}(\mathsf{L}, (pk, m, (t, \sigma, c_1, c_2)));$

418 **if** $\mathrm{cnt} = i_0$ **then**

419      $C_0 \leftarrow (t, \sigma, c_1, c_2);$

420 **return** $(t, \sigma, c_1, c_2);$

421 $\mathcal{O}_{\mathsf{Usc}}(pk, C): \quad \mathcal{O}_{\mathsf{N}}(pk, C):$

422 **if** $pk = pk_{\mathrm{sd}}$ and $C = C_0 \neq \bot$ **then**

$\mathcal{O}_{\mathsf{Usc}}$ $\mathcal{O}_{\mathsf{N}}$
423 **return** $m_0;$ abort $\leftarrow 1;$

424 Parse C as $(t, \sigma, c_1, c_2);$

E_1, E_2, E_3
425 **if** $c_1 = \bar{c}_1$ **then return** $\bot;$

426 $(\tau_1, \tau_1', \tau_2, \tau_2') \leftarrow \mathsf{Dcp}(sk_{\mathrm{rcv}}, c_1); m \leftarrow \mathsf{D}(\tau_1, c_2);$

427 $\tau_3 \leftarrow \mathsf{Prf}(\tau_2, m); \hat{m} \leftarrow \mathsf{H}(\tau_0, (pk, \tau_2, \tau_2', \tau_3, c_1, c_2, pk_{\mathrm{rcv}}));$

428 $d \leftarrow \mathsf{Vrfy}(pk_{\mathrm{sd}}, \hat{m}, \sigma); t' \leftarrow \mathsf{Prf}(\tau_1', \sigma);$

429 **if** $d = 1$ and $t = t'$ **then**

$\mathcal{O}_{\mathsf{Usc}}$ $\mathcal{O}_{\mathsf{N}}$
430 **return** $m;$ $nr \leftarrow (\tau_1, \tau_1', \tau_2, \tau_2'); \mathsf{Apd}(\mathsf{L}_1, (pk, nr, C)); $ **return** $nr;$

431 **else return** $\bot;$

432 Finalization:

433 **if** $\mathcal{A}$ outputs (C^*, m^*, nr^*) such that:

   (i) $(pk_{\mathrm{rcv}}, m, C^*) \in \mathsf{L}$ for some $m \in \mathbf{M},$ ▶ C^* *was generated by* $\mathcal{O}_{\mathsf{Sc}}(\cdot, \cdot)$ *on input* $(pk_{\mathrm{rcv}}, m).$

   (ii) $1 = d \leftarrow \mathsf{PV}(C^*, m^*, nr^*, pk_{\mathrm{sd}}, pk_{\mathrm{rcv}}),$ and

(iii) $(pk_{\mathsf{sd}}, nr^*, C^*) \notin \mathsf{L}_1$,   ▶ nr^* *was not generated by* $\mathcal{O}_{\mathsf{N}}(\cdot, \cdot)$ *on a query on* (pk_{sd}, C^*);

(iv) and $C^* = C_0 = (\bar{t}, \bar{\sigma}, \bar{c}_1, \bar{c}_2)$;   ▶ *the simulator guessed correctly;*

then

434   Parse nr^* as $(\tau_1^*, \tau'^*_1, \tau_2^*, \tau'^*_2)$; return (τ_2^*, τ'^*_2)

435 **else** return $\perp$;

We consider the experiments E_i, for $i = 0, 1, 2, 3$. In E_0 $\mathcal{A}$ plays Game 6; the simulator guesses the execution of the signcryption oracle wherein C^* will be generated, and answers $\mathcal{A}$'s queries consistently. Let Ev be the event $\mathcal{A}$ succeeds and Guess be the event the simulator's guess is correct. If Ev $\wedge$ Guess occurs, the simulator outputs (τ_2^*, τ'^*_2) such that $\hat{m}_0 \leftarrow \mathsf{H}(\tau_0, (pk, \tau_2^*, \tau'^*_2, \tau_3^*, c_1, c_2, pk_{\mathsf{rcv}}))$ wherein $\tau_3^* \leftarrow \mathsf{Prf}(\tau_2^*, m_0)$. As the guess's correctness is independent from $\mathcal{A}$'s success,

$$\Pr(\mathsf{Ev} \wedge \mathsf{Guess}) = \Pr(\mathsf{Ev})/q_{\mathsf{Sc}}. \tag{12}$$

Let out_i denote the event Ev $\wedge$ Guess in experiment E_i, for $i = 0, 1, 2, 3$. We now consider the experiment E_1, wherein instead of generating $(\bar{\tau}_1, \bar{\tau}'_1, \bar{\tau}_2, \bar{\tau}'_2, \bar{c}_1)$ for the guessed Sc query (see at lines 403 and 409), the simulator receives $(\bar{\tau}_1, \bar{\tau}'_1, \bar{\tau}_2, \bar{\tau}'_2, \bar{c}_1)$ from a KEM challenger as $\mathsf{Chall}_{\mathcal{K}_{E_0}}$. In E_1, when $\mathcal{A}$ provides the $\mathcal{O}_{\mathsf{Usc}}$ or $\mathcal{O}_{\mathsf{N}}$ oracles with a signcrypted cipher text (t, σ, c_1, c_2) with $c_1 = \bar{c}_1$, the simulator returns $\perp$. Indeed, for such a query to succeeds (except C_0, which is allowed only for $\mathcal{O}_{\mathsf{Usc}}$), it must hold that $t = t' \leftarrow \mathsf{Prf}(\bar{\tau}'_1, \sigma)$. As $(t, \sigma, c_1, c_2) \neq (\bar{t}, \bar{\sigma}, \bar{c}_1, \bar{c}_2)$, if $(t, \sigma) \neq (\bar{t}, \bar{\sigma})$, this yields a PRF MAC forgery, otherwise (we must have $(c_1, c_2) \neq (\bar{c}_1, \bar{c}_2)$) we obtain a collision for H or colliding signatures. Hence

$$|\Pr(\mathsf{out}_0) - \Pr(\mathsf{out}_1)| \leqslant \varepsilon_{\mathsf{Prf}}(k) + (q_{\mathsf{Usc}} + q_{\mathsf{N}})/|\mathbf{K}| + \varepsilon_{\mathcal{S}}(k) + \varepsilon_{\mathsf{H}}(k).$$

We consider the experiment E_2, where the only difference compared to E_1 is that $(\bar{\tau}_1, \bar{\tau}'_1, \bar{\tau}_2, \bar{\tau}'_2, c_1)$ is received from a KEM challenger as $\mathsf{Chall}_{\mathbf{K}_{E_1}}$ instead of $\mathsf{Chall}_{\mathcal{K}_{E_0}}$. It holds that

$$|\Pr(\mathsf{out}_1) - \Pr(\mathsf{out}_2)| \leqslant \varepsilon_{\mathcal{K}}(k).$$

In experiment E_3, the challenger receives $(\bar{\tau}_1, \bar{\tau}'_1, \bar{\tau}_2, \bar{\tau}'_2, c_1)$ as $\mathsf{Chall}_{\mathcal{K}_{E_1}}$ from the KEM challenger, however it does not use $\bar{\tau}_2$ and $\bar{\tau}'_2$, instead the values of $\bar{\tau}_2$ and $\bar{\tau}'_2$ are generated by a pre-image challenger, as $\bar{\tau}_2$ and $\bar{\tau}'_2$ are generated following the same distribution as at the KEM challenger, it follows that

$$\Pr(\mathsf{out}_2) = \Pr(\mathsf{out}_3).$$

Now if out_3 occurs, the simulator succeeds in its pre-image game. So, from Lemma 1,

$$\Pr(\mathsf{out}_3) \leqslant 1/|\mathbf{K}| + \varepsilon_{\mathsf{H}}(k).$$

And then,

$$\Pr(\mathsf{Ev})/q_{\mathsf{Sc}} = \Pr(\mathsf{out}_0) \leqslant |\Pr(\mathsf{out}_0) - \Pr(\mathsf{out}_1)| + |\Pr(\mathsf{out}_1) - \Pr(\mathsf{out}_3)| + \Pr(\mathsf{out}_3)$$
$$\leqslant \varepsilon_{\mathsf{Prf}}(k) + (q_{\mathsf{Usc}} + q_{\mathsf{N}} + 1)/|\mathbf{K}| + \varepsilon_{\mathcal{S}}(k) + \varepsilon_{\mathcal{K}}(k) + 2\varepsilon_{\mathsf{H}}(k).$$

$\square$

5   Comparison with Previous Constructions

As far as we are aware, only Chiba *et al.* [10] propose generic constructions of insider secure signcryption schemes (in the dynamic multi-user model) in the standard model. They propose two generic designs, we refer to by CMSM1 [10, Sect. 4.1] and CMSM2 [10, Sect. 4.2]. Both constructions use as building blocks:

– an IND-CCA–secure symmetric encryption scheme (only semantic security is required for CMSM2), and
– a sUF-CMA–secure signature scheme.

The construction CMSM1 uses also an IND-CCA–secure tag–based–KEM (a KEM which takes a tag as additional input for encapsulation/decapsulation).
The design CMSM2 uses as additional building blocks:

– an IND-CCA–secure KEM, and
– a one-to-one and sUF–OT secure MAC.

In comparison, in our design, we use as building blocks:

– a semantically secure symmetric encryption scheme,
– a sUF-CMA–secure signature scheme,
– an IND-CCA–secure KEM,
– a collision resistant hash function, and
– a secure pseudo-random function.

Although tag-based-KEMs can be built from any IND-CCA–secure public key encryption scheme [10], KEMs seem to be more common. For instance, cryptography standards, such as HPKE [6], use KEMs as building block, not tag-based-KEMs. And, any tag-based KEM can be transformed into a KEM, by using an empty tag. In this respect, compared to CMSM1, the SN scheme uses more common low level primitives.

The construction CMSM2 uses very common low level primitives. Unfortunately, to achieve strong unforgeability, there is a significant restriction on the MAC, which is required to be one-to-one, *i. e.* it is required that given a key τ and a message m, there is *one and only one* t such that $\mathsf{MAC}(\tau, m) = t$. This requirement excludes a large class of hash based MACs such as HMAC [16], UMAC [17], or KMAC [15]. The same restriction exists on the encryption scheme; this precludes the use a randomized encryption scheme, such as a bloc cipher with a mode of operation using a (pseudo-)random initialization vector, for instance. In comparison, in the SN construction, we require the signature scheme to be resistant against colliding signatures and the encryption scheme to be resistant against clustering key attacks. In many signatures, wherein the message to be signed is hashed first (the Full Domain Hash [14], for instance), colliding signatures yield a digest collision. The requirement is then naturally achieved in usual signature schemes. And, given the commonly required avalanche effect in substitution permutation network based encryption schemes (each cipher-text bit is changed with probability 1/2, when a single bit of the key is modified), one can reasonably expect common encryption schemes to be resistant against key clustering attacks. To instantiate the PFR, given the public parameter τ_0 and a secure block cipher, from the PFR–PRP switching lemma [9, p. 134], $\mathsf{Prf}(\tau, x)$ can be computed using the instructions:

500 $\mathsf{Prf}(\tau, x)$:
501 $x' \leftarrow \mathsf{H}(\tau_0, x); t \leftarrow \mathsf{E}(\tau, x');$ return t;

It appears that, compared to CMSM2, the SN scheme offers a wider range of choices for an instantiation of the low level primitives. This may be of prime importance in a constrained environment wherein only a limited number of low level primitives can be implemented.

Contrary to Tan's design [23] and the generic constructions from [2] and [19], the SN scheme does not require the registered key model; it then offers a superior security. Also, compared to the constructions from [20–22], SN does not use the random oracle model. Another security advantage of the SN scheme compared to these constructions is its generic nature; it can be instantiated with adequate present and future (including quantum-resistant) primitives.

From an efficiency perspective, the computational cost of the CMSM1, CMSM2, and SN schemes, comes mainly from the asymmetric operations (the cost of the symmetric operations is usually neglected): encapsulation and signature for signcryption, and decapsulation and signature verification, for unsigncryption. Given that any tag-based-KEM can be transformed (for free) into a KEM, for any instantiation of CMSM1 or CMSM2, there is an instantiation of SN that achieves the same efficiency for the asymmetric operations, if not better. For a comparison with direct constructions [20–23], SN can be instantiated with any signature scheme $\mathcal{S}$ and symmetric encryption scheme $\mathcal{E}$, and an appropriate KEM, PRF and hash function, provided $\mathcal{S}$ is strongly unforgeable and $\mathcal{S}$ is semantically secure and the KEM is IND-CCA–secure. Given that hash and PRF evaluations are negligible compared to signature and KEM operations, SN will yield a comparable efficiency.

The bit length of a CMSM1 signcrypted cipher-text corresponding to a message m is the bit length of m (assuming that the encryption scheme $\mathcal{E}$ is length preserving) added with that of a signature on m and that of a encapsulated key, i.e. $\mathsf{sz}(m) + \mathsf{sz}(\mathsf{Sign}(sk_{\mathsf{sd}}, m)) + \mathsf{sz}(\mathsf{Ecp}(sk_{\mathsf{sd}}, pk_{\mathsf{rcv}}))$, where sk_{sd} and pk_{rcv} are respectively the sender's private key and the receiver's public key. The CMSM2 and SN schemes add to this quantity the size of a MAC (a PRF based MAC in the case of SN). So, the SN and CMSM2 have the same communication overhead, which is slightly greater than that of CMSM1.

An interesting feature of the SN scheme, is that all the security reductions are tight, except for the unforgeability of non-repudiation evidence wherein we use a guessing strategy. A concrete instance of SN may be re-analyzed for unforgeability of non-repudiation evidence, if the underlying KEM is build upon a random self-reducible problem.

A   Proof of Lemma 1

Let $\mathcal{A}$ be an adversary playing Game 1. We build an adversary $\mathcal{B}$ against the collision (with identical prefix) resistance of H a follows.

1) $\mathcal{B}$ receives $\tau_0 \leftarrow_{\mathsf{R}} \mathbf{K}$ from its challenger and sends τ_0 to $\mathcal{A}$.
2) When $\mathcal{B}$ receives (p_0, m_0, s_0) from $\mathcal{A}$, it chooses $(\tau, \tau') \leftarrow_{\mathsf{R}} \mathbf{K}^2$ and computes $\tau_0'' \leftarrow \mathsf{Prf}(\tau', m_0)$, $\hat{m}_0 \leftarrow \mathsf{H}(\tau_0, (p_0, \tau, \tau', \tau'', s_0))$ and sends $\hat{m}_0$ to $\mathcal{A}$.

3) When $\mathcal{A}$ outputs (τ^*, τ'^*) such that $\hat{m}_0 = \hat{m}_0^* \leftarrow \mathsf{H}(\tau_0, (p_0, \tau^*, \tau'^*, \tau''^*, s_0))$ wherein $\tau''^* \leftarrow \mathsf{Prf}(\tau'^*, m_0)$, if $(\tau, \tau') \neq (\tau^*, \tau'^*)$ then $\mathcal{B}$ outputs (s, s') wherein $s = (p_0, \tau, \tau', \tau'', s_0)$ and $s' = (p_0, \tau^*, \tau'^*, \tau''^*, s_0)$ as messages with identical prefix p_0 and colliding hashes under τ_0.

Let bad be the event: the chosen pair (τ, τ') is such that for all $(\bar{\tau}, \bar{\tau}') \neq (\tau, \tau')$, $\hat{m}_0 \neq \mathsf{H}(\tau_0, (p_0, \bar{\tau}, \bar{\tau}', \bar{\tau}'', s_0))$, i. e. there is no other pair $(\bar{\tau}, \bar{\tau}') \in \mathbf{K}^2$ such that $\mathsf{H}(\tau_0, (p_0, \bar{\tau}, \bar{\tau}', \bar{\tau}'', s_0)) = \mathsf{H}(\tau_0, (p_0, \tau, \tau', \tau'', s_0))$. It holds that

$$\Pr(\mathsf{bad}) \leqslant |\mathbf{T}|/|\mathbf{K}|^2.$$

If $\mathsf{Succ}_{\mathcal{A},\mathsf{H}}$ denotes the event $\mathcal{A}$ succeeds in Game 1,

$$\begin{aligned}\Pr(\mathsf{Succ}_{\mathcal{A},\mathsf{H}}) &= \Pr(\mathsf{Succ}_{\mathcal{A},\mathsf{H}} \wedge \mathsf{bad}) + \Pr(\mathsf{Succ}_{\mathcal{A},\mathsf{H}} \wedge \neg\mathsf{bad}) \\ &\leqslant \Pr(\mathsf{bad}) + \Pr(\mathsf{Succ}_{\mathcal{A},\mathsf{H}} \wedge \neg\mathsf{bad}).\end{aligned}$$

Now let Eq be the event $(\tau, \tau') = (\tau^*, \tau'^*)$.

$$\Pr(\mathsf{Succ}_{\mathcal{A},\mathsf{H}} \wedge \neg\mathsf{bad}) = \Pr(\mathsf{Succ}_{\mathcal{A},\mathsf{H}} \wedge \neg\mathsf{bad} \wedge \mathsf{Eq}) + \Pr(\mathsf{Succ}_{\mathcal{A},\mathsf{H}} \wedge \neg\mathsf{bad} \wedge \neg\mathsf{Eq}).$$

Now, as if $\mathsf{Succ}_{\mathcal{A},\mathsf{H}} \wedge \neg\mathsf{bad}$ occurs, there at least one $(\tau^*, \tau'^*) \neq (\tau, \tau')$ such that $\hat{m}_0 = \hat{m}_0^* \leftarrow \mathsf{H}(\tau_0, (p_0, \tau^*, \tau'^*, \tau''^*, s_0))$, and $\mathcal{A}$ has no information about (τ, τ') besides $\hat{m}_0$, it holds that

$$\Pr(\mathsf{Succ}_{\mathcal{A},\mathsf{H}} \wedge \neg\mathsf{bad} \wedge \mathsf{Eq}) \leqslant \Pr(\mathsf{Succ}_{\mathcal{A},\mathsf{H}} \wedge \neg\mathsf{bad} \wedge \neg\mathsf{Eq}).$$

Hence

$$\Pr(\mathsf{Succ}_{\mathcal{A},\mathsf{H}}) \leqslant |\mathbf{T}|/|\mathbf{K}|^2 + 2\Pr(\mathsf{Succ}_{\mathcal{A},\mathsf{H}} \wedge \neg\mathsf{bad} \wedge \neg\mathsf{Eq}).$$

And, whenever $\mathsf{Succ}_{\mathcal{A},\mathsf{H}} \wedge \neg\mathsf{bad} \wedge \neg\mathsf{Eq}$ occurs $\mathcal{B}$ outputs s, s' with identical prefix such that $\mathsf{H}(\tau_0, s) = \mathsf{H}(\tau_0, s')$. □

References

1. An, J.H., Rabin, T.: Security for signcryption: the two-user model. In: Dent, A., Zheng, Y. (eds.) Practical Signcryption, pp. 21–42. Springer, Heidelberg (2010). https://doi.org/10.1007/978-3-540-89411-7_2
2. Arriaga, A., Barbosa, M., Farshim, P.: On the joint security of signature and encryption schemes under randomness reuse: efficiency and security amplification. In: Bao, F., Samarati, P., Zhou, J. (eds.) ACNS 2012. LNCS, vol. 7341, pp. 206–223. Springer, Heidelberg (2012). https://doi.org/10.1007/978-3-642-31284-7_13
3. Badertscher, C., Banfi, F., Maurer, U.: A constructive perspective on signcryption security. In: Catalano, D., De Prisco, R. (eds.) SCN 2018. LNCS, vol. 11035, pp. 102–120. Springer, Cham (2018). https://doi.org/10.1007/978-3-319-98113-0_6
4. Baek, J., Steinfeld, R.: Security for signcryption: the multi-user model. In: Dent, A., Zheng, Y. (eds.) Practical Signcryption, pp. 43–53. Springer, Heidelberg (2010). https://doi.org/10.1007/978-3-540-89411-7_3
5. Baek, J., Steinfeld, R., Zheng, Y.: Formal proofs for the security of signcryption. J. Cryptol. **20**(2), 203–235 (2007)

6. Barnes, R., Bhargavan, K., Lipp, B., Wood, C.: RFC 9180: Hybrid public key encryption (2022)
7. Bao, F., Deng, R.H.: A signcryption scheme with signature directly verifiable by public key. In: Imai, H., Zheng, Y. (eds.) PKC 1998. LNCS, vol. 1431, pp. 55–59. Springer, Heidelberg (1998). https://doi.org/10.1007/BFb0054014
8. Bjørstad, T.E., Dent, A.W.: Building better signcryption schemes with tag-KEMs. In: Yung, M., Dodis, Y., Kiayias, A., Malkin, T. (eds.) PKC 2006. LNCS, vol. 3958, pp. 491–507. Springer, Heidelberg (2006). https://doi.org/10.1007/11745853_32
9. Boneh, D., Shoup, V.: A graduate course in applied cryptography. Draft 0.6 (2023). https://toc.cryptobook.us/
10. Chiba, D., Matsuda, T., Schuldt, J.C.N., Matsuura, K.: Efficient generic constructions of signcryption with insider security in the multi-user setting. In: Lopez, J., Tsudik, G. (eds.) ACNS 2011. LNCS, vol. 6715, pp. 220–237. Springer, Heidelberg (2011). https://doi.org/10.1007/978-3-642-21554-4_13
11. Ducklin, P.: Serious security: google finds fake but trusted SSL certificates for its domains, made in France. Naked Security-Award-Winning Computer Security, News, Opinion, Advice and Research from SOPHOS, pp. 09–12 (2013)
12. Fan, J., Zheng, Y., Tang, X.: Signcryption with non-interactive non-repudiation without random oracles. In: Gavrilova, M.L., Tan, C.J.K., Moreno, E.D. (eds.) Transactions on Computational Science X. LNCS, vol. 6340, pp. 202–230. Springer, Heidelberg (2010). https://doi.org/10.1007/978-3-642-17499-5_9
13. Fisher, D.: Final Report on DigiNotar Hack Shows Total Compromise of CA Servers. Threatpost, 10/31/12. https://threatpost.com/final-report-diginotar-hack-shows-total-compromise-ca-servers-103112/77170/
14. Kakvi, S.A., Kiltz, E.: Optimal security proofs for full domain hash, revisited. In: Pointcheval, D., Johansson, T. (eds.) EUROCRYPT 2012. LNCS, vol. 7237, pp. 537–553. Springer, Heidelberg (2012). https://doi.org/10.1007/978-3-642-29011-4_32
15. Kelsey, J., Chang, S.J., Perlner, R.: SHA-3 derived functions: cSHAKE, KMAC, TupleHash, and ParallelHash. NIST Special Publication, vol. 800, p. 185 (2016)
16. Krawczyk, H., Bellare, M., Canetti, R.: RFC2104: HMAC: Keyed-hashing for message authentication (1997)
17. Krovetz, T. (Ed.): RFC 4418: UMAC: Message Authentication Code using Universal Hashing (2006)
18. Malone-Lee, J.: Signcryption with non-interactive non-repudiation. Des. Codes Cryptogr. 37(1), 81–109 (2005)
19. Matsuda, T., Matsuura, K., Schuldt, J.C.N.: Efficient constructions of signcryption schemes and signcryption composability. In: Roy, B., Sendrier, N. (eds.) INDOCRYPT 2009. LNCS, vol. 5922, pp. 321–342. Springer, Heidelberg (2009). https://doi.org/10.1007/978-3-642-10628-6_22
20. Ngarenon, T., Sarr, A.P.: A Computational Diffie-Hellman based Insider Secure Signcryption with Non Interactive Non Repudiation (full version) (2022). https://hal.science/hal-03628351/document
21. Ngarenon, T., Sarr, A.P.: A computational Diffie-Hellman based insider secure signcryption with non-interactive non-repudiation. In: Rushi Kumar, B., Ponnusamy, S., Giri, D., Thuraisingham, B., Clifton, C.W., Carminati, B. (eds.) ICMC 2022. Springer Proceedings in Mathematics & Statistics, vol. 415. Springer, Cham (2023). https://doi.org/10.1007/978-981-19-9307-7_8
22. Sarr, A.P., Seye, P.B., Ngarenon, T.: A practical and insider secure signcryption with non-interactive non-repudiation. In: Carlet, C., Guilley, S., Nitaj, A., Souidi, E.M. (eds.) C2SI 2019. LNCS, vol. 11445, pp. 409–429. Springer, Cham (2019). https://doi.org/10.1007/978-3-030-16458-4_24

23. Tan, C.H.: Signcryption scheme in multi-user setting without random oracles. In: Matsuura, K., Fujisaki, E. (eds.) IWSEC 2008. LNCS, vol. 5312, pp. 64–82. Springer, Heidelberg (2008). https://doi.org/10.1007/978-3-540-89598-5_5

24. Zheng, Y.: Digital signcryption or how to achieve cost(signature & encryption) ≪ cost(signature) + cost(encryption). In: Kaliski, B.S. (ed.) CRYPTO 1997. LNCS, vol. 1294, pp. 165–179. Springer, Heidelberg (1997). https://doi.org/10.1007/BFb0052234

High-Order Collision Attack Vulnerabilities in Montgomery Ladder Implementations of RSA

Arnaud Varillon$^{(\boxtimes)}$ (ID), Laurent Sauvage, and Jean-Luc Danger

LTCI, Telecom Paris, Institut Polytechnique de Paris, 19, place Marguerite Perey, CS 20031, 91123 Palaiseau Cedex, France
{arnaud.varillon,laurent.sauvage,jean-luc.danger}@telecom-paris.fr

Abstract. This paper describes a straightforward methodology which allows mounting a specific kind of single-trace attacks called collision attacks. We first introduce the methodology (which operates at the algorithmic level) and then provide empirical evidence of its soundness by locating the points of interest involved in all existing collisions and then attacking an unmasked RSA implementation whose modular exponentiation is based on the Montgomery Ladder. The attacks we performed, albeit slightly worse than the theoretical prediction, are very encouraging nonetheless: the whole secret exponent can be retrieved (i.e., a success rate equal to 100%) using only 10 traces. Lastly, we describe how this could allow for the introduction of high-order attacks, which are known to break some protected implementations of symmetric cryptography, in the context of asymmetric cryptography.

Keywords: Side-Channel · Electromagnetic · Montgomery Ladder · RSA · Leakage Assessment · Collision Attack

1 Introduction

The RSA Cryptosystem. RSA [25] is one of the ubiquitous cryptosystems powering many common operations ranging from banking to authentication in computer systems. It leverages the factorization problem to encrypt/decrypt a message m (the input) using, like in any asymmetric cryptosystem, a pair of keys (the public one (n, e), and the private one, (d, p, q)) in a modular exponentiation. For instance, for the decryption of a ciphertext g, the formula is:

$$m = g^d \mod n$$

Side-Channel Attacks and RSA. Among the many threats targeting the cryptographic libraries used for these purposes, side-channel attacks make for a lesser-known to the public, yet especially acute concern. This kind of crypt-analytic attacks exploits oversights in the implementation of a cryptographic algorithm as well as side effects of the execution of the latter. In techniques like the one we propose, this is usually done using a divide-and-conquer app-roach which greatly reduces the number of computations required to recover the private key.

Asymmetric cryptography is a prime target of these attacks. More specifically, RSA has been extensively studied in the side-channel context (e.g. [7,23]). Over the years, two main trends have emerged: (cache-)timing attacks (e.g. [1]) and horizontal attacks (e.g. [29]). Nonetheless, with the advent of (noise-resistant and deep) neural networks in the field, profiling (i.e., vertical) attacks are on the rise (e.g. [7,24]), and are likely to become the most prominent side-channel threat for asymmetric cryptography.

Related Works. Several algorithms exist which can compute the modular exponentiation [15,17] in RSA. Among these, the Montgomery Ladder [19] (Algo-rithm 1) has been brought to the side-channel realm [16] by Joye et al. as a safer alternative to some of the then well-known techniques such as Square & Multiply and Square & Multiply Always. In their paper, they emphasize on its regularity which, they claim, makes it resistant to horizontal attacks (related to Simple Power Attacks (SPAs)) provided that the uses of its two registers (i.e., variables, in this context) are indistinguishable from one another.

The most notorious (by number of citations) vulnerability of the Montgomery Ladder is the unsupervised vertical exploitation of some leakage of the secret exponent bit being processed in the conditional swapping of operands [13,21,22, 24]. However, since the first side-channel attack on RSA [23], the most popular countermeasures for this cryptosystem [3,9,10,23] (e.g., blinding) mainly pre-vent vertical attacks. As a consequence, in recent years, attacks using a single trace, such as horizontal collision attacks [7,8,14,29,31], have become a major concern for RSA: now that vertical leakage is much more difficult to reveal and subsequently exploit, the best attacks against state-of-the-art countermeasures (and probably those to come as well) are increasingly likely to be horizontal and to require a single trace. This has shifted the focus of research works to horizon-tal countermeasures to complement the vertical ones, like blinding, which are now deemed insufficient: Most papers in the field advocate for their combined use in secure implementations. The interested reader may skip to Sect. 2 where we expand on the literature related to one kind of such attacks for the Mont-gomery Ladder before discussing throughout the rest of the paper the extent to which high-order variants of the main contribution of this paper could defeat horizontal countermeasures.

Goal of This Paper. This paper introduces a methodology for the detection of (high-order) collision attack vulnerabilities in the Montgomery Ladder which, to the best of our knowledge, is different from the state of the art. It aims to extend the mix of collision identification (1) and POI selection (2) suggested by Carbone et al. [7] by introducing a systematic procedure for (1) and making (2) more general.[1] In particular, unlike many attacks from the literature on this topic, our technique does not require chosen inputs. All this should provide for a more accurate evaluation, in later papers, of the security of other modular exponentiation techniques and other cryptosystems (for instance, elliptic curve cryptography) in the context of recent first-order (e.g. [7,8]) or future high-order horizontal collision attacks.

This contribution is structured as follows: in Sect. 2, we present these attacks and show, in Sect. 3, that the Montgomery Ladder is, in theory, vulnerable to them using our methodology. Then, in Sect. 4, we assess the validity of this approach in practice on real traces by locating the POIs involved in the existing collisions and then mounting the corresponding first-order attacks. Lastly, in Sect. 5, we briefly review the consequences of this work for the security of RSA in the side channel context and provide a few perspectives for future research works.

2 Related Works

Introducing Collisions into the Side-Channel Context. Although cryptographic devices constantly leak (possibly sensitive) data through physical means as they function, the true extent of this leakage at critical timestamps is seldom (if ever) evaluated accurately because of modeling issues [6]. Existing leakage models seek to explain the variability observed in the acquired traces (each of which comprises samples obtained during a single execution of the cryptographic code) by describing in mathematical terms the behavior of the hardware of the target with respect to the data being processed. For attacks which are based on physical properties of this hardware, such as Differential Power Attacks (DPAs) which rely on the toggling count of registers, this approach appears to be sound. However, this makes the models device-specific which, in turn, lessens the performance of the leakage assessment: in a black-box setting, the hardware of a given target can be very challenging to analyze, and technological dispersion implies that a model which has been tuned for a device may not be valid for another device from the same batch.

Collisions, which are defined at the algorithmic rather than hardware level, do not suffer from this defect. They correspond to the reuse of intermediate values during a cryptographic operation in several computations [20]. Whenever this reuse depends on some (small enough) part of the secret, there is a vulnerability which can lead to a side-channel attack.[2] The presence of such a collision

---

[1] Their leakage assessment works for their specific target only.

[2] As it turns out, symmetric and asymmetric cryptography behave differently in this respect. In the symmetric case, the confusion introduced by the likes of S-Boxes makes collisions probabilistic. In the RSA case, collisions happen with probability equal to either 0 or 1, meaning that the value of the part of the secret being processed directly determines whether there is a collision. Theoretically, a single execution of the modular exponentiation is therefore enough to recover the whole exponent.

is evaluated assuming that the processing of equal values leads to equal leakage. Each point of interest (POI—i.e., sample statistically related to some sensitive variable) in the observed leakage is interpreted relatively to another one, rather than individually like in a DPA for instance. Therefore, detecting collisions does not require the knowledge of the exact leakage model of the device: it is assumed to be the same for all samples, so a proxy like a numerical model of the computations is enough. Such an approximation retains all the information which is relevant for the comparisons. In fact, as we demonstrate, it is not even required to know the values being handled by the hardware: thanks to the physics of the latter, it is possible to evaluate whether two values are equal by comparing the corresponding leakages as measured using the oscilloscope. This does not involve any kind of estimation of the contents of the hardware registers.

RSA and Side-Channel Collision Attacks. Regarding RSA, **when a collision exists for a given bit value only and not the other, it is possible to retrieve the latter from the detection of the collision**: this is the working principle of the collision attacks considered in this paper. Because, regarding RSA, the existence of collisions is linked to the value of the secret exponent only, **such attacks are naturally immune to message and modulus blinding** when it is performed once and for all at the beginning of the computation (as is usually done) and, for those which require only one trace, to exponent blinding as well. So far, various such attacks [2,7,8,12,14,29–31] have been suggested in the literature, yet apart from [2,12,30,31] and from [14] with a few modifications, these do not apply to the Montgomery Ladder and, apart from [7], appear to struggle in the presence of noise in the traces.

Indeed, the Big Mac attack from [29] tries to match one of the two operands of the multiplication in each iteration of the sliding window with one of the precomputed powers of the message using the Euclidean distance. Since no such lookup table exists for the Montgomery Ladder, this attack does not apply to it. The Horizontal Correlation Analysis from [8] aims to determine whether the conditional multiplication in the Square & Multiply algorithm is performed. To do so, the authors recommend correlating trace segments corresponding to the processing of digits of the operands with the Hamming weights of those of the input message.[3] This collision attack is specific to this algorithm and cannot be extended to the Montgomery Ladder if only because it is regular. Lastly, the collision attack mounted in [7] works against the Square & Multiply Always algorithm only. It seeks to find out whether the result of the multiplication has been discarded by comparing a common input between this operation, which has been carried out for a given exponent bit, and the squaring associated with the following one. Since the Montgomery Ladder is truly regular [16] (its does not use dummy computations) this work does not apply to it as well.

Regarding the attacks which do apply to the Montgomery Ladder, the technique from [31] requires, as a doubling attack, two traces much like the original

---

[3] Other internal variables have been suggested as well, yet in the end, it all boils down to finding whether the input message is involved in certain operations.

one [11]. Although the vulnerability they rely on is somewhat similar to one of those we introduce, it does not allow for a single-trace attack and is, as a consequence, thwarted by blinding. The comparative (power) analysis pioneered by Homma et al. in [14] uses even more traces since a pair of inputs must be crafted for every exponent bit which is to be guessed.[4] The Online Template Attack (OTA) from [2], which improves on this constraint by building templates *after* acquiring the trace to attack, still suffers from this 'defect', although to a lesser extent.[5] The approach proposed in [30], which consists in computing the correlation between sets of aggregates covering complete modular operations (one aggregate per operation) which are gathered over multiple traces, requires many traces as well.[6] Last, the attack from [12] does not work well in a single trace on the Montgomery Ladder, especially if one uses the Pearson correlation coefficient as we do here. It involves computing a mean profile over all the operations in a given trace which is then subtracted to each of them to reduce the prevalence of noise. Then, an elaborate POI selection is performed to allow for the detection of collision by comparing the extracted sub-traces which are made up of many samples. Last, the authors added an error correction step to make for potential mistakes made in the latter. Thus, this could arguably be described as the most complex collision attack in the literature.[7] Yet, the probability to accurately recover the secret is still strictly less than 1 (0.926 in the best case). All in all, these attacks do not attain the best performance predicted by the theory which remains stubbornly out of reach to this day. One should also note that the various distinguishers coming from classical pattern matching which are used in these papers for the detection of collisions (Euclidean distance, Pearson corre-

---

[4] Although it is not mentioned in the paper, their technique can be extended to the Montgomery Ladder using their forward estimation method. This amounts to comparing, for a pair chosen according to the guideline they provide, the squaring done in the first iteration which processes the input message (the corresponding bit is equal to 1) and the one carried out for the bit which is currently unknown. Like in the paper, the estimation of a given exponent bit requires that all the preceding ones be known, therefore an error on index j affects all the following indices.

[5] However, we acknowledge that, unlike the OTA, our methodology is not portable. In fact, in collision attacks (to which OTA belongs to some extent) at least, there seems to exist a balance to find between portability and the cost of profiling. The authors of [2] appear to have chosen to prioritize portability by making the template building phase "online". Therefore, each attack requires a profiling phase. We have decided to proceed differently. Our attack is not portable, but on the plus side, profiling needs be done only once. Consequently, the more keys an attacker targets for a given pair (board, software), the better our methodology gets in respect to OTA which requires one template per scalar bit every time.

[6] The authors report using 5000 traces yet do not provide any success rate.

[7] For instance, we claim that our contribution, which comprises only two steps and does not require any error correction, is somewhat simpler. Moreover, in addition to the vulnerability mentioned there, we describe another one which happens in the processing of a single bit.

lation coefficient) are intrinsically sensitive to noise, and thus perform poorly when applied to patterns spanning complete group operations (e.g.: squaring).[8]

The selection of points suggested by Carbone et al. in [7] as an input step to their attack reduces significantly the impact of noise on its success rate since the samples used by the distinguisher all hold a high enough (thanks to the tuning performed for the POIs selection criteria) level of information about the target variable. This preprocessing of the traces, which is very common in other sub-branches, was non-existent in the realm of collision attacks on asymmetric cryptography which favored other approaches akin to windowing. However, like in all the other papers we mentioned, Carbone et al. focus on a specific variable or operation and as a consequence miss other existing collision attack vulnerabilities which could be used in the same way (in first-order attacks) or in higher-order settings targeting several variables at the same time as is commonplace for symmetric cryptography.

The Montgomery Ladder. The original algorithm used for the modular exponentiation in RSA is Square & Multiply [17]. Its main flaw is the fact that the multiplication is performed only when the current bit of d is equal to 1. The Square & Multiply Always variant [9] attempts to fix this vulnerability by computing the multiplication regardless of the value of the current exponent bit and throwing the result away when required. This makes the modular exponentiation regular since the same operations are carried out irrespective of the value of this bit. However, in both cases, the conditional use of the result from multiplication makes the modular exponentiation insecure. The main concern is a conditional collision which happens between the inputs of the multiplication done for the bit d_j of the exponent, and those of the squaring computed for the following one d_{j-1}.

From a more formal perspective, given $d = \sum_{i=0}^{i=T-1} d_i \cdot 2^i$, the result of the classical left-to-right modular exponentiation is:

$$g^d = ((\ldots (g^{d_{T-1}})^2 \cdot g^{d_{T-2}} \ldots)^2 \cdot g^{d_0})$$

In this equation, one can notice that the squaring is always performed whereas the multiplication can be omitted when the exponent bit is 0 since $g^0 = 1$. Let $D^{(j)} = \sum_{i=j}^{T-1} d_i 2^i$, then[9] the value computed at the end of the $(T-j)$-th iteration is either $g^{2D^{(j+1)}}$ if d_j is equal to 0, or $g^{2D^{(j+1)}+1} = g^{D^{(j+1)}} \cdot g^{D^{(j+1)}+1}$ if it is equal to 1. The latter computation uses all possible results from d_{j+1} (without and with a multiplication). It is therefore possible to make the Square & Multiply algorithm regular without using dummy operations by performing the multiplication irrespective of d_j, and using two variables which hold, in turns, these two results based on its value. This rewrite of the exponentiation makes

---

[8] This is especially so for the STM32F407 board, which we used for this paper, which is arguably noisier than other platforms commonly targeted such as ChipWhisperer.
[9] This sum is assumed to be equal to zero when it is empty.

every operation contribute towards the result, and could be used as a solution to the aforementioned shortcoming.

The Montgomery Ladder [16] is built upon this observation.[10] In their paper, Joye et al. proposed an implementation of this trick by means of two variables, R_0 and R_1. R_0 holds the result of the correct computation given d_j, and R_1, the other one.[11] Furthermore, they provided the corresponding algorithm for which we recall the pseudocode (Algorithm 1).

3   Our Collision Attack Vulnerability Analysis of the Montgomery Ladder

Considering the small survey we propose (Sect. 2), we argue that the existing literature (symmetric and asymmetric) does not feature any formal definition for collisions in general, and as far as RSA and this paper are concerned, in high-order settings. To remedy this, we start with a generic yet familiar definition (collisions on values) which we gradually tailor to RSA (collisions on variables involving at least two operations).

Definition 1 (Collisions). *Let Γ denote the set of operations which make up a cryptographic computation. A collision on a value v is defined as the use (as an operand—read—or the result—write) of v in several operations $\gamma_1, \ldots \gamma_r$, $(\gamma_1, \ldots, \gamma_r) \in \Gamma^r$.*

In RSA, the structure of the modular exponentiation implies that v is linked to a single variable V. The collisions on values which are exploited in the literature we reviewed [7,8,14,29,31] can therefore be lifted to the algorithmic level as follows. From now on, the word 'collision' is used as a shorthand for 'collision in RSA'.

Definition 2 (Collisions in RSA). *Let Γ_m and V_m respectively denote the set of operations and the set of variables in the modular exponentiation which processes the secret exponent $d = (d_{T-1} \ldots d_0)_2$ bit by bit. A collision on a variable $V \in V_m$ is defined as the use of V in two distinct operations γ_s and $\gamma_t, (\gamma_s, \gamma_t) \in (\Gamma_m)^2$ coming from the processing of two exponents bits d_i and d_j ($i \leq j$), without being overwritten in the meantime. Furthermore, a collision becomes an attack vulnerability when the collision exists for one possible value of d_j, but not for the other one $\neg d_j$.*

The condition upon which a collision becomes an attack vulnerability comes from the fact that V is always used in γ_s, but in γ_t as well for one of the two possible values for d_j only. As a consequence, detecting the reuse of V in γ_t allows for the estimation of d_j. For this reason, we suggest calling γ_s the source of the collision, and γ_t, its target. In the rest of this paper, we may, to refer to Definition 2, then

---

[10] Our mathematical derivation is a reformulation of the one available in the original paper.

[11] Therefore, at the beginning of each iteration of the loop, the following is always true: $R_1 = g \cdot R_0$.

synonymously say that the collision happens on V, or between γ_s and γ_t. Now, if more than two operations take part in a collision (as defined in Definition 1), then, according to the state of the art, there are as many vulnerabilities as conditional reuses of V: each entity involved in a collision comes from a single operation. This implies that high-order collision attack vulnerabilities, in which **a combination of multiple variables coming from a set of operations is reused in another set of operations**, cannot exist. Thus, we propose the following extension which is more suitable for such vulnerabilities.

Definition 3 (High-order Collisions in RSA). *Let Γ_m and V_m respectively denote the set of operations and the set of variables used in the modular exponentiation. A high-order collision on a variable V is a collision in which V can be described as a linear combination $f : \prod_{i=1}^{l} K_i \to \mathbb{Z}_n$ of multiple components (i.e., other variables) coming from different operations $(\gamma_1, \ldots \gamma_l) \in (\Gamma_m)^l$:*

$$V = f(V_1, \ldots, V_l)$$

where $(V_1, \ldots, V_l) \in (V_m)^l$, and the $(K_i)_{1 \leq i \leq l}$ are the spaces of the $(V_i)_{1 \leq i \leq l}$. Like a collision, it may become an attack vulnerability.

In this definition, unlike in the first-order case, **the collision may exist at the algorithmic level only**. Indeed, at this level, in the first-order case, the operands of each operation each correspond to a single variable (e.g.: g in the Montgomery Ladder), whereas in the high-order case, these operands may each be the image of a function f which combines other variables originating from computations which may not be part of the modular exponentiation (e.g.: $r_0 \cdot g$ in the Montgomery Ladder, where r_0 is a random integer, and the multiplication is performed before the Montgomery Ladder). In fact the $(\gamma_i)_{1 \leq i \leq l}$ may include γ_s and γ_t (the original variables are blinded during the modular exponentiation), be computed as part of each of those two operations (idem), or be unrelated to them (the original variables are blinded outside the modular exponentiation). For instance, if a horizontal 'randomization' (i.e. blinding-like)[12] countermeasure such as [10] were to be implemented alongside the Montgomery Ladder, the values used in γ_s and γ_t would not be equal even though Definition 2 applies to V: its original contents would frequently be randomized. Nevertheless, provided that the attacker is able to combine leakages owing to the various variables being input to the function f which gives rise to those values, such collision vulnerabilities would break this protected implementation. Using this framework, we may now, in the following theorems, propose a collision analysis for the Montgomery Ladder which is both more thorough than in the previous literature and exhaustive by considering all variables rather than a single one. To help the reader better understand the collisions we study, we use a specific nomenclature (Table 1) every time we refer to them.

---

[12] Countermeasures which shuffle the order of the operations do not remove the first-order vulnerabilities since the collisions still exist. An attacker who is able to detect γ_s and γ_t irrespective of their position in the trace may proceed as previously described. As such, these are not taken into consideration here.

Table 1. Taxonomy of collisions (T: bit-length of d).

Bits involved in the collision	Name
$d_j, j \in [\![0, T-1]\!]$	d_j collisions
$d_{j:j-1}, j \in [\![0, T-1]\!]$	$d_j\text{-}d_{j-1}$ collisions
$(d_i, d_k), (i,k) \in [\![0, T-1]\!]^2$	$d_i\text{-}d_k$ collisions

3.1 d_j Collisions

To illustrate the previous definitions using a familiar setting, let us first apply them to the Montgomery Ladder by considering *the values* held by the variables, as is usual in the existing literature, rather than the variables themselves. The question we will therefore answer in the next few paragraphs is the following: which values could possibly be involved in a collision during one iteration of the loop from the Montgomery ladder? We know (Algorithm 1) that the latter uses two variables: $V_m = \{R_0, R_1\}$. Moreover, the same two operations are performed (Fig. 1, vertical dashed blue line in the middle), irrespective of the value of the exponent bit d_j being processed: $\Gamma_m = \{\text{Multiply}, \text{Square}\}$.

To compute the contents of these variables at any time, it is enough to notice that, at the beginning of every iteration of the loop (line 2, Algorithm 1), the following relation is true [16]: $R_1 = g \cdot R_0$. Let g^x denote the content of R_0 at the beginning of the iteration associated with an exponent bit $d_j, j \in [\![0, T-1]\!]$, then R_1 holds the value g^{x+1} (Fig. 1—green part, initial values in 2nd and 3rd lines of both upper and lower halves). When $d_j = 0$ (upper half), R_1 gets the result of the multiplication and R_0, that of the squaring. Hence, the value $g^x \cdot g^{x+1} = g^{2x+1}$ is assigned to R_1 ('$\rightarrow R_1$', 1st line in the upper part, multiplication), and the value $(g^x)^2 = g^{2x}$, to R_0 ('$\rightarrow R_0$', 1st line in the upper part, squaring).

Now that we have computed the contents of both variables with respect to d_j, how can we spot first, existing collisions, and then, those which are attack vulnerabilities? The selection criterion to apply to the contents of R_0 and R_1 is the following (Definition 2): which values are used in the two operations? Only g^x, g^{x+1} and g^{2x+1} meet this rule. Yet, among these candidates, which ones are used in the squaring for one value of d_j only? As we show in the following lines, the answer is: g^x and g^{x+1}. Indeed, g^x is read as an input to, first, the multiplication ('yes' entry in the 4th line, multiplication) and then, the squaring (idem, squaring). Since the variable holding that value, R_0, is not used to store the result of the multiplication, it is not overwritten ('no' entry in the 4th line, multiplication) between those two points in the execution. This matches Definition 2, where $V = R_0$ and $(\gamma_s, \gamma_t) = (\text{Multiply}, \text{Square})$, so this is a collision (solid burgundy arrow in the upper half). The same logic indicates that g^{x+1} takes in part in a collision as well (solid yellow arrow in the lower half). However, this alone is not a threat: the corresponding vulnerability exists only if there is no collision on g^x for the other possible value for d_j (Definition 2). One may then notice that when $d_j = 1$ (lower half), the values g^{2x+1} and g^{2x+2} are assigned to, respectively, R_0 and R_1.[13] Interestingly, this implies that g^x is no longer used as an input to the squaring (dashed burgundy arrow in the lower half). Therefore, the collision does not exist anymore, and there is, in fact, a collision attack vulnerability (Definition 2). The same kind of logic applies to g^{x+1} which is involved in a collision attack vulnerability as well (dashed yellow arrow in the upper half). Overall, one can follow two attack paths to estimate the value of d_j. In particular, one could try to combine them to mount a 'high-order' attack.

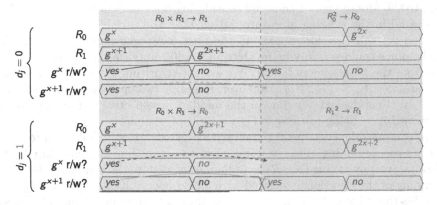

Fig. 1. Evolution and expected activity for the contents of R_0 and R_1 in the Montgomery Ladder for an exponent bit $d_j, j \in [\![0, T - 1]\!]$. g^x is read in both operations when $d_j = 0$ ('yes' entries in the 'g^x r/w?' line + red arrow in the upper half), but only in the multiplication when $d_j = 1$ (no collision, idem + dashed red arrow in the lower half): this is a collision attack vulnerability on R_0 between the inputs of both operations. Lastly, g^x is never written. Likewise, the pair (g^{x+1}, R_1) follows a similar pattern: the roles of both halves are swapped, so R_1 takes part in a similar collision attack vulnerability. (Color figure online)

Since, in the matter of RSA, values are bijectively linked to variables (Definition 2), let us now extend our formal framework to the present matter. As will become apparent by the end of the present paper, this will allow for the precise identification of the root cause of all existing collision attack vulnerabilities in the Montgomery Ladder.[14] This will make their description simpler compared to the preceding considerations. Furthermore, this formalization will enable us

---

[13] Changes between the two possible values for d_j have been highlighted in purple.

[14] This could, in turn, render the usual 'randomization' countermeasures ineffective against high-order collision attacks. This latter point will be expanded on in a future paper. For the time being, only exponent blinding can prevent the attacks analyzed in this paper.

to show that there does not exist other collision attack vulnerabilities in the processing of a single exponent bit than the ones which we studied in the previous paragraphs.

Theorem 1 (d_j collisions). *In the Montgomery Ladder, within the processing of a single exponent bit, there exists only two collision attack vulnerabilities which happen between the inputs of the multiplication and those of the following squaring. Moreover, these vulnerabilities are equivalent: only the interpretation of the presence of a collision changes.*

Proof. To find out which vulnerabilities exist in a single iteration of the loop from the Montgomery Ladder, let us examine its pseudocode (Algorithm 1). A comparison of the two branches reveals that the variable used in the squaring is the one which has not been used to store the result of the multiplication. More formally, lines 4 and 6 of the listing can be summarized using the following relation which is parametrized by the exponent bit being processed:

$$R_{\neg d_j} \leftarrow R_0 R_1; R_{d_j} \leftarrow (R_{d_j})^2 \tag{1}$$

Since d_j can take only two values, 0 and 1, a symmetry exists between the operands specified for the two branches (Eq. (1)). This fact has three implications. Firstly, since $R_{\neg d_j}$ holds the result of the first operation whereas R_{d_j} is used in the second operation, R_{d_j} is read in both operations but is never overwritten in between which provides grounds for collisions between the input of the multiplication and that of the squaring (Definition 2). Secondly, the variable on which the collision happens changes with d_j, so there are two possible collisions corresponding to the two values which d_j can take. Lastly, another way to formulate this property is that, for a given variable (e.g., R_0), d_j conditions the presence of a collision. As a consequence (Definition 2), these collisions are, in fact, collision attack vulnerabilities.

Since the source and the target of these vulnerabilities are the same, only the interpretation of the presence of a collision changes with d_j. This entails that the vulnerabilities are equivalent. In addition, we considered all possible variables in this proof, so there cannot exist any other collision attack vulnerability in a single iteration of the loop.   □

All in all, the symmetry between the two branches is the root cause of the vulnerabilities **between the inputs of both operations** which we have just exposed. There is, unfortunately, no easy fix to it since it is part of the working principle of the Montgomery Ladder (Sect. 2). One may combine both leakages to improve the performance of the distinguisher when necessary. This would make for a 'simulated' high-order collision attack (Definition 3) whose variable does not actually exist. Lastly, the value associated with the leakage in the selected points of interest must be known to allow for the estimation of d_j: the presence of a collision is not linked to the same value of d_j for the two numerical models.

3.2 d_j-d_{j-1} Collisions

Now that we have looked for collision attack vulnerabilities regarding a single exponent bit $d_j, j \in [\![0, T - 1]\!]$, let us look at those happening between two consecutive exponent bits $d_{j:j-1}, j \in [\![0, T - 1]\!]$. Surprisingly, the same symmetry generates another kind of collision attack vulnerability between two adjacent exponent bits. Like in d_j collisions, R_{d_j} is not overwritten during the multiplication (Fig. 2). Consequently, it holds a result coming from the processing of the previous bit, d_{j+1}. The same logic as in the previous subsection can then be used to prove the existence of vulnerabilities, as we show in later paragraphs.

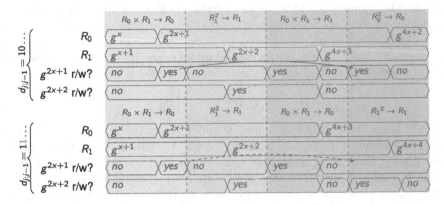

Fig. 2. Evolution and expected activity for the contents of R_0 and R_1 in the Montgomery Ladder for two consecutive exponent bits $d_{j:j-1} = 1 \ldots, j \in [\![1, T - 1]\!]$. Using the same technique as in Fig. 1, we highlight a collision attack vulnerability on R_0 ('g^{2x+1} r/w ?' lines) between the output of the 1st multiplication and input of the 2nd squaring. Likewise, R_1 takes part in a collision attack vulnerability between the output of the 1st squaring and the input of the 2nd squaring.

Although the vulnerabilities may seem identical to the one reported in [31], we emphasize on the fact that they are different for the targeted functions as well as the part of the latter which is used as a reference when detecting the presence of a collision (here, the output of the operations) are not the same. In particular, our work does not call for a comparison between traces acquired from chosen messages: a single trace from a randomly generated message is, in theory, enough.

Theorem 2 (d_j-d_{j-1} collisions). *In the Montgomery Ladder, within the processing of a two adjacent exponent bits, there exist two collision attack vulnerabilities whose sources are the outputs of, respectively, the multiplication and the squaring associated with the first bit. The target of these collisions is the same in both cases: it is the squaring performed for the second bit.*

Proof. Let us come back to the symmetry between the two branches (Algorithm 1). Its mathematical formulation (Eq. (1)) has two consequences. Firstly, it implies that when $d_{j-1} = \neg d_j$, the variable which holds the result of the multiplication done for d_j ($R_{\neg d_j}$) is reused in the squaring computed for d_{j-1}. Indeed, from the relation between d_j and d_{j-1}, the following is true:

$$R_{\neg d_j} = R_{d_{j-1}}$$

Secondly, it entails that when $d_j = d_{j-1}$, the variable which stores the output of the squaring carried out for d_j (R_{d_j}) is reused in the squaring associated with d_{j-1}. Of course, from the relation between d_j and d_{j-1}, the following is true:

$$R_{d_j} = R_{d_{j-1}}$$

As in Theorem 1, in both cases, the targeted variable is not overwritten between the two operations under consideration (Eq. (1)), therefore there exist two collisions between the processings of d_j and d_{j-1} (Definition 2). Furthermore, the previous paragraph highlights that fact that d_{j-1} conditions the presence of the latter so, these are collision attack vulnerabilities (Definition 2).   □

This theorem proves a property which, in hindsight, is rather simple. Like in the d_j case, **the target must be an input**.[15] Since we are now looking for collisions over two bits, **the source must now be a destination**.[16] The arrows in Fig. 2 thus correspond to all collisions satisfying these constraints. Contrary to the first kind of collision attack vulnerability, this one does not directly yield the value of the $(d_j)_{0 \leq j \leq T-1}$: it merely indicates the type of relation which links them. In practice, getting their values is only a matter of fixing the first one, d_{T-1}, deducing a possible value for the rest of the candidate exponent from this piece of information, and trying the latter out to determine whether this hypothesis is correct. However, unlike in the d_j case, here d_j must be known to estimate d_{j-1}: the values involved in a collision and the interpretation of its presence depend on it. This makes this attack path especially challenging (Footnote 4). Lastly, there cannot be any other collision attack vulnerability since after the processing of two adjacent bits, both R_0 and R_1 have been overwritten. In particular, bits which are further apart cannot take part in a collision, and there exists no d_i-d_k collision in the Montgomery Ladder.

4 Experimental Validation

4.1 Identification of POIs

Experimental Setup. Now that we have applied our methodology to the Montgomery Ladder to find existing collision attack vulnerabilities at the algorithmic level, we analyze a few experiments to assess its soundness in practice. For this purpose, we acquired EM traces by sampling the near field emissions of

---

[15] If it is a destination, then it has just changed. This runs counter to Definition 2.
[16] Same justification as before, since both R_0 and R_1 get overwritten in an iteration of the loop.

a STM32F407 microcontroller executing the FF_WWW_skpow function from the MIRACL library [27]: it implements the Montgomery Ladder and uses it in a CRT-RSA decryption. The board was running at its maximum speed: 168 MHz. Furthermore, in these experiments, we used a Langer Near Field RF Passive probe for ECB Emissions which we placed over a decoupling capacitor on the power line. We sampled these EM emissions at 5 GSa/s using an Agilent Infiniium DSO90404A oscilloscope which was connected to a computer over the network for the transfer of traces. Lastly, we paid attention to the experimental setting to minimize the amount of jitter in the traces. This allowed us to get perfect constant-time executions for the loop in the Montgomery Ladder, and therefore, traces (reasonably well)[17] aligned at the acquisition level by placing the corresponding trigger right before this piece of code. In particular, we emphasize on the fact that these traces have not undergone any kind of preprocessing before the analyses which we present.

Observing Collisions in Traces. To visualize the collisions we highlighted in Sect. 2, we used their fundamental assumption which we recall here to underline its importance: we assume that the handling of equal values leads to equal leakages. Observing collisions in practice is, therefore, tantamount to applying a statistical analysis to the traces to find where their associated values are manipulated by the hardware and to make the corresponding differences in amplitude visible. To this end, we used NICV [5] which is ideal for the detection of collisions[18] since, like collisions, it does not rely on the perfect knowledge of the hardware leakage model for the target. The formula for this metric is the following:

$$NICV = \frac{\text{Var}[\mathbb{E}[Y|X]]}{\text{Var}[Y]}$$

where X is the random variable representing the numerical model and Y, the one associated with the traces. In accordance with Sect. 2, here X can be any of the values g^z, with $z \in \{x, x+1, 2x, 2x+1, 2x+2\}$. The number of partitions required to compute the numerator of this fraction grows exponentially with the bit-length of X. Thus, in practice, at most only 8 bits (a byte) can be studied at a time. We performed the analyses on all bytes for each numerical model, but describe the results for the least significant one only. Lastly, to keep only the interesting pieces of information during the statistical analyses we are about to present, for each of these, we generated a fixed set of keys meeting some criteria related to the numerical model, and let the messages vary freely at random. This way, NICV is able to average out pretty well the variations which are not covered by the model.

To keep this discussion short enough for this paper, we show the results of the practical experiments for d_j-d_{j-1} collisions only. Nevertheless, we stress

---

[17] The span of a given instant in the executions covers about 3 samples which is less than a CPU cycle.

[18] During an attack, since the values for such models are unknown, NICV cannot be used. It can only be used during the profiling phase, not the exploitation phase.

that the figures, the reasoning involved in the interpretation of the results, and the conclusions are similar as far as d_j collisions are concerned: the phenomena reported in Sect. 2 can be made visible.

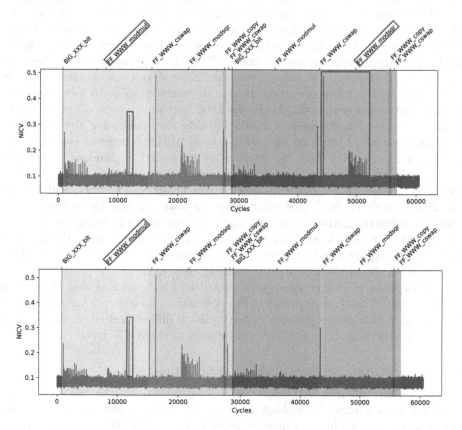

Fig. 3. NICV on $g[7:0]$ computed using 49152 traces (top: $d = (10\ldots)_2$, bottom: $d = (11\ldots)_2$). All activity linked to the collision attack vulnerability on R_0 (= g— Fig. 2, g^{2x+1} line) is visible (red rectangles): the source is located next to the 10,000 mark in the 1st FF_WWW_modmul, and the target, around the 50,000 mark in the 2nd FF_WWW_modsqr. The difference between the two resulting traces ($d_{j-1} \in \{0,1\}$) exposes the collision attack vulnerability: the target exists only when $d_{j-1} = 0$ (upper graph), it is not there when $d_{j-1} = 1$ (lower graph). (Color figure online)

Results for d_j-d_{j-1} Collisions and Discussion. For each numerical model, there are four cases to consider (Fig. 2) which are the four values $d_{j:j-1}$ can take: 00, 01, 10 and 11. Once again, for the same reasons as in the previous paragraph, we consider the last two only. We focused on the processing of the first two bits $d_{T-1:T-2}$ of the secret exponent during the acquisitions of traces, therefore $x = 0$

and the numerical models of interest are[19] $g^{2x+1} = g$ and $g^{2x+2} = g^2$. In the resulting 'NICV' traces (Figs. 3 and 6): the x-axis depicts the execution timing, in cycles, starting from the beginning of the first iteration of the loop (Algorithm 1), and the y-axis reports the NICV metric for each sample in the (aligned) traces.

All the expected activity (and more) has been captured (Fig. 3, related to g): the graphs feature peaks with amplitudes well above 0.1 everywhere the timing diagrams indicate that there should be a statistical dependency (the 'yes' entries in the 'r/w' lines for the numerical model g^{2x+1}). In other words, everywhere the variable (and therefore the value, Definition 2) related to the numerical model is handled by the hardware, there is a peak in the graphs. In fact, there are multiple peaks per such event due to the ratio between the size of the hardware registers and that of the integers handled during the operations: a typical CRT-RSA operand is 512 bits long whereas a typical hardware register can only hold 32 bits at a time; thus these big integers are processed in chunks. We outlined these peaks using red rectangles. Surprisingly, there are some peaks in other locations as well (next to the 0 mark in the 1st FF_WWW_modmul, and around the 20,000 mark in the 1st FF_WWW_modsqr, in both traces). These peaks are a consequence of the initialization of R_0 to 1, and should not be taken into account for they do not exist in subsequent iterations of the loop. Lastly, the collision between the inputs of the two operations is there only when $d_{T-2} = 0$ which concurs with the predictions from the timing diagrams.

For the sake of completeness with regard to Fig. 2, we included the results for g^2 as well (Fig. 6, in appendix). The discussion, however, is the same: only the interpretation of the presence of the collision differs. Indeed, in this case, it is associated with $d_{T-2} = 1$, which can be seen in the NICV trace.

4.2   Exploitation of Identified Vulnerabilities

First-Order Collision Attacks. So far, we have made the collisions stand out from other samples by looking at a ratio of variances after partitioning the traces according to a model whose values were known. In real-life conditions, an attacker would not be able to classify traces like this since the value of the secret exponent d is to be guessed, not known. Still, the methodology we described can be used as a profiling step which, since the traces are aligned, gives the indices of the samples in the traces which should be input to the attack step: these are the same for all traces. Next, an attacker can use another statistical tool which, given these samples, can estimate whether they amount to a collision which, in turn, eventually yields d_j (Sect. 2). Since the collisions we highlighted are amenable to first-order attacks, we do not mount higher-order attacks to validate this exploitation phase.

In addition to the quick survey of hands-on techniques we did earlier, other (more theoretical) contributions exist, albeit for symmetric cryptography. In particular, in [6], the authors formalize and then study the success rates of, among

---

[19] The timing diagrams indicate that $g^{2\cdot0} = 1$ should be discussed as well. However, since it is a constant, it is not possible to analyze the variations for these samples in the traces. As consequence, we discarded it.

others distinguishers, the ones we mentioned before and which we recall here: Euclidean distance and correlation. The results of their simulations show that using the correlation between a few selected samples yields a satisfactory success rate within a few traces: their stochastic collision distinguisher is defined for S-Boxes, and cannot be easily transferred to our problem.

However, we have not been able to extract enough points of interest in each operation (source and target) in a single trace to perform the attack horizontally: many of the peaks in the NICV traces (Figs. 3 and 6) are simply too small. They do not hold enough information about g or g^2 to make for a robust estimation of the real correlation. As a consequence, we mixed this horizontal approach with ideas from the vertical (timing) correlation-enhanced collision attack described in [20]. Instead of gathering the points of interest in each of the two operations in a single trace before computing the correlation between the two resulting sets, we simply build these sets over N traces (same secret exponent d, yet different messages $(g_i)_{1 \leq i \leq N}$) by taking, in each trace and for each operation involved in the collision attack vulnerability being exploited, the sample associated with the highest peak in the NICV trace. It may look like this technique, which readily applies to the d_j-d_{j-1} case, might not work in the d_j case for the same parts of the same operations are targeted, possibly leading to the same peaks in the NICV graphs.[20] This is nevertheless incorrect since for both numerical models, the equality is verified for one value of d_j only. It is therefore always possible to detect the presence of a collision, and from there, to estimate d_j. We provide an overview of the whole process (Fig. 4).

We carried out the corresponding first-order attacks for d_j as well as d_j-d_{j-1} collisions: we attempted to retrieve one bit only, and give the evolution of the corresponding success rates as a function of N (Fig. 5). For d_j collisions, this is also the proportion of bits of d one can hope to recover with this attack since the exponent bits can be estimated independently of one another. In our case, an average of 98.5% of all the bits are correctly guessed after 150 traces. The attack did not get any better by further increasing N. The rest of d may then be corrected using classical cryptanalytical techniques such as [18] or other means like [26]. For d_j-d_{j-1} collisions however, the probability of guessing d correctly is p^T where p is the success rate. As hinted in Footnote 4, this implies that the number of erroneous bits output by this attack cannot be known, thus any success rate smaller than 100% is not acceptable. Fortunately, this lower bound is met after 10 traces only (Fig. 5). Even if these figures seem to show that d_j-d_{j-1} collisions work better than d_j collisions, there is no reason for this to be true. This difference in performance probably stems from the choice of the NICV peak which was probably less optimal in the d_j case than in the other case even though we did take the biggest ones available in each case.

We stress that, by paying more attention to the experimental setting, one should be able to get equal leakage levels for all bytes in the colliding values

---

[20] In fact, since the two variables (R_0, R_1) are treated one at a time by the hardware, there will be an offset (a few cycles) between the sets of peaks related to both numerical models. The peaks will always be distinct.

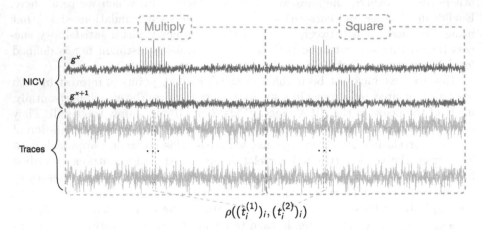

$$\rho((t_i^{(1)})_i, (t_i^{(2)})_i)$$

Fig. 4. Working principle of the proposed collision attack methodology. Once the indices of the POIs involved in collisions in a trace have been identified using NICV for γ_s and γ_t, we pick the one associated with the highest leakage level in each operation (here, one POI for the multiplication and one POI for the squaring). We then collect the corresponding pairs of samples every time we use a new trace during the attack. Lastly, once a fixed threshold has been reached for the number N of processed traces, we compute the correlation between the two groups of samples to detect the presence of a collision.

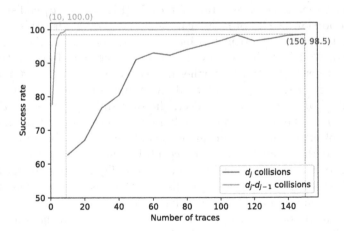

Fig. 5. Evolution of the success rate against the number of traces used in the correlation-based collision attacks. Best performance: 100% success rate for d_j-d_{j-1} collisions in 10 traces, 98.5% success rate for d_j collisions in 150 traces. Note that d_j collisions should perform as good, the selection of points of interest (same technique in both cases) is most likely the root cause of the difference.

and all critical timestamps, unlike in this paper (Figs. 3 and 6). It would then definitely be possible to select the samples in a single trace, as described in Sect. 4.2. In particular, we obtained promising early results by ensuring that the sampling frequency is a multiple of that of the CPU of the microcontroller, and reducing the latter so that the clock signal input to the board does not get shifted at random by pieces of circuitry like prescalers. This helped us further improve the alignment of the traces which, in turn, caused bigger peaks, thus enabling us to build the two sets of points of interest in a single trace by selecting the maximums of a fixed number of the latter rather than over multiple trace as we did. This would make for the single-trace attack predicted by the theory. In particular, classical blinding countermeasures, which protect from vertical attacks only, would then become ineffective. We plan to use and describe this new experimental setting in later papers once we reliably attain this upper bound.

Towards High-Order Collision Attacks. Since we have been able to find collisions on several variables (R_0 and R_1, but this methodology would have revealed other ones if more variables had been involved) one could use these to build attacks on multiple variables at the same time. For instance, in blinding-like horizontal countermeasures on modular exponentiation such as [10], at some point, the microcontroller processes the random element like any other variable. Thus, to retrieve values which are now masked during the operation (in our case, the contents of R_0 and R_1), one could, using the technique we presented in this paper, locate leakages owing to those values and to the random element, and then try to infer from these samples the unmasked values or, even more directly, the value of d_j. Since this paper proposes a complete first-order evaluation of the Montgomery Ladder, adapting this contribution to high-order evaluations requires changes in the exploitation phase only: the profiling phase would be the same. Consequently, we claim that the only remaining obstacle to such attacks is the fact that, to this day, in the literature, to the best of our knowledge, no paper has suggested a way to combine the leakages for unmasking like in high-order attacks targeting symmetric cryptography (e.g. [4,28]).

5   Conclusion

We have introduced a methodology for the detection of collision attack vulnerabilities in the Montgomery Ladder which comprises two steps: a theoretical assessment of the possible numerical models for the collisions, and a practical validation of the usability of the latter. We then provided evidence for the soundness of this approach by mounting matching first-order attacks whose success rates are already satisfactory (100% success rate in the best case after 10 traces) without combining the leakages associated with multiple collision attack vulnerabilities. Last we described how this methodology could be used in high-order collision attacks and discussed the remaining issue to tackle before doing so. This work shows that the Montgomery Ladder is not secure in practice and that its use as a countermeasure is not sufficient anymore: collision attacks like the ones we presented reveal the secret exponent rather easily. In light of our findings, and in accordance with the state of the art of the field, it is now mandatory to add multiple countermeasures to any RSA implementation to meet a security level which is acceptable in practice: for instance, our best attack can be thwarted by blinding.

This paper leaves a few avenues for future research regarding our methodology and its sensitivity to blinding, such as the possibility of a single-trace attack (as sketched in Sect. 4.2) on an implementation of RSA whose only countermeasure is the Montgomery Ladder (a straightforward extension of this work) or on other implementations adding a combination of countermeasures like [10] or [3]. In addition, to remedy the lesser performance of d_j collisions in practice, one could, following our remark, use (deep) neural networks which may be better suited for the selection of points of interest. We plan to tackle these open questions in later papers.

Acknowledgements. This work has been funded by the French Ministry of Armed Forces through its Agence de l'Innovation de la Défense.

A   The Montgomery Ladder

Algorithm 1: Pseudocode for the Montgomery Ladder (RSA).

Input: $g, d = (d_{T-1}, \ldots, d_0)_2$
Output: $m = g^d$

1 $R_0 \leftarrow 1; R_1 \leftarrow g$;
2 for $j = T - 1$ downto 0 do
3 | if $d_j = 0$ then
4 | | $R_1 \leftarrow R_0 R_1; R_0 \leftarrow (R_0)^2$;
5 | else
6 | | $R_0 \leftarrow R_0 R_1; R_1 \leftarrow (R_1)^2$;
7 | end
8 end
9 return R_0

B Observing Collisions Involving g^2

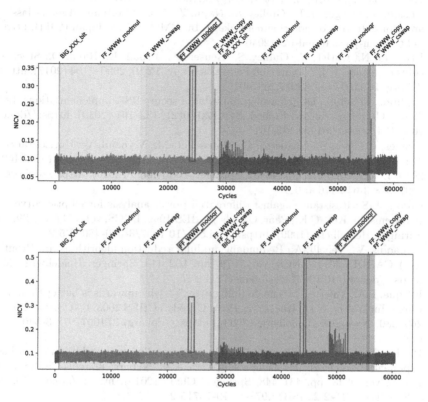

Fig. 6. NICV on $g^2[7:0]$ computed using 49152 traces (top: $d = (10\ldots)_2$, bottom: $d = (11\ldots)_2$). All activity linked to the collision attack vulnerability on R_1 ($= g^2$— Fig. 2, g^{2x+2} line) is visible (red rectangles). Like in Fig. 3, the difference between the two resulting traces ($d_{j-1} \in \{0, 1\}$) exposes the collision attack vulnerability. (Color figure online)

References

1. Aldaya, A.C., García, C.P., Tapia, L.M.A., Brumley, B.B.: Cache-timing attacks on RSA key generation. IACR Trans. Cryptogr. Hardw. Embed. Syst. **2019**, 213–242 (2018). https://doi.org/10.13154/tches.v2019.i4.213-242
2. Batina, L., Chmielewski, L., Papachristodoulou, L., Schwabe, P., Tunstall, M.: Online template attacks. J. Cryptogr. Eng. **9**, 21–36 (2017). https://doi.org/10.1007/s13389-017-0171-8
3. Bauer, A., Jaulmes, E., Prouff, E., Wild, J.: Horizontal and vertical side-channel attacks against secure RSA implementations. In: Dawson, E. (ed.) CT-RSA 2013. LNCS, vol. 7779, pp. 1–17. Springer, Heidelberg (2013). https://doi.org/10.1007/978-3-642-36095-4_1

4. Benadjila, R., Prouff, E., Strullu, R., Cagli, E., Dumas, C.: Deep learning for sidechannel analysis and introduction to ASCAD database. J. Cryptogr. Eng. **10**(2), 163–188 (2020). https://doi.org/10.1007/s13389-019-00220-8
5. Bhasin, S., Danger, J.-L., Guilley, S., Najm, Z.: NICV: normalized inter-class variance for detection of side-channel leakage. In: EMC, Tokyo, Japan (2014). https://hal.telecom-paris.fr/hal-02412040
6. Bruneau, N., Carlet, C., Guilley, S., Heuser, A., Prouff, E., Rioul, O.: Stochastic collision attack. IEEE Trans. Inf. Forensics Secur. **12**(9), 2090–2104 (2017). https://doi.org/10.1109/TIFS.2017.2697401
7. Carbone, M., et al.: Deep learning to evaluate secure RSA implementations. IACR Trans. Cryptogr. Hardw. Embed. Syst. **2019**(2), 132–161 (2019). https://doi.org/10.13154/tches.v2019.i2.132-161
8. Clavier, C., Feix, B., Gagnerot, G., Roussellet, M., Verneuil, V.: Horizontal correlation analysis on exponentiation. In: Soriano, M., Qing, S., López, J. (eds.) ICICS 2010. LNCS, vol. 6476, pp. 46–61. Springer, Heidelberg (2010). https://doi.org/10.1007/978-3-642-17650-0_5
9. Coron, J.-S.: Resistance against differential power analysis for elliptic curve cryptosystems. In: Koç, Ç.K., Paar, C. (eds.) CHES 1999. LNCS, vol. 1717, pp. 292–302. Springer, Heidelberg (1999). https://doi.org/10.1007/3-540-48059-5_25
10. Dupaquis, V., Venelli, A.: Redundant modular reduction algorithms. In: Prouff, E. (ed.) CARDIS 2011. LNCS, vol. 7079, pp. 102–114. Springer, Heidelberg (2011). https://doi.org/10.1007/978-3-642-27257-8_7
11. Fouque, P.A., Valette, F.: The doubling attack – why upwards is better than downwards. In: Walter, C.D., Koç, Ç.K., Paar, C. (eds.) CHES 2003. LNCS, vol. 2779, pp. 269–280. Springer, Heidelberg (2003). https://doi.org/10.1007/978-3-540-45238-6_22
12. Hanley, N., Kim, H.S., Tunstall, M.: Exploiting collisions in addition chain-based exponentiation algorithms using a single trace. In: Nyberg, K. (ed.) CT-RSA 2015. LNCS, vol. 9048, pp. 431–448. Springer, Cham (2015). https://doi.org/10.1007/978-3-319-16715-2_23 ISBN: 978-3-319-16715-2
13. Heyszl, J., Ibing, A., Mangard, S., De Santis, F., Sigl, G.: Clustering algorithms for non-profiled single-execution attacks on exponentiations. In: Francillon, A., Rohatgi, P. (eds.) CARDIS 2013. LNCS, vol. 8419, pp. 79–93. Springer, Cham (2014). https://doi.org/10.1007/978-3-319-08302-5_6 ISBN: 978-3-319-08302-5
14. Homma, N., Miyamoto, A., Aoki, T., Satoh, A., Shamir, A.: Collision-based power analysis of modular exponentiation using chosen-message pairs. In: Oswald, E., Rohatgi, P. (eds.) CHES 2008. LNCS, vol. 5154, pp. 15–29. Springer, Heidelberg (2008). https://doi.org/10.1007/978-3-540-85053-3_2 ISBN: 978-3-540-85053-3
15. Jajodia, S., van Tilborg, H.C.: Encyclopedia of Cryptography and Security. Springer, New York (2011). https://doi.org/10.1007/978-1-4419-5906-5. ISBN: 038723473X
16. Joye, M., Yen, S.-M.: The montgomery powering ladder. In: Kaliski, B.S., Koç, K., Paar, C. (eds.) CHES 2002. LNCS, vol. 2523, pp. 291–302. Springer, Heidelberg (2003). https://doi.org/10.1007/3-540-36400-5_22
17. Knuth, D.E.: The Art of Computer Programming, Volume 2: Seminumerical Algorithms. Addison-Wesley (1981)
18. Micheli, G.D., Heninger, N.: Recovering cryptographic keys from partial information, by example. Cryptology ePrint Archive, Paper 2020/1506 (2020). https://eprint.iacr.org/2020/1506

19. Montgomery, P.L.: Speeding the pollard and elliptic curve methods of factorization. Math. Comput. **48**(177), 243–264 (1987). https://doi.org/10.1090/S0025-5718-1987-0866113-7

20. Moradi, A., Mischke, O., Paar, C., Li, Y., Ohta, K., Sakiyama, K.: On the power of fault sensitivity analysis and collision side-channel attacks in a combined setting. In: Preneel, B., Takagi, T. (eds.) CHES 2011. LNCS, vol. 6917, pp. 292–311. Springer, Heidelberg (2011). https://doi.org/10.1007/978-3-642-23951-9_20 ISBN: 978-3-642-23951-9

21. Nascimento, E., Chmielewski, L: Applying horizontal clustering side-channel attacks on embedded ECC implementations. In: Eisenbarth, T., Teglia, Y. (eds.) CARDIS 2017. LNCS, vol. 10728, pp. 213–231. Springer, Cham (2018). https://doi.org/10.1007/978-3-319-75208-2_13

22. Nascimento, E., Chmielewski, L, Oswald, D., Schwabe, P.: Attacking embedded ECC implementations through cmov side channels. In: Avanzi, R., Heys, H. (eds.) SAC 2016. LNCS, vol. 10532, pp. 99–119. Springer, Cham (2017). https://doi.org/10.1007/978-3-319-69453-5_6

23. Kocher, P.C.: Timing attacks on implementations of Diffie-Hellman, RSA, DSS, and other systems. In: Koblitz, N. (ed.) CRYPTO 1996. LNCS, vol. 1109, pp. 104–113. Springer, Heidelberg (1996). https://doi.org/10.1007/3-540-68697-5_9

24. Perin, G., Chmielewski, L., Batina, L., Picek, S.: Keep it unsupervised: horizontal attacks meet deep learning. IACR Trans. Cryptogr. Hardw. Embed. Syst. **2021**(1), 343–372 (2020). https://doi.org/10.46586/tchesv2021.i1.343-372

25. Rivest, R.L., Shamir, A., Adleman, L.: A method for obtaining digital signatures and public-key cryptosystems. Commun. ACM **21**(2), 120–126 (1978). https://doi.org/10.1145/359340.359342. ISSN: 0001-0782

26. Schindler, W., Wiemers, A.: Power attacks in the presence of exponent blinding. J. Cryptogr. Eng. **4**, 213–236 (2014). https://doi.org/10.1007/s13389-014-0081-y

27. Scott, M.: MIRACL Core Cryptographic Library (2019). https://github.com/miracl/core

28. Waddle, J., Wagner, D.: Towards efficient second-order power analysis. In: Joye, M., Quisquater, J.-J. (eds.) CHES 2004. LNCS, vol. 3156, pp. 1–15. Springer, Heidelberg (2004). https://doi.org/10.1007/978-3-540-28632-5_1 ISBN: 978-3-540-28632-5

29. Walter, C.D.: Sliding windows succumbs to big mac attack. In: Koç, Ç.K., Naccache, D., Paar, C. (eds.) CHES 2001. LNCS, vol. 2162, pp. 286–299. Springer, Heidelberg (2001). https://doi.org/10.1007/3-540-44709-1_24

30. Witteman, M.F., van Woudenberg, J.G.J., Menarini, F.: Defeating RSA multiply-always and message blinding countermeasures. In: Kiayias, A. (ed.) CT-RSA 2011. LNCS, vol. 6558, pp. 77–88. Springer, Heidelberg (2011). https://doi.org/10.1007/978-3-642-19074-2_6 ISBN: 978-3-642-19074-2

31. Yen, S.-M., Ko, L.-C., Moon, S.J., Ha, J.C.: Relative doubling attack against montgomery ladder. In: Won, D.H., Kim, S. (eds.) ICISC 2005. LNCS, vol. 3935, pp. 117–128. Springer, Heidelberg (2006). https://doi.org/10.1007/11734727_11 ISBN: 978-3-540-33355-5

On the Masking-Friendly Designs for Post-quantum Cryptography

Suparna Kundu[1]([✉]) [iD], Angshuman Karmakar[1,2] [iD], and Ingrid Verbauwhede[1] [iD]

[1] COSIC, KU Leuven, Kasteelpark Arenberg 10, Bus 2452, 3001 Leuven-Heverlee, Belgium
{suparna.kundu,angshuman.karmakar,ingrid.verbauwhede}@esat.kuleuven.be
[2] Indian Institute of Technology Kanpur, Kanpur, India

Abstract. Masking is a well-known and provably secure countermeasure against side-channel attacks. However, due to additional redundant computations, integrating masking schemes is expensive in terms of performance. The performance overhead of integrating masking countermeasures is heavily influenced by the design choices of a cryptographic algorithm and is often not considered during the design phase.

In this work, we deliberate on the effect of design choices on integrating masking techniques into lattice-based cryptography. We select Scabbard, a suite of three lattice-based post-quantum key-encapsulation mechanisms (KEM), namely Florete, Espada, and Sable. We provide arbitrary-order masked implementations of all the constituent KEMs of the Scabbard suite by exploiting their specific design elements. We show that the masked implementations of Florete, Espada, and Sable outperform the masked implementations of Kyber in terms of speed for any order masking. Masked Florete exhibits a 73%, 71%, and 70% performance improvement over masked Kyber corresponding to the first-, second-, and third-order. Similarly, Espada exhibits 56%, 59%, and 60% and Sable exhibits 75%, 74%, and 73% enhanced performance for first-, second-, and third-order masking compared to Kyber respectively. Our results show that the design decisions have a significant impact on the efficiency of integrating masking countermeasures into lattice-based cryptography.

Keywords: Post-quantum cryptography · Key-encapsulation mechanism · Side-channel attacks · Scabbard · Higher-order masking

1 Introduction

Physical attacks such as fault injection and side-channel attacks are potent threats to any cryptosystem deployed in the public domain. Classical cryptographic schemes such as elliptic-curve cryptography [25] and RSA [27] went through decades of testing, analysis, and invention of different physical attacks and their countermeasures to generate enough confidence to be successfully deployed in the real world. In comparison, post-quantum cryptography (PQC),

F. Regazzoni et al. (Eds.): SPACE 2023, LNCS 14412, pp. 162–184, 2024.
https://doi.org/10.1007/978-3-031-51583-5_10

or specifically lattice-based cryptography (LBC) has gone through significantly less amount of investigation in the context of physical attacks. Therefore, although the United States government's National Institute of Standards and Technology (NIST) has recently proposed some standard PQC schemes [1], for a successful transition to PQC, it is imperative that we concentrate our research efforts in this direction.

Masking [11] is an interesting countermeasure against passive physical attacks or side-channel attacks (SCA) such as power analysis, electromagnetic radiation analysis, etc. On a fundamental level, masking works by splitting the secret into multiple random shares and performing the same computation as the unmasked version on each share. Thus, the security of masking is based on the same information-theoretic principles, such as Shamir's secret sharing [29] or multi-party computation [30]. Masking can provide provably secure countermeasures against side-channel attacks. Nevertheless, due to the duplication of computations, the runtime of a masked implementation theoretically grows significantly with the increase in the order of masking. For example, in the case of Kyber, a post-quantum key-encapsulation mechanism (KEM) scheme that has been selected as standard in the NIST's procedure, the runtime of the first, second, and third order of masked implementation is 12, 20, and 30 times of the unmasked implementation on ARM Cortex-M4 platform [10].

Our primary motivation in this work is to assess how the design decisions of a lattice-based KEM scheme, such as the choice of quotient polynomial, distribution of secrets and errors, underlying hard problems, modulus, etc., influence their masking performance. We also want to test how close we can get to the theoretical upper bound of efficiency in masking. For our experiments, we have chosen the post-quantum KEM suite Scabbard [5] with 3 different lattice-based schemes. First, a ring-learning with rounding (RLWR) based scheme Florete with ring size comparable to NewHope [2], second a module-learning with rounding (MLWR) based scheme Sable with ring size similar to Saber [15] and Kyber [8], and finally an MLWR-based scheme Espada with unique smaller ring size. The choice of Scabbard helps us to demonstrate our methods on diverse KEM schemes with many variations in the design. Scabbard was proposed to improve the NIST PQC finalist KEM Saber [15]. The designers of Scabbard argued that all the design decisions of Scabbard had been propelled by the experience gained in the research and developments in the field of lattice-based cryptography of previous years. Therefore, it inherits all the advantages of Saber *i.e.* less randomness due to rounding, power-of-two modulus for efficient masking, simple algorithms for efficiency and faster deployment on diverse platforms, etc. Further, the design of Scabbard improves in areas like suitability for parallel implementation, flexibility, efficiency, and adaptation of faster masking schemes. We will discuss the schemes of Scabbard in Sect. 2.1. In the original publication [5], the authors have provided different implementations on hardware and software platforms to prove their claims on efficiency. It was shown before that the design of Saber is highly conducive to masking [4]. Due to these reasons, Scabbard is an ideal choice to demonstrate the interplay between design choices and masking performance in lattice-based KEMs.

In this work, we propose arbitrary-order masked implementations of all the KEMs in the suite Scabbard. We implement and benchmark them on an ARM Cortex-M4 microcontroller platform using the PQM4 [21] library to prove the masking friendliness of its design. The ring size of the polynomial length matches the number of message bits, which is 256 for Saber or Kyber as well as Sable. So, the encoding of message bits to the ciphertext polynomial is trivial in these cases. However, this is not the case for Florete and Espada, and these schemes use `original_msg` function for message decoding and `arrange_msg` function for message encoding. This work introduces a higher-order masked version of `original_msg` and `arrange_msg` function. These functions can be applied to all LWR-based KEMs with different ring sizes than 256 and even learning with errors (LWE) based KEMs with some modifications. The schemes of Scabbard use different centered binomial distributions compared to Saber or Kyber. For this purpose, we modified the masked centered binomial distribution (CBD) algorithms proposed by Schneider et al. [28] for each scheme of Scabbard and optimized it for them. Public and re-encrypted ciphertext comparison is an important part of the Fujisaki-Okamoto transformation used in LWE-/LWR-based KEM. It is faster for unmasked or first-order masking but becomes computationally expensive for higher-order maskings. Here, we modified the ciphertext comparator of [23] for each scheme of Scabbard to obtain better performance. These masked components are faster in Scabbard than Kyber, thanks to the choice of RLWR/MLWR hard problem, power-of-two moduli and slightly reduced parameter sets.

As performance results, the overhead factor we obtained for masked Florete for the first-, second-, and third-order are approximately 2.7×, 5×, and 7.7×, compared to the unmasked implementation. For Espada, the overhead cost of the first-, second-, and third-order masked versions are roughly 1.8×, 2.8×, and 4× than the unmasked one. The performance cost of masked Sable for the first-, second-, and third-order are around 2.4×, 4.3×, and 6.3× over the unmasked version. We compare the masked implementations of Florete, Espada, and Sable with the state-of-the-art masked implementation of Kyber and Saber. We show that the masked implementations of all the schemes of Scabbard surpass the masked implementations of Kyber in terms of performance for any order masking, and masked implementations of Florete and Sable outperform masked implementations of Saber for arbitrary order. More specifically, masked Florete performs 73%, 71%, and 70% better than masked Kyber, corresponding to the first-, second-, and third-order. Espada shows 56%, 59%, and 60% performance improvement for first-, second- and third-order masked implementations compared to Kyber. Masked Sable exceeds the execution time of masked Kyber by 75%, 74%, and 73% for the first-, second-, and third-order. Our masked implementations are available at https://github.com/Suparna-Kundu/Masked_Scabbard.git.

To conclude this section, we want to draw attention to the fact that although the NIST standardization procedure for PKE/KEM has been finalized with Kyber, we firmly believe that further investigations and innovations are required to improve side-channel secure PQC schemes. The NIST procedure opened the possibility of exploring different possibilities to improve various aspects of PQC schemes. We have witnessed this throughout the course and even after the NIST procedure. For example, Mitaka [16] has been proposed, which is a masking-friendly version of Falcon [17], a NIST standard for digital signatures. Kyber-90s version of Kyber was proposed to use the advanced encryption standard (AES) as a pseudo-random number generator instead of the slower Keccak extended output function. Similarly, Saber-90s and uSaber were proposed as alternate versions of the NIST PQC standardization finalist scheme Saber to improve efficiency and ease of masking. As discussed earlier, Scabbard [5] was an improvement of Saber. The design of Scabbard has further influenced the design of PQC KEM Smaug [12], which is a candidate scheme from ongoing Korean PQC standardization [22]. Therefore, exploring various design choices and their effect on different aspects of the performance of existing PQC schemes is an interesting research direction.

2 Preliminaries

For a positive integer q, the set of integers modulo q is denoted by $\mathbb{Z}_q$. The quotient ring $\mathbb{Z}_q[x]/f(x)$ is denoted by $\mathcal{R}_q^n$, where $f(x)$ is a n degree cyclotomic polynomial over $\mathbb{Z}_q[x]$. We use lowercase letters to denote an element of this ring, which is a polynomial. We indicate the ring of l length vectors over the ring $\mathcal{R}_q^n$ as $(\mathcal{R}_q^n)^l$ and use bold lowercase letters to denote an element of this ring which is a vector of polynomials. The ring of $l \times l$ length matrices over the ring $\mathcal{R}_q^n$ as $(\mathcal{R}_q^n)^{l \times l}$. The elements of this ring are $l \times l$ matrices of polynomials and are represented by uppercase letters. $x \leftarrow \chi(S)$ represents that x is sampled from the set S and follows the distribution χ. When x is generated using a pseudo-random number generator expanding a seed $seed_x$ over the set S, we denote it as $x \leftarrow \chi(S; seed_x)$. We use $\mathcal{U}$ to denote the uniform distribution and the CBD whose standard deviation $\sqrt{\mu/2}$ is presented by β_μ. We denote the rounding operator with $\lfloor \cdot \rceil$, which returns the closest integer and is rounded upwards during ties. These operations can be extended over the polynomials by applying them coefficient-wise. The polynomial multiplication between two polynomials of length n is represented using $n \times n$ multiplication. We use $\{x_i\}_{0 \leq i \leq t}$ to represent the set $\{x_0, x_1, \ldots, x_t\}$ which contains $t + 1$ elements of the ring $\mathcal{R}$.

2.1 Scabbard: A Post-quantum KEM Suite

Scabbard is a suite of post-quantum KEMs proposed by Mera et al. [5] that improved state-of-the-art LBC schemes by incorporating different design choices and newer developments in the field. The security of the schemes in the Scabbard depends on some variants of learning with rounding (LWR) problems, more specifically, module-LWR (MLWR) and ring-LWR (RLWR) problems. Banerjee et al. [3] introduced the LWR problem and also showed that the LWR problem is as hard as the LWE problem. If $A \leftarrow \mathcal{U}((\mathbb{Z}_q)^{l \times l})$, secret $\mathbf{s} \leftarrow \beta_\mu((\mathbb{Z}_q)^l)$, error $\mathbf{e} \leftarrow \beta_{\mu_e}((\mathbb{Z}_q)^l)$, and $\mathbf{b} \leftarrow \mathcal{U}((\mathbb{Z}_q)^l)$ then distinguishing between $(A, As + e)$ and (A, b) is hard and this problem is known as the decision version of LWE problem. The decision version of the LWR problem states that if $A \leftarrow \mathcal{U}((\mathbb{Z}_q)^{l \times l})$, secret $\mathbf{s} \leftarrow \beta_\mu((\mathbb{Z}_q)^l)$, and for some $p < q$, $\mathbf{b} \leftarrow \mathcal{U}((\mathbb{Z}_p)^l)$ then distinguishing between $(A, \lfloor (q/p)As \rceil)$ and (A, b) is hard [3]. In the LWR problem, the explicit sampling of error $\mathbf{e}$ in the LWE is replaced by the rounding operation. In case of the MLWR problem, $A \leftarrow \mathcal{U}((\mathcal{R}_q^n)^{l \times l})$, $\mathbf{s} \leftarrow \beta_\mu((\mathcal{R}_q^n)^l)$, $\mathbf{b} \leftarrow \mathcal{U}((\mathcal{R}_p^n)^l)$ and the MLWR problem states that $(A, \lfloor (q/p)As \rceil)$ and (A, b) are computationally indistinguishable [24]. In standard LWR-based and RLWR-based constructions, the ranks of underlying matrices are respectively l and n, with very high probability. On the other hand, MLWR-based constructions are proposed as a trade-off between standard LWR-based and RLWR-based structures. The rank of underlying matrices in MLWR-based schemes is $l \times n$. It makes the structures of MLWR-based constructions more generic, as we can convert the MLWR-based scheme to a standard LWR-based one by fixing $n = 1$ and an RLWR-based one by setting $l = 1$. Therefore, we use MLWR notations to describe the schemes in Scabbard below. A KEM needs to be secure against chosen ciphertext attacks (IND-CCA/IND-CCA2: indistinguishable against a-posteriori chosen-ciphertext attacks). In LWR-based KEM, it is accomplished by applying Jiang et al.'s version [20] of Fujisaki-Okamoto (FO) transformation [18] over the generic LWR-based public-key encryption (PKE), where the PKE needs to be secure against chosen plaintext attacks (IND-CPA: indistinguishable against chosen plaintext attack). We denote generic LWR-based PKE as LWR.PKE and generic LWR-based KEM as LWR.KEM, which are shown respectively in Fig. 1 and Fig. 2. In LWR.KEM, $\mathcal{H}$, $\mathcal{G}$, and KDF three hash functions are required as part of FO transformation. This suite of KEMs consists of three schemes: (i) Florete, (ii) Espada, and (iii) Sable. We briefly describe these three schemes with their specific features below.

LWR.PKE.KeyGen()

1. $seed_A \leftarrow \mathcal{U}(\{0,1\}^{256})$
2. $A \leftarrow \mathcal{U}((\mathcal{R}_q^n)^{l \times l}; seed_A)$
3. $r \leftarrow \mathcal{U}(\{0,1\}^{256})$
4. $\mathbf{s} \leftarrow \beta_\mu((\mathcal{R}_q^n)^l; r)$
5. $\mathbf{b} = ((A^T\mathbf{s} + \mathbf{h}) \bmod q) \gg (\epsilon_q - \epsilon_p) \in (\mathcal{R}_p^n)^l$
6. **return** $(pk = (seed_A, \mathbf{b}), sk = (\mathbf{s}))$

LWR.PKE.Dec$(sk = \mathbf{s}, c = (\mathbf{u}, v))$

1. $u'' = \mathbf{u}^T(\mathbf{s} \bmod p) \in \mathcal{R}_p^n$
2. $m'' = (u'' - 2^{\epsilon_p - \epsilon_t - B}v + h_2) \bmod p$
3. $m' = m'' \gg (\epsilon_p - B) \in \mathcal{R}_{2^{B_t}}^n$
4. **return** m'

LWR.PKE.Enc$(pk = (seed_A, \mathbf{b}), m \in R_2; r)$

1. $A \leftarrow \mathcal{U}((\mathcal{R}_q^n)^{l \times l}; seed_A)$
2. **if:** r is not specified:
3. $\quad r \leftarrow \mathcal{U}(\{0,1\}^{256})$
4. $\mathbf{s'} \leftarrow \beta_\mu((\mathcal{R}_q^n)^l; r)$
5. $\mathbf{u} = ((A\mathbf{s'} + \mathbf{h}) \bmod q) \gg (\epsilon_q - \epsilon_p) \in (\mathcal{R}_p^n)^l$
6. $c_m = \mathbf{b}^T(\mathbf{s'} \bmod p) \in \mathcal{R}_p^n$
7. $v = (c_m + h_1 - 2^{\epsilon_p - B}m \bmod p) \gg (\epsilon_p - \epsilon_t - B) \in \mathcal{R}_{2^{B_t}}^n$
8. **return** $c = (\mathbf{u}, v)$

Fig. 1. Generic LWR.PKE [5]

LWR.KEM.KeyGen()	LWR.KEM.Encaps($pk = (seed_A, \boldsymbol{b})$)
1. $(seed_A, \boldsymbol{b}, \boldsymbol{s}) = $ LWR.PKE.KeyGen()	1. $m' \leftarrow \mathcal{U}(\{0,1\}^{256})$
2. $pk = (seed_A, \boldsymbol{b})$	2. $m = $ arrange_msg(m')
3. $pkh = \mathcal{H}(pk)$	3. $m = \mathcal{H}(m)$
4. $z \leftarrow \mathcal{U}(\{0,1\}^{256})$	4. $(\hat{K}, r) = \mathcal{G}(\mathcal{H}(pk), m)$
5.	5. $c = $ LWR.PKE.Enc($pk, m; r$)
return $(pk = (seed_A, \boldsymbol{b}), sk = (\boldsymbol{s}, z, pkh))$	6. $K = $ KDF($\hat{K}, \mathcal{H}(c)$)
	7. **return** (c, K)

LWR.KEM.Decaps($sk = (\boldsymbol{s}, z, pkh), pk = (seed_A, \boldsymbol{b}), c$)

1. $m'' = $ LWR.PKE.Dec($\boldsymbol{s}, c$)
2. $m' = $ original_msg(m'')
3. $(\hat{K}', r') = \mathcal{G}(pkh, m')$
4. $c_* = $ LWR.PKE.Enc($pk, m'; r'$)
5. **if:** $c = c_*$
6.   **return** $K = $ KDF($\hat{K}', \mathcal{H}(c)$)
7. **else:**
8.   **return** $K = $ KDF($z, \mathcal{H}(c)$)

Fig. 2. Generic LWR.KEM [5]

2.1.1 Florete This scheme is based on the RLWR problem *i.e.* $l = 1$ in Fig. 1 and designed for faster running time. Here, the cyclotomic polynomial used to construct the quotient rings $\mathcal{R}_q^n$, $\mathcal{R}_p^n$, and $\mathcal{R}_t^n$ is $(x^{768} - x^{384} + 1)$. In Florete, one message bit is encoded in three coefficients of the polynomial v in line 7 of LWR.PKE.Enc algorithm of Fig. 1. So, during the encapsulation process, as shown in line 2 of LWR.KEM.Encaps algorithm of Fig. 2, a conversion from 256 bits of message to a polynomial of length 768 is performed with the help of arrange_msg function and it is defined as: arrange_msg(m') = $m'||m'||m'$. The inverse of arrange_msg function is used in the LWR.KEM.Decaps algorithm named as original_msg, and the original_msg : $\mathbb{Z}_2^{768} \longrightarrow \mathbb{Z}_2^{256}$ is defined as if original_msg(m'') = m' and $b \subset [0, 1, \ldots, 255\}$ then $m'[b] = \begin{cases} 0 & \text{if } m''[b] + m''[b + 256] + m''[b + 512] \le 1 \\ 1 & \text{otherwise} \end{cases}$. In Florete, 768×768 polynomial multiplication is used, and it is performed using the combination of Toom-Cook 3-way, Toom-Cook 4-way, 2 levels of Karatsuba, and 16×16 schoolbook multiplication.

2.1.2 Espada This scheme is designed to reduce the memory footprint on software platforms. It is based on the MLWR problem, and the cyclotomic polynomial is used to construct the underlying quotient ring of the lattice problem $\mathcal{R}_q^n$ is $(x^{64} + 1)$. The polynomial length here is 64, so the dimension of vectors of polynomial l is taken equal to 12 to maintain security. In Espada, the 256 bit message is encoded inside the 64 length polynomial v, so four message bits are encoded in a coefficient of the polynomial v. The arrange_msg : $\mathbb{Z}_2^{256} \longrightarrow \mathbb{Z}_4^{64}$ and the function is defined as: $\mathtt{arrange\_msg}(m') = m''$, where for $b \in \{0, 1, \ldots, 63\}$

$$m''[b] = m'[4*b+3]||m'[4*b+2]||m'[4*b+1]||m'[4*b]. \tag{1}$$

The $\mathtt{original\_msg} : \mathbb{Z}_4^{64} \longrightarrow \mathbb{Z}_2^{256}$ function is defined as: $\mathtt{original\_}$ $\mathtt{msg}(m'') = m'$ and follows Eq. 1. Lastly, the 64×64 polynomial multiplication is performed using 2 levels of Karatsuba and 16×16 schoolbook multiplication.

2.1.3 Sable This scheme can be interpreted as an alternate version of Saber and is designed to improve performance with less memory footprint. It is also based on the MLWR problem, and similar to Saber, the cyclotomic polynomial used here in the quotient rings is $(x^{256} + 1)$. The $\mathtt{arrange\_msg}$ function and $\mathtt{original\_msg}$ function are described as: $\mathtt{arrange\_msg}(m') = m'$ and $\mathtt{original\_msg}(m'') = m'' = m'$, respectively. The polynomial multiplication used in Sable is identical to Saber. The 256×256 polynomial multiplication is realized by the combination of Toom-Cook 4-way, 2 levels of Karatsuba, and 16×16 schoolbook multiplication.

The concrete security of these schemes depends on the parameter set, which includes the three power-of-two ring moduli $t < p < q$, the length of a polynomial n, the dimension of the vector of polynomial l, the CBD parameter μ, and the number of message-bit encoded in a coefficient of the polynomial is represented by B. Table 1 presents the parameter sets for all three schemes that achieve the NIST security level 3. We humbly refer to the original Scabbard paper [5] for more insightful details.

Table 1. Parameters of Scabbard suite

Scheme Name	Ring/Module Parameters		PQ Security	Failure probability	Moduli		CBD (β_η)	Encoding	Key sizes for KEM (Bytes)	
Florete	n:	768	2^{157}	2^{-131}	ϵ_q:	10	$\eta = 1$	B = 1	Public key:	896
					ϵ_p:	9			Secret key:	1152
	l:	1			ϵ_t:	3			Ciphertext:	1248
Espada	n:	64	2^{128}	2^{-167}	ϵ_q:	15	$\eta = 3$	B = 4	Public key:	1280
					ϵ_p:	13			Secret key:	1728
	l:	12			ϵ_t:	3			Ciphertext:	1304
Sable	n:	256	2^{169}	2^{-143}	ϵ_q:	11	$\eta = 1$	B = 1	Public key:	896
					ϵ_p:	9			Secret key:	1152
	l:	3			ϵ_t:	4			Ciphertext:	1024

2.2   Masking

The effectiveness of masking against SCA has been well demonstrated for symmetric-key block ciphers [13,26] and recently extended for LBC [4,9,23]. In n-th order masking, we split the sensitive data x into $(n+1)$ shares and perform all the operations on each share separately. So, an adversary with a limited number of probes, such as at most n probes, does not receive any advantages compared to another adversary who does not have access to those probes. The nth order masking technique can prevent up to nth order differential power attacks. However, the integration of masking techniques in LBC schemes affects the performance of the algorithm significantly with the increment of the masking order. The design decision of cryptographic schemes affects the performance of masked versions of the lattice-based schemes. This is why even though the unmasked performance of NIST finalist Saber is almost the same as Kyber, the masked version of Saber is way faster than masked Kyber for any masking order. Masked version Saber gains this advantage thanks to the choice of LWR problem and power-of-two moduli. The KEMs in the suite Scabbard also use power-of-two moduli and further improve the efficiency of the LWR-based schemes. In this work, we investigate whether the efficiency of Scabbard will translate to the masked domain.

3   Masking Scabbard

The CCA-secure KEM schemes are used to share secrets among communicating parties. Here, the secret key is non-ephemeral *i.e.* the key generation is run once to generate a long-term secret key that can be used for multiple sessions and communicating with multiple entities. Therefore, in a KEM scheme, only the decapsulation is executed multiple times to retrieve the secret data from multiple entities through multiple sessions. However, this is also advantageous for an adversary. The adversary can run the decapsulation operation multiple times to improve the precision of its fault injection or take multiple side-channel traces to reduce noise in its measurements, thus improving its success probability. Mounting attacks on other operations, such as key generation and encapsulation, are relatively harder. Once an adversary compromises the secret key, it can use it to expose the secret keys of multiple sessions. Therefore, protecting the decapsulation operation from side-channel attacks is critical for the side-channel security of a KEM. We display the flow of the decapsulation algorithm of generic LWR-based KEM in Fig. 3 and denoted vulnerable operations in the color gray. Here original_msg and arrange_msg functions are shown by OMsg and AMsg. In this section, we will describe the masking methods of all the components susceptible to SCA in the decapsulation operation of the Scabbard schemes.

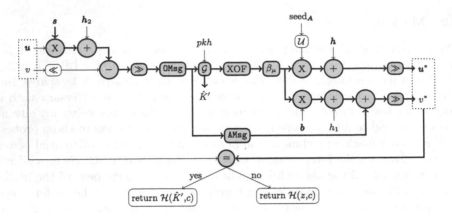

Fig. 3. Decapsulation of LWR-based KEM. The operations in color gray are involved with the long-term secret *s* and are susceptible to side-channel attacks

Here, we have used two masking techniques: (i) arithmetic masking and (ii) Boolean masking to mask the Scabbard suite's schemes because these schemes consist of some operations that are cheaper to mask using arithmetic masking and some are easy to mask using Boolean masking. In both the t-order arithmetic and Boolean masking techniques, first we split the sensitive operand $x \in \mathbb{Z}_q = \mathbb{Z}_{2^{\epsilon_q}} = \mathbb{Z}_2^{\epsilon_q}$ into $(t + 1)$ shares, such as $x_0, x_1, \ldots, x_t \in \mathbb{Z}_q$. However, for arithmetic masking the relation between x and $(t + 1)$ shares of x is $x = (x_0 + x_1 + \cdots + x_t) \bmod q$, and in Boolean masking the relation between x and $(t+1)$ shares of x is $x = (x_0 \oplus x_1 \oplus \cdots \oplus x_t)$.

3.1 Arithmetic Operations

It can be seen from Fig. 3 that the decapsulation algorithm of each KEM of the suite Scabbard consists of mostly arithmetic operations, such as polynomial multiplications, polynomial addition, and polynomial subtractions. These operations can be masked efficiently utilizing arithmetic masking. Here, we need to duplicate these operations for each arithmetic share and perform them separately. The performance cost of these operations grows linearly with the increase of arithmetic shares.

Although this part is more or less similar for all the LWE/LWR-based KEMs (for example, Kyber and Saber), the parameter set impacts the performance of unmasked and masked versions of these operations. This also helps the schemes of Scabbard to achieve better performance compared to other LBC-based KEMs in some scenarios. The performance cost of the masked arithmetic operations in Sable is less than Saber or Kyber because the total cost of arithmetic operations of Sable is less than Saber or Kyber in the unmasked domain. It happens because Sable uses a slightly reduced parameter set than Saber. However, the performance cost of arithmetic operations in Florete or Espada is more than Saber or Kyber, as is the case in the unmasked domain.

3.2   Compression

Compression operation is the final step of the LWR.PKE.Dec algorithm, and in this step, encoded message bits are retrieved from the polynomial m'' after performing the reconciliation. For Florete and Sable, only the most significant bit is extracted, and for Espada, the four most significant bits are extracted from each coefficient of the polynomial m''. After that, these message bits are used as input in SHA3-512 hash function for computing the seed s' for the re-encryption procedure. These message bits are also needed to construct the session key. The extraction of the most significant bits is performed by using a logical shift operation in LWR-based KEM. This operation is easy to protect with Boolean masking. However, in the masked setting, the input of the compression operation is arithmetically masked, as its previous steps consisted of arithmetic operations. So, in the masked compression operation, first, we apply arithmetic to Boolean (A2B) conversion, and then we perform coefficient-wise $\epsilon_p - B$ bit right shift operation [23].

This compress operation in Sable is very similar to the one used in Saber, except for the value of ϵ_p. The value of the parameter ϵ_p is smaller in Sable than in Saber. So, the performance of A2B conversion is relatively better in Sable compared to Saber. Hence, the overall performance of the masked compress operation is better in Sable than in Saber. The compress operation of Florete is also similar to the compress operation used in Saber. The value of parameters ϵ_p in Florete is the same as Sable and so a little smaller than in Saber. However, the degree of the message containing part of the ciphertext polynomial is 768 in Florete, while it is 256 in Saber. So, the number of coefficients in Florete is three times compared to Saber. The performance cost of A2B conversion and $\epsilon_p - 1$ right shift operation in Florete is approximately three times the performance cost of these operations in Saber. Therefore, the performance of the masked compress operation in Florete takes approximately three times the cycles compared to the masked compress operation in Saber. The scheme Espada encodes four message bits in a single coefficient of ciphertext, and the polynomial size in Espada is 64, which is 1/4th of the polynomial size in Saber. The value of ϵ_p in Espada is slightly bigger than in Saber. However, the A2B conversion component is faster in Espada than in Saber due to the small polynomial size. Also, for the same reason, the coefficient-wise $\epsilon_p - 4$ bit right shift operation in Espada is faster than the coefficient-wise $\epsilon_p - 1$ bit right shift operation of Saber. Overall, the performance of the masked compress operation of Espada is roughly four times faster compared to the masked compress operation in Saber. As Kyber uses prime moduli, the masked compress operation of Kyber is far more complicated and has some extra steps. These extra steps includes conversion of arithmetic shares from $\mathbb{Z}_q$ to power-of-two modulus $\mathbb{Z}_{2^{k_q}}$, where $\log q < 2^{k_q}$. These are computationally quite expensive operations. Due to the power-of-two moduli, schemes in Scabbard and Saber do not need these additional steps. This results in more efficient masked compress operation for these schemes.

3.3   Message Decoding and Encoding

For Florete and Espada, the bit length of the message $i.e$ 256 is not equal to
the sizes of the polynomial ring, which are 768 and 64, respectively. Authors
of Scabbard proposed techniques to encode and decode the message into the
polynomial named $\texttt{arrange\_msg}$ and $\texttt{original\_msg}$ respectively. The encoding
and decoding operation where the polynomial ring length is the same as the
message length is very straightforward, and we do not need any special masking
gadget for $\texttt{original\_msg}$ and $\texttt{arrange\_msg}$ functions. However, we need to use a
special masking component to mask the $\texttt{original\_msg}$ function when polynomial
length equals r times message bits, where $r > 1$, e.g., Florete, NewHope [2]. We
use r coefficients to hide one message bit in this case. We also have to use
a special masking gadget to mask the $\texttt{arrange\_msg}$ function if the number of
message bits equals B times a polynomial length, where $B > 1$, e.g., Espada.
In these schemes, B message bits are hidden in a coefficient. We discuss these
gadgets below.

Message Decoding: In Florete, 3 coefficients had been used to hide one message
bit. The $\texttt{original\_msg} : \mathbb{Z}_2^{768} \longrightarrow \mathbb{Z}_2^{256}$ is defined here as if $\texttt{original\_msg}(m'') =$
m' and $b \in \{0, 1, \ldots, 255\}$ then $m'[b] = \begin{cases} 0 & \text{if } m''[b] + m''[b + 256] + m''[b + 512] \leq 1 \\ 1 & \text{otherwise} \end{cases}$.
First, we perform secure additions ($\texttt{SecAdd}$) over Boolean shared data to mask
this function, and the possible output must be one of $\{0, 1, 2, 3\}$. Notice that
it is always a two-bit number for any bit b. The output of the $\texttt{original\_msg}$ is
equal to the most significant bit, which is the 2nd bit. So, after performing the
masked addition, we extract the most significant bit of the masked output shares
(2nd bit). At last, we return the most significant bit as output $\texttt{original\_msg}$ for
each bit $b \in \{0, 1, \ldots, 255\}$. We present this masked function in Algorithm 1.

Algorithm 1: Masked $\texttt{original\_msg}$ function for Florete

Input : $\{m_i''\}_{1 \leq i \leq n}$ where $m_i'' \in \mathbb{Z}_2^{768}$ such that $\bigoplus_{i=1}^n m_i'' = m''$
Output : $\{m_i'\}_{1 \leq i \leq n}$ where $m_i' \in \mathbb{Z}_2^{256}$, $\bigoplus_{i=1}^n m_i' = m'$ and
$\quad\quad\quad$ $\texttt{original\_msg}(m'') = m'$

1 **for** j=0 **to** 255 **do**
2 $\quad$ $\{x_i[j]\}_{1 \leq i \leq n} \leftarrow m_i''[j]$; $\{y_i[j]\}_{1 \leq i \leq n} \leftarrow m_i''[256 + j]$;
$\quad\quad$ $\{z_i[j]\}_{1 \leq i \leq n} \leftarrow m_i''[512 + j]$
3 $\{w_i\}_{1 \leq i \leq n} \leftarrow \texttt{SecAdd}(\{x_i\}_{1 \leq i \leq n}, \{y_i\}_{1 \leq i \leq n})$
4 $\{w_i'\}_{1 \leq i \leq n} \leftarrow \texttt{SecAdd}(\{w_i\}_{1 \leq i \leq n}, \{z_i\}_{1 \leq i \leq n})$
5 $\{m_i'\}_{1 \leq i \leq n} \leftarrow \{w_i'\}_{1 \leq i \leq n} \gg 1$
6 **return** $\{m_i'\}_{1 \leq i \leq n}$

Message Encoding: In Florete and Sable, a co-efficient of the message polynomial carries a single message bit. Here, `arrange_msg` is defined by `arrange_msg` : $\mathbb{Z}_2^{256} \longrightarrow \mathbb{Z}_2^{768}$ and `arrange_msg` : $\mathbb{Z}_2^{256} \longrightarrow \mathbb{Z}_2^{256}$ for Florete and Sable respectively. The Boolean masked output of this function then takes part in the modular addition in the next step of the re-encryption stage as the message polynomial. As the shares of each coefficient of the message polynomial are in $\mathbb{Z}_2$, the Boolean shares are equivalent to the arithmetic shares. Hence, we can skip the Boolean to arithmetic conversion here. However, for Espada, we encode four message bits in a single co-efficient of the message polynomial, and `arrange_msg` is defined by `arrange_msg` : $\mathbb{Z}_2^{256} \longrightarrow \mathbb{Z}_4^{64}$. So, we need to convert Boolean shares of each coefficient of message polynomial to arithmetic shares using the `B2A` algorithm. After that, we perform the modular addition with two arithmetically masked inputs.

3.4   Hash Functions

Decapsulation algorithm uses one hash functions G (`SHA3-512`) and one pseudo-random number generator XOF (`SHAKE-128`). These functions are different instances of the sponge function Keccak-f[1600] [6]. It consists of five steps: (i) θ, (ii) ρ, (iii) π, (iv) χ, and (v) ι. Among the five steps, θ, ρ, and π are linear diffusion steps and ι is a simple addition. As all these four steps are linear operations over Boolean shares, in masked settings, we repeat all these operations on each share separately. Only χ is a degree 2 non-linear mapping and thus requires extra attention to mask. Overall, Keccak-f[1600] is less expensive to mask by using Boolean masking. Here, we use the higher-order masked Keccak proposed by Gross et al. [19]. Due to the compact parameter choices, Scabbard schemes require fewer pseudo-random numbers than Saber. Eventually, this leads to fewer invocations of the sponge function Keccak in Florete and Sable than in Espada. Moreover, the output length of `SHAKE-128` is the same for Florete and Sable, which is even smaller than Espada. To sum up, the performance cost of the masked XOF `SHAKE-128` is lower in Florete, Sable, and Espada compared to Saber.

3.5   Centered Binomial Sampler

The re-encryption part of the decapsulation algorithm contains a centered binomial sampler for sampling the vector $\mathbf{s}'$. This sampler outputs `HW`(x) − `HW`(y), where x and y are pseudo-random numbers and `HW` represents hamming weight. The bit size of pseudo-random numbers x and y depends on the scheme. These pseudo-random numbers are produced employing `SHAKE-128`. As mentioned in the previous section, these function is efficient if we mask with the help of Boolean masking. Hence, the shares generated from `SHAKE-128` are Boolean. However, upon constructing the $\mathbf{s}'$, we need to perform modular multiplication with inputs $\mathbf{s}'$ and public-key $\mathbf{b}$. This is efficient if we use arithmetic masking. Therefore, we need to perform Boolean to arithmetic conversion in the masked-centered binomial sampler. Schneider et al. [28] proposed two centered binomial samplers, Sampler$_1$ and Sampler$_2$. Sampler$_1$ first converts Boolean shares of x and y to arithmetic shares then computes $\text{HW}(x) - \text{HW}(y)$ by using arithmetic masking technique. Sampler$_2$ first computes $z = \text{HW}(x) - \text{HW}(y) + k$, where $k \geq \mu/2$ using Boolean masking. After that, it converts Boolean shares of z to arithmetic shares and then performs $z - k$ using the arithmetic masking technique to remain with arithmetic shares of $\text{HW}(x) - \text{HW}(y)$. Sampler$_1$ uses a bit-wise masking procedure, while sampler$_2$ uses the bitslicing technique on some parts of the algorithm for receiving better throughput. We have adopted these two samplers and optimized them to mask the CBD function of each KEM of the Scabbard suite. We could not directly use the optimized CBD used in Saber [23], as that one is optimized for β_8, and schemes of Scabbard use smaller CBD to sample the vector $\mathbf{s}'$. Schemes like Kyber and NewHope [2,28] use prime modulus. So, a few components there are different, for example, the B2A conversion and extra modular addition. As Scabbard uses power-of-two moduli, these components can be implemented in a much cheaper way for them. We describe the optimized masked CBD samplers for these schemes below.

3.5.1 Florete and Sable

In these two schemes, we take advantage of the centered binomial sampler with a small standard deviation, β_2. For β_2, x and y are 1-bit pseudo-random numbers. We have adopted Sampler$_1$ and Sampler$_2$, with these specification. As Sampler$_2$ is designed to provide a better performance, we started with the adaptation of Sampler$_2$ for β_2 named MaskCBDSampler$_A$ as shown in Algorithm 2. In this algorithm, first, we perform SecBitSub on Boolean shares of x and y to calculate Boolean shares of $\text{HW}(x) - \text{HW}(y)$. Second, we add constant 1 with the output shares of SecBitSub to avoid negative numbers. Third, we convert the output from Boolean shares to arithmetic shares with the help of the B2A conversion algorithm proposed in [7]. In the last step, we subtract the added constant in step-2, which converts secret shares from $\{0, 1, 2\}$ to $\{-1, 0, 1\}$.

Algorithm 2: MaskCBDSampler$_A$ ([28], using sampler$_2$)

Input : $\{x_i\}_{0 \leq i \leq n}, \{y_i\}_{0 \leq i \leq n}$ where $x_i, y_i \in \mathbb{R}_2$ such that
$\bigoplus_{i=0}^{n} x_i = x, \bigoplus_{i=0}^{n} y_i = y$
Output : $\{A_i\}_{0 \leq i \leq n}$ where $A_i \in \mathbb{R}_q$ and $\sum_{i=0}^{n} A_i = (\text{HW}(x) - \text{HW}(y)) \bmod q$

1 $\{z_i\}_{0 \leq i \leq n} \leftarrow \text{SecBitSub}(\{x_i\}_{0 \leq i \leq n}, \{y_i\}_{0 \leq i \leq n})$
2 $z_0[0] \leftarrow z_0[0] \oplus 1$
3 $\{A_i\}_{0 \leq i \leq n} \leftarrow \text{B2A}(\{z_i\}_{0 \leq i \leq n})$ [7]
4 $A_1 \leftarrow (A_1 - 1) \bmod q$
5 **return** $\{A_i\}_{0 \leq i \leq n}$

Algorithm 3: MaskCBDSampler$_B$ ([28], using sampler$_1$)

Input : $\{x_i\}_{0 \leq i \leq n}, \{y_i\}_{0 \leq i \leq n}$ where $x_i, y_i \in \mathbb{R}_2$ such that
$\bigoplus_{i=0}^{n} x_i = x, \bigoplus_{i=0}^{n} y_i = y$
Output : $\{A_i\}_{0 \leq i \leq n}$ where $A_i \in \mathbb{R}_q$ and $\sum_{i=0}^{n} A_i = (\text{HW}(x) - \text{HW}(y)) \bmod q$

1 $\{T1_i\}_{0 \leq i \leq n} \leftarrow$ B2A($\{x_i\}_{0 \leq i \leq n}$) [7]; $\{T2_i\}_{0 \leq i \leq n} \leftarrow$ B2A($\{y_i\}_{0 \leq i \leq n}$) [7]
2 **for** $i=0$ **to** n **do**
3 $\quad \lfloor A_i \leftarrow (T1_i - T2_i)$
4 **return** $\{A_i\}_{0 \leq i \leq n}$

Algorithm 4: MaskCBDSampler$_C$ ([28], using sampler$_2$)

Input : $\{x_i\}_{0 \leq i \leq n}, \{y_i\}_{0 \leq i \leq n}$ where $x_i, y_i \in \mathbb{R}_2^3$ such that
$\bigoplus_{i=0}^{n} x_i = x, \bigoplus_{i=0}^{n} y_i = y$
Output : $\{A_i\}_{0 \leq i \leq n}$ where $A_i \in \mathbb{R}_q$ and $\sum_{i=0}^{n} A_i = (\text{HW}(x) - \text{HW}(y)) \bmod q$

1 $\{z_i\}_{0 \leq i \leq n} \leftarrow$ SecBitAdd($\{x_i\}_{0 \leq i \leq n}$) [4]
2 $\{z_i\}_{0 \leq i \leq n} \leftarrow$ SecBitSub($\{z_i\}_{0 \leq i \leq n}, \{y_i\}_{0 \leq i \leq n}$) [28]
3 **for** $i=0$ **to** n **do**
4 $\quad \lfloor z_i[2] \leftarrow (z_i[2] \oplus z_i[1])$
5 $z_0[2] \leftarrow z_0[2] \oplus 1$
6 $\{A_i\}_{0 \leq i \leq n} \leftarrow$ B2A($\{z_i\}_{0 \leq i \leq n}$) [7]
7 $A_1 \leftarrow (A_1 - 4) \bmod q$
8 **return** $\{A_i\}_{0 \leq i \leq n}$

As the bit size of x and y is small for β_2, the bitslice technique for addition and subtraction does not improve the throughput much. So, for comparison purposes, we have adopted the technique of the sampler$_1$ for β_2. We name this algorithm MaskCBDSampler$_A$, and present in Algorithm 3. In this algorithm, we conduct B2A conversions over x and y and then perform share-wise subtraction between arithmetic shares of x and y.

3.5.2 Espada We use the centered binomial sampler, β_6, in this scheme. For β_6, x and y are 3-bit pseudo-random numbers. We have adopted a bit-sliced implementation of Sampler$_2$ from [28] for β_6 to achieve better efficiency as the standard deviation of the CBD is large. We name this masked sampler as MaskCBDSampler$_C$, and it is shown in Algorithm 4. Similar to MaskCBDSampler$_B$, MaskCBDSampler$_C$ begins with the SecBitAdd operation, which is performed on Boolean shares of x and generates Boolean shares of HW(x). Then SecBitSub is conducted over the Boolean output shares and Boolean shares of y and outputs Boolean shares of HW(x) $-$ HW(y). After that, the constant 4 is added with the output shares of SecBitSub to avoid negative numbers. In the next step, we convert the output from Boolean shares to arithmetic shares with the help of B2A conversion algorithm proposed in [7]. Finally, we subtract the added constant in step-7 and transform secret shares from $\{1, 2, 3, 4, 5, 6, 7\}$ to $\{-3, -2, -1, 0, 1, 2, 3\}$.

The masked CBD sampler (β_8) used in Saber is faster than the masked CBD of Kyber because of the power-of-two moduli. MaskCBDSampler$_A$ and MaskCBDSampler$_B$ are optimized implementation of β_2, which has been used in Florete and Sable. MaskCBDSampler$_C$ is designed for Espada, which is optimized implementation of β_6. For β_2 and β_6, the B2A conversion is much faster than β_8 thanks to the smaller coefficients size in the input polynomial. Therefore, the performance cost of the masked CBD is less for all the schemes in Scabbard compared to Saber or Kyber. A more detailed performance cost analysis of masked CBD implementations for Scabbard is presented in Sect. 4.1.

3.6 Ciphertext Comparison

It is one of the costliest components for masked implementations of lattice-based KEMs, which is a part of the FO transformation. Previously, many methods have been proposed to perform this component efficiently [9,14,23]. For the masked ciphertext comparison part of each KEM of Scabbard, we have adopted the improved simple masked comparison method used in the higher-order masked implementation of Saber [23]. To the best of our knowledge, this is currently the most efficient masked ciphertext comparison implementation available. Through this process, we compare the arithmetically masked output of the re-encryption component before the right shift operation ($\tilde{u}$, $\tilde{v}$) with the unmasked public ciphertext, (u, v). Additionally, note that $\mathbf{u}' = \tilde{\mathbf{u}} \gg (\epsilon_q - \epsilon_p)$ and $v' = \tilde{v} \gg (\epsilon_p - \epsilon_t - B)$. At first, we perform A2B conversion step over the arithmetically masked shares of the output and transform these to Boolean shares, and then we follow the right shift operation. After that, we subtract the unmasked public ciphertext (u, v) from a share of the Boolean masked output of the A2B operation with the help of the XOR operation. Finally, we proceed with checking that all the returned bits of the subtract operation are zero with the BooleanAllBitsOneTest algorithm. This algorithm returns 1 only if it receives all the bits encoded in each coefficient of the polynomials is 1; else it returns 0. All these aforementioned steps are presented in Algorithm 5. For further details, we refer to the higher-order masked Saber paper [23].

The parameter settings are different for each KEM of the Scabbard suite. Due to this, byte sizes of the masked inputs of the functions A2B and BooleanAllBitsOneTest are different for each KEM of the suite, and we show these numbers in Table 2. For reference, we also provide the byte sizes of the masked inputs of A2B and BooleanAllBitsOneTest for Saber in this table. These differences in the input bytes also affect the performances of corresponding masked implementations. The masked input sizes of both the functions A2B and BooleanAllBitsOneTest for Sable are less than Saber. On account of this, the performance cost of masked ciphertext comparison is cheaper for Sable than Saber. The masked input sizes of both functions A2B and

---

Algorithm 5: Simple masked comparison algorithm [23]

Input   : Arithmetic masked re-encrypted ciphertext ($\{\tilde{\mathbf{u}}_i\}_{0 \leq i \leq n}$, $\{\tilde{v}_i\}_{0 \leq i \leq n}$) and public ciphertext ($\mathbf{u}$ and v) where each $\tilde{\mathbf{u}}_i \in \mathbb{R}_{2^{\epsilon_q}}^{\Gamma}$ and $\tilde{v}_i \in \mathbb{R}_{2^{\epsilon_p}}$ and $\sum_{i=0}^{n} \tilde{\mathbf{u}}_i \bmod q = \dot{\mathbf{u}} \sum_{i=0}^{n} \tilde{v}_i \bmod q = \tilde{v}$.

Output : $\{bit\}_{0 \leq i \leq n}$, where with each $bit_i \in \mathbb{Z}_2$ and $\bigoplus_{i=0}^{n} bit_i = 1$ iff $\mathbf{u} = \mathbf{u}' \gg (\epsilon_q - \epsilon_p)$ and $v = v' \gg (\epsilon_p - \epsilon_t - B)$, otherwise 0.

1 $\{\mathbf{y}_i\}_{0 \leq i \leq n} \leftarrow$ A2B($\{\tilde{\mathbf{u}}_i\}_{0 \leq i \leq n}$); $\{x_i\}_{0 \leq i \leq n} \leftarrow$ A2B($\{\tilde{v}_i\}_{0 \leq i \leq n}$)

2 $\{\mathbf{y}_i\}_{0 \leq i \leq n} \leftarrow (\{\mathbf{y}_i\}_{0 \leq i \leq n} \gg (\epsilon_q - \epsilon_p))$; $\{x_i\}_{0 \leq i \leq n} \leftarrow (\{x_i\}_{0 \leq i \leq n} \gg (\epsilon_p - \epsilon_t - B))$

3 $\mathbf{y}_1 \leftarrow \mathbf{y}_1 \oplus \mathbf{u}$; $x_1 \leftarrow x_1 \oplus v$

   /* Boolean circuit to test all bits of $(\mathbf{y}, x)$ are 0   */

4 $\mathbf{y}_0 \leftarrow \neg \mathbf{y}_0$; $x_0 \leftarrow \neg x_0$

5 $\{bit_i\}_{0 \leq i \leq n} \leftarrow$ BooleanAllBitsOneTest ($\{\mathbf{y}_i\}_{0 \leq i \leq n}, \{x_i\}_{0 \leq i \leq n}, \epsilon_p, \epsilon_t$)

6 **return** $\{bit_i\}_{0 \leq i \leq n}$

Table 2. Size of inputs of the A2B and BooleanAllBitsOneTest functions situated in Algorithm 5 for Scabbard's schemes and Saber

Function	Input Bytes			
	Florete	Sable	Espada	Saber
A2B	1824	1344	1544	1568
BooleanAllBitsOneTest	1248	1024	1304	1088

BooleanAllBitsOneTest for Florete are greater than Saber. So, the masked ciphertext comparison component of Florete needs more cycles than Saber. The masked input size of the function A2B of Espada is less than Saber, but the input size of BooleanAllBitsOneTest for Espada is bigger than Saber. So, the first-order masked comparison component is faster for Espada compared to Saber, but the second and third-order masked comparison component is slower in Espada than in Saber. However, the performance of each scheme's masked ciphertext comparison component in the suite Scabbard is better than Kyber because of the prepossessing steps needed in Kyber [14].

4   Performance Evaluation

We implemented all our algorithms on a 32-bit ARM Cortex-M4 microcontroller, STM32F407-DISCOVERY development board. We used the popular post-quantum cryptographic library and benchmarking framework PQM4 [21] for all measurements. The system we used to measure the performance of the masked implementations includes the compiler `arm-none-eabi-gcc` version `9.2.1`. The PQM4 library uses the system clock to measure the clock cycle, and the frequency of this clock is 24 MHz. We employ random numbers to ensure the independence of the shares of the masked variable in masking algorithms. For this purpose, we use the on-chip TRNG (true random number generator) of the ARM Cortex-M4 device. This TRNG has a different clock frequency than the main system clock, which is 48 MHz. It generates a 32-bit random number in 40 clock cycles, equivalent to 20 clock cycles for the main system clock. Our implementations can be used for any order of masking. In this section, we provide the performance details of first-, second-, and third-order masking.

Table 3. Performance of MaskCBDSampler$_A$ and MaskCBDSampler$_B$

Order	×1000 clock cycles		
	1st	2nd	3rd
MaskCBDSampler$_A$	**178,591**	504,101	1,226,224
MaskCBDSampler$_B$	182,714	**499,732**	**909,452**

4.1 Analyzing the Performance of Masked CBD Samplers

As discussed in Sect. 3.5, MaskCBDSampler$_A$ and MaskCBDSampler$_B$ can be used for both Florete and Sable. Performance comparisons between MaskCBDSampler$_A$ and MaskCBDSampler$_B$ for different shares are provided in Table 3. Overall, we observe from the table that MaskCBDSampler$_B$ performs better than MaskCBDSampler$_A$ for higher-order masking. As a result, we use MaskCBDSampler$_B$ in the masked implementations of Florete and Sable.

4.2 Performance Measurement of Masked Scabbard Suite

Tables 4, 5, and 6 provide the clock cycles required to execute the masked decapsulation algorithm of Florete, Espada, and Sable, respectively. The overhead factors for the first-, second-, and third-order masked decapsulation operation of Florete are 2.74×, 5.07×, and 7.75× compared to the unmasked version. For Espada, the overhead factors for the first-, second-, and third-order decapsulation algorithm compared to the unmasked decapsulation are 1.78×, 2.82×, and 4.07, respectively. Similarly, for Sable, the overhead factors for the first-, second-, and third-order decapsulation algorithm are 2.38×, 4.26×, and 6.35× than the unmasked one. As mentioned earlier, the masked algorithm needs fresh random numbers to maintain security. Generating random numbers is a costly procedure. So, for a better understanding of the improvements, we also present the requirement of random bytes for Florete, Espada, and Sable in Table 7.

Table 4. Performance of Florete

Order	Unmask	×1000 clock cycles		
		1st	2nd	3rd
Florete CCA-KEM-Decapsulation	954	2,621 (2.74×)	4,844 (5.07×)	7,395 (7.75×)
CPA-PKE-Decryption	248	615 (2.47×)	1,107 (4.46×)	1,651 (6.65×)
Polynomial arithmetic	241	461 (1.91×)	690 (2.86×)	917 (3.80×)
Compression *original_msg*	6	153 (25.50×)	416 (69.33×)	734 (122.33×)
Hash $\mathcal{G}$ (SHA3-512)	13	123 (9.46×)	242 (18.61×)	379 (29.15×)
CPA-PKE-Encryption	554	1,744 (3.14×)	3,354 (6.05×)	5,225 (9.43×)
Secret generation	29	427 (14.72×)	982 (33.86×)	1,663 (57.34×)
XOF (SHAKE-128)	25	245 (9.80×)	484 (19.36×)	756 (30.24×)
CBD (β_2)	4	182 (45.50×)	497 (124.25×)	907 (226.75×)
Polynomial arithmetic *arrange_msg*	524	943 (2.51×)	1,357 (4.52×)	1,783 (6.79×)
Polynomial Comparison		373	1,014	1,778
Other operations	138	139 (1.00×)	140 (1.01×)	140 (1.01×)

Table 5. Performance of Espada

Order	Unmask	×1000 clock cycles		
		1st	2nd	3rd
Espada CCA-KEM-Decapsulation	2,422	4,335 (1.78×)	6,838 (2.82×)	9,861 (4.07×)
CPA-PKE-Decryption	70	137 (1.95×)	230 (3.28×)	324 (4.62×)
Polynomial arithmetic	69	116 (1.68×)	170 (2.46×)	225 (3.26×)
Compression *original_msg*	0.4	20 (50.00×)	60 (150.00×)	99 (247.50×)
Hash $\mathcal{G}$ (SHA3-512)	13	123 (9.46×)	243 (18.69×)	379 (29.15×)
CPA-PKE-Encryption	2,215	3,950 (1.78×)	6,240 (2.81×)	9,031 (4.07×)
Secret generation	57	748 (13.12×)	1,650 (28.94×)	3,009 (52.78×)
XOF (SHAKE-128)	51	489 (9.58×)	968 (18.98×)	1,510 (29.60×)
CBD (β_6)	6	259 (43.16×)	681 (113.50×)	1,498 (249.66×)
Polynomial arithmetic *arrange_msg*	2,157	2,865 (1.44×)	3,593 (2.12×)	4,354 (2.79×)
Polynomial Comparison		259	996	1,667
Other operations	124	124 (1.00×)	124 (1.00×)	126 (1.01×)

Table 6. Performance of Sable

Order	Unmask	×1000 clock cycles		
		1st	2nd	3rd
Sable CCA-KEM-Decapsulation	1,020	2,431 (2.38×)	4,348 (4.26×)	6,480 (6.35×)
CPA-PKE-Decryption	130	291 (2.23×)	510 (3.92×)	745 (5.73×)
Polynomial arithmetic	128	238 (1.85×)	350 (2.73×)	465 (3.63×)
Compression *original_msg*	2	52 (26.00×)	160 (80.00×)	280 (140.00×)
Hash $\mathcal{G}$ (SHA3-512)	13	123 (9.46×)	242 (18.61×)	379 (29.15×)
CPA-PKE-Encryption	764	1,903 (2.49×)	3,482 (4.55×)	5,241 (6.85×)
Secret generation	29	427 (14.72×)	984 (33.93×)	1,666 (57.44×)
XOF (SHAKE-128)	25	245 (9.80×)	484 (19.36×)	756 (30.24×)
CBD (β_2)	4	182 (45.50×)	499 (124.75×)	909 (227.25×)
Polynomial arithmetic *arrange_msg*	734	1,187 (2.00×)	1,640 (3.40×)	2,086 (4.86×)
Polynomial Comparison		287	856	1,488
Other operations	112	113 (1.00×)	113 (1.00×)	113 (1.00×)

Table 7. Random number requirement for all the masked schemes of Scabbard

	# Random bytes								
	Florete			**Espada**			**Sable**		
Order	1st	2nd	3rd	1st	2nd	3rd	1st	2nd	3rd
CCA-KEM-Decapsulation	15,824	52,176	101,280	11,496	39,320	85,296	12,496	39,152	75,232
CPA-PKE-Decryption	2,560	10,176	20,352	304	1,216	2,432	832	3,328	6,656
Polynomial arithmetic	0	0	0	0	0	0	0	0	0
Compression	2,496	9,984	19,968	304	1,216	2,432	832	3,328	1,152
original_msg	64	192	384	0	0	0	0	0	0
Hash $\mathcal{G}$ (SHA3-512)	192	576	1,152	192	576	1,152	192	576	67,424
CPA-PKE-Encryption	13,072	41,424	79,776	11,000	37,528	81,712	11,472	35,248	6,656
Secret generation	6,528	16,512	29,952	4,896	14,688	35,520	6,528	16,512	29,952
XOF (SHAKE-128)	384	1,152	2,304	768	2,304	4,608	384	1,152	2,304
CBD (Binomial Sampler)	6,144	15,360	27,648	4,128	12,384	30,912	6,144	15,360	27,648
Polynomial arithmetic	0	0	0	0	0	0	0	0	0
arrange_msg	0	0	0	256	768	2,048	0	0	0
Polynomial Comparison	6,544	24,912	49,824	5,848	22,072	44,144	4,944	18,736	37,472
Other operations	0	0	0	0	0	0	0	0	0

4.3   Performance Comparison of Masked Scabbard Suite with the State-of-the-Art

We analyze the performance and random number requirements for masked decapsulation algorithms of Scabbard's schemes in comparison to the state-of-the-art masked implementations of LBC. We compare our masked Scabbard implementation with Bronchain et al.'s [10] and Bos et al.'s [9] masked implementations of Kyber and Kundu et al.'s [23] masked implementations of Saber in Table 8.

Table 8. Performance comparison of masked Scabbard implementations with the state-of-the-art

Scheme	Performance			# Randm numbers		
	(×1000 clock cycles)			(bytes)		
	1st	2nd	3rd	1st	2nd	3rd
Florete (this work)	2,621	4,844	7,395	15,824	52,176	101,280
Espada (this work)	4,335	6,838	9,861	11,496	39,320	85,296
Sable (this work)	**2,431**	**4,348**	**6,480**	12,496	39,152	75,232
Saber [23]	3,022	5,567	8,649	12,752	43,760	93,664
uSaber [23]	2,473	4,452	6,947	10,544	36,848	79,840
Kyber [10]	10,018	16,747	24,709	–	–	–
Kyber [9]	3,116*	44,347	115,481	12,072*	902,126	2,434,170

*: optimized specially for the first-order masking

First-, second- and third-order masked decapsulation implementations of Florete are respectively 73%, 71%, and 70% faster than Bronchain et al.'s [10] masked implementation of Kyber. Bos et al. optimized their algorithm specifically for the first-order masking of Kyber. Even though it is 15% slower than the first-order masked decapsulation of Florete. Bos et al.'s [9] second- and third-order masked implementations of Kyber are respectively 89% and 93% slower than Florete. The random byte requirements in the masked version of Florete compared to Kyber are 94% less for the second order and 95% less for the third order. Florete also performs better than Saber. Florete needs 13%, 12%, and 14% fewer clock cycles than Saber for first-, second-, and third-order masking.

Masked decapsulation implementation of Espada performs 56%, 59%, and 60% better than Bronchain et al.'s [10] masked implementation of Kyber for first-, second-, and third-order, respectively. Second-, and third-order masked implementations of Espada are faster than Bos et al.'s [9] masked Kyber by 84% and 91%, respectively. The random bytes requirements in Espada compared to Kyber are 95% less for the second-order and 96% less for the third-order masking. Espada also uses fewer random numbers than Saber. Espada requires 9% fewer random bytes in first-order masking, 10% fewer random bytes in second-order masking, and 8% fewer random bytes in third-order masking than Saber.

We show that the masked implementation of Sable performs better than masked Kyber and Saber for first-, second-, and third-order (like Florete). Sable performs 75%, 74%, and 73% better than Bronchain et al.'s [10] masked implementation of Kyber and 21%, 90%, and 94% better than Bos et al.'s [9] masked implementation of Kyber first-, second-, and third-order, respectively. Compared to Kyber, Sable requires 95% and 96% less random bytes for second- and third-order masking. The performance of masked Sable is better than masked Saber by 19% for first-order, 21% for second-order, and 25% for third-order masking. Masked Sable uses 2%, 10%, and 19% less number of random bytes for first-, second-, and third-order than masked Saber, respectively. uSaber is a masking-friendly variant of Saber proposed during the third round of NIST submission. We notice that masked Sable is also faster than masked uSaber for arbitrary order. Masked Sable is 1% faster for first-order, 2% for second-order, and 6% for third-order than masked uSaber. Although first- and second-order masked Sable needs more random bytes than uSaber, third-order masked Sable requires 5% less random bytes than uSaber.

Implementations of masked Scabbard schemes achieve better performance and use fewer random bytes than masked Kyber because the schemes of Scabbard use the RLWR/ MLWR problem as an underlying hard problem and Kyber uses the MLWE problem as the hard problem. The decapsulation operation of RLWR/ MLWR-based KEM has fewer components compared to the decapsulation operation of RLWE/ MLWE-based KEM due to the requirement of sampling error vectors and polynomials generations in the re-encryption step of RLWE/ MLWE-based KEMs. RLWR/ MLWR-based KEMs also benefit due to the use of power-of-two moduli. Computationally expensive components, such as A2B or B2A conversions, are cheaper when using power-of-two moduli. The schemes of Scabbard also use slightly smaller parameters than Kyber, which also contributes to achieving better performance and requirements of fewer random bytes for masked implementation of Scabbard's KEMs compared to Kyber.

5   Conclusions

In this work, we presented the impact of different design decisions of LBC on masking. We analyzed each component where masking is needed and discussed each design decision's positive and negative impact on performance. As we mentioned at the beginning of the paper, it is possible to improve different practical aspects, such as masking overheads, by modifying the existing designs of PQC. This highlights the necessity of further research efforts to improve existing PQC designs.

Acknowledgements. This work was partially supported by Horizon 2020 ERC Advanced Grant (101020005 Belfort), CyberSecurity Research Flanders with reference number VR20192203, BE QCI: Belgian-QCI (3E230370) (see beqci.eu), and Intel Corporation. Angshuman Karmakar is funded by FWO (Research Foundation - Flanders) as a junior post-doctoral fellow (contract number 203056/1241722N LV).

References

1. Alagic, G., et al.: Status report on the third round of the NIST post-quantum cryptography standardization process (2022). Accessed 26 June 2023
2. Alkim, E., Ducas, L., Pöppelmann, T., Schwabe, P.: Post-quantum key exchange - a new hope. In: Holz, T., Savage, S. (eds.) 25th USENIX Security Symposium, USENIX Security 2016, Austin, TX, USA, 10–12 August 2016, pp. 327–343. USENIX Association (2016)
3. Banerjee, A., Peikert, C., Rosen, A.: Pseudorandom functions and lattices. In: Pointcheval, D., Johansson, T. (eds.) EUROCRYPT 2012. LNCS, vol. 7237, pp. 719–737. Springer, Heidelberg (2012). https://doi.org/10.1007/978-3-642-29011-4_42
4. Beirendonck, M.V., D'Anvers, J.P., Karmakar, A., Balasch, J., Verbauwhede, I.: A side-channel resistant implementation of SABER. Cryptology ePrint Archive, Report 2020/733 (2020)
5. Bermudo Mera, J.M., Karmakar, A., Kundu, S., Verbauwhede, I.: Scabbard: a suite of efficient learning with rounding key-encapsulation mechanisms. IACR Trans. Cryptogr. Hardw. Embed. Syst. **2021**(4), 474–509 (2021)
6. Bertoni, G., Daemen, J., Peeters, M., Van Assche, G.: Keccak. In: Johansson, T., Nguyen, P.Q. (eds.) EUROCRYPT 2013. LNCS, vol. 7881, pp. 313–314. Springer, Heidelberg (2013). https://doi.org/10.1007/978-3-642-38348-9_19
7. Bettale, L., Coron, J., Zeitoun, R.: Improved high-order conversion from Boolean to arithmetic masking. IACR Trans. Cryptogr. Hardw. Embed. Syst. **2018**(2), 22–45 (2018)
8. Bos, J., Ducas, L., Kiltz, E., Lepoint, T., Lyubashevsky, V., Schanck, J.M., Schwabe, P., Seiler, G., Stehlé, D.: CRYSTALS - kyber: a CCA-secure module-lattice-based KEM. Cryptology ePrint Archive, Report 2017/634 (2017)
9. Bos, J.W., Gourjon, M., Renes, J., Schneider, T., van Vredendaal, C.: Masking kyber: first- and higher-order implementations. IACR Cryptology ePrint Archive, p. 483 (2021)
10. Bronchain, O., Cassiers, G.: Bitslicing arithmetic/Boolean masking conversions for fun and profit with application to lattice-based KEMs. Cryptology ePrint Archive, Report 2022/158 (2022)

11. Chari, S., Jutla, C.S., Rao, J.R., Rohatgi, P.: Towards sound approaches to counteract power-analysis attacks. In: Wiener, M. (ed.) CRYPTO 1999. LNCS, vol. 1666, pp. 398–412. Springer, Heidelberg (1999). https://doi.org/10.1007/3-540-48405-1_26

12. Cheon, J.H., Choe, H., Hong, D., Yi, M.: SMAUG: pushing lattice-based key encapsulation mechanisms to the limits. Cryptology ePrint Archive, Paper 2023/739 (2023)

13. Coron, J.-S.: Higher order masking of look-up tables. In: Nguyen, P.Q., Oswald, E. (eds.) EUROCRYPT 2014. LNCS, vol. 8441, pp. 441–458. Springer, Heidelberg (2014). https://doi.org/10.1007/978-3-642-55220-5_25

14. D'Anvers, J., Beirendonck, M.V., Verbauwhede, I.: Revisiting higher-order masked comparison for lattice-based cryptography: algorithms and bit-sliced implementations. IEEE Trans. Comput. **72**(2), 321–332 (2023)

15. D'Anvers, J.-P., Karmakar, A., Sinha Roy, S., Vercauteren, F.: Saber: module-LWR based key exchange, CPA-secure encryption and CCA-secure KEM. In: Joux, A., Nitaj, A., Rachidi, T. (eds.) AFRICACRYPT 2018. LNCS, vol. 10831, pp. 282–305. Springer, Cham (2018). https://doi.org/10.1007/978-3-319-89339-6_16

16. Espitau, T., et al.: MITAKA: a simpler, parallelizable, maskable variant of FALCON. In: Dunkelman, O., Dziembowski, S. (eds.) EUROCRYPT 2022. LNCS, vol. 13277, pp. 222–253. Springer, Cham (2022). https://doi.org/10.1007/978-3-031-07082-2_9

17. Fouque, P.A., et al.: FALCON: Fast-Fourier lattice-based compact signatures over NTRU (2018). Accessed 28 June 2023

18. Fujisaki, E., Okamoto, T.: How to enhance the security of public-key encryption at minimum cost. In: Imai, H., Zheng, Y. (eds.) PKC 1999. LNCS, vol. 1560, pp. 53–68. Springer, Heidelberg (1999). https://doi.org/10.1007/3-540-49162-7_5

19. Gross, H., Schaffenrath, D., Mangard, S.: Higher-order side-channel protected implementations of KECCAK. Cryptology ePrint Archive, Report 2017/395 (2017)

20. Jiang, H., Zhang, Z., Chen, L., Wang, H., Ma, Z.: Post-quantum IND-CCA-secure KEM without additional hash. IACR Cryptology ePrint Archive 2017/1096 (2017)

21. Kannwischer, M.J., Rijneveld, J., Schwabe, P., Stoffelen, K.: PQM4: post-quantum crypto library for the ARM Cortex-M4. https://github.com/mupq/pqm4

22. KpqC: Korean PQC competition (2022). https://www.kpqc.or.kr/competition.html. Accessed 30 June 2023

23. Kundu, S., D'Anvers, J.P., Van Beirendonck, M., Karmakar, A., Verbauwhede, I.: Higher-order masked saber. In: Galdı, C., Jarecki, S. (eds.) SCN 2022. LNCS, vol. 13409, pp. 93–116. Springer, Cham (2022). https://doi.org/10.1007/978-3-031-14791-3_5

24. Langlois, A., Stehlé, D.: Worst-case to average-case reductions for module lattices. Des. Codes Cryptogr. **75**(3), 565–599 (2015). https://doi.org/10.1007/s10623-014-9938-4

25. Miller, V.S.: Use of elliptic curves in cryptography. In: Williams, H.C. (ed.) CRYPTO 1985. LNCS, vol. 218, pp. 417–426. Springer, Heidelberg (1986). https://doi.org/10.1007/3-540-39799-X_31

26. Rivain, M., Prouff, E.: Provably secure higher-order masking of AES. In: Mangard, S., Standaert, F.-X. (eds.) CHES 2010. LNCS, vol. 6225, pp. 413–427. Springer, Heidelberg (2010). https://doi.org/10.1007/978-3-642-15031-9_28

27. Rivest, R.L., Shamir, A., Adleman, L.M.: A method for obtaining digital signatures and public-key cryptosystems. Commun. ACM **21**(2), 120–126 (1978)

28. Schneider, T., Paglialonga, C., Oder, T., Güneysu, T.: Efficiently masking binomial sampling at arbitrary orders for lattice-based crypto. In: Lin, D., Sako, K. (eds.) PKC 2019. LNCS, vol. 11443, pp. 534–564. Springer, Cham (2019). https://doi.org/10.1007/978-3-030-17259-6_18
29. Shamir, A.: How to share a secret. Commun. ACM **22**(11), 612–613 (1979)
30. Yao, A.C.: Protocols for secure computations. In: 23rd Annual Symposium on Foundations of Computer Science (SFCS 1982), pp. 160–164 (1982)

Spliced Region Detection and Localization in Digital Images Based on CNN Learning Guided by Color Transitions and Surface Texture

Debjit Das(✉)🆔, Ranit Das(✉)🆔, and Ruchira Naskar(✉)🆔

Department of Information Technology, Indian Institute of Engineering Science
and Technology, Shibpur, Howrah 711103, West Bengal, India
{debjit.rs2020,ruchira}@it.iiests.ac.in,
2021itm002.ranit@students.iiests.ac.in

Abstract. In this paper, we deal with the problem of localization of image splicing, which has proven to be one of the major types of digital image forgery today, where an adversary combines regions from multiple source images, to create a natural-looking composite image. This type of composition, difficult to identify by the naked eye, many times proves to be beneficial in synthetic image generation tasks for media, photography and advertisement industries. However, when performed with mal-intention, it needs to be detected in order to prevent various social perils ranging from privacy violations and the spread of fake news, to more serious threats of fake identity generation in terrorist activities and money laundering cases. In this work, we propose a Convolutional Neural Network (CNN) model that accurately identifies the forged regions in a spliced image. We introduce three pre-processing steps on the forged image to identify the color transitions between pixels, overall surface texture and zones with the most prominent colors. It generates three new images from the forged image. We merged them together to make a single image, which is used to train our neural network model. The proposed method identifies the boundary pixels if they are authentic or forged, and subsequently finds the pattern to detect the boundary of the forged region. The model has been rigorously evaluated, and the experiment results obtained are extremely encouraging on the CASIA 2.0 dataset.

Keywords: Color transition · CNN · Digital image forgery · Spliced surface textures · Splicing localization

1 Introduction

The rapid progress of technology and globalization has revolutionized the field of photography, granting widespread access to affordable electronic devices and fuelling the growing popularity of digital cameras. In fact, smartphones today have impressive camera setups that can rival even the most advanced Digital Single-Lens Reflex (DSLR) cameras. Consequently, photography has become an integral part of the modern digital world, with nearly everyone capturing and sharing photos effortlessly. As the availability of electronic devices and digital cameras increased, so did the tools for modifying

F. Regazzoni et al. (Eds.): SPACE 2023, LNCS 14412, pp. 185–196, 2024.
https://doi.org/10.1007/978-3-031-51583-5_11

(a)   (b)   (c)   (d)

Fig. 1. Image splicing example from CASIA 2.0 dataset. (a), (b) Two authentic images (c) Spliced image (d) Ground truth of the spliced image

and manipulating photographs. Originally intended to refine and enhance image quality, these technologies have now become widely accessible and affordable even to layman users. However, this accessibility has also given rise to a significant concern – the creation of fake or counterfeit images. The harm inflicted by such counterfeit photos can be critical, and, in some cases, irreparable.

Image tampering can be approached from two angles: active and passive. Active approaches involve incorporating digital signatures and watermarks into images to establish authenticity and ownership. These methods provide a level of protection against unauthorized usage or manipulation. On the other hand, passive approaches encompass various techniques, including copying, splicing, image morphing, retouching, and enhancement. Each technique presents different challenges and can be employed to deceive viewers by creating misleading or false representations.

This paper deals with a specific form of image forgery, viz. *digital image splicing*. We address the problem of identifying and locating spliced portions in a digital image. In Fig. 1(a) and (b) represent two authentic images, and (c) is the result of a splicing attack on the two images, where we can see a region from image (a) has been spliced onto the image (b), and (d) represents the ground truth of the spliced image. This is an example of image forgery using the *splicing* technique.

In recent decades, researchers have developed various strategies for identifying the forgery of digital images [1, 13]. However, detecting image splicing forgery poses a greater challenge than other tamper detection methods. This is primarily due to the post-processing techniques employed to eliminate visible differences after tampering in a splicing attack. As illustrated in the example in Fig. 1, it remains difficult for the human eye to discern the tampered area even with a meticulous inspection.

Traditional image forgery tracking algorithms typically rely on detecting specific artefacts within a manipulated image to identify instances of forgery [8]. However, in recent times, Convolutional Neural Networks (CNN) have gained popularity in the field of computer vision. In this particular problem too, CNNs have achieved remarkable success. This is due to two key factors. Firstly, CNN exploits the strong correlation among neighbouring pixels. Rather than establishing direct connections between every pair of pixels, CNN prioritizes regionally clustered interconnections. This approach enables CNN to capture spatial relationships within an image effectively. Secondly,

CNN employs weight sharing via a convolutional process to generate feature maps. This means that learned characteristics from training images can be applied to identify subtle and imperceptible forgeries. Leveraging these characteristics, CNN offers a promising approach for detecting forgeries within images. By constructing a CNN-based network, we can effectively analyse the various artefacts present in a manipulated image [15, 17, 21]. Among recent deep learning-based approaches, Liu et al. [9] proposed PSCC-Net, which analyses images using a two-path technique. In [18] Wu et al. employed a CNN to extract block-like features from a picture, calculate the similarity between distinct blocks, and discover the matched ones. Another note-worthy deep neural network developed by Wu et al. in recent times is *ManTra-Net* [19], which is a CNN network that can handle an image of any resolution and various types of forgery.

In this paper, we propose a CNN-based model to detect and localize spliced regions within an image that aims to identify these artefacts, which arise due to discrepancies between the characteristics of the source image and the forged region.

The rest of the paper is structured as follows. A review of the literature on image forgery detection approaches is presented in Sect. 2. The proposed methodology for localizing forged regions in a spliced image is presented in Sect. 3. Our experiments and results are discussed in Sect. 4. Section 5 presents the conclusion and future scope for this work.

2   Literature Review

Different methods are available to address image forgery detection and localization, ranging from conventional techniques to more recent approaches based on deep learning. While conventional methods primarily focus on detecting specific artefacts left by forgeries, deep learning-based techniques, which will be discussed below, have emerged as a relatively new and promising approach. This discussion will begin with classical methods and progressively explore the advancements in deep learning-based approaches. The detection of image splicing forgery using traditional methods can be roughly divided into four types based on the differences in attributes between the tampered region and the authentic region. In [11], the authors propose a method for identifying forgery based on the varying illumination of different components within an image. This technique involves comparing the illumination directions of the forged and authentic parts of the image. Another approach discussed in [10] focuses on error-level analysis for image forgery detection. This method involves analyzing the error levels in different image regions to identify potential forgeries. Habibi et al. [6] utilize the contourlet transform to recover edge points to detect image forgery. Examining the edge points, they aim to identify indications of image manipulation. Furthermore, the research work in [3] explores conventional image falsification detection methods. This study examines various techniques commonly used for identifying forged images. These references provide insights into different approaches used in the field of image forgery detection, including illumination-based analysis, error level analysis, contourlet transform, and conventional detection methods.

Among the deep learning-based approaches, Liu et al. [9] proposed PSCC-Net, which analyses images using a two-path technique. In [18], Wu et al. employed a CNN to extract block-like features from a picture, calculate the similarity between distinct blocks, and discover the matched ones. Wu et al. also developed ManTra-Net, a CNN network that can handle an image of any resolution and various forging kinds, discussed in [19]. In [7], Kniaz et al. trained four models at once: GA, GR, DA, and DR, which evaluate the output of GA and GR. The work in [12] develops a technique for mapping sets of image areas to a value that indicates whether they include the same or separate forensic evidence.

3   Proposed Model

Here, we present a CNN-based model to identify and localize image splicing. CNNs have recently attracted much attention as a viable solution for solving real-world problems. Filter banks in a CNN are groups of weights that capture graphical features. They can also be used to study variations in picture properties between tampered and background regions, as well as to address the drawbacks of current splicing detection algorithms that focus on particular elements of an image. Furthermore, a CNN has light-transformation resistance, deformation resistance, and geometric invariance, which could assure the robust detectability of the proposed approach.

In order to prepare the training data for our model, we gather the following sample sets: tampered (spliced) images, the corresponding ground truths representing spliced vs. non-spliced regions in the form of a binary image, and two original images that were used to create the forged image (as seen in Fig. 1). Only spliced images are taken as input for the preprocessing steps.

Before applying any convolution operation to the tampered image, we perform some pre-processing steps to enhance the detection quality and performance. We employ three subsequent pre-processing methods on a spliced image to enable the working of our model. These are detailed next.

3.1   Finding Color Transitions

To enhance the detection of color transitions between pixels and gather information on color transitions between forged and authentic regions, we first convert the image to YCbCr color space and normalize it. Luminosity (Y), red-difference chrominance (Cr), and blue-difference chrominance (Cb) channels are then separated. Next, we try to obtain the color transitions between the forged and authentic regions of the image. This is obtained using a filtering operation on the input binary image using a specified kernel size. The input image is convolved with the filter and subsequently normalized by mapping the minimum and maximum pixel values to the range of 0 to 1. The already separated Cr and Cb channels are taken as input to this subroutine. Additionally, the absolute difference image between Cb and Cr channels is also fed as input to this procedure. This generates a total of three images, which are merged together, resulting in the final output consisting of color transitions between pixels (refer to Fig. 2).

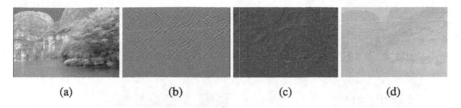

(a)   (b)   (c)   (d)

Fig. 2. Sample undergoing three stages of pre-processing. (a) Actual spliced sample (b) Resultant showing color transitions between pixels (c) Overall surface textures (d) Most prominent color zones.

3.2 Finding the Surface Textures

The next step in pre-processing involves extracting overall surface texture of the image. To achieve this, first, we divide the image into blocks of specific sizes. For each block, a sub-image is extracted from the original image based on the current block's position and size. Then we apply Discrete Cosine Transform (DCT) on the sub-image. We find the mean and median of the DCT coefficients of a particular sub-image, and find their product. This product is repeated multiple times to generate an equal sized (corresponding) block in the output image.

To capture the image surface texture We apply this operation on two different channels: (A) the Cr channel, (B) the product of Cb and Cr. The two resultant images are then merged alongside the original Y channel, which gives us an image capturing the overall surface texture of the tampered image, as evident from Fig. 2.

3.3 Finding Prominent Color Zones

The final pre-processing step tries to find the image portions demonstrating the most visibly distinct or prominent color zones. We transform the input image using singular value decomposition (SVD) and encoding based on color and difference information to achieve this.

The following formula gives the SVD of M × N matrix A,

$$A = UW^{T} \tag{1}$$

where, U is $M \times N$ matrix of orthogonal eigenvectors of AA^{T} and V^{T} is the transpose of a $N \times N$ matrix containing the orthogonal eigenvectors of $A^{T}A$ and W is a $N \times N$ diagonal matrix of the singular values which are the square roots of the eigenvalues of $A^{T}A$.

In this pre-processing step, we compute the absolute difference in each channel between each pixel and its neighbours. The resultant difference arrays are then padded to match the shape of the original image. Then, we create a new matrix which consists of six channels, the original normalized values of Y, Cb, and Cr, and the other three channels are created by taking the absolute difference of each channel for each pixel and its neighbours. This 3D matrix is then reshaped into a 2D array; the first dimension is the product of the height and width of the matrix and the second dimension

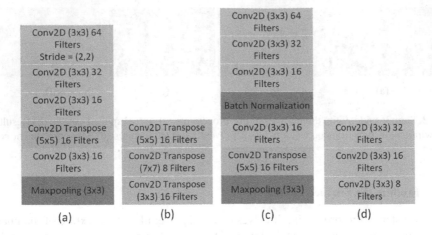

Fig. 3. Building blocks of proposed model. (a) Block 1 (b) Block 2 (c) Block 3 (d) Block 4.

is the number of channels, here, six. SVD is then performed on this 2D matrix. The result consists of singular values (s), left singular vectors (U), and right singular vectors (V). Top three singular vectors and singular values are taken for encoding. The 2D matrix is then multiplied element-wise (dot product) with the transpose of the newly obtained matrix of singular vectors. The result which is obtained by this operation is reshaped back to the original shape (height, width, 3), hence we multiply each channel of the reshaped image with its corresponding top singular value to enhance the encoded information. The modified Y, Cb, and Cr channels are merged back together. By this, we obtain an image which highlights the portions of the tampered image depicting the most prominent color zones, which is an indicator of probable forged locations. (See Fig. 2.) The preprocessing steps are not self-sufficient to provide the necessary information to our model in order to localize the spliced region, but together they produce relevant information regarding the region of forgery. Using prominent color zones along with color transitions helps us to identify the most color-dense areas in the image, and the transitions of colors of various density between multiple zones. In our dataset, we have noticed that most of the spliced images, have some sort of color distortion between spliced and authentic regions. These steps together helps us to find these types of information to successfully identify the forged regions.

All three images generated by the three pre-processing stages are merged to create a single image. Each one of these images has three channels, so our merged image contains nine channels altogether. Every image in our dataset is pre-processed as described above. Alongside this, we took the ground truth of each spliced image with its edges marked using a Canny edge detector, used as target labels in our training.

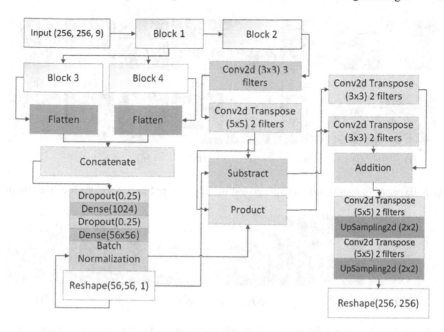

Fig. 4. Proposed model architecture.

3.4 Proposed Network Model

Now the data is prepared to be fed into the neural network model. The proposed method predicts whether a pixel belongs to the boundary between the spliced region and the background image, or not. Our detection is performed at pixel level. The proposed model aims to generate a mask to highlight the tampered regions in a given spliced image.

The input shape considered by the proposed model is (256, 256, 9). This indicates each image is of dimensions 256×256 and consists of nine channels. The proposed neural network is programmatically divided into some functional blocks, out of which, the first block consists of multiple convolutional layers followed by a transposed convolutional layer and a max pooling layer. The second block defines operations that involve transposed convolutions. It takes an input layer and performs a series of transposed convolutional operations. The third block defines a block of operations that involves convolutional and transposed convolutional layers, as well as batch normalization and max pooling. It takes an input layer and performs a series of operations. The fourth block again introduces a series of convolution operations. These blocks are illustrated in Fig. 3. Using these blocks, the rest of the network is built.

Subtract and product are two intermediate stages in our model in which we are doing these two operations on the results gained from previous stages. Reshape (56, 56, 1) is used because of the output from the previous Dense(56×56) layer. It indicates that after this reshaping, the image will be of size 56×56 and has one colour channel. After applying reshape (256, 256), which is the last layer in our model, the model produces

Fig. 5. Experiment results. (a)–(h) Spliced test images. (i)–(p) Spliced regions localized output.

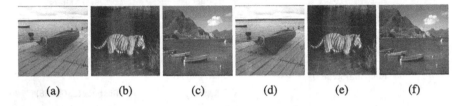

Fig. 6. Experiment results. (a)–(c) Authentic test images (d)–(f) Detection performance

the predicted binary image and it is of size 256×256, which is also the size of the original ground truth of the spliced images provided in the dataset.

The proposed neural network is an end-to-end deep learning system, as depicted in Fig. 4. It features multiple convolution and deconvolution layers, followed by upsampling layers to retain image information. To categorise pixels into the foreground (tampered) and background segments, which is simply a binary classification of pixels, we must train the framework to identify the tampered and non-tampered regions. We use Sigmoid activation in the last layer and ReLU activation in the rest. We use binary cross-entropy loss function to determine the loss in the training phase.

4   Experimental Results

The proposed model is constructed and tested using Keras and TensorFlow frameworks on NVIDIA RTX 3070 8 GB GPU. We employ the Casia v2.0 dataset in our experiment. It consists of 12,614 images including 5,123 tampered images and 7,491 genuine images. CASIA 2.0 includes images of interiors, nature, scenery, people, plants, articles, architecture, textures, and animals. This dataset contains images with resolutions ranging from 800×600 to 384×256. We adopted batch size of six and the model is trained for over 200 epochs. The training and test set split is done in the ratio 90:10.

Table 1. Batch-wise performance evaluation

Method	F-Measure	Precision	Recall	Accuracy (%)
Batch 1	0.8577	0.8649	0.8713	96.21%
Batch 2	0.8402	0.8573	0.8782	96.38%
Batch 3	0.8547	0.8625	0.8795	97.21%
Batch 4	0.8589	0.8613	0.8792	97.57%
Batch 5	0.8610	0.8728	0.8802	97.82%
Batch 6	0.8762	0.8835	0.8986	98.05%

4.1 Performance Evaluation

We compute the model's performance accuracy primarily based on the percentage of correctly identified boundary pixels. We reshaped all images to the dimensions of 256×256 pixels. Tampered images and their corresponding masks are fed as a pair to train the model. We perform the pre-processing mentioned in Sect. 3 to predict the masks. Finally, we use the masks to mark the boundaries of the forged regions (using the red color channel). The model achieves over 98% detection accuracy and a validation loss of 1.1134×10^{-4}. Visual results obtained by the proposed model for eight random experiments with spliced test images are presented in Fig. 5, and, for authentic test images detection performance is presented in Fig. 6. The training and test accuracies and validation loss of the model over the first 200 epochs are presented in Fig. 7. Also, we present the performance of the proposed model for six subsequent training batches in Table 1.

4.2 Comparative Analysis

As stated above, the model's performance is evaluated based on the fraction of correctly identified boundary pixels. For example, *True Positive* case represents the fraction of spliced boundary pixels, correctly identified as spliced; whereas *False Positive* represents authentic boundary pixels falsely detected to be spliced. In order to make a quantitative evaluation of the experimental results of this experiment, we select precision, recall, F-measure, and accuracy as the evaluation index.

$$\text{Precision} = \frac{\text{True Positives (TP)}}{\text{True Positives (TP)} + \text{False Positives (FP)}}$$

$$\text{Recall} = \frac{\text{True Positives (TP)}}{\text{True Positives (TP)} + \text{False Negatives (FN)}}$$

$$\text{F-Measure} = \frac{2 \times \text{Precision} \times \text{Recall}}{\text{Precision} + \text{Recall}}$$

$$\text{Accuracy (\%)} = \frac{\text{TP} + \text{TN}}{\text{TP} + \text{TN} + \text{FP} + \text{FN}} \times 100\%$$

We tested the model on the Casia v2 dataset. Several groups of test result images are chosen at random from the results of the tests. This study's detection results are

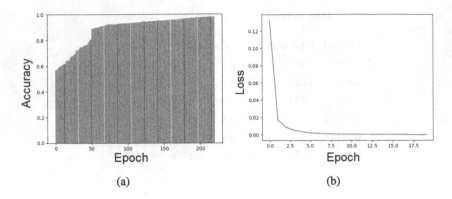

Fig. 7. Model performance. (a) Test Accuracy vs. Epoch (b) Validation Loss vs. Epoch.

Table 2. Results of comparative analysis

Method	F-Measure	Precision	Recall	Accuracy
CFA (2009) [5]	0.2026	0.1439	0.6973	34.88%
NADQ (2019) [2]	0.2847	0.2777	0.4555	72.74%
FCN (2017) [16]	0.5470	0.6654	0.5308	93.69%
U-Net (2015) [14]	0.5978	0.6869	0.6121	94.62%
C2RNet (2020) [20]	0.6758	0.5810	0.8080	–
RRU-Net (2019) [2]	0.8410	0.8480	0.8340	–
DU-DC-EC (2020) [22]	0.6830	–	–	97.82%
DCU-Net (2023) [4]	0.8667	0.8772	0.8893	97.93%
Proposed Model	**0.8762**	**0.8835**	**0.8986**	**98.05%**

shown above. The detection findings show that the proposed model suggested in this work achieves good results and can perform accurate pixel-level tamper location. Due to hardware limitations, we trained our models with batch/chunks of data. Each batch size is 300. Performance results per batch are given in Table 1.

The proposed model is compared with six recent splicing localization models. The comparison results are shown in Table 2. Among the selected techniques, NADQ [2] and CFA [5] are approaches based on feature extraction, FCN [16] and C2RNet [20] are based on semantic segmentation, and RRU-Net [2], DU-DC-EC-Net [22] and DCU-Net [4] are models based on U-Net model branching. It is evident from Table 2 that the proposed model outperforms the state-of-the-art in terms of performance efficiency, closely followed by DCU-Net and DU-DC-EC-Net architectures.

– NADQ, 2019 [2]: based on the derivation of a unified statistical model that characterizes DCT coefficients when aligned or misaligned double JPEG compression is applied; the statistical model is used to generate a likelihood map that shows the probability of each 8×8 image block being double compressed.

- CFA [5]: the techniques are based on computing a single feature and a simple threshold-based classifier. By interpreting the locally nonexistent CFA artefacts as tampering evidence, the proposed scheme takes the forgery graph of the credible probability of each small pixel block as the output.
- FCN [16]: this method is used to classify images at the pixel level, thus solving the problem of image segmentation at the semantic level. FCN is applied for detecting image splicing, which can automatically learn image tampering features.
- U-Net [14]: as one of the models of full convolution network structure, it can also be used for pixel-level classification. Compared with FCN, the most important improvement is to add a skip connection structure to reduce the loss of information.

5 Conclusions and Future Work

In this paper, we propose a CNN model for image splicing detection and localization. The model performs tampered region localization at the pixel level. To achieve more precise positioning, we propose three pre-processing stages. In the first stage, we see the color transitions, the second stage captures the overall surface texture of the image, and in the third stage, we try to find zones with the most prominent color. For the final detection and localisation, The three resultants are combined and fed to the proposed CNN for forgery localization. The proposed method has been tested on the Casia 2.0 dataset and has been compared with other existing methods.

Future research will include the development of generalized forgery localization schemes encompassing diverse forgery types such as region duplication attacks.

References

1. Asghar, K., Habib, Z., Hussain, M.: Copy-move and splicing image forgery detection and localization techniques: a review. Aust. J. Forensic Sci. **49**(3), 281–307 (2017)
2. Bi, X., Wei, Y., Xiao, B., Li, W.: RRU-Net: the ringed residual U-Net for image splicing forgery detection. In: Proceedings of the IEEE/CVF Conference on Computer Vision and Pattern Recognition Workshops (2019)
3. Christlein, V., Riess, C., Jordan, J., Riess, C., Angelopoulou, E.: An evaluation of popular copy-move forgery detection approaches. IEEE Trans. Inf. Forensics Secur. **7**(6), 1841–1854 (2012)
4. Ding, H., Chen, L., Tao, Q., Fu, Z., Dong, L., Cui, X.: DCU-Net: a dual-channel U-shaped network for image splicing forgery detection. Neural Comput. Appl. **35**(7), 5015–5031 (2023). https://doi.org/10.1007/s00521-021-06329-4
5. Dirik, A.E., Memon, N.: Image tamper detection based on demosaicing artifacts. In: 2009 16th IEEE International Conference on Image Processing (ICIP), pp. 1497–1500. IEEE (2009)
6. Habibi, M., Hassanpour, H.: Splicing image forgery detection and localization based on color edge inconsistency using statistical dispersion measures. Int. J. Eng. **34**(2), 443–451 (2021)
7. Kniaz, V.V., Knyaz, V., Remondino, F.: The point where reality meets fantasy: mixed adversarial generators for image splice detection. In: Advances in Neural Information Processing Systems, vol. 32 (2019)

8. Kwon, M.J., Yu, I.J., Nam, S.H., Lee, H.K.: CAT-Net: compression artifact tracing network for detection and localization of image splicing. In: Proceedings of the IEEE/CVF Winter Conference on Applications of Computer Vision, pp. 375–384 (2021)

9. Liu, X., Liu, Y., Chen, J., Liu, X.: PSCC-Net: progressive spatio-channel correlation network for image manipulation detection and localization. IEEE Trans. Circ. Syst. Video Technol. **32**(11), 7505–7517 (2022)

10. Luo, W., Huang, J., Qiu, G.: JPEG error analysis and its applications to digital image forensics. IEEE Trans. Inf. Forensics Secur. **5**(3), 480–491 (2010)

11. Matern, F., Riess, C., Stamminger, M.: Gradient-based illumination description for image forgery detection. IEEE Trans. Inf. Forensics Secur. **15**, 1303–1317 (2019)

12. Mayer, O., Stamm, M.C.: Forensic similarity for digital images. IEEE Trans. Inf. Forensics Secur. **15**, 1331–1346 (2019)

13. Meena, K.B., Tyagi, V.: Image forgery detection: survey and future directions. In: Shukla, R.K., Agrawal, J., Sharma, S., Singh Tomer, G. (eds.) Data, Engineering and Applications, pp. 163–194. Springer, Singapore (2019). https://doi.org/10.1007/978-981-13-6351-1_14

14. Ronneberger, O., Fischer, P., Brox, T.: U-Net: convolutional networks for biomedical image segmentation. In: Navab, N., Hornegger, J., Wells, W.M., Frangi, A.F. (eds.) MICCAI 2015. LNCS, vol. 9351, pp. 234–241. Springer, Cham (2015). https://doi.org/10.1007/978-3-319-24574-4_28

15. Rony, J., Belharbi, S., Dolz, J., Ayed, I.B., McCaffrey, L., Granger, E.: Deep weakly-supervised learning methods for classification and localization in histology images: a survey. arXiv preprint arXiv:1909.03354 (2019)

16. Shelhamer, E., Long, J., Darrell, T.: Fully convolutional networks for semantic segmentation. IEEE Trans. Pattern Anal. Mach. Intell. **39**(4), 640–651 (2017)

17. Verdoliva, L.: Media forensics and deepfakes: an overview. IEEE J. Sel. Top. Sig. Process. **14**(5), 910–932 (2020)

18. Wu, Y., Abd-Almageed, W., Natarajan, P.: Image copy-move forgery detection via an end-to-end deep neural network. In: 2018 IEEE Winter Conference on Applications of Computer Vision (WACV), pp. 1907–1915. IEEE (2018)

19. Wu, Y., AbdAlmageed, W., Natarajan, P.: ManTra-Net: manipulation tracing network for detection and localization of image forgeries with anomalous features. In: Proceedings of the IEEE/CVF Conference on Computer Vision and Pattern Recognition, pp. 9543–9552 (2019)

20. Xiao, B., Wei, Y., Bi, X., Li, W., Ma, J.: Image splicing forgery detection combining coarse to refined convolutional neural network and adaptive clustering. Inf. Sci. **511**, 172–191 (2020)

21. Zhang, M., Zhou, Y., Zhao, J., Man, Y., Liu, B., Yao, R.: A survey of semi-and weakly supervised semantic segmentation of images. Artif. Intell. Rev. **53**, 4259–4288 (2020). https://doi.org/10.1007/s10462-019-09792-7

22. Zhang, R., Ni, J.: A dense U-Net with cross-layer intersection for detection and localization of image forgery. In: ICASSP 2020–2020 IEEE International Conference on Acoustics, Speech and Signal Processing (ICASSP), pp. 2982–2986. IEEE (2020)

UN-SPLIT: Attacking Split Manufacturing Using Link Prediction in Graph Neural Networks

Lilas Alrahis[1(✉)], Likhitha Mankali[2], Satwik Patnaik[3], Abhrajit Sengupta[2], Johann Knechtel[1], and Ozgur Sinanoglu[1]

[1] New York University Abu Dhabi, Abu Dhabi, UAE
{lma387,johann,ozgursin}@nyu.edu
[2] New York University, New York, USA
{likhitha.mankali,as9397}@nyu.edu
[3] University of Delaware, Newark, USA
satwik@udel.edu

Abstract. We explore a new angle for attacking split manufacturing aside from relying only on physical design hints. By learning on the structure, composition, and the front-end-of-line (FEOL) interconnectivity of gates in a given design (or design library/dataset), along with key hints from physical design, we obtain a model that can predict the missing back-end-of-line (BEOL) connections. We formulate this as a link-prediction problem and solve it using a graph neural network (GNN). Furthermore, we utilize post-processing techniques that analyze the GNN predictions and apply common domain knowledge to further enhance the accuracy of our attack methodology.

Keywords: Split manufacturing · Graph neural networks · Link prediction · Machine learning · Hardware security

1 Introduction

The globalized integrated circuit supply chain enables the industry to meet semiconductor demands efficiently. Fabless design companies focus on intellectual property (IP) development and outsource manufacturing, assembly, packaging, and testing. While this integration model offers cost savings and faster deployment, it also introduces security concerns like IP piracy. Researchers have investigated design-for-trust approaches to restore trust and counter hardware-based security attacks [17].

Split manufacturing was proposed by the Intelligence Advanced Research Projects Activity (IARPA) agency to reduce manufacturing costs and, more importantly, enhance security and IP protection [14]. A high-level illustration of split manufacturing is depicted in Fig. 1. The process is to literally split the

---

The work of Satwik Patnaik was done when he was at Texas A&M University, College Station, USA.

F. Regazzoni et al. (Eds.): SPACE 2023, LNCS 14412, pp. 197–213, 2024.
https://doi.org/10.1007/978-3-031-51583-5_12

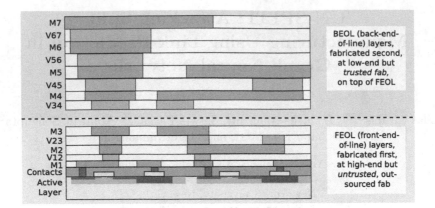

Fig. 1. Conceptual illustration of the split manufacturing process.

design into front-end-of-line (FEOL) and back-end-of-line (BEOL) layers and then have them manufactured at different foundries. The FEOL is fabricated at an untrusted high-end foundry to access advanced technology nodes, whereas the BEOL is fabricated later on at a trusted low-end foundry, which integrates these layers on top of the FEOL. Split manufacturing is promising to mitigate illegal overproduction, IP piracy, and targeted hardware Trojan insertion, all conducted by the untrusted FEOL foundry. This is because the FEOL foundry only has access to a "sea of gates" that is not fully connected; the FEOL foundry does not have access to the full design.

However, various attacks on split manufacturing have succeeded in exploiting the deterministic nature of electronic design automation (EDA) tools to decipher the BEOL connections [12,13,16,18,19]. Because EDA tools optimize for power, performance, and area (PPA), the solutions found by such tools typically have some specific and common features. For example, placement engines tend to place all connected gates close to one another to reduce wirelength. Such a feature is referred to as the "proximity hint." By exploiting this and other physical design hints, adversaries may be able to infer a considerable part of the missing BEOL connections.

In our work, we explore a new angle for attacking split manufacturing by utilizing graph representation learning. Through learning on some design dataset about the composition of gates and their interconnects, i.e., the design's structure, along with the functionality of gates, we can infer how gates are likely to be connected in a target design. Next we discuss the contributions of our UN-SPLIT platform.

1. **Developing a platform that converts circuits into graphs (Sect. 3.2).** The platform incorporates several features that are automatically extracted from the circuits (layout files), such as the location and type of gates and the FEOL connectivity between different parts of the circuit.
2. **Formulating an attack on split manufacturing as a link prediction task (Sect. 3.3),** where the goal is to predict the presence or absence of edges between different parts of the circuit that are split between the foundries.

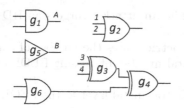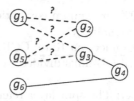

Netlist with missing connections   Inferring the missing connections as a link prediction problem

Fig. 2. High-level idea of our proposed UN-SPLIT platform: inferring missing BEOL connection by solving a link prediction problem.

An example of this formalism is illustrated in Fig. 2, where the dashed links represent missing connections, and the solid links indicate readily available connections in the FEOL. The objective is to estimate the likelihood for each dashed link, representing possible BEOL connections, and identify the ones with the highest likelihood to be incorporated the into yet-incomplete netlist hold by the FEOL-based adversary. We solve the link prediction problem using a graph neural network (GNN) that captures and understands the structure and behavior of circuits.

3. **Proposing a post-processing stage that rectifies misclassifications made by the GNN (Sect. 3.4).** This stage takes advantage of additional information about the circuit, such as the feasibility or infeasibility of certain connections, to improve the overall accuracy.

Key Results. In our extensive experiments on various ITC-99 combinational benchmarks for *split layers* M6 and M8, UN-SPLIT achieves a *correct connection rate (CCR)* of up to 100%, meaning it correctly recovers the entire netlist.

2   Background and Related Work

2.1   Threat Model

Residing in the offshore FEOL foundry, an adversary can obtain the gate-level netlist by reverse-engineering the GDSII layout file of a design. However, in the context of split manufacturing, this netlist is incomplete, as the BEOL layers are implemented only later on in another, trusted foundry.

Given only the FEOL, the goal of the attacker is to infer the BEOL links to retrieve the original design. The attacker has no access to an oracle as the chip is yet to be manufactured.

2.2   Terminology and Metrics

Hamming Distance, HD: In the context of split manufacturing, this well-known metric measures the bit-level difference for output patterns of the design as recovered by an attacker versus the original design. A designer aims to enforce an HD of 50% (maximum corruption), while an attacker targets an HD of 0% (correct functionality).

Correct Connection Rate, CCR: This metric states the number of correctly determined BEOL links divided by the total number of missing BEOL connections.

Split Layer: The split layer refers to the top metal layer in the FEOL which is still available to the attacker.

Open Pin: An open pin is a start point in the split layer for a missing/undisclosed connection up into the BEOL.

Target Pin, Candidate Pins: A target pin is an open pin that is currently under consideration, by an attacker, for reconnecting to its correct counterpart among all candidate pins. A candidate pin is a feasible option, meaning that, e.g., pins that would connect one gate's output pin to another gate's output pin are excluded from candidate pins.

Split Net: A split net is a net that is split across FEOL and BEOL. Split nets are differentiated by their type: source or sink. A source split net connects, only within the FEOL, an output pin of one single gate or one primary input (PI) to zero or more input pin(s) of other gate(s). A sink split net connects, also only within the FEOL, to some input pin(s) of some gate(s) and/or to primary output (PO).

2.3   Attacks and Defenses on Split Manufacturing

We provide a brief overview of attacks and defenses related to proximity as background information. The literature includes other attacks and defenses beyond the scope of this discussion.

The seminal proximity attack [16] is based on the fact that EDA tools partition cells into modules such that total wire length between the partitions is minimized. The attack exploits such deterministic implementation, by connecting each target pin to its nearest candidate pin.

The network flow attack (NFA) [18] shares a similar concept with the proximity attack, as it selects BEOL connections that minimize wire length. However, unlike the proximity attack, which applies only to hierarchical designs, the NFA can handle flattened netlists. The NFA constructs a network flow model and utilizes a minimum-cost flow algorithm to determine the best-cost approach to connect the pins, with cost being the total BEOL wire length.

Magaña et al. [12,13] propose various proximity measures. Their goal is to reduce the search space, by defining a close neighborhood and limiting the number of candidates links to consider for each target pin. Thereafter, an attacker can leverage other hints to elect one candidate, such as avoidance of combinational loops. Magaña et al. [12,13] demonstrate that routing-based proximity information is more effective than placement-based proximity information. However, the authors also conclude that proximity alone is not sufficient in narrowing down the list of candidates.

Magaña et al. [12,13] also propose a defense method: insert routing blockages at the split layer and below so that more nets have to be routed above the split layer, thereby significantly increasing the complexity for proximity attacks. In our work, we employ a similar defense technique to thoroughly test the strength of our proposed attack.

Please note that a direct comparison of ours with prior art is not practical. Since the problem of attacking split manufacturing hinges on intricacies of physical layouts, such comparison would require the very same layouts as used in prior art; however, prior art typically did not release layouts.

2.4 Link Prediction

Link prediction algorithms estimate the likelihood of a connection between two target nodes, taking into account the network structure and node attributes [11].

Consider an undirected graph $\mathcal{G} = (V, E, \boldsymbol{X})$, where V represents the set of nodes, E denotes the observed edges, and $\boldsymbol{X}$ is the node feature matrix. The adjacency matrix $\boldsymbol{A}$ represents the connections in the graph. Let $T \notin E$ be the set of missing links. In a link prediction algorithm, scores are assigned to all links in T based on heuristics, and links with scores above a threshold are predicted to exist.

Traditional link prediction algorithms rely on specific heuristics based on graph and node properties, such as the number of common neighbors, to calculate the likelihood of a link existing in a graph. However, these heuristics are sometimes dependent on the type of graph. Instead of fixating on a specific heuristic, GNNs have been utilized to learn about links in a graph, enabling generalization to various graph structures and offering a learning-based approach to predict the likelihood of a link's existence, as opposed to relying on manual engineering of these heuristics. In short, GNNs leverage the inherent graph structure and node features to extract meaningful link features, surpassing the performance of traditional methods [20].

2.5 Graph Neural Networks

A GNN generates an *embedding* (i.e., vector representation) for each node in the graph, arranging similar nodes close together in the embedding space [21].

In general, the embedding of a target node, denoted as v, is updated through *message passing*. Thereby, the features of neighboring nodes $\mathcal{N}(v)$ are combined to create an aggregated representation. This aggregated information, along with the features of the target node, is used to update its embedding.

After L rounds of message passing, each node is aware of its own features, the features of neighboring nodes, and the graph structure within the L-hop neighborhood. The message passing phase can be summarized as follows:

$$a_v^{(l)} = AGG^{(l)} \left(\left\{ z_u^{(l-1)} : u \in \mathcal{N}(v) \right\} \right) \tag{1}$$

$$z_v^{(l)} = COMBINE^{(l)} \left(z_v^{(l-1)}, a_v^{(l)} \right) \tag{2}$$

The embedding of node v at the l-th round, represented as $z_v^{(l)}$, is obtained through a two-step process. Firstly, the embeddings of neighboring nodes $z_u^{(l-1)}$

are aggregated using the aggregation function $AGG^{(l)}$. Secondly, the previous embedding $z_v^{(l-1)}$ of node v and the aggregated information $a_v^{(l)}$ are combined using the $COMBINE^{(l)}$ function. Different GNN architectures vary based on the choices of $AGG(\cdot)$ and $COMBINE(\cdot)$.

2.6 Related Work: GNN-Based Attacks on Logic Locking

In the field of hardware security, GNNs have demonstrated excellent performance in analyzing circuits due to their natural graph representation [1,2,9]. They have primarily been used to launch attacks on logic locking [6]. The objective of logic locking is to protect a design's IP by introducing new key-controlled elements, commonly referred to as key-gates, into the design. The design only functions correctly when the correct key is applied. Attacks on logic locking typically target either deciphering the locking key or entirely removing the protection logic.

For instance, GNNUnlock [3,5] targets logic locking implementations that introduce an entire logic block (e.g., a comparator or a Hamming distance checker) to inject errors into the design when the correct key is not applied. With the assistance of a GNN, GNNUnlock can classify nodes (gates) in the gate-level netlist and identify the protection logic, subsequently removing it. Note that this attack is not applicable to split manufacturing since there is no additive logic to be removed in that scenario. Another GNN-based attack is OMLA [8], which focuses on logic locking that inserts XOR/XNOR key-gates into the design. OMLA can learn the properties of the subcircuits surrounding the key-gates and predict the secret key. This attack is also unsuitable for attacking split manufacturing because split manufacturing cannot be modeled by XOR/XNOR insertion but rather by MUX-controlled key-gates.

UNTANGLE [4] and MuxLink [7] specifically perform link prediction to attack MUX-based locking. These attacks transform MUX-based locking into a link prediction problem and solve it using GNNs.

Although some of these attacks have a similar approach as our work, there are numerous technical differences. For example, both UNTANGLE and MuxLink begin with a gate-level netlist or a design in the so-called bench format. In contrast, our work starts with the actual design exchange format (DEF) layout file, converting it into a graph, as we will explain in Sect. 3. We also extract problem-specific layout information such as pin locations, which were not considered by these prior attacks. Moreover, the problem we are addressing is considerably more complex. In the case of logic locking, there were only two link options per MUX locality, making reliance on GNN predictions sufficient. However, in our case, we have significantly larger localities, necessitating the proposal of a post-processing algorithm to aid in design recovery.

3   Proposed UN-SPLIT Attack Platform

The key ideas in terms of GNN processing are to first extract a subgraph around each target link, which contains information about the surrounding circuitry.

Second, by performing graph classification, the label of the target link becomes the label of its corresponding subgraph. In this section, we present the flow of UN-SPLIT in detail, which is also depicted in Fig. 3.

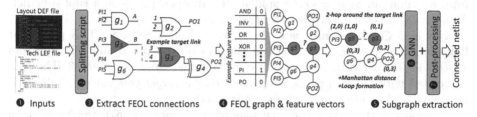

Fig. 3. Proposed UN-SPLIT overall flow.

3.1   Emulating Split Manufacturing

The DEF layout file and the related standard-cell library exchange format file (i.e., the technology LEF file) are taken as inputs (Fig. 3 ❶).

These inputs are processed as follows (Fig. 3 ❷). First, given a split layer, all the data describing the BEOL routing above that split layer is ignored, except when compiling ground truths for training (see further below). Second, all split nets are listed out, with their type (source or sink; recall Sect. 2.2), their connected cell instance(s), their connected PI(s)/PO(s), if any, and their open pin(s) including coordinates. Note that the latter are derived from the via locations connecting the FEOL to the BEOL. Also note that, only for training and evaluation purposes, the true BEOL connections are also listed out. The output of this stage are the annotated FEOL connections (Fig. 3 ❸).

3.2   Representing FEOL Connections as a Graph

The above obtained information is then used to construct a graph $\mathcal{G}$ (Fig. 3 ❹) that represents the FEOL of the target circuit as follows.

Node Creation, Basic Features: UN-SPLIT adds nodes to the graph, where each node represents a cell, a PI, or a PO. Each node is assigned a feature vector, e.g., including a hot-encoding of the cell's Boolean functionality. In our work, the vector's part describing the latter has a size of 32; this size depends on the technology library and its gates/Boolean functionalities. The feature vector also indicates whether it is a PI or PO, e.g., the feature vector associated with node $PI3$ in Fig. 3 ❹ indicates that this node represents a PI. The feature vector will later be expanded with additional features.

Edge Establishment: Based on the FEOL connectivity (Sect. 3.1), UN-SPLIT establishes edges between nodes, representing the wires/nets running between components in the lower metal layers. To enable efficient message passing operations, edges are added in both directions, creating an undirected graph. However, we also maintain a directed graph $\mathcal{G}_d$, which is later used for annotation of combinational loops.

Target Links: To determine the links to be considered by the GNN, i.e., all the possible BEOL connections, UN-SPLIT utilizes the split nets identified by the parsing stage (Sect. 3.1). UN-SPLIT enumerates all possible connections from an open pin p_1 in a source split net to an open pin p_2 in a sink split net. This list of target links is stored separately from the graph.

In Fig. 3 ❸, an example is outlined by a dashed red line. This particular link shall describe the connection between $g5$'s output pin B and $g3$'s input pin 4—this is abstracted into an actual target link that connects $g5$ to $g3$. The gate associated with an open pin p_i is referred to as a *target gate/node* and denoted as v_{p_i}. $g5$ and $g3$ are example target gates/nodes.

Normalized Distances: For each pair of open pins (p_1, p_2), the Manhattan Distance is computed as $\mid x_1 - x_2 \mid + \mid y_1 - y_2 \mid$. Next, the distance values are normalized with respect to the longest distance observed across all designs in the dataset. The purpose is to focus on relative distances for pairs of open pins, as the absolute distances vary significantly across designs. The normalized distances are then stored along with the corresponding target links, in the list of links.

3.3 Link Prediction Based on Graph Neural Networks

The graph, list of links, and corresponding normalized distances (Sect. 3.2) are used for link prediction, with the help of the GNN platform SEAL [20], as follows.

Subgraph Extraction. First, we group target nodes into a set called S. For instance, if we are interested in predicting the likelihood of a link between nodes v_{p_1} and v_{p_2}, we initialize S as $\{(v_{p_1}, v_{p_2})\}$. Second, given the overall graph $\mathcal{G}$, we extract an h-hop enclosing subgraph for S, denoted as $\mathcal{G}_{(S,h)}$, around that pair of target nodes. The subgraph $\mathcal{G}_{(S,h)}$ is obtained by considering the vertices that are within a shortest path distance of h from any vertex in S.

In Fig. 3 ❺, an example of subgraph extraction with $h = 2$ is shown. The target nodes are $g5$ and $g3$, respectively, highlighted in red. To construct the subgraph, all nodes within a 2-hop distance from these two target nodes are included, while the remaining nodes of $\mathcal{G}$ are ignored for this specific target link. Note that, by considering the pair of target nodes, we are "virtually bridging" the missing BEOL connection between the underlying source and sink split nets, albeit only for GNN subgraph processing and to enable link prediction.

Subgraph extraction is performed for each target link under consideration. As a result, a distinct subgraph is associated with each link, and these subgraphs are subsequently passed to the GNN (Fig. 3 ❻) for link prediction.

Node-Level Distance and Other Features. In the extracted subgraph, each node is assigned a basic feature vector as discussed in Sect. 3.2. Additionally, node-level distance encoding is performed to emphasize on the structural properties of the design and to focus on the target link. Our distance encoding technique involves the following steps:

Computing Shortest Paths: UN-SPLIT calculates the shortest-path distances from a) the target node v_{p_1} of the source split net (that node is also called target output node) to all other nodes in the subgraph and b) from the target node v_{p_2} of the sink split net (that node also called target input node) to all other nodes in the subgraph. In cases where there is no direct path between a pair of nodes, i.e., the two nodes are separated through source and sink split nets, respectively, a distance pseudo-value of zero is assigned.

Distance Encoding: UN-SPLIT assigns a distance vector to each node based on its shortest distance to the target nodes. All non-zero distances are shifted by +1 and then limited to a practical maximal value, e.g., 10 in this work. This shifting is done to obtain unique vectors for the output/input target nodes, i.e., $(1,0)/(0,1)$, respectively, which allows the GNN to readily distinguish the two ends of the target link from all other nodes in the subgraph.

An example is given in Fig. 3 ⑤. The target input node $g3$ is assigned a unique vector $(0,1)$, indicating its distinction from other nodes. Similarly, the target output node $g5$ is represented by the vector $(1,0)$. Furthermore, node $g4$ is labeled with the vector $(0,2)$, indicating that it is a) not directly connected to the target output node $g5$ and b) located 1-hop away from the target input node $g3$, considering the value is shifted by +1.

Finally, the distance vectors are converted into one-hot encoded vectors of size equal to the maximum distance value plus one (for zero-value pseudo distances), i.e., 11 in this work.

Feature Vector Extension: All basic feature vectors are extended as follows. First, they are concatenated with the above one-hot-encoded vectors for node-level distances within the subgraph. Such augmented feature vector enables the GNN to better capture the spatial relationship between all subgraph nodes and the target nodes. Furthermore, another feature is concatenated that indicates whether adding the target link to the netlist would result in any combinational loop(s); this is determined using the directed graph version $\mathcal{G}_d$.

Finally, the extracted normalized Manhattan distance from the physical design for each link (as explained in Sect. 3.2) is concatenated to the feature vector of the nodes representing that link in the subgraph.

GNN Model and Classification. UN-SPLIT provides flexibility in choosing the type/model of GNN to use for the task at hand. Without loss of generality, we utilize the deep graph convolutional neural network (DGCNN) [21], which has shown superior performance for graph classification tasks.

Note that the graph convolutional layer in DGCNN operates as follows: given an input embedding $Z^l \in \mathbb{R}^{n \times k_l}$ from the $(l-1)$-th layer, the layer applies a linear feature transformation $Z^l W^l$, where $W^l \in \mathbb{R}^{k_l \times k_{l+1}}$ is a trainable weight matrix, to map the k_l feature channels to k_{l+1} channels. This is followed by aggregation of node information to neighboring vertices, including the node itself, and normalization using the degree matrix $\tilde{D}$ to ensure consistent feature scaling. Multiple convolutional layers can be stacked to capture multi-scale sub-structure features. The outputs from each layer are concatenated to form a

Table 1. Comparison of average locality sizes for output nodes between proximity attack and UN-SPLIT for M6 split layer

Benchmark	Proximity Attack	UN-SPLIT
b14_C	41	18
b15_C	316	38
b20_C	200	20
b21_C	316	38
b22_C	397	10
Average	**254**	**22**

single representation $Z^{1:L}$ of the graph. A sorting and pooling layer then sorts the tensor row-wise, based on the last layer's output Z^L, and reshapes it to select a fixed number of representative nodes. Finally, the resulting embedding is passed through 1-D convolutional layers with filter and step size $\sum_{l=1}^{L} k_l$ for graph classification.

3.4 Post-processing

The key contribution of UN-SPLIT is its GNN-based approach, which greatly reduces the number of links to be considered. In the post-processing stage, individual output nodes are evaluated, and the best links from the possible connections are selected to determine the final set of connections and recover the netlist. The selection process takes into account the likelihood scores, obtained via the GNN link prediction, and normalized distances of all potential links. Algorithm 1 describes the pseudo-code of the post-processing stage.

By setting a threshold (L_{th}) for likelihood scores, only links with scores greater than L_{th} are considered potential correct connections. This threshold-based approach enables a substantial decrease in the number of possible links for each output node, which we refer to as the *locality size*.

Compared to a proximity-based attack that relies solely on normalized distances or proximity as hints, the incorporation of GNN predictions leads to a remarkable reduction in the locality size, approximately 12 times smaller, as illustrated in Table 1 for M6 split layer. This reduction in locality size is a significant advantage, highlighting the effectiveness of GNNs in simplifying the post-processing stage.

The remaining links are sorted in ascending order based on their distances, and the link with the least distance is chosen as the correct connection for each output node. Additionally, the validity of the chosen connections is checked to ensure that they result in a valid netlist with no combinational loops. If a combinational loop is found, the links involved in the loop are removed, and the post-processing is repeated for the corresponding output nodes. Finally, the gate-level-netlist is recovered by connecting the missing connections (split nets) as returned by the post-processing stage.

Algorithm 1: Post-processing algorithm

Input: Likelihood L; Normalized distance D; Likelihood threshold L_{th}; Possible links T; Split Design Y_{split};

Output: Final recovered design $\mathcal{Y}$

```
1  for i = 1 to len(T) do
2  │   if L[i] < L_th then
3  │   │   T.pop(i)
4  │   │   L.pop(i)
5  │   └   D.pop(i)

6  D_sort, T_sort ←Sort_Ascending(D, T)
7  O ← {}
8  for u ∈ T_sort do
9  │   node ←Find_Output_Node(u)
10 └   O.append(node)

11 O ←set(O)
12 T_pred ← {}
13 for v ∈ O do
14 │   links ←Get_Links(T_sort, v)
15 │   link_pred ← links[0]
16 └   T_pred.append(link_pred)

17 G ←Create_Graph(Y_split)
18 Done ← False
19 while Done == False do
20 │   for u ∈ T_pred do
21 │   └   G.add_edge(u)
22 │   loop ←Find_Cycle(G)
23 │   if len(loop) == 0 then
24 │   └   Done ← True

25 │   else
26 │   │   for e ∈ loop do
27 │   │   │   T_pred.remove(e)
28 │   │   │   T_sort.remove(e)
29 │   │   │   node ←Find_Output_Node(e)
30 │   │   │   links ←Get_Links(T_sort, node)
31 │   │   │   link_pred ← links[0]
32 │   │   └   T_pred.append(link_pred)

33 Y ←Get_Recovered_Design(Y_split, T_pred)
34 return Y
```

3.5   Dataset Generation

To train and evaluate UN-SPLIT, without loss of generality, we use the ITC-99 combinational benchmarks suite. For each benchmark to attack/test, we train an individual model. For each model, all other benchmarks are used for training and validation. More specifically, 10 DEF files are generated per benchmark, with all 10 generated layouts considered for benchmarks designated for training, whereas 1 out of the 10 generated layouts is randomly selected for the benchmark under test (and the remaining 9 layouts for that benchmark are ignored for this model). Training is configured for the same split layer as used for the attack.

Positive and negative subgraph samples, i.e., correct and incorrect BEOL connections, are extracted from the above layout dataset to form the actual training dataset for the GNN. To balance the training dataset, an equal number of negative samples are selected, randomly, as there are positive samples. For validation, 10% of the positive and negative links are set aside to assess the model's performance on unseen data.

4   Experimental Evaluation

4.1   Setup

We summarize the experimental setup and tool flow for UN-SPLIT in Fig. 4. Next, more details are provided.

Implementation: The emulation of split manufacturing is implemented in *C++* code and utilizes the *Cadence LEF/DEF Open Source Distribution, Product Version 5.8* for parsing of DEF and LEF files. The scripts for circuit-to-graph conversion are implemented in *Perl*. We utilize the *PyTorch* implementation of SEAL/DGCNN [20] for link prediction. Post-processing is implemented in *Python*.

Runtime Environment: UN-SPLIT runs on a single machine utilizing 10 cores (2x Intel(R) Xeon(R) CPU E5-2680 v4@2.4GHz).

IC Design: Gate-level netlists are obtained using the *Cadence RTL compiler* and the NanGate Open Cell Library. Then, layout generation is performed using *Cadence Innovus*.

Benchmarks and Split Layers: We consider the following combinational ITC-99 benchmarks: b14_C, b15_C, b20_C, b21_C, b22_C, and b17_C. We consider the split layers M8 and M6. Also recall the process of dataset generation in Sect. 3.5.

GNN Configuration: We train the DGCNN on the extracted enclosing subgraphs for 500 epochs with an initial learning rate of 0.0001 and save the model with the best performance on the 10% validation set. The GNN consists of 4 graph convolution layers with 32, 32, 32, and 1 output channels, respectively. For the *SortPooling* layer of DGCNN, we set k such that 100% of graphs hold $\leq k$ nodes. We fix k this way so that none of the nodes get dropped from the final representation of the corresponding subgraphs. Next, we employ two 1-D convolutional layers with 16 and 32 output channels, respectively, followed by a single fully-connected layer of 128 neurons. A *MaxPooling* layer is stacked after the first 1-D convolutional layer with filter size of 2 and stride of 2; the second 1-D convolutional layer has filter size of 5 a stride of 1. A *Dropout* layer with a dropout rate of 0.5 is employed after the fully-connected layer, followed by a *Softmax* layer of two output units for classification. Similarly to [21], we use the

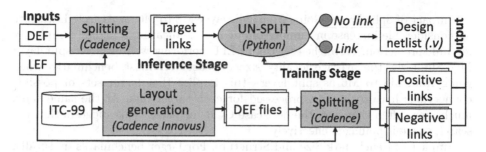

Fig. 4. Experimental setup and tool flow. The UN-SPLIT oval encompasses graph creation, subgraph extraction, node labeling, and the GNN.

hyperbolic tangent ($tanh$) activation function in the graph convolution layers and the rectified linear unit ($ReLU$) function in the rest of the layers. We use stochastic gradient descent with the *Adam* updating rule [10].

Protected Designs: Prior art like [12,13] proposed placement and/or routing perturbations for defending against split manufacturing attacks. In this work, we follow similar strategies. More specifically, we employ random insertion of routing blockages into metal layers below the split layer, such that timings overheads do not exceed 5% and such that layouts remain free of DRC violations after re-routing. More details are provided in [15].

4.2 Metrics

We report the number of cut nets P, which represent the total of positive BEOL connections. We further list the GNN accuracy for correctly predicting positive BEOL connections (true positive rate, TPR) and negative BEOL connections (true negative rate, TNR). We additionally report the total accuracy calculated as follows:

$$\text{Total Accuracy} = \frac{\text{TPR} \times P + \text{TNR} \times N}{P + N}$$

where N is the number of negative samples. We further report the threshold and corresponding locality size.

The *best-case CCR* assesses the presence of correct BEOL connections within the locality extracted for each target link, following the GNN-based link prediction and likelihood thresholding steps. That is, if the correct connection is within the extracted locality, the corresponding best-case CCR is 100%; if not, it is 0%. The final best-case CCR is averaged across all target links. The post-processing CCR assess the netlist after actual post-processing as described in Sect. 3.4. Finally, we report the HD for the recovered designs.

4.3 Experimental Results

Regular Designs. Table 2 shows the results for UN-SPLIT on regular designs, i.e., without any dedicated protection.

Impact of Split Layer: Going from split layer M8 to M6, as expected, we note an considerable increase in number of cut nets, indicating a higher complexity for link prediction. Nevertheless, UN-SPLIT performs well even on split layer M6. Similarly, the average locality size increases for most benchmarks when going from M8 to M6 as split layer—this implies that larger sets of possible connections have to be post-processed for each target link. At the same time, much more often than not, the best-case CCR increases. This suggests that the search space is managed effectively.

Impact of Benchmark Size and Structure: For larger benchmarks, naturally, there is an increase in complexity for link prediction. For example, comparing the smaller b14_C benchmark (around 3,461 gates) to the larger b20_C benchmark (around 7,741 gates), the number of cut nets for M8 split layer increases from 13 to 61. Additionally, the average locality size provided by UN-SPLIT increases from 7 for b14_C to 12 for b20_C, reflecting the larger number of possible connections to consider for each target link. UN-SPLIT still performs well. For instance, the best-case CCR for b20_C is 96.72% whereas for b14_C it is 84.62%. However, there are also outliers, namely for b22_C and b17_C at split layer M6. Whereas most of the considered benchmarks include repetitive circuitry, b17_C has a different design underlying, where the model may struggle to generalize, given the dataset is focused on these other, more repetitive structures.

Overall, these observations indicate that UN-SPLIT generally remains effective when handling larger benchmarks and can well manage the complexity of the underlying link prediction problem. For further scalability, one might consider larger and more diverse datasets for training.

Post-processing: UN-SPLIT achieves a final CCR up to 100% by performing post-processing as shown in Table 2. We observe an average post-processing CCR of 70.42% and 33.88% for the benchmarks split at the M8 and M6 layers, respectively. This result showcases that post-processing can almost achieve the best-case CCR for some benchmarks.

HD Analysis: UN-SPLIT recovers a valid netlist by applying post-processing. Thus, we can calculate HD for the recovered netlists to quantify the difference in functionality between the original and recovered designs. UN-SPLIT obtains an average HD of 1.38% and 6.83% for designs split at M8 and M6 layers, respectively, as shown in Table 2. These results indicate that the functionality of the recovered design is close to the original for most of the designs. For instance, for b14_C design split at M8 layer, UN-SPLIT could recover the complete functionality of the design, thus obtaining HD of 0. Furthermore, we observe that the HD obtained by UN-SPLIT is better than randomly connecting the missing connections in the split design. For instance, for designs split at the M8 layer, we observe that the HD obtained by 6.4× lesser than the HD obtained by randomly connecting the missing connections.

Table 2. UN-SPLIT results for attacking regular ITC-99 benchmarks split at layers M6 and M8

Benchmark	Split Layer	# Cut Nets	TPR (%)	TNR (%)	Total Accuracy (%)	Threshold	Avg. Locality Size	Best-Case CCR (%)	Post-Processing CCR (%)	HD (%)
b14_C	M8	13	84.62	50.35	53.21	0.50	7	100.00	100.00	0
b15_C		77	100.00	75.35	75.89	0.50	12	100.00	68.83	0.49
b20_C		61	96.72	71.07	71.71	0.50	12	96.72	70.49	0.99
b21_C		56	92.86	69.03	69.68	0.50	12	94.64	92.86	0.01
b22_C		104	82.69	83.99	83.97	0.50	11	82.69	70.19	1.17
b17_C		3,756	29.26	99.38	98.96	0.01	3	41.69	20.10	5.67
b14_C	M6	48	100.00	55.80	56.91	0.50	18	100.00	85.42	1.16
b15_C		1,361	90.96	66.72	6.93	0.50	38	91.40	15.79	6.43
b20_C		585	97.78	75.93	76.20	0.50	20	98.12	35.72	6.30
b21_C		850	93.76	70.68	70.87	0.50	38	93.88	33.76	10.28
b22_C		875	30.63	96.59	96.35	0.50	10	31.31	21.83	11.15
b17_C		12,879	44.98	98.25	98.13	0.01	8	44.98	10.76	5.67

Table 3. UN-SPLIT results for attacking protected ITC-99 benchmarks split at layers M6 and M8

Benchmark	Split Layer	# Cut Nets	TPR (%)	TNR (%)	Total Accuracy (%)	Threshold	Avg. Locality Size	Best-Case CCR (%)	Post-Processing CCR (%)	HD (%)
b14_C	M8	1,998	67.01	87.20	86.51	0.10	4	63.51	39.09	5.59
b15_C		3,828	88.91	89.04	89.04	0.10	14	81.77	23.14	10.31
b20_C		3,907	74.37	78.56	78.52	0.10	18	72.33	17.35	14.67
b21_C		3,702	90.73	84.51	84.57	0.10	15	85.98	48.73	1.82
b22_C		4,294	93.73	83.68	83.75	0.10	21	91.66	35.72	0.87
b17_C		5,329	39.55	97.80	97.64	0.10	5	30.70	16.94	12.56
b14_C	M6	3,381	64.35	81.21	81.04	0.10	16	55.13	19.67	19.83
b15_C		6,576	81.75	82.82	82.82	0.10	34	78.04	15.36	24.31
b20_C		7,885	82.87	81.35	81.36	0.10	47	79.40	17.98	8.80
b21_C		6,112	89.25	79.67	79.70	0.10	57	85.59	16.67	9.88
b22_C		10,698	37.58	91.11	90.99	0.10	30	29.36	1.86	11.85
b17_C		18,385	47.39	98.04	97.98	0.10	12	38.19	13.61	10.36

Protected Designs. To further evaluate the robustness of UN-SPLIT, we apply the models trained on regular/unprotected layouts[1] to also predict links in designs protected using random routing obfuscation (Sect. 4.1).

Routing Perturbations: Comparing the results presented in Table 3 to those for regular designs (Table 2), we observe a degradation in performance, as expected. However, UN-SPLIT can remain effective even on these protected designs. For example, for the b15_C benchmark and split layer M8, the number of cut nets significantly increases from 77 to 3,828, i.e., around 50 times. Despite this massively larger search space, the best-case CCR only drops to 81.77%.

Post-Processing: On average, UN-SPLIT can obtain a post-processing CCR of 30.16% and 14.19% for split layers M8 and M6, respectively. This result indicates that the protected designs still leak some structural hints that can be exploited by the GNN. However, it is also more challenging for UN-SPLIT to recover protected designs when compared to regular split designs. As indicated above, this is mainly because of the considerable increase in cut nets induced by routing perturbations.

---

[1] UN-SPLIT could also be separately trained on protected designs, potentially further enhancing its performance. We will consider this for future work.

HD Analysis: We observe an average HD of 7.64% and 14.17% for the protected designs split at M8 and M6 layers, as shown in Table 3.

5   Limitations

Attacking split manufacturing is a complex problem, especially when lower metal layers are considered for splitting. The complexity arises from the larger number of connections to be considered and the limited information available to the attacker for inferring these connections. Although our GNN-based approach aims to reduce this complexity by prioritizing links with high likelihood scores from the GNN, it still must consider every possible link in order to make predictions.

In terms of computations, the UN-SPLIT approach for subgraph extraction can be parallelized, allowing us to make predictions on multiple links simultaneously. However, besides computational complexity, as the split layer descends lower, the GNN has access to less information — all links start to appear similar, i.e., show similar likelihood scores. It is important to note that, for lower split layers, layout and placement information can become more dominant over the functionality hints considered by the GNN model. Since the model needs to observe some connections and learn about their functionality, UN-SPLIT seems better suited for higher metal layers.

6   Conclusions

In our UN-SPLIT work, we present the first exploration of using GNNs for attacking split manufacturing. The motivation behind using a GNN was to explore and learn a new type of attack hint, specifically gate composition, and integrate it for the first time in an attack against split manufacturing.

Please note that a direct comparison with prior art is not practical. Since the problem of attacking split manufacturing hinges on intricacies of physical layouts, such comparison would require the very same layouts as used in prior art; however, prior art typically did not release layouts.

References

1. Alrahis, L., Knechtel, J., Klemme, F., Amrouch, H., Sinanoglu, O.: GNN4REL: graph neural networks for predicting circuit reliability degradation. IEEE Trans. Comput. Aided Des. Integr. Circuits Syst. 41(11), 3826–3837 (2022). https://doi.org/10.1109/TCAD.2022.3197521
2. Alrahis, L., Knechtel, J., Sinanoglu, O.: Graph neural networks: a powerful and versatile tool for advancing design, reliability, and security of ICs. In: Asia and South Pacific Design Automation Conference (ASP-DAC), pp. 83–90 (2023)
3. Alrahis, L., Patnaik, S., Hanif, M.A., Saleh, H., Shafique, M., Sinanoglu, O.: GNNUnlock+: a systematic methodology for designing graph neural networks-based oracle-less unlocking schemes for provably secure logic locking. IEEE Trans. Emerg. Top. Comput. 10(3), 1575–1592 (2022). https://doi.org/10.1109/TETC.2021.3108487

4. Alrahis, L., Patnaik, S., Hanif, M.A., Shafique, M., Sinanoglu, O.: UNTANGLE: Unlocking routing and logic obfuscation using graph neural networks-based link prediction. In: International Conference On Computer Aided Design (ICCAD), pp. 1–9 (2021). https://doi.org/10.1109/ICCAD51958.2021.9643476
5. Alrahis, L., et al.: GNNUnlock: graph neural networks-based oracle-less unlocking scheme for provably secure logic locking. In: Design, Automation & Test in Europe Conference & Exhibition (DATE), pp. 780–785 (2021)
6. Alrahis, L., Patnaik, S., Shafique, M., Sinanoglu, O.: Embracing graph neural networks for hardware security. In: International Conference On Computer Aided Design (ICCAD), pp. 1–9 (2022)
7. Alrahis, L., Patnaik, S., Shafique, M., Sinanoglu, O.: MuxLink: circumventing learning-resilient MUX-locking using graph neural network-based link prediction. In: Design, Automation & Test in Europe Conference & Exhibition (DATE), pp. 694–699 (2022). https://doi.org/10.23919/DATE54114.2022.9774603
8. Alrahis, L., Patnaik, S., Shafique, M., Sinanoglu, O.: OMLA: an oracle-less machine learning-based attack on logic locking. IEEE Trans. Circuits Syst. II Express Briefs 69(3), 1602–1606 (2022). https://doi.org/10.1109/TCSII.2021.3113035
9. Alrahis, L., et al.: GNN-RE: graph neural networks for reverse engineering of gate-level netlists. IEEE Trans. Comput. Aided Des. Integr. Circuits Syst. 41(8), 2435–2448 (2022). https://doi.org/10.1109/TCAD.2021.3110807
10. Kingma, D.P., Ba, J.: Adam: a method for stochastic optimization. arXiv preprint: arXiv:1412.6980 (2014)
11. Liben-Nowell, D., Kleinberg, J.: The link-prediction problem for social networks. Am. Soc. Inf. Scie. Tech. 58(7) (2007)
12. Magaña, J., Shi, D., Melchert, J., Davoodi, A.: Are proximity attacks a threat to the security of split manufacturing of integrated circuits? TVLSI 25(12), 3406–3419 (2017). https://doi.org/10.1109/TVLSI.2017.2748018
13. Magaña, J., et al.: Are proximity attacks a threat to the security of split manufacturing of integrated circuits? In: ICCAD (2016). https://doi.org/10.1145/2966986.2967006
14. McCants, C.: Trusted integrated chips (TIC) program (2016). https://www.ndia.org/-/media/sites/ndia/meetings-and-events/divisions/systems-engineering/past-events/trusted-micro/2016-august/mccants-carl.ashx
15. Patnaik, S.: GitHub - DfX-NYUAD/Randomized routing perturbation (2020). https://github.com/DfX-NYUAD/Randomized_routing_perturbation. Accessed 30 Oct 2023
16. Rajendran, J., Sinanoglu, O., Karri, R.: Is split manufacturing secure? In: DATE, pp. 1259–1264 (2013). https://doi.org/10.7873/DATE.2013.261
17. Rostami, M., Koushanfar, F., Karri, R.: A primer on hardware security: models, methods, and metrics. Proc. IEEE 102, 1283–1295 (2014)
18. Wang, Y., Chen, P., Hu, J., Li, G., Rajendran, J.: The cat and mouse in split manufacturing. TVLSI 26(5), 805–817 (2018). https://doi.org/10.1109/TVLSI.2017.2787754
19. Zeng, W., Zhang, B., Davoodi, A.: Analysis of security of split manufacturing using machine learning. TVLSI 27(12), 2767–2780 (2019). https://doi.org/10.1109/TVLSI.2019.2929710
20. Zhang, M., Chen, Y.: Link prediction based on graph neural networks. In: NIPS, pp. 5171–5181 (2018)
21. Zhang, M., Cui, Z., Neumann, M., Chen, Y.: An end-to-end deep learning architecture for graph classification. In: AAAI Conference AI (2018)

Logarithmic-Size (Linkable) Ring Signatures from Lattice Isomorphism Problems

Xuan Thanh Khuc[1]([✉]) [iD], Anh The Ta[3] [iD], Willy Susilo[1] [iD],
Dung Hoang Duong[1] [iD], Fuchun Guo[1] [iD], Kazuhide Fukushima[2] [iD],
and Shinsaku Kiyomoto[2] [iD]

[1] Institute of Cybersecurity and Cryptology, School of Computing and Information Technology, University of Wollongong, Wollongong, Australia
xtk929@uowmail.edu.au, {wsusilo,hduong,fuchun}@uow.edu.au
[2] Information Security Laboratory, KDDI Research, Inc., Fujimino, Japan
{ka-fukushima,kiyomoto}@kddi-research.jp
[3] CSIRO's Data61, Sydney, Australia
theanh.ta@csiro.au

Abstract. The Lattice Isomorphism Problem (LIP) asks whether two given lattices are isomorphic via an orthogonal linear transformation. At Eurocrypt 2022, Ducas and van Woerden provide a solid foundation for LIP as a promising candidate for post-quantum cryptography. They then propose a digital signature HAWK from LIP in the hash-then-sign framework, whose module version was recently investigated by Ducas et al. at Asiacrypt 2022. HAWK is one of the brightest prospects at round one of the NIST for additional digital signatures. In this paper, we build the first (linkable) ring signature schemes based on the hardness of LIP. The proposed signatures have the logarithmic size in the number of ring users. Our signature size is significantly smaller than several ring signatures based on other underlying problems when the number of users in the ring is large.

To this end, we leverage group action properties of LIP and follow the Merkle tree-based construction of Beullens, Katsumata and Pintore at Asiacrypt 2020 in the context of isogeny-based cryptography, with suitable adaptions to lattice isomorphism group actions.

Keywords: ring signatures · linkable ring signatures · lattice isomorphism problems · group actions

1 Introduction

With the rapid development in building increasingly larger quantum computers in recent years [26], post-quantum cryptography has become critical for protecting our data from powerful quantum adversaries. The transition to the secure post-quantum world has been in preparation for a long time [32], and will soon become standards. A critical turning point is that, after many years of investigation, the National Institute of Standards and Technology (NIST) has chosen

F. Regazzoni et al. (Eds.): SPACE 2023, LNCS 14412, pp. 214–241, 2024.
https://doi.org/10.1007/978-3-031-51583-5_13

the key management mechanism CRYSTAL-Kyber [37], signatures CRYSTAL-Dilithium [30] and FALCON [35]- all lattice-based - and a hash-based signature SPHINCS$^+$ for post-quantum cryptography standardisation [33]. While lattices have a dominating position in this area, it is both necessary and essential to have alternative solutions. Indeed, NIST has just started a new competition for additional post-quantum digital signature schemes with almost 50 submissions based on various hardness problems [34]. The quest is then naturally extended to the whole field of post-quantum cryptography: while many advanced cryptographic functionalities (advanced signatures, proof systems, etc.) have been realised from lattice assumptions, it is important to have constructions for such primitives based on alternative post-quantum hardness assumptions. In this paper, we make contributions in this research direction by giving secure constructions for advanced signatures, logarithmic ring signature schemes and their linkable variants from newly proposed post-quantum hardness assumptions, the lattice isomorphism problems that underlie the recent NIST additional signature submission HAWK [25].

Ring signatures (RS), first introduced by Rivest, Shamir and Tauman in [36], allow any member in a group of users - called the *ring* - sign messages on behalf of the whole group and at the same time no one can tell which user is the real signer. In other words, RS schemes provide the *anonymity* property for their users which is important in privacy-preserving applications. In addition, a signer can dynamically form a ring by simply collecting users' public keys without the need for agreement from other members. There has been an active line of research to design compact ring signatures. As the number N of users increases, the size of ring signatures often grows linearly in N. However, several works have reduced the growth of ring signature sizes to $\log(N)$ [6,9,18,23,28,39]. Such logarithmic ring signatures are obtained via the Fiat-Shamir transform from different constructions of one-out-of-many or zero-knowledge proof of knowledge. Schemes in [9,23,28] are based on classical number theoretic assumption, while [6,18,39] use lattice-based or isogeny-based hardness assumptions, hence achieve post-quantum security. There have been several candidates for post-quantum cryptography. Among them, lattice-based cryptography seems to take a lot of attention due to its attractive features such as high asymptotic efficiency and parallelism, security under worst-case intractability assumptions, e.g., learning with errors (LWE) problem or short integer solution (SIS) problem, flexibility in enabling many advanced constructions such as fully homomorphic encryption [10,14], attribute-based encryption [5,22], multi signatures [2,8], etc.

In this paper, we focus on another lattice assumption, namely the *lattice isomorphism problem* (LIP). While lattice isomorphism problems have been studied already by Haviv and Regev in [24], Ducas and van Woerden [17] have recently revitalised the research direction of using lattice isomorphism problems in cryptography [4,15,16]. In [17], Ducas and van Woerden provide a new reformulation of lattice isomorphisms in terms of quadratic forms. They then introduce two computational problems: the lattice isomorphism problem in terms of quadratic forms (sLIP^Q) and the distinguishing lattice isomorphism problem ($\Delta\mathsf{LIP}^{Q_0,Q_1}$), in both search and decision versions following the efficient discrete Gaussian sampling algorithm. In [17], they showed that lattice isomorphism problems are new and promising candidates for post-quantum cryptographic hardness assumptions. In particular, they admit worse-case to average-case reductions [17, Section 3.3] which are essential for building secure cryptographic primitives. Cryptanalysis works on LIP have also appeared recently [12,15]. There are also many exciting connections between LIP with coding theory and number theory, we refer to [4,17] for further details. It raises then a natural question *"whether other primitives can be built based on this new type of hardness assumptions?"*. Up to now, there is only a handful of cryptographic constructions based on lattice isomorphisms: two zero-knowledge proofs due to Haviv-Regev [24] and Ducas-van Woerden [17], a key encapsulation mechanism [17], a hash-then-sign signature scheme and its variant for module lattices [16,17], and an encryption scheme due to Bennett *et al.* in [4]. This paper focuses on constructing (linkable) ring signatures from LIP.

Our Contribution. In this paper, we provide the first construction of logarithmic (linkable) ring signatures from LIP. The core idea is to construct an OR proof of knowledge from LIP from which a ring signature is obtained via the Fiat-Shamir transformation. We depart from the approach of Beullens, Katsumata and Pintore in [6] in which they provided a general framework for constructing OR proof of knowledge from secure cryptographic group actions. In addition to concrete constructions of logarithmic ring signatures from CSIDH and MLWE group actions, they also introduced a series of optimisation methods to boost the efficiency and security of group actions based OR proof of knowledge. Follow-up works [1] and [13] have adapted the techniques of [6] to build logarithmic ring signatures from the code-equivalence problem and alternating trilinear form equivalence, respectively.

The lattice isomorphism problem is a relatively new post-quantum assumption with various distinct features. This makes the task of adapting methods from previous works a challenging one. Firstly, the group is $GL(n, \mathbb{Z})$ is both non-commutative and infinite, making it impossible to uniform sample the secrets as in previous works. In addition, GMW style [21] sigma protocol of Ducas and van Woerden [17] does not fit into the current framework; we need to suitably modify it in our Protocol 3.1. Secondly, the distribution of D over a set of group actions is very specific to the LIP setting. Unlike previous works in which secret keys can be obtained by simply uniform sampling, the distribution D of pairs of public and secret keys in the case of LIP is defined as the output distribution of a polynomial time sampling algorithm. We need additional parameters to run the sampling algorithm. Moreover, we do not have a method to sample the secret keys directly. What we can do is to sample a public key from the distribution D, and at the same time obtain an element uniformly randomly from the finite set of lattice equivalences. These differences lead to a series of changes we must make throughout the steps of zero-knowledge proofs to obtain correct constructions; see the protocols in Sect. 3.

Since our scheme is based on LIP, our scheme avoids using the rejection sampling algorithm, where the signer must rerun the signing algorithm when some condition is not satisfied as several ring signatures based on lattice problem (MSIS, MLWE) [6]. Our ring signature schemes' size only depends on $\log N$, where N denotes the ring size. For NIST I (128-bit security) in the ring size $N = 2^6$, our ring signature size is 40KB. This size is approximate to Falafl [6]. However, our size is larger than Calamari [6], LESS [1] and ATFE-GMW-FS [7]. Although RAPTOR [29], DualRing-LB [38], MRr-DSS [3], and MatRiCT [19] have shorter signature sizes than ours when the ring size is small, their size significantly increases when the number of participants rises. For NIST V (256-bit security), our ring signature size is much smaller than the KKW [27] (Table 1).

Table 1. Comparison of the signature size (KB) between our schemes and others

	N					Hardness assumption	Security level
	2^1	2^3	2^6	2^{12}	2^{21}		
Calamari [6]	3.5	5.4	8.2	14	23	CSIDH-512	*
RAPTOR [29]	2.5	10	81	5161	/	NTRU	100 bits
MatRiCT [19]	/	18	19	59	/	MSIS, MLWE	NIST I
Falafl [6]	29	30	32	35	39	MSIS, MLWE	NIST I
DualRing-LB [38]	/	4.6	6	106.6	/	MSIS, MLWE	NIST I
MRr-DSS [3]	/	27	36	422	/	MinRank	NIST I
LESS [1]	/	10.8	13.7	19.7	28.6	Code Equiv.	NIST I
ATFE-GMW-FS [7]	8.9	10.5	12.9	17.7	24.9	ATFE	NIST I
Ours - 128 bits	**35**	**37**	**40**	**45**	**54**	**LIP**	NIST I
KKW [27]	/	/	250	456	/	LoWMC	NIST V
Ours - 256 bits	**162**	**169**	**181**	**203**	**237**	**LIP**	NIST V

Organization. Our paper is organised into five sections. After giving an introduction in Sect. 1, we recall the necessary backgrounds on lattice isomorphism problems and definitions of relevant cryptographic primitives in Sect. 2. In Sect. 3, we discuss the differences between LIP and group actions considered in previous works [1,6,13], and present our constructions of proofs of knowledge and signatures. The parameter selection is also shown in this section. We conclude our paper in Sect. 4.

2   Preliminaries

2.1   Lattice Isomorphism Problems

This section recalls the basics of lattice isomorphism problems from [17]. An n-dimensional full rank lattice $L \subset \mathbb{R}^n$ can be given as the set of integer linear combinations $L = \{x_1\mathbf{b}_1 + \cdots + x_n\mathbf{b}_n : x_1, \ldots, x_n \in \mathbb{Z}\}$ of column vectors in a basis B of L: $B = [\mathbf{b}_1, \ldots, \mathbf{b}_n] \in GL(n, \mathbb{R})$. We also write the lattice L generated from B as either $\mathcal{L}(B)$ or $B \cdot \mathbb{Z}^n$, interchangeably. For $O \in \mathbb{R}^{n \times n}$, define the lattice $O \cdot L = \{O\mathbf{x} : \mathbf{x} \in L\}$. By definition, two lattices $\mathcal{L}_1, \mathcal{L}_2$ are isomorphic if there exists an orthonormal matrix $O \in O(n, \mathbb{R})$ such that $\mathcal{L}_2 = O \cdot \mathcal{L}_1$. The lattice isomorphism problem (LIP) states as follows.

Definition 2.1 (LIP - Lattice version, [17,24]). *Given two isomorphic lattices* $\mathcal{L}_1, \mathcal{L}_2 \subset \mathbb{R}^n$, *find an orthonormal matrix* $O \in O(n, \mathbb{R})$ *such that* $\mathcal{L}_2 = O \cdot \mathcal{L}_1$.

Two basis matrices B_1, B_2 generate the same lattice $\mathcal{L}(B_1) = \mathcal{L}(B_2)$ iff there is a unimodular matrix $U \in GL(n, \mathbb{Z})$ such that $B_2 = B_1 U$. Thus, for isomorphic lattices $\mathcal{L}_1 = \mathcal{L}_1(B_1)$ and $\mathcal{L}_2 = \mathcal{L}_2(B_2)$, LIP actually asks to find a pair of matrices $(O, U) \in O(n, \mathbb{Z}) \times GL(n, \mathbb{Z})$ such that $B_2 = OB_1U$.

Since O has real coefficients, it isn't easy to use the equivalence $B_2 = OB_1U$ for algorithmic purposes. To overcome this problem, Ducas and van Woerden [17] reformulate LIP in terms of quadratic forms as follows. The set $Sym^+(n, \mathbb{R})$ of quadratic forms of dimension n consists of all positive definite symmetric matrices of size $n \times n$. Given a lattice $L = \mathcal{L}(B)$, one can associate a quadratic form $Q = \gamma(B) = B^t B$ to L. In fact, this Gram map γ gives an identification between quadratic forms $Sym^+(n, \mathbb{R})$ and lattice isomorphic classes $O(n, \mathbb{R}) \backslash GL(n, \mathbb{R})$ as $\gamma^{-1}(B^t B) = \{OB : O \in O(n, \mathbb{R})\}$. A crucial observation is that if all the entries of B are integers, then so is Q. We then consider only the set $Sym^+(n, \mathbb{Z})$ of integer-valued quadratic forms.

The group of basis equivalences, i.e. unimodular matrices $U \in GL(n, \mathbb{Z})$, acts on $Q \in Sym^+(n, \mathbb{Z})$ via $\rho_U(Q) = U^t QU$. Given two bases $B_2 = OB_1U$ of the lattice $\mathcal{L}(B_2) = \mathcal{L}(B_1)$, their associated quadratic forms $Q_1 = B_1^t B_1$ and $Q_2 = B_2^t B_2$ satisfies $Q_2 = B_2^t B_2 = U^t B_1^t O^t OB_1U = U^t B_1^t B_1U = U^t Q_1U = \rho_U(Q_1)$.

Definition 2.2 (Quadratic form equivalence, [17]). *We have two quadratic forms* $Q_1, Q_2 \in Sym^+(n, \mathbb{Z})$ *are equivalent, if there exists a unimodular matrix* $U \in GL(n, \mathbb{Z})$ *such that* $Q_2 = \rho_U(Q_1) = U^t Q_1U$. *Denote by* $[Q]$ *the equivalence class of* Q.

Given quadratic form Q associated with a lattice L, the Cholesky decomposition $Q = B_Q^t B_Q$ gives a unique upper-triangular integer-valued matrix B_Q, and B_Q is a basis of L. The correspondence between lattice and quadratic form formulations allows representing lattice vectors $B\mathbf{x} \in \mathcal{L}(B) \subset \mathbb{R}^n$ by canonical vectors $\mathbf{x} \in \mathbb{Z}^n$. However, the distance induced by quadratic forms differs from the standard one in $\mathbb{Z}^n$. The inner product with respect to Q is $\langle \mathbf{x}, \mathbf{y} \rangle_Q = \mathbf{x}^t Q\mathbf{y}$, and the induced norm is $|\mathbf{x}|_Q^2 = \mathbf{x}^t Q\mathbf{x}$, instead of the standard $|\mathbf{x}|^2 = \mathbf{x}^t \mathbf{x}$.

Define the i-th minimal distance $\lambda_i(Q)$ as the smallest $r > 0$ such that $\{\mathbf{x} \in \mathbb{Z}^n : |\mathbf{x}|_Q \leq r\}$ spans a vector space of dimension at least i, for $i = 1, \ldots, n$.

Definition 2.3 (wc-sLIP^Q, [17]). *Given* $Q \in Sym^+(n, \mathbb{Z})$, *the worse case search lattice isomorphism problem* wc-sLIP^Q *asks for any* $Q' \in [Q]$ *to find a* $U \in GL(n, \mathbb{Z})$ *such that* $Q' = \rho_U(Q) = U^t QU$.

Note that wc-sLIP^Q is an equivalent formulation of LIP: given a solution U of wc-sLIP^Q, we can extract a solution O for LIP by computing the orthogonal matrix $O = B_2(B_1U)^{-1}$. The automorphism group $Aut(Q) = \{V \in GL(n, \mathbb{Z}) : V^tQV = Q\}$ is finite for any fixed Q, and the the set of all equivalences from Q to Q' is $\{VU : V \in Aut(Q)\}$ given a solution U of wc-sLIP^Q.

Ducas and van Woerden [17] also consider the worse case distinguishing lattice isomorphism problem wc-ΔLIP^{Q_0,Q_1}.

Definition 2.4 (wc-ΔLIP^{Q_0,Q_1}, [17]). *Given $Q_0, Q_1 \in Sym^+(n, \mathbb{Z})$, the problem wc-$\Delta$LIP^{Q_0,Q_1} asks for any quadratic form $Q' \in [Q_b]$, where $b \in \{0,1\}$ is a uniformly random bit, to find the bit b.*

A unique feature of quadratic form equivalence is the existence of many arithmetic and geometric invariants, called genus, which are efficiently computable. To avoid these distinguishers, we always need to make sure that genuses of Q_0, Q_1 are the same for wc-ΔLIP^{Q_0,Q_1}. See Section 7 of [17] for further details. The hardness of quadratic form equivalence problems wc-sLIP^Q and wc-ΔLIP^{Q_0,Q_1} is always understood with respect to an infinite family of quadratic forms $(Q_n)_n$ and $((Q_0)_n, (Q_1)_n)$, $n = 1, 2, \ldots$, respectively.

2.2 Discrete Gaussian Distribution and Sampling Algorithm for Lattice Isomorphisms

To use the hardness assumptions for cryptographic primitives, one needs to define average case versions of lattice isomorphism problems. This goal is achieved in the work of Ducas and van Woerden [17], in which they define probability distribution and build an efficient sampling algorithm on equivalent classes of quadratic forms. Their approach is inspired by works on discrete Gaussian sampling and lattice trapdoors in lattice-based cryptography [11,20,31]. We recall the necessary constructions from [17], especially their polynomial time discrete Gaussian sampling algorithm.

Discrete Gaussian Distribution with Respect to a Quadratic Form. Given a quadratic form $Q \in Sym^+(n, \mathbb{Z})$, the Gaussian function on $\mathbb{R}^n$ with respect to the form Q, parameter $s > 0$ and center $\mathbf{c} \in \mathbb{R}^n$ is defined as the function $\rho_{Q,s,\mathbf{c}} : \mathbb{R}^n \to (0, 1]$:

$$\rho_{Q,s,\mathbf{c}}(\mathbf{x}) = \exp\left(\frac{-\pi|\mathbf{x} - \mathbf{c}|_Q^2}{s^2}\right). \tag{2.1}$$

The discrete Gaussian distribution $\mathcal{D}_{Q,s,\mathbf{c}}$ for a quadratic form Q, with parameter $s > 0$ and center $\mathbf{c} \in \mathbb{R}^n$ is then defined as follows

$$\Pr_{X \leftarrow \mathcal{D}_{Q,s,\mathbf{c}}}[X = \mathbf{x}] = \begin{cases} \frac{\rho_{Q,s,\mathbf{c}}(\mathbf{x})}{\rho_{Q,s,\mathbf{c}}(\mathbb{Z}^n)} & \text{if } \mathbf{x} \in \mathbb{Z}^n, \\ 0 & \text{if } \mathbf{x} \notin \mathbb{Z}^n, \end{cases} \tag{2.2}$$

where the total weight is $\rho_{Q,s,\mathbf{c}}(\mathbb{Z}^n) = \sum_{\mathbf{x} \in \mathbb{Z}^n} \rho_{Q,s,\mathbf{c}}(\mathbf{x})$. Write $\mathcal{D}_{Q,s}$ for $\mathcal{D}_{Q,s,\mathbf{c}}$ when $\mathbf{c} = 0$. We refer to the original paper [17] for many important properties (smoothing parameter, min-entropy, etc.) of the distribution $\mathcal{D}_{Q,s,\mathbf{c}}$.

Discrete Gaussian Sampling Algorithm. We recall the sampling algorithm from the Gaussian distribution $\mathcal{D}_s([Q])$ of [17]. First, one needs an efficient method for sampling lattice points from discrete Gaussian distribution.

Lemma 2.5 ([11]). *There is a polynomial time algorithm $\textbf{Sample}(Q, s, \mathbf{c})$ that on input a quadratic form $Q \in Sym^+(n, \mathbb{Z})$, parameter $s \geq |B_Q^*| \cdot \sqrt{\log(2n + 4))/\pi}$ and center $\mathbf{c} \in \mathbb{R}^n$, it returns a sample from the distribution $\mathcal{D}_{Q,s,\mathbf{c}}$.*

The second subroutine is a reduction algorithm that, on given a quadratic form and a set of short vectors of full rank, returns a well-reduced equivalent quadratic form.

Lemma 2.6 ([31]). *There is a polynomial time algorithm $\textbf{Extract}: (R, U) \leftarrow \textbf{Extract}(Q, Y)$ that on input a quadratic form Q and vectors $Y = (\mathbf{y}_1, \ldots, \mathbf{y}_m) \in \mathbb{Z}^{n \times m}$ such that $\text{rk}(\mathcal{L}(Y)) = n$, outputs a matrix $U \in GL(n, \mathbb{Z})$ and a quadratic form $R = U^t Q U$ equivalent to Q such that $|B_Q^*| \leq \max\limits_{i \in [m]} |\mathbf{y}_i|_Q$.*

An important observation of [17] is that the output distribution of **Extract** is well-defined, that is the extracted form depends only on the geometry of the input vectors, not on the particular representative of the equivalent class $[Q]$.

Lemma 2.7 ([17]). *Let $Y = (\mathbf{y}_1, \ldots, \mathbf{y}_m) \in \mathbb{Z}^{n \times m}$ such that $\text{rk}(\mathcal{L}(Y)) = n$. If $(R, U) \leftarrow \textbf{Extract}(Q, Y)$ and $(R', U') \leftarrow \textbf{Extract}(V^t Q V, V^{-1} Y)$ for some unimodular matrix $V \in GL(n, \mathbb{Z})$, then $R' = R$ and $U' = V^{-1} U$.*

Finally, the distribution $\mathcal{D}_s([Q])$ is defined as follows.

Definition 2.8 ([17]). *Given a quadratic form $Q \in Sym^+(n, \mathbb{Z})$, the Gaussian distribution $\mathcal{D}_s([Q])$ of quadratic forms over the set $[Q]$ of forms equivalent to Q, with parameter $s > 0$ is defined as the output distribution of the following procedure:*

1. *Let $C = 1 - \frac{1}{1+e^{-\pi}}$, $m = \lceil \frac{2n}{C} \rceil$.*
   Sample m vectors $Y = (\mathbf{y}_1, \ldots, \mathbf{y}_m)$ from $\mathcal{D}_{Q,s}$ by $\textbf{Sample}(Q, s)$.
   Repeat until $\text{rk}(Y) = n$.
2. *$(R, U) \leftarrow \textbf{Extract}(Q, Y)$.*
3. *Return R.*

To obtain an efficient sampling algorithm from $\mathcal{D}_s([Q])$, one needs a lower bound on the parameter s based on the reducedness of Q so that Step 1 in Definition 2.8 terminates quickly. [17] points out that it suffices to take $s \geq \lambda_n(Q)$.

Algorithm 2.9 (Algorithm 1, Lemma 3.4, [17]). *For $Q \in Sym^+(n, \mathbb{Z}^n)$, $s \geq \max\{ \lambda_n(Q), |B_Q^*| \cdot \sqrt{\log(2n + 4)/\pi} \}$, the sampling algorithm from $\mathcal{D}_s([Q])$ of Ducas-van Woerden [17] given Definition 2.8, called $\textbf{QSample}(Q, s)$, runs in polynomial time.*

The output of **QSample** is (R, U) where R is a sample from $\mathcal{D}_s([Q])$, and conditioned on R, U is uniformly distributed over the set of isomorphisms from Q to R. Having defined the distribution $\mathcal{D}_s([Q])$, and the sampling algorithm **QSample**(Q, s), we can now state average-case versions of lattice isomorphism problems.

Definition 2.10 (ac-sLIP$_s^Q$, [17]). *Given a quadratic form $Q \in Sym^+(n, \mathbb{Z})$ and $s > 0$, the problem ac-sLIP$_s^Q$ asks for a given quadratic form Q' sampled from $\mathcal{D}_s([Q])$ to find a unimodular matrix U such that $Q' = U^t Q U$.*

Definition 2.11 (ac-ΔLIP$_s^{Q_0, Q_1}$, [17]). *Given two quadratic forms Q_0, $Q_1 \in Sym^+(n, \mathbb{Z})$ and $s > 0$, the problem ac-ΔLIP$_s^{Q_0, Q_1}$ asks for a given quadratic form Q' sampled from $\mathcal{D}_s([Q_b])$, where $b \leftarrow \{0, 1\}$ is a uniform random bit, to find b.*

Similar to lattice problems, LIPs also enjoy the important average-case to worst-case reductions. Conversely, it was shown in [17] that when s is large enough, the average-case LIPs become at least as hard as any worst-case instance.

2.3 (Linkable) Ring Signatures

Definition 2.12. *A ring signature RS is a tuple of 4 PPT algorithms (RS.Setup, RS.KeyGen, RS.Sign, RS.Verify):*

- RS.Setup(1^λ): *Given a security level λ as input, it returns public parameters pp.*
- RS.KeyGen(pp): *It takes as input the public parameters and outputs a pair (sk, pk) of the public key pk and secret key sk for each user.*
- RS.Sign(R, sk_i, m): *An user with the secret key sk_i and a ring $R = \{pk_1, \ldots, pk_N\}$, where pk_i is the public key corresponding to sk_i, produces a signature σ on the message m with respect to the ring R.*
- RS.Verify(σ, m, R): *Given a signature σ, it outputs 1 (accept) if σ is a valid ring signature with respect to the message m and the ring R, and 0 (reject) otherwise.*

Security of the ring signature scheme is defined with correctness, anonymity and unforgeability properties (See Appendix A).

Definition 1 (Linkable ring signatures). *A linkable ring signature scheme LRS consists of the 4 PPT algorithms of a Ring signature scheme and one additional PPT algorithm LRS.Link such that:*

- LRS.Link(σ_1, σ_0): *On input two signature σ_0 and σ_1, it outputs either 1 or 0, where 1 indicate that the signatures are generated by using the same secret key.*

Along with the correctness property, we require the linkability, linkable anonymity, and non-frameability properties of a linkable ring signature scheme (See Appendix B).

2.4   Admissible Group Actions

Definition 2.13 ([6]). *Let G be an additive group, S_1, S_2 two symmetric subsets of G, $\mathcal{X}$ a finite set, $\delta \in [0,1]$. Let $D_{\mathcal{X}}$ be a distribution over a set of group actions $G \times \mathcal{X} \to \mathcal{X}$. The tuple $\mathsf{AdmGA} = (G, \mathcal{X}, S_1, S_2, D_{\mathcal{X}})$ is a δ-admissible group action with respect to $X_0 \in \mathcal{X}$ if the following holds:*

1. *There exist efficient algorithms to perform the following tasks: compute $g \cdot X$ for all $g \in S_1 \cup S_2$ and all $X \in \mathcal{X}$, sample uniformly from S_1, S_2 and $D_{\mathcal{X}}$, and represent elements of G and $\mathcal{X}$ uniquely.*
2. *The intersection of the sets $\{S_2 \cdot g\}_{g \in S_1}$ is sufficiently large: if we denote $S_3 = \cap_{g \in S_1} S_2 \cdot g$, then $|S_3| = \delta|S_2|$. There is an efficient algorithm to check if an element $g \in G$ belongs to S_3.*
3. *It is difficult to output $g \in S_2 \cdot S_3$ such that $g' \cdot X_0 = X$ with non-negligible probability, given $X = g \cdot X_0$ for some g sampled uniformly from S_1.*

Note that the group actions in [6] are commutative, like class group and MLWE group actions, while the group action in our case, as well as in the case of code equivalence in [1], are non-commutative. This difference leads to several problems in designing signatures based on lattice isomorphisms following the framework of [6]. We will discuss the specific details in Sect. 3.1.

3   OR Proof of Knowledge and Ring Signature from Lattice Isomorphisms

In this section, we give details of how to construct OR proofs of knowledge of quadratic form equivalence.

3.1   Group Action in the Setting of Lattice Isomorphisms

Given a quadratic form $Q_0 \in Sym^+(n, \mathbb{Z})$, the group $G = GL(n, \mathbb{Z})$ acts on $\mathcal{X} = [Q_0] = \{Q \in Sym^+(n, \mathbb{Z}) : Q \sim Q_0\}$ - the set of quadratic forms equivalent to Q_0. A special feature, compared to other cryptographic group actions, is that in this case both the group and the ambient space are infinite. The action of G on $\mathcal{X}$ is specified by $(U, Q) \mapsto \rho_U(Q) = U^t Q U$ which is transitive. The Group Action Inverse Problem (GAIP) for $(G, \mathcal{X}, \rho)$ can be stated as the $\mathsf{ac\text{-}sLIP}_s^{Q_0}$ problem thanks to the discrete Gaussian sampling algorithm.

While the original definition of admissible group actions of [6] in Definition 2.13 does not apply directly to our setting here, we can make simple modifications to it to adapt to the setting of lattice isomorphism. Note that the work of [1] also makes some similar modifications in order to apply methods from [6] to code equivalence problems. We list the changes in the following and refer to the Definition 2.13 for comparison.

1. The group is $G = GL(n, \mathbb{Z})$ which is noncommutative, and both G and $\mathcal{X}$ are infinite sets. The distinguished point $X_0 \in \mathcal{X}$ is $X_0 = Q_0$. The two symmetric subsets S_1, S_2 are taken to be the entire group G, hence $\delta = 1$.

2. The distribution $D_{\mathcal{X}}$ over a set of group action of G on $\mathcal{X}$ is very specific to the lattice isomorphism setting. It is the output distribution of **QSample**(Q_0, s) which can be identified with

$$(Q, U) \leftarrow \mathcal{D}_s([Q_0]) \times (\mathsf{Uniform}(Aut(Q_0))|Q).$$

As such, we always need a public parameter s such that $s \geq \max\{\lambda_n(Q_0), |B^*_{Q_0}| \cdot \sqrt{\log(2n+4)/\pi}\}$ to run the sampling algorithm.

3. In addition, we do not have a method to sample uniformly random from the group $G = GL(n, \mathbb{Z})$. What we can do is to sample a point $X \in \mathcal{X}$ from the distribution $\mathcal{D}_s([Q_0])$, and at the same time obtain an element $g = U \in G$ uniformly randomly from the finite set of equivalences between X_0 and X.

4. Assume the hardness of the ac-sLIP$_s^{Q_0}$ problem, it follows that given (Q_1, Q_0) where $Q_1 \leftarrow \mathcal{D}_s([Q_0])$ via **QSample**, it is difficult to find $U' \in G$ such that $\rho_{U'}(Q_0) = U_1$.

3.2   Proof of Knowledge for Lattice Equivalence

In [17, Section 4.1], Ducas and van Woerden describe a proof of knowledge of a secret element $U \in G$ such that $\rho_U(Q_0) = Q_1$ for public equivalent forms $Q_0, Q_1 \in \mathcal{X}$, following the classical GMW [21] proof for graph isomorphisms. We observe that this protocol does not fit into the group action framework of [6]. Thus, for our purpose we need a modified protocol: in the response phase, the prover sends $U_1^{1-c}V_1$, instead of $U_1^{-c}V_1$ as in [17], to the verifier.

Protocol 3.1. *Public data: The public parameters are two equivalent forms* (Q_0, Q_1) *and a parameter* s *such that*

$$s \geq \max\{\lambda_n(Q_0), \max\{|B^*_{Q_0}|, |B^*_{Q_1}|\} \cdot \sqrt{\log(2n+4)/\pi}\}. \tag{3.1}$$

The secret information of which the prover wants to prove his knowledge to the verifier is an equivalence U_1 *from* Q_0 *to* $Q_1 : \rho_{U_1}(Q_0) = U_1^t Q_0 U_1 = Q_1.$

- **Round 1 - $\mathcal{P}_1(Q_0, Q_1, s)$:** *The prover* $\mathcal{P}_1(Q_1, s)$ *runs* **QSample**(Q_1, s) *to sample* $Q' \leftarrow \mathcal{D}_s([Q_1])$, *together with* $V_1 \in G$ *uniformly random from the set of equivalences from* Q_1 *to* Q', *such that* $Q' = \rho_{V_1}(Q_1) = V_1^t Q_1 V_1$. *He sends the commitment* $cmt = Q'$ *to the verifier.*
- **Round 2 - $\mathcal{V}_1$:** *The verifier* $\mathcal{V}_1$ *sample a random bit challenge* $c \leftarrow \{0, 1\}$ *and sends it to the prover.*
- **Round 3 - $\mathcal{P}_2(U, c)$:** *Upon receiving* c, *the prover* $\mathcal{P}_2(U_1)$ *proceeds as follows:*
  - *if* $c = 0$, *the response is* $rsp = U_1 V_1$;
  - *if* $c = 1$, *then response is* $rsp = V_1$.
- **Round 4 - $\mathcal{V}_2(Q_0, Q_1)$:** *The verifier* $\mathcal{V}_2(Q_0, Q_1, c)$ *works as follows:*
  - *when* $c = 0$, *he checks whether* $\rho_{rsp}(Q_0) = cmt$, *that is* $(U_1 V_1)^t Q_0 (U_1 V_1) = V_1^t Q_1 V_1 = Q'$;
  - *when* $c = 1$, *the verifier checks whether* $\rho_{rsp}(Q_1) = cmt$, *that is* $V_1^t Q_1 V_1 = Q'$.

Theorem 3.2. *Protocol 3.1 satisfies correctness, soundness and zero-knowledge properties.*

Proof. See Appendix D.

Furthermore, this sigma protocol is also recoverable, which later allows us to use challenge instead of commitment and obtain a shorter signature. Next, we extend the Protocol 3.1 to obtain OR proof of lattice equivalence. In the beginning, we are given a fixed public quadratic form Q_0. For each user i, one runs **QSample** on $[Q_0]$ to generate a public key $pk_i = Q_i$ and the corresponding secret key $sk_i = U_i : \rho_{U_i}(Q_0) = Q_i$. For running the **QSample** in polynomial time, we need an additional public parameter s such that

$$s \geq \max\{\lambda_n(Q_0), \max\{|B^*_{Q_0}|, |B^*_{Q_1}|, \ldots, |B^*_{Q_N}|\} \cdot \sqrt{\log(2n+4)/\pi}\}. \quad (3.2)$$

Suppose the prover in our OR proof is the user $I \in \{1, \ldots, N\}$. He can collect the public keys Q_i's to form the ring $R = \{Q_1, \ldots, Q_N\}$. In addition, the prover knows the secret key $sk_I = U_I$, but he does not know any other secret key due to the hardness of the lattice isomorphism problem. One can easily extend the Protocol 3.1 to obtain an OR proof of knowledge for the prover to prove his knowledge of the secret key $sk_I = U_I$ such that $\rho_{U_I} = Q_I$ and hide his identity I in the ring R from the verifier. Note that one needs to use a random shuffle in the commitment, and for verification, one either checks a set membership or a set equality.

3.3   OR Sigma Protocols

We give details of how to implement the base OR sigma protocol Π^{base} for quadratic form isomorphism with $G = GL(n, \mathbb{Z})$, $X_0 = Q_0$, $\mathcal{X} = [Q_0]$, and the distribution $D_{\mathcal{X}} = \mathsf{Output}(\mathbf{QSample}(Q_0, s))$. Each user uses the public parameters Q_0, s to run **QSample**, and at output obtain its key pair $(pk = Q, sk = U) \in \mathcal{X} \times G$.

The prover is an user of index $I \in \{1, \ldots, N\}$ who can gather public keys to form a ring $R = \{pk_1 = Q_1, \ldots, pk_N = Q_N\}$. The base OR sigma protocol $\Pi^{base} = (\mathcal{P}^{base} = (\mathcal{P}^{base}_1, \mathcal{P}^{base}_2), \mathcal{V}^{base} = (\mathcal{V}^{base}_1, \mathcal{V}^{base}_2))$ is a proof of knowledge for $(sk_I = U_I, I) \in (G, [N])$ such that $\rho_{U_I}(Q_0) = Q_I$.

In the first round, the prover generates a random seed **seed** from a pseudorandom number generator **Expand**. He then generates further random strings $\{\mathsf{seed}_i\}_{i \in [N]}$, and uses seed_i as a random seed for running **QSample** for each user $i \in [N]$. He then runs **QSample** for each user i using seed_i to obtain $Q'_i \leftarrow \mathcal{D}_s([Q_i])$, $V_i \in GL(n, \mathbb{Z}) : Q'_i = \rho_{V_i}(Q_i)$, and uses Q'_i as a commitment $C_i = Q'_i$. He builds a Merkle tree with leaves $(C_1, \ldots, C_N)$ on a root **root**. The prover sends **root** to the verifier.

In the second round, the verifier samples a bit $ch \in \{0, 1\}$ uniformly at random, and sends it to the prover.

In the third round, the prover considers two cases:

- If $ch = 0$, then the prover computes $z = U_I V_I$. He sends z and the path $\mathsf{path}(C_I)$ connecting C_I to the root of the Merkle tree to the verifier.

– If $ch = 1$, then prover responses with $z = (V_1\|\ldots\|V_N)$. He actually sends only $rsp = $ seed to the verifier, who can use it to run the pseudorandom generator Expand to recover seed$_i$'s, then V_i's for each $i \in [N]$.

In the fourth round, the verifier considers two cases:

– If $ch = 0$, the verifier computes $Q'' = \rho_z(Q_0)$, then set the leaf $C'' = Q''$. He then uses path(C_I) to reconstruct the root root$''$. Finally, he checks whether root$'' = $ root.
– If $ch = 1$, the verifier uses seed to run the pseudorandom generator to recover seed$_i$'s, then V_i's for each $i \in [N]$. He then reconstructs the Merkle tree and checks whether its root is root.

The full description of the base OR sigma protocol is given in Protocol 3.3. Note that, we use index-hiding Merkle tree and seed tree techniques to construct protocol (See Appendix C).

Protocol 3.3 (Base OR sigma protocol)
$\Pi^{base} = (\mathcal{P} = (\mathcal{P}_1^{base}, \mathcal{P}_2^{base}), \mathcal{V} = (\mathcal{V}_1^{base}, \mathcal{V}_2^{base}))$:

– **Round 1:** $\mathcal{P}_1^{base}(R, (U_I, I); \mathcal{O})$
  1. seed $\leftarrow \{0,1\}^\lambda$
  2. $(\text{seed}_1, \ldots, \text{seed}_N) \leftarrow$ Expand(seed), seed$_i \in \{0,1\}^\lambda$
  3. For $i = 1, \ldots, N$:
     $(Q_i', V_i) \leftarrow$ **QSample**$(Q_0, s\|\text{seed}_i)$
     $C_i = Q_i'$
  4. (root, tree) $\leftarrow$ MerkleTree$(C_1, \ldots, C_N)$.
  5. $cmt = $ root.
  6. Send cmt to the verifier.
– **Round 2:** $\mathcal{V}_1^{base}$ responds with a uniformly random bit $ch \leftarrow \{0,1\}$.
– **Round 3:** $\mathcal{P}_2^{base}((U_I, I), ch)$
  1. If $ch = 0$:
     $z = U_I V_I$
     path$(C_I) \leftarrow$ getMerklePath(tree, I)
     $rsp = (z, \text{path}(C_I))$
  2. If $ch = 1$:
     $rsp = $ seed
  3. Send rsp to the prover.
– **Round 4:** $\mathcal{V}_2^{base}(cmt, ch, rsp; \mathcal{O})$
  1. root $= cmt, c = ch$.
  2. If $c = 0$:
     Parse $(z, \text{path}) \leftarrow rsp$
     $Q'' = \rho_z(Q_0)$
     $C'' = Q''$
     root$'' \leftarrow$ ReconstructRoot(C'', path)
     Output 1 if root$'' = $ root, else output 0.

3. If $c = 1$:

    seed $= rsp$

    Run the computations in steps 2–5 of $\mathcal{P}_1^{base}$ on seed to obtain root''

    Output 1 if root'' = root, else output 0.

Theorem 3.4. *For the following relations*

$$R = \{((Q_1, \ldots, Q_N), (U_I, I)) : Q_i's \text{ are quadratic forms and } \rho_{U_I}(Q_0) = Q_I\},$$

$$\tilde{R} = \{((Q_1, \ldots, Q_N), w) : Q_i's \text{ are quadratic forms,}$$

$$\text{and } \left((w = (U_I, I) : \rho_{U_I}(Q_0) = Q_I\right)$$

$$\text{or } (w = (x, x') : x \neq x', \mathcal{H}(x) = \mathcal{H}(x'))\},$$

the OR proof of knowledge Π^{base} is correct, relaxed special sound for the relations $(R, \tilde{R})$ and honest-verifier zero-knowledge.

Proof. See Appendix E.

3.4   Main OR Sigma Protocol

Since the base OR sigma protocol has only binary challenge space, a naive approach to achieve λ bits of security is to simply run Π^{base} totally λ times in parallel. To further improve the efficiency and security of the resulting ring signature, [6] proposes several optimization techniques to turn Π^{base} into the main sigma protocol Π^{main} with larger challenge space and better efficiency. Below, we summarize their methods, and then incorporate them into the main OR sigma protocol.

The first optimization idea of [6] is the use of unbalanced challenge space. From the observation that response in the case $ch = 0$ is more costly than when $ch = 1$, [6] proposes to choose integers M, K such that $\binom{M}{K} > 2^\lambda$, then perform Π^{base} totally M times, $M > \lambda$, of which exactly K times with $ch = 0$ and $M - K$ times with $ch = 1$. The challenge space is now the set $C_{M,K}$ of all strings in $\{0,1\}^M$ with exactly K bits equal 0.

The second optimization idea is to use a seed tree for responses when $ch = 1$ [6]. Among M executions of Π^{base} in parallel, there are exactly $M - K$ runs with $ch = 1$ in those cases, the output is simply the random seed. Instead of generating independent seeds for each run, one can generate M seeds using the seed tree. Then the place of $M - K$ seeds, the prover outputs seeds$_{\text{internal}}$ = ReleaseSeeds(seed$_{\text{root}}$, $\mathbf{c}$), where $\mathbf{c}$ is the challenge sampled from $C_{M,K}$. Later, to recover the $M - K$ seeds, one runs RecoverLeaves on seeds$_{\text{internal}}$ and $\mathbf{c}$.

The third optimization idea from [6] is adding salt to provide tighter security proof for the zero-knowledge property. This technique does not give efficiency improvement but helps avoid multi-target attacks. In particular, in the first round of Π^{base} the prover picks a salt of 2λ bits, then runs the i-th instance of Π^{base} with the random oracle $\mathcal{O}_i(.) = \mathcal{O}(\text{salt}\|i\|\cdot)$. The prover also salts the seed tree construction.

Protocol 3.5 (Main OR sigma protocol)

$\Pi^{main} = (\mathcal{P} = (\mathcal{P}_1^{main}, \mathcal{P}_2^{main}), \mathcal{V} = (\mathcal{V}_1^{main}, \mathcal{V}_2^{main}))$:

- **Round 1:** $\mathcal{P}_1^{main}(R, (U_I, I); \mathcal{O})$
  1. $seed_{root} \leftarrow \{0, 1\}^\lambda$
  2. $salt \leftarrow \{0, 1\}^{2\lambda}$, $\mathcal{O}' = \mathcal{O}(salt\|\cdot)$
  3. $(seed_1, \ldots, seed_M) \leftarrow \mathsf{SeedTree}(seed_{root}, M; \mathcal{O}')$
  4. *For* $i = 1, \ldots, M$:

     $\mathcal{O}_i = \mathcal{O}(salt\|i\|\cdot)$

     $cmt_i \leftarrow \mathcal{P}_1^{base}(R, (U_I, I); \mathcal{O}_i, seed_i)$
  5. $cmt = (salt, cmt_1, \ldots, cmt_M)$.
  6. *Send cmt to the verifier.*
- **Round 2:** $\mathcal{V}_1^{main}$ *responds with a uniformly challenge* $ch = \mathbf{c} \leftarrow \mathcal{C}_{M,K}$.
- **Round 3:** $\mathcal{P}_2^{main}((U_I, I), ch; \mathcal{O})$
  1. *Parse* $\mathbf{c} = (c_1, \ldots, c_M) = ch$
  2. *For* $i \in [M]$ *such that* $c_i = 0$, $rsp_i \leftarrow \mathcal{P}_2^{base}((U_I, I), c_i; \mathcal{O}, seed_i)$
  3. $\mathcal{O}' = \mathcal{O}(salt\|\cdot)$
  4. $seeds_{internal} \leftarrow \mathsf{ReleaseSeeds}(seed_{root}, salt, \mathbf{c}; \mathcal{O}')$
  5. $rsp = (seeds_{internal}, \{rsp_i\}_{i \in [M]:c_i=0})$
  6. *Send rsp to the prover.*
- **Round 4:** $\mathcal{V}_2^{main}(cmt, ch, rsp; \mathcal{O})$
  1. *Parse*

     $cmt = (salt, cmt_1, \ldots, cmt_M)$

     $ch = \mathbf{c} = (c_1, \ldots, c_M)$

     $rsp = (seeds_{internal}, \{rsp_i\}_{i \in [M]:c_i=0})$
  2. $\mathcal{O}' = \mathcal{O}(salt\|\cdot)$
  3. $(\{rsp_i\}_{i \in [M]:c_i=0}) \leftarrow \mathsf{RecoverLeaves}(seeds_{internal}, \mathbf{c}; \mathcal{O}')$
  4. *For* $i = 1, \ldots, N$:

     $\mathcal{O}_i(\cdot) = \mathcal{O}(salt\|i\|\cdot)$

     Output 0 if $\mathcal{V}_2^{base}(cmt_i, c_i, rsp_i; \mathcal{O}_i)$ *outputs 0, and aborts the protocol.*
  5. *Output 1.*

Security Proof of Π^{main}. Given the security of the base sigma protocol Π^{base}, one can derive the security of the main sigma protocol Π^{main} by using properties of $\mathsf{SeedTree}$ by suitably modifying the analysis in [6, Section 3.5].

Correctness. As the base protocol runs without aborts, the verifier accepts transcripts of honest executions of Π^{main} almost surely thanks to the correctness property of the $\mathsf{SeedTree}$.

Relaxed Special Soundness. Given two accepting transcripts $(cmt, \mathbf{c}, rsp)$ and $(cmt, \mathbf{c}', rsp')$ with $\mathbf{c} \neq \mathbf{c}'$, one can find an index $j \in [M]$ such that their j-th bit satisfies $c_j \neq c_j'$. Assume that $c_j = 0, c_j' = 1$. Let $rsp = (seeds_{internal}, \{rsp_i\}_{i \in S}$, where $S = \{i : c_i = 0\}$. Then $\mathcal{V}_2(cmt_j, 0, rsp_j) = 1$. Let $\{seed_i'\}_{i:c_i'=1} = \mathsf{RecoverLeaves}(seeds_{internal}', \mathbf{c}')$. Then, $\mathcal{V}_2(cmt_j, 1, seed_j') = 1$.

One applies the extractor of Π^{base} to $(cmt_j, 0, rsp_j)$ and $(smt_j, 1, seed_j')$ to extract a witness. If the witness is a collision $W = (Q\|\text{bits}, Q'\|\text{bits}')$ for the oracle $\mathcal{O}_i$ in $\mathcal{P}_1$, the collision for $\mathcal{O}$ is $(salt\|i\|Q\|\text{bits}, salt\|i\|Q'\|\text{bits}')$.

Special Zero-Knowledge. At this point, the zero-knowledge property of Π^{main} follows from the zero-knowledge property of the base sigma protocol Π^{base} and properties of SeedTree, and in fact, the proof in [6, Theorem 3.6] does not use any additional information of concrete group actions compared to the proof of [6, Theorem 3.3].

In particular, given the special honest-verifier zero-knowledge property of Π^{base} and the security of SeedTree, one obtains that Π^{main} is special zero-knowledge: there is a simulator Sim such that for any relation (X, W), any challenge ch, any computationally unbounded adversary $\mathcal{A}$ making q queries of the form $\mathsf{salt}\|\cdot$ to the random oracle $\mathcal{O}$, one has

$$\left| \Pr[\mathcal{A}(\mathcal{P}(X, W, ch)) = 1] - \Pr[\mathcal{A}(\mathsf{Sim}(X, ch)) = 1] \right| \leq \frac{3q}{2^\lambda}.$$

3.5   Ring Signature from the Main OR Sigma Protocol

To obtain ring signature from the main OR sigma protocol, we use the general approach of Fiat-Shamir transform, in which the challenge is modelled as the output of a hash function $\mathcal{H}_{FS}$ with range $C_{M,K}$. The hash function is treated as a random oracle and the resulting signature is secure in the random oracle model.

Algorithm 3.6. *We obtain a ring signature from the main OR sigma protocol Π^{main} via Fiat-Shamir transform as follows.*

- KeyGen(pp):
  1. $(Q, U) \leftarrow \mathbf{QSample}(Q_0, s)$
  2. $pk = Q, sk = U$
  3. *Return* (pk, sk)
- Sign(sk_I, I, m, R):
  1. *Parse* $R = (pk_1, \ldots, pk_N)$
  2. $cmt = (\mathsf{salt}, (cmt_i)_{i \in [M]}) \leftarrow \mathcal{P}_1^{main}(R, (sk_I, I); \mathcal{O})$
  3. $ch = \mathcal{H}_{FS}(m, R, cmt)$
  4. $rsp = \mathcal{P}_2^{main}((sk_I, I), ch)$
  5. *Return* $\sigma = (cmt, ch, rsp)$
- Verify(R, m, σ):
  1. *Parse* $R = (pk_1, \ldots, pk_N)$
  2. *Parse* $\sigma = (cmt, ch, rsp)$
  3. *If* $\mathcal{V}_2^{main}(cmt, ch, rsp; \mathcal{O}) = 1$ *and* $ch = \mathcal{H}_{FS}(m, R, cmt)$, *then return 1, else return 0.*

It follows from well-known general arguments that correctness, honest verifier zero-knowledge, special soundness properties of the underlying OR sigma protocol imply the correctness, anonymity and unforgeability of the ring signature, see [6,23].

3.6   Logarithmic Linkable Ring Signature

In [6], Beullens, Katsumata and Pintore also give a general receipt for building logarithmic linkable ring signature from pairs of group action $\star : G \times \mathcal{X} \to \mathcal{X}$ and $\bullet : G \times \mathcal{T} \to \mathcal{T}$ and a function Link $: \mathcal{T} \times \mathcal{T} \to \{0,1\}$. The pair of group actions needs to satisfy the following properties:

- Correctness: for any $T \in \mathcal{T}$, Link$(T, T) = 1$.
- Linkability: it is hard to find secret keys s and s' such that $s' \star X_0 = s \star X_0$ and Link$(s \bullet T_0, s' \bullet T_0) = 0$.
- Linkable anonymity: for a random secret key s, the distribution $(s \star X_0, s \bullet T_0)$ and $(X, T) \leftarrow \mathcal{X} \times \mathcal{T}$ are indistinguishable.
- Non-frameability: given $X = s \star X_0$ and $T = s \bullet T_0$, it is hard to find s' such that Link$(s' \bullet T_0, T) = 1$.

It is evident that the required properties - linkability, linkable anonymity and non-frameability - of linkable ring signature follow from the above properties of admissible pairs of group actions. Elements of $\mathcal{T}$ are used as a tag for checking the link between signatures.

In [6], the authors provide instantiations of pairs of group actions based on isogeny and lattice assumptions. For isogeny-based constructions, the group action $\bullet$ is $g \bullet x = g \star (g \star x)$. An additional hardness assumption, called Squaring Decisional CSIDH (sdCSIDH), is required for the security of the resulting linkable signature. For the lattice-based construction from module LWE assumption, [6] uses a second, independent LWE group action for linkability. In particular, the group actions take the form $(\mathbf{s}, \mathbf{e}, \tilde{\mathbf{e}}) \star \mathbf{w} = \mathbf{A}\mathbf{s} + \mathbf{e} + \mathbf{w}$ and $(\mathbf{s}, \mathbf{e}, \tilde{\mathbf{e}}) \bullet \mathbf{w} = \mathbf{B}\mathbf{s} + \tilde{\mathbf{e}} + \mathbf{w}$ for independent matrices $\mathbf{A}, \mathbf{B}$. We refer to [6] for further details on the concrete constructions.

In [1,13], linkable ring signature from code equivalence problem and alternating trilinear from equivalence problem are also obtained following the framework of [6]. It is observed that the ad-hoc approach of square decisional version of code equivalence problem and alternating trilinear from equivalence leads to problems with linkability. Instead, the group action $\bullet$ for case of code equivalence problem in [1] and alternating trilinear from equivalence in [13] is taken to be the inverse group action, that is instead of using $g \star x = g \cdot x$, one uses $g \bullet x = g^{-1} \cdot x$.

For the lattice isomorphism problem, we follow the approach of [1] and use the inverse group action of lattice isomorphism for $\bullet$. In particular, in the setting of lattice isomorphisms with $g = U$ and $x = Q$, we use $g \star x = \rho_U(Q)$ and $g \bullet x = \rho_{U^{-1}}(Q)$. Notice that other choices for $\bullet$ in [6], like square action or generating T_0 from $\mathcal{D}_s([Q_0])$ by a trusted party and use $\bullet = \star$, do not work for lattice isomorphism due to non-commutativity of the group action, which makes linkability very hard to achieve.

On public data $Q_0 \in Sym^+(n, \mathbb{Z})$ and suitable positive s, run **QSample**(Q_0, s) to obtain a secret $sk = U$ and a public key $pk = Q$ such that $Q = \rho_U(Q_0)$. Let $T_0 = Q_0$. Then the associated tag is $T = \rho_{U^2}(Q_0)$. The Link function simply checks if the two tags T, T' are the same matrices.

The linkability property can be deduced as follows. Suppose for contradiction that we found $s = U$, $s' = U'$ such that $Q = Q'$, which means $\rho_U(Q_0) = \rho_{U'}(Q_0)$, and $T \neq T'$, which means $\rho_{U^{-1}}(Q_0) \neq \rho_{U'^{-1}}(Q_0)$, then we would have $Q_0 = \rho_{U^{-1}U'}(Q_0)$ and $Q_0 \neq \rho_{UU'^{-1}}(Q_0)$. Thus, while $U^{-1}U'$ is an automorphism of Q_0, UU'^{-1} is not, which gives us a contradiction as the set of automorphisms of Q_0 is a finite group with respect to matrix multiplication.

Linkable anonymity follows from the way we generate keys and tag. The distribution of Q is $\mathcal{D}_s([Q_0])$ and U is uniformly random from the set of isomorphisms from Q_0 to Q, thus the distribution of T is $\mathcal{D}'_s([Q_0]) := \{\rho_{U^{-1}}(Q_0) : (Q, U) \leftarrow \mathcal{D}_s([Q_0])\}$. Hence, $(Q, T) = (\rho_U(Q_0), \rho_{U^{-1}}(Q_0))$ distributes as the public distribution $\mathcal{D}_s([Q_0]) \times \mathcal{D}'_s([Q_0])$.

Finally, for non-frameability, it is necessary that for given $Q = \rho_U(Q_0)$ and $T = \rho_{U^{-1}}(Q_0)$, it is difficult to find a unimodular matrix U' such that $T = \rho_{U'^{-1}}(Q_0)$. Given such U', we obtain an isomorphism UU' of quadratic form from T to Q which solves the search lattice isomorphism problem.

3.7 Parameter Selection

For parameter choices of lattice isomorphism problems, we follow the specification of the digital signature HAWK [25] whose implementation has been publicly released in the NIST additional digital signature competition [34]. Specifically, the dimension n is chosen as a power of 2, the initial quadratic form Q_0 is the trivial form on $\mathbb{Z}^{2n}$ - that is Q_0 is the $2n \times 2n$ identity matrix, the secret U is a basis of $SL(2, \mathbb{Z}[X]/(X^n + 1))$ which is generated in the style of FALCON [35] for efficiency. The detailed KeyGen algorithm is given in Algorithm 1 of HAWK [25]. The public key is then simply $Q_1 = U^t \cdot U$. For the NIST I level of security, one takes $n = 2^9$, while for the NIST V level of security $n = 2^{10}$. Other parameters for optimal key generation are detailed in Table 2 of HAWK [25].

Our (non-linkable) ring signature is $\sigma = (cmt, ch, rsp)$. Since our base OR sigma protocol is commitment recoverable, there is an efficient deterministic algorithm inputting the statement R, the challenge ch and response rsp that can recover the unique cmt. Hence, we can use only salt instead of cmt in our signature. This leads to the following computational cost (in bits):

$$\text{Our signature size} = \mathsf{Salt} + Ch + \mathsf{Seed}_{\mathsf{internal}} \cdot (M - K) + (z + (\text{hash values}) \log N) \cdot K.$$

In order to achieve 128-bit security (NIST I), we choose integers $M = 250$ and $K = 30$, where $\binom{250}{30} > 2^{128}$ with $K = 30$ challenge $ch = 0$ and $M - K = 220$ challenge $ch = 1$. We use 256-bit salts, hash values and 128-bit seeds. We consider parameter sets for HAWK-512 [25].

In order to achive 256-bit security (NIST V), we choose integers $M = 494$ and $K = 59$, where $\binom{494}{59} > 2^{256}$ with $K = 59$ challenge $ch = 0$ and $M - K = 435$ challenge $ch = 1$. We use 512-bit salts, hash values and 256-bit seeds. We consider parameter sets for HAWK-1024 [25].

4 Conclusion

Lattice isomorphism problem (LIP) has recently gained interest as a promising foundation for post-quantum cryptography [4,15–17]. While it is desirable to build cryptographic primitives based on LIP, only a handful of encryption and signature schemes have been constructed so far. In this paper, we build a logarithmic ring signature and its linkable variant from LIP. Our approach regards LIP as an instance of group action and follows the general framework of [6] with suitable modifications for the case of LIP. In future work, we will consider implementation for our proposed ring signatures.

Acknowledgements. We are grateful to the SPACE 2023 anonymous reviewers for their helpful comments. This work is partially supported by the Australian Research Council Linkage Project LP190100984.

A Ring Signatures Properties

We require the following properties of ring signatures.

Correctness: means that a correctly generated ring signature is surely accepted. Given the security level λ, for every ring size $N = \mathsf{poly}(\lambda)$, and every message m, if $pp \leftarrow \mathsf{RS.Setup}(1^\lambda)$, $(sk_i, pk_i) \leftarrow \mathsf{RS.KeyGen}(pp)$, for $i \in [N]$, $R = (pk_1, \ldots, pk_N)$ and $\sigma \leftarrow \mathsf{RS.Sign}(R, sk_j, m)$ for some $j \in [N]$, then $\Pr[\mathsf{RS.Verify}(\sigma, m, R) = 1] = 1$.

Anonymity: requires that it is infeasible to determine the signer even if all users' secret keys in the ring are revealed. Formally, a ring signature RS is anonymous against full key exposure if for any $N = \mathsf{poly}(\lambda)$, any PPT adversary $\mathcal{A}$ has negligible advantage against a challenger in the following game:

1. The challenger runs $\mathsf{RS.Setup}(1^\lambda)$ to obtain pp, and uses randomness $rand_i$ to run $\mathsf{RS.KeyGen}(pp, rand_i)$ to generate key pairs (sk_i, pk_i) for each user $i \in [N]$.
2. The challenger samples a random bit $b \in \{0,1\}$ and keeps it secret.
3. The challenger sends pp and all $rand_i$ to the adversary.
4. The adversary provides a challenge (m, R, i_0, i_1) to the challenger, where i_0, i_1 are indices of two users in the ring R.
5. The challenger uses his secret bit b to sign $\sigma^* = \mathsf{RS.Sign}(R, sk_{i_b}, m)$, and sends the signature σ^* back to the adversary.
6. The adversary guesses a bit $b^* \in \{0,1\}$.
7. The adversary wins the game if $b^* = b$.
   The advantage of $\mathcal{A}$ in this game is $\mathsf{Adv}_{\mathsf{RS}}^{\mathsf{anonymity}} = |\Pr[\mathcal{A} \text{ wins}] - \frac{1}{2}|$.

Unforgeability: means that it is infeasible to forge a valid ring signature without knowing the secret key of some user in the ring. Formally, a ring signature RS is unforgeable with respect to insider corruption if, for any $N = \mathsf{poly}(\lambda)$, any PPT adversary $\mathcal{A}$ has negligible advantage against a challenger in the following game:

1. The challenger runs RS.Setup(1^λ) to obtain pp, and uses randomness $rand_i$ to run RS.KeyGen($pp, rand_i$) to generate key pairs (sk_i, pk_i) for each user $i \in [N]$.
2. The challenger forms a ring $PK = \{pk_i\}_{i \in [N]}$ and initialises two sets $SL = \emptyset$, $CL = \emptyset$.
3. The challenger sends pp and PK to the adversary.
4. The adversary can make arbitrary polynomially many signing and corruption queries as follows:
   - Signing query (sign, i, m, R): the challenger checks if i is a user in the ring R: $pk_i \in R$. If i is a user, then the challenger signs $\sigma = $ RS.Sign(R, sk_i, m). He sends the signature σ to the adversary and adds (i, m, R) to the signing set $SL = SL \cup \{(i, m, R)\}$.
   - Corruption query (corrupt, i): the challenger sends the randomness $rand_i$ of user i to the adversary, and pk_i to the corruption set $CL = CL \cup \{pk_i\}$.
5. The adversary guesses a ring signature (σ^*, m^*, R^*).
6. The adversary wins the game if RS.Verify(σ^*, m^*, R^*) = 1, $R^* \subset PK - CL$, and (i, m^*, R^*) $\notin SL$.

B Linkable Ring Signatures Properties

We require the following properties of linkable ring signatures.

Correctness: For every security parameter $\lambda \in \mathbb{N}, N = \mathsf{poly}(\lambda), j \in [N]$, sets $D_0, D_1 \subseteq [N]$ such that $j \in D_0 \cap D_1$, and every message m_0, m_1, if $pp \leftarrow$ LRS.Setup (1^λ), (pk_i, sk_i) $\leftarrow$ LRS.KeyGen(pp) for all $i \in [N]$, $R_b := \{pk_i\}_{i \in D_b}, \sigma_b \leftarrow$ LRS.Sign (sk_j, m_b, R_b) for all $b \in \{0, 1\}$ then LRS.Verify(R_b, m_b, σ_b) = 1, for all $b \in \{0, 1\}$ and LRS.Link(σ_0, σ_1) = 1.

Linkability: A linkable ring signature scheme LRS is linkable if, for all $\lambda \in \mathbb{N}$ and $N = \mathsf{poly}(\lambda)$, any PPT adversary $\mathcal{A}$ has at most negligible advantage in the following game:

1. The challenger runs $pp \leftarrow$ LRS.Setup(1^λ) and provides pp to $\mathcal{A}$.
2. $\mathcal{A}$ outputs $PK := \{pk_i\}_{i \in [N]}$ and a set of tuples ($\sigma_i, m_i, R_i)_{i \in [N+1]}$;
3. We say the adversary $\mathcal{A}$ wins if the following conditions hold:
   - For all $i \in [N + 1]$, we have $R_i \subseteq PK$;
   - For all $i \in [N + 1]$, we have LRS.Verify(R_i, m_i, σ_i) = 1;
   - For all $i, j \in [N + 1]$ such that $i \neq j$, we have LRS.Link(σ_i, σ_j) = 0.

Linkable Anonymity: A linkable ring signature scheme LRS is linkable anonymous if, for all $\lambda \in \mathbb{N}$ and $N = \mathsf{poly}(\lambda)$, any PPT adversary $\mathcal{A}$ has at most negligible advantage in the following game:

1. The challenger runs $pp \leftarrow$ LRS.Setup(1^λ) and generates key pairs (pk_i, sk_i) = LRS.KeyGen(pp, rr_i) for all $i \in [N]$ using random coins rr_i. It also samples a random bit $b \leftarrow \{0, 1\}$;
2. The challenger provides pp and $PK := \{pk_i\}_{i \in [N]}$ to $\mathcal{A}$;

3. $\mathcal{A}$ outputs two challenge verification keys $pk_0^*, pk_1^* \in PK$ to the challenger. The secret keys corresponding to pk_0^*, pk_1^* are denoted by sk_0^*, sk_1^*, respectively;
4. The challenger provides all random coins rr_i of the corresponding $pk_i \in PK - \{pk_0^*, pk_1^*\}$;
5. $\mathcal{A}$ queries for signatures on input a verification key $pk \in \{pk_0^*, pk_1^*\}$, a message m and a ring R such that $\{pk_0^*, pk_1^*\} \subseteq R$:
   - If $pk = pk_0^*$, then the challenger returns $\sigma \leftarrow$ LRS.Sign(sk_b^*, m, R);
   - If $pk = pk_1^*$, then the challenger returns $\sigma \leftarrow$ LRS.Sign(sk_{1-b}^*, m, R);
6. $\mathcal{A}$ outputs a guess b^*. If $b^* = b$, we say the adversary $\mathcal{A}$ wins. The advantage of $\mathcal{A}$ in this game is $\mathsf{Adv}_{\mathsf{LRS}}^{\mathsf{anonymity}} = |\Pr[\mathcal{A} \text{ wins}] - \frac{1}{2}|$.

Non-frameability: A linkable ring signature scheme LRS is non-frameable if, for all $\lambda \in N$ and $N = \mathsf{poly}(\lambda)$ any PPT adversary $\mathcal{A}$ has at most negligible advantage in the following game played against a challenger.

1. The challenger runs $pp \leftarrow$ LRS.Setup(1^λ) and generates key pairs $(pk_i, sk_i) \leftarrow$ LRS.KeyGen$(pp; rr_i)$ for all $i \in [N]$ using random coins rr_i. It sets $PK := \{pk_i\}_{i \in [N]}$ and initializes two empty set SL and CL.
2. The challenger provides pp and PK to $\mathcal{A}$.

- $\mathcal{A}$ can make signing and corruption queries an arbitrary polynomial number of times:
  - (sign, i, m, R) : The challenger checks if $pk_i \in R$ and if so it computes the signature $\sigma \leftarrow$ LRS.Sign(sk_i, m, R). The challenger provides σ to $\mathcal{A}$ and adds (i, m, R) to SL;
  - (corrupt, i) : The challenger adds pk_i to CL and returns rr_i to $\mathcal{A}$.
- $\mathcal{A}$ outputs (R^*, m^*, σ^*). We say the adversary $\mathcal{A}$ wins if the following conditions are satisfied:
  - LRS.Verify$(R^*, m^*, \sigma^*) = 1$ and $(\cdot, m^*, R^*) \notin SL$;
  - LRS.Link$(\sigma^*, \sigma) = 1$ for some σ returned by the challenger on a signing query $(i, m, R) \in SL$, where $pk_i \in PK - CL$.

C   Proof of Knowledge

A proof of knowledge scheme is a two-party interactive protocol in which a prover $\mathcal{P}$ tries to prove his knowledge about some statement to a verifier $\mathcal{V}$. The parties take turns one by one to act in the protocol. First, the prover sends a commitment cmt to the verifier. The verifier generates a challenge ch_1 and returns it to the prover. The prover answers by sending a response rsp_1 to the verifier. The verifier again generates the second challenge ch_2 and sends it to the prover. The prover again answers by sending the second response rsp_2 to the verifier. The parties repeat sending challenges and responses n times. After receiving the last response rsp_n, the verifier returns 1 (accept), which means that he is convinced that the prover possesses the knowledge, or 0 (reject), which means that he is not. With n pairs of challenges-responses, we call this a $(2n + 1)$-round proof of knowledge.

Definition C.1. *Consider a relation* $\mathcal{R} = \{(x, w) : x \in L, w \in W(x)\}$, *where L is an NP language, x is a statement in L and $W(x)$ is the set of witnesses of x. Proof of knowledge for the relation $\mathcal{R}$ is a two-party interactive protocol in which the prover tries to convince the verifier that he knows a witness for each statement in the given language. We require two properties for proof of knowledge: correctness and soundness.*

Correctness: If $(x, w) \in \mathcal{R}$, then a prover who knows the witness w can surely convince the verifier of this knowledge: $\Pr[\langle \mathcal{P}(x, w), \mathcal{V}(x) \rangle = 1] = 1$.

Soundness: Intuitively, soundness means that a prover who does not know the witness cannot convince the verifier that he knew with nonnegligible probability. Otherwise, an efficient solver would exist for the hard problem of finding witnesses for statements in $\mathcal{R}$. Formally, a proof of knowledge has soundness error ε if for any PPT prover $\mathcal{P}'$ such that $\varepsilon' = \Pr[\langle \mathcal{P}'(x, w), \mathcal{V}(x) \rangle = 1] > \varepsilon$, there exists a PPT algorithm extractor $\mathcal{E}$ which outputs a witness w' for x in time $\mathsf{poly}(\lambda, \frac{1}{\varepsilon' - \varepsilon})$ with probability at least $\frac{1}{2}$. Here, the extractor $\mathcal{E}$ has a rewindable black-box access to $\mathcal{P}'$, meaning that $\mathcal{E}$ can copy the state of $\mathcal{P}'$ at any moment in the protocol, relaunch $\mathcal{P}'$ from a previously copied state, and query $\mathcal{P}'$ on input messages.

Honest-Verifier Zero-Knowledge: A proof of knowledge between $\mathcal{P}$ and $\mathcal{V}$ is an honest-verifier zero-knowledge proof if there exists a PPT algorithm simulator $\mathcal{S}$ whose output distribution is indistinguishable from the distribution of transcripts produced by the interactive protocol between $\mathcal{P}$ and $\mathcal{V}$, for an honest verifier $\mathcal{V}$.

C.1   Index-Hiding Merkle Trees

Given a list of elements $A = [a_1, \ldots, a_N]$, one can use the Merkle tree to hash A into a single value called the root so that it will be efficient to prove that an element is in the list A. For OR proofs of knowledge, we need a variant of the Merkle tree introduced in [6], which has an additional property that also hides the position of an element in the list when proving that this element is in A.

Definition C.2 ([6]). *An index-hiding Merkle tree is given as a tuple of 3 algorithms* (genTree, getPath, ReconRoot), *together with a public hash function* $H : \{0, 1\}^* \to \{0, 1\}^{2\lambda}$.

- genTree(A) $\to$ (root, tree): *takes as input a list of 2^k elements $A = (a_1, \ldots, a_{2^k})$, it constructs a binary tree of depth k: the leaf nodes are $\{\ell_i = H(a_i)\}_{i \in [2^k]}$, and every inside node h with children nodes h_{left} and h_{right} equals the hash digest of a concatenation of h_{left} and h_{right}. For hiding indices, instead of using the standard concatenation $h_{left} \| h_{right}$, we order the two children nodes with the lexicographical order. This modified concatenation is denoted by $(h_{left}, h_{right})_{lex}$. The algorithm outputs the root of the Merkle tree and a description of the entire tree as (root, tree).*

- getPath(tree, I) → path: *takes as input the tree description* tree *and an index $I \in [2^k]$, outputs the list* path *containing the sibling node of ℓ_I and the sibling of all ancestor nodes of ℓ_I ordered by decreasing depth.*
- ReconRoot(u, path) → root: *takes as input an element a in the list A and a path* path $= (n_1, \ldots, n_k)$, *outputs a reconstructed root* root$'= h_k$ *calculated by putting $h_0 = H(a)$ and defining $h_i = H((h_i, n_i)_{lex})$ for each $i \in [k]$.*

If H is collision-resistant, then the Merkle tree construction is binding, which means that for any $b \notin A$, it is infeasible to construct a path to prove that $b \in A$. The use of the lexicographical order to concatenate two children nodes in the Merkle tree construction implies that the output path of getPath information-theoretically hides the input index $I \in [N]$.

C.2   Seed Tree

In [6], the authors introduce a primitive called seed tree to generate several pseudorandom values and later disclose an arbitrary subset without revealing information on the remaining values. A seed tree is a complete binary tree of λ-bit seed values such that the left/right child node of a seed seed$_h$ is the left/right half of Expand($seed\|h$), where Expand is a pseudorandom generator (PRG). The unique identifier h of the parent seed is appended to separate the input domains of different calls to the PRG. A sender can efficiently reveal the seed values associated with a subset of the set of leaves by revealing the appropriate set of inside seeds in the tree.

Definition C.3 ([6]). *Let* Expand $: \{0,1\}^{\lambda + \lceil \log_2(M-1) \rceil} \to \{0,1\}^{2\lambda}$ *be a PRG for $\lambda, M \in \mathbb{N}$ instantiated by a random oracle $\mathcal{O}$. A seed tree is a tuple of 4 $\mathcal{O}$-oracle calling algorithms* (SeedTree, ReleaseSeeds, RecoverLeaves, SimulateSeeds).

- SeedTree(seed$_{root}$, M; $\mathcal{O}$) → $\{leaf_i\}_{i \in [M]}$: *takes as input a root seed* seed$_{root} \in \{0,1\}^\lambda$ *and an integer M, constructs a complete binary tree with M leaves by recursively expanding each seed to obtain its children seeds. Oracle calls are of the form $\mathcal{O}(\text{Expand}\|\text{seed}_h\|h)$, where $h \in [M-1]$ is a unique identifier for the position of seed in the binary tree.*
- ReleaseSeeds(seed$_{root}$, $\mathbf{c}$; $\mathcal{O}$) → seeds$_{internal}$: *takes as input a root seed* seed$_{root} \in \{0,1\}^\lambda$ *and a challenge $\mathbf{c} \in \{0,1\}^M$, outputs the list of seeds* seeds$_{internal}$ *that covers all the leaves with index i such that $c_i = 1$. A set of nodes D covers a set of leaves S if the union of the leaves of the subtrees rooted at each node $v \in D$ is exactly the set S.*
- RecoverLeaves(seeds$_{internal}$, $\mathbf{c}$; $\mathcal{O}$) → $\{leaf_i\}_{i:c_i=1}$: *takes as input a set* seeds$_{internal}$ *and a challenge $\mathbf{c} \in \{0,1\}^M$, computes and outputs all the leaves of subtrees rooted at seeds in* seeds$_{internal}$ *which is exactly the set $\{leaf_i\}_{i:c_i=1}$.*
- SimulateSeeds($\mathbf{c}$; $\mathcal{O}$) → seeds$_{internal}$: *takes as input a challenge $\mathbf{c} \in \{0,1\}^M$, computes the set of nodes covering the leaves with index i such that $c_i = 1$. Then random samples a seed from $\{0,1\}^\lambda$ for each of these nodes and outputs the set of these seeds as* seeds$_{internal}$.

Such a seed tree is correct and hiding in a sense that:

(i) the leaves $\{leaf_i\}_{i:c_i=1}$ output by SeedTree(seed$_{\text{root}}$, M) are the same as those output by RecoverLeaves(ReleaseSeeds(seed$_{\text{root}}$, c), c) for any c $\in$ $\{0,1\}^M$;

(ii) SimulateSeeds helps to show that the seeds associated with all the leaves with index i such that $c_i = 0$ are indistinguishable from uniformly random values for a recipient that is only given seeds$_{\text{internal}}$ and c.

C.3   Proof of Knowledge for Group Actions

Proof of Group Actions. Consider a group action $G \times \mathcal{X} \to \mathcal{X}, (g, x) \mapsto g \cdot x$ of a group G on a set $\mathcal{X}$. Fix a public element $X_0 \in \mathcal{X}$.

For two public elements $X_0, X \in \mathcal{X}$, we want to prove knowledge of a secret group element g such that $g \cdot X_0 = X$. Following the classical proof of knowledge of graph isomorphism, a proof of group actions is obtained as follows. The prover commits to $cmt = r \cdot X$, where $r \in G$ is a random group element. The verifier selects a random bit challenge $ch \in \{0,1\}$. If $ch = 0$, then the prover responds with $rsp = r \cdot g$. The verifier subsequently checks whether $rsp \cdot X_0 = cmt$. If $ch = 1$, then the prove sets $rsp = r$. The verifier checks whether $rsp \cdot X = cmt$.

OR Proof of Group Actions. For public elements $X_0, X_1, \ldots, X_N$ of $\mathcal{X}$, the OR proof of knowledge for group actions aims to prove knowledge of a secret group element g such that $g \cdot X_0 = X_I$ for some index $I \in \{1, \ldots, N\}$. One can easily extend the proof of knowledge above to obtain a secure OR proof of group actions as follows.

For each index $i = 1, \ldots, N$, the prover samples a random group element $r_i \in G$ and commits to $cmt_i = r_i \cdot X_i$. Then, the verifier chooses a random bit challenge $ch \in \{0,1\}$. If $ch = 0$, the prover sets his response as $rsp = r_I \cdot g$. The verifier then checks whether $rsp \cdot X_0 \in \{cmt_1, \ldots, cmt_N\}$. If $ch = 1$, then the prover sets $rsp = (r_1, \ldots, r_N)$. The verifier checks whether $\{r_1 \cdot X_1, \ldots, r_N \cdot X_N\} = \{cmt_1, \ldots, cmt_N\}$. Sending the commitments in a random order helps to hide the index I as the equation $rsp \cdot X_0 \in \{cmt_1, \ldots, cmt_N\}$ provides no information about the index I in $rsp = r_I \cdot g$. If we did not randomly shuffle the commitments, then from $rsp \cdot X_0 = cmt_I$ one would see directly that the signer is I.

Using Merkle Tree to Reduce the Size of the OR Proof to Logarithmic Size. When $ch = 1$, the commitment in OR proof consists of N elements of $\mathcal{X}$, which make the proof size linear in the number of users N. A key idea of Beullens, Katsumata and Pintore in [6] is to use the Merkle tree to hash the list of commitments and send only the root as the commitment. Consequently, when $ch = 0$, we need to send a path in the Merkle tree for correct verification as part of the response. This method reduces the OR proof's size to be logarithmic in the number of users N.

Given a list of elements $A = [a_1, \ldots, a_N]$, one can use the Merkle tree to hash A into a single value called the root so that it will be efficient to prove that an element is in the list A. For OR proofs of knowledge, we need a variant of the Merkle tree introduced in [6], which has an additional property that also hides the position of an element in the list when proving that this element is in A.

Another important technique of [6] to reduce proof size is to use unbalanced challenge spaces. Upon applying Merkle tree hashing, opening to the case $ch = 1$ is much cheaper than when $ch = 0$. To achieve λ bits of security, instead of repeating the OR proof λ times in parallel, one can choose integers M, K such that $\binom{M}{K} \geq 2^\lambda$ and $M > \lambda, K \ll \lambda$, then repeat totally M times the execution of OR proof with exactly K times with challenge $ch = 0$. Since the more expensive case of $ch = 0$ is repeated much less frequently, the proof size is significantly reduced. Note that among M parallel executions of the binary challenge OR proofs, $M - K$ times are used for $ch = 1$ in which, one simply returns the random seed. The seed tree optimises this step: instead of choosing independent seeds for different runs, one generates the seeds using the seed tree. Instead of responding with total $M - K$ seeds, the prover outputs the released seeds from the root seed and the challenge $\mathbf{c}$.

D   Proof of Theorem 3.2

Correctness: If the protocol is executed correctly, the response is $rsp = U_1^{1-c}V_1$. The verification equation reads $Q' = \rho_{V_1}(Q_1) = \rho_{U_1^{1-c}V_1}(\rho_{U_1^{c-1}}(Q_1)) = \rho_{rsp}(Q_c)$, which is correct.

Soundness: Suppose that on the same commitment Q', we have two valid transcripts $(Q', 0, rsp_0), (Q', 1, rsp_1)$. One has two verification equations $\rho_{rsp_0}(Q_0) = Q'$ and $\rho_{rsp_1}(Q_1) = Q'$. It follows that $\rho_{rsp_0}(Q_0) = \rho_{rsp_1}(Q_1)$, hence we have $\rho_{rsp_1}^{-1}(\rho_{rsp_0}(Q_0)) = \rho_{rsp_1^{-1}}(\rho_{rsp_0}(Q_0)) = \rho_{rsp_0 \cdot rsp_1^{-1}}(Q_0) = Q_1$. In particular, $rsp_0 \cdot rsp_1^{-1}$ is an isomorphism from Q_0 to Q_1. We obtain the soundness property under the assumption that the worst-case lattice isomorphism problem is hard.

Zero-Knowledge: We need to simulate the transcript of our protocol on given public quadratic forms Q_0, Q_1 without knowing the secret isomorphism U_1. Sampling (Q', V) with **QSample**(Q_0, s) gives Q' of distribution $\mathcal{D}_s([Q_0])$, and V is a uniformly random isomorphism from Q_0 to Q'. Next, we sample a random bit c. If $c = 1$, the Protocol 3.1 actually does not use the secret isomorphism U_1, so one can simulate the conversation by proceeding the same way as in the protocol with $c = 1$. The transcript is simply $(Q', 1, V)$. When $c = 0$, we run **QSample**(Q_1, s) on Q_1 to obtain (Q'', V'') where $Q'' = \rho_{V''}(Q_1)$. Thus, $(Q'', 0, V'')$ is a suitable simulated transcript when $c = 0$, as the distributions of Q'', V'' are $\mathcal{D}_s([Q_1]) = \mathcal{D}_s([Q_0])$ and uniformly random isomorphism from Q_0 to Q'', which are the same as in the case $c = 0$ of the Protocol 3.1.

E   Proof of Theorem 3.4

Correctness. If we run $\varPi^{base}$ honestly with prover's input (U_I, I) which satisfies $\rho_{U_I}(Q_0) = Q_I$, then the verifier accepts almost surely. If $ch = 0$, then $z =$

$U_I V_I$, and we have $\rho_z(Q_0) = \rho_{U_I V_I}(Q_0) = \rho_{V_I}(\rho_{U_I}(Q_0)) = \rho_{V_I}(Q_I) = Q_I'$. As the prover computes $C_I = Q_I'$ in $\mathcal{P}_1$, root$''$ ← ReconstructRoot(C'', path) reconstructed from the I-th leaf of the Merkle tree in $\mathcal{V}_2$ will match the root root in $\mathcal{P}_1$, hence the verifier accepts. If $ch = 1$, then in $\mathcal{V}_2$ the verifier repeats the calculation in $\mathcal{P}_1$ with $seed = rsp$, and obtains the same root root$''$ = root, hence the verifier accepts.

Relaxed Special Soundness. Given two accepting transcripts (root, 0, (z, path)) and (root, 1, seed), we can extract a witness as either $U \in GL(n, \mathbb{Z})$ such that $\rho_U(Q_0) = Q_I$ for some $I \in [N]$, or a collision in $\mathcal{H}$, or a collision for the random oracle $\mathcal{O}$, as follows. One first expands $(\text{seed}_1, \ldots, \text{seed}_N) \leftarrow \mathcal{O}(\text{Expand}\|\text{seed})$ to obtain $\text{seed}_i \in \{0, 1\}^\lambda$, then computes (root$'$, tree) ← MerkleTree($C_1, \ldots, C_N$), where $C_i = Q_i'$ is obtained via **QSample**($Q_0, s\|\text{seed}_i$). From the two valid transcripts, one obtains that root$'$ = root and ReconstructRoot(C'', path) = root with $C'' = Q'' = \rho_z(Q_0)$. If $C'' \neq C_i$ for all $i \in [N]$, then one can use the Merkle tree extractor to find a collision of $\mathcal{H}$ from (tree, C'', path). If there exists $I \in [N]$ such that $C'' = C_I$, one checks whether $Q'' \neq \rho_U(Q_I)$, if so, then the pairs $Q'', \rho_U(Q_I)$ is a collision of $\mathcal{O}$. When in addition $Q'' = \rho_U(Q_I)$, one has $\rho_{U_I^{-1} z}(Q_0) = Q_I$, hence $U_I^{-1} z$ is an isomorphism between Q_0, Q_I.

Honest-Verifier Zero-Knowledge. One needs to build a simulator Sim such that for any valid relation (X, W), and any challenge ch, any computationally unbounded adversary $\mathcal{A}$ making q queries to the random oracle $\mathcal{O}$, one has

$$\left| \Pr[\mathcal{A}(\mathcal{P}(X, W, ch)) = 1] - \Pr[\mathcal{A}(\text{Sim}(X, ch)) = 1] \right| \leq \frac{2q}{2^\lambda}.$$

In the framework of [6], the proof of zero-knowledge property in [6, Theorem 3.3] is an extension of the proof for graph isomorphism protocol and uses the following ingredients: the problem ac-sLIP$_s^{Q_0}$ is hard, seed and bits$_i$'s have high min-entropy and information-theoretically hidden from $\mathcal{A}$, and that the distributions of root and path does not depend on the value of I. For lattice isomorphism sigma protocol, we refer to [17,24] for proofs of zero-knowledge property in a similar line. One defines Sim for each case of $ch = 1$ and $ch = 0$ separately as follows:

- When $ch = 1$, the prover does not need a secret key to run the protocol, Sim just runs the prover on input $(X, ch = 1)$ and uses the same output as the prover. As the prover does not use the witness in this case, transcripts when $ch = 1$ are simulated perfectly.
- When $ch = 0$, Sim runs $(Q', V) \leftarrow$ Algorithm 2.9(Q_0, s), let $z = V$. It sets $C_1 = \rho_z(Q_0)$, and sets the remaining commitments $C_2, \ldots, C_N$ to be uniformly random strings from $\{0, 1\}^{2\lambda}$. It generates a Merkle tree (tree, root) ← MerkleTree($C_1, \ldots, C_N$), then extracts a path path ← getMerklePath(tree, 1). Finally, Sim sets its output in this case as (root, 0, $rsp = (z, \text{path})$). When $ch = 0$, one simulates the transcript by randomising its parts one by one to obtain a sequence of simulators Sim$_i$. Fix an adversary $\mathcal{A}$ and a relation (X, W). Define the event E_i as $\mathcal{A}(\text{Sim}_i(X, 0)) = 1$.

- Sim_1: This simulator runs the same procedure as the honest prover $\mathcal{P}_1$, but it uses uniformly random bit strings seed_i's. The adversary only spots the difference in the transcript if he has made a query exactly on seed, which happens with the probability less than $\frac{q}{2^\lambda}$. Thus, $\left| \Pr[\mathcal{A}(\mathcal{P}(X, W, 0)) = 1] - \Pr[E_1] \right| \leq \frac{q}{2^\lambda}$.
- Sim_2: This simulator is the same as Sim_1 except that it uses uniformly random bit string for commitments C_i in $\mathcal{P}_1$. The adversary only sees the difference in the transcript if he has queried on a commitment Q'_i. Assume that all the Q_i are distinct. Let q_i be the number of queries of the form Q'_i. Then the probability that $\mathcal{A}$ has made queries exactly on input Q'_i is at most $\frac{q_i}{2^\lambda}$. The probability that $\mathcal{A}$ can spot the difference in the transcript by making queries on some commitment Q'_i is at most $\sum_{i=1}^{N} \frac{q_i}{2^\lambda} \leq \frac{q}{2^\lambda}$, which implies $\left| \Pr[E1] - \Pr[E2] \right| \leq \frac{q}{2^\lambda}$.
- Sim_3: This simulator is the same as Sim_2 except that Sim_2 reruns $(Q'_I, V_I) \leftarrow \mathbf{QSample}(Q_0, s)$ and uses this new $Q'_I = \rho_{V_I}(Q_0)$ in the step 2 of $\mathcal{V}_2$. This does not change the distribution of output of Sim_2, so $|\Pr[E2] - \Pr[E3]| = 0$.
- Sim_4: The is the final simulator which is different from Sim only by using $I = 1$ instead of the value of I in the true witness. Since different values of I do not affect the distribution of root and path, one has $|\Pr[E3] - \Pr[E4]| = 0$.

After randomising all parts of the transcript, the probability that the adversary can spot changes in the distributions is negligible $\left| \Pr[\mathcal{A}(\mathcal{P}(X, W, 0)) = 1] - \Pr[E_4] \right| \leq \frac{2q}{2^\lambda}$.

References

1. Barenghi, A., Biasse, J., Ngo, T., Persichetti, E., Santini, P.: Advanced signature functionalities from the code equivalence problem. Int. J. Comput. Math. Comput. Syst. Theory **7**(2), 112–128 (2022)
2. Bellare, M., Neven, G.: Multi-signatures in the plain public-key model and a general forking lemma. In: Proceedings of the 13th ACM Conference on Computer and Communications Security, pp. 390–399 (2006)
3. Bellini, E., Esser, A., Sanna, C., Verbel, J.: MR-DSS - smaller MinRank-based (ring-)signatures. In: Cheon, J.H., Johansson, T. (eds.) PQCrypto 2022. LNCS, vol. 13512, pp. 144–169. Springer, Cham (2022). https://doi.org/10.1007/978-3-031-17234-2_8
4. Bennett, H., Ganju, A., Peetathawatchai, P., Stephens-Davidowitz, N.: Just how hard are rotations of $\mathbb{Z}^n$? algorithms and cryptography with the simplest lattice. Cryptology ePrint Archive, Paper 2021/1548, to appear at EUROCRYPT2023 (2021). https://eprint.iacr.org/2021/1548
5. Bethencourt, J., Sahai, A., Waters, B.: Ciphertext-policy attribute-based encryption. In: 2007 IEEE Symposium on Security and Privacy (SP 2007), pp. 321–334. IEEE (2007)
6. Beullens, W., Katsumata, S., Pintore, F.: Calamari and Falafl: logarithmic (linkable) ring signatures from isogenies and lattices. In: Moriai, S., Wang, H. (eds.) ASIACRYPT 2020. LNCS, vol. 12492, pp. 464–492. Springer, Cham (2020). https://doi.org/10.1007/978-3-030-64834-3_16

7. Bläser, M., et al.: On digital signatures based on isomorphism problems: QROM security, ring signatures, and applications. Cryptology ePrint Archive (2022)
8. Boneh, D., Drijvers, M., Neven, G.: Compact multi-signatures for smaller blockchains. In: Peyrin, T., Galbraith, S. (eds.) ASIACRYPT 2018. LNCS, vol. 11273, pp. 435–464. Springer, Cham (2018). https://doi.org/10.1007/978-3-030-03329-3_15
9. Bootle, J., Cerulli, A., Chaidos, P., Ghadafi, E., Groth, J., Petit, C.: Short accountable ring signatures based on DDH. In: Pernul, G., Ryan, P.Y.A., Weippl, E. (eds.) ESORICS 2015. LNCS, vol. 9326, pp. 243–265. Springer, Cham (2015). https://doi.org/10.1007/978-3-319-24174-6_13
10. Brakerski, Z., Gentry, C., Vaikuntanathan, V.: (Leveled) fully homomorphic encryption without bootstrapping. ACM Trans. Comput. Theory (TOCT) **6**(3), 1–36 (2014)
11. Brakerski, Z., Langlois, A., Peikert, C., Regev, O., Stehlé, D.: Classical hardness of learning with errors. In: STOC 2013. Association for Computing Machinery, New York (2013)
12. Budroni, A., Chi-Domínguez, J.-J., Kulkarni, M.: Lattice isomorphism as a group action and hard problems on quadratic forms. Cryptology ePrint Archive, Paper 2023/1093 (2023). https://eprint.iacr.org/2023/1093
13. Chen, Z., Duong, D.H., Nguyen, T.N., Qiao, Y., Susilo, W., Tang, G.: On digital signatures based on isomorphism problems: QROM security and ring signatures. IACR Cryptology ePrint Archive, p. 1184 (2022)
14. Chillotti, I., Gama, N., Georgieva, M., Izabachène, M.: Faster fully homomorphic encryption: bootstrapping in less than 0.1 seconds. In: Cheon, J.H., Takagi, T. (eds.) ASIACRYPT 2016. LNCS, vol. 10031, pp. 3–33. Springer, Heidelberg (2016). https://doi.org/10.1007/978-3-662-53887-6_1
15. Ducas, L., Gibbons, S.: Hull attacks on the lattice isomorphism problem. Cryptology ePrint Archive, Paper 2023/194, to appear at PKC2023 (2023). https://eprint.iacr.org/2023/194
16. Ducas, L., Postlethwaite, E.W., Pulles, L.N., van Woerden, W.: HAWK: module LIP makes lattice signatures fast, compact and simple. In: Agrawal, S., Lin, D. (eds.) ASIACRYPT 2022. LNCS, vol. 13794, pp. 65–94. Springer, Cham (2022). https://doi.org/10.1007/978-3-031-22972-5_3
17. Ducas, L., van Woerden, W.: On the lattice isomorphism problem, quadratic forms, remarkable lattices, and cryptography. In: Dunkelman, O., Dziembowski, S. (eds.) EUROCRYPT 2022. LNCS, vol. 13277, pp. 643–673. Springer, Cham (2022). https://doi.org/10.1007/978-3-031-07082-2_23
18. Esgin, M.F., Steinfeld, R., Sakzad, A., Liu, J.K., Liu, D.: Short lattice-based one-out-of-many proofs and applications to ring signatures. In: Deng, R.H., Gauthier-Umaña, V., Ochoa, M., Yung, M. (eds.) ACNS 2019. LNCS, vol. 11464, pp. 67–88. Springer, Cham (2019). https://doi.org/10.1007/978-3-030-21568-2_4
19. Esgin, M.F., Zhao, R.K., Steinfeld, R., Liu, J.K., Liu, D.: MatRiCT: efficient, scalable and post-quantum blockchain confidential transactions protocol. In: Proceedings of the 2019 ACM SIGSAC Conference on Computer and Communications Security, pp. 567–584 (2019)
20. Gentry, C., Peikert, C., Vaikuntanathan, V.: Trapdoors for hard lattices and new cryptographic constructions. In: STOC 2008. Association for Computing Machinery, New York (2008)
21. Goldreich, O., Micali, S., Wigderson, A.: Proofs that yield nothing but their validity or all languages in np have zero-knowledge proof systems. J. ACM **38**(3), 690–728 (1991)

22. Goyal, V., Pandey, O., Sahai, A., Waters, B.: Attribute-based encryption for fine-grained access control of encrypted data. In: Proceedings of the 13th ACM Conference on Computer and Communications Security, pp. 89–98 (2006)
23. Groth, J., Kohlweiss, M.: One-out-of-many proofs: or how to leak a secret and spend a coin. In: Oswald, E., Fischlin, M. (eds.) EUROCRYPT 2015. LNCS, vol. 9057, pp. 253–280. Springer, Heidelberg (2015). https://doi.org/10.1007/978-3-662-46803-6_9
24. Haviv, I., Regev, O.: On the lattice isomorphism problem. In: Proceedings of the Twenty-Fifth Annual ACM-SIAM Symposium on Discrete Algorithms, SODA 2014, pp. 391–404. Society for Industrial and Applied Mathematics (2014)
25. Huang, T.P., Postlethwaite, E.W., Prest, T., Pulles, L.N., van Woerden, W.: https://hawk-sign.info
26. IBM. IBM unveils 400 qubit-plus quantum processor and next-generation IBM quantum system two (2022)
27. Katz, J., Kolesnikov, V., Wang, X.: Improved non-interactive zero knowledge with applications to post-quantum signatures. In: Proceedings of the 2018 ACM SIGSAC Conference on Computer and Communications Security, pp. 525–537 (2018)
28. Libert, B., Peters, T., Qian, C.: Logarithmic-size ring signatures with tight security from the DDH assumption. In: Lopez, J., Zhou, J., Soriano, M. (eds.) ESORICS 2018. LNCS, vol. 11099, pp. 288–308. Springer, Cham (2018). https://doi.org/10.1007/978-3-319-98989-1_15
29. Lu, X., Au, M.H., Zhang, Z.: Raptor: a practical lattice-based (linkable) ring signature. In: Deng, R.H., Gauthier-Umaña, V., Ochoa, M., Yung, M. (eds.) ACNS 2019. LNCS, vol. 11464, pp. 110–130. Springer, Cham (2019). https://doi.org/10.1007/978-3-030-21568-2_6
30. Léo, D., et al.: Crystals: cryptographic suite for algebraic lattices
31. Micciancio, D., Goldwasser, S.: Complexity of Lattice Problems: A Cryptographic Perspective. SECS, Springer, Heidelberg (2002). https://doi.org/10.1007/978-1-4615-0897-7
32. NIST. NIST asks public to help future-proof electronic information (2016)
33. NIST. NIST announces first four quantum-resistant cryptographic algorithms (2022)
34. NIST. Post-quantum cryptography: digital signature schemes. Round 1 additional signatures (2023)
35. Pierre-Alain, F., et al. Falcon: Fast Fourier lattice-based compact signatures over NTRU
36. Rivest, R.L., Shamir, A., Tauman, Y.: How to leak a secret. In: Boyd, C. (ed.) ASIACRYPT 2001. LNCS, vol. 2248, pp. 552–565. Springer, Heidelberg (2001). https://doi.org/10.1007/3-540-45682-1_32
37. Roberto, A., et al.: Crystals: cryptographic suite for algebraic lattices
38. Yuen, T.H., Esgin, M.F., Liu, J.K., Au, M.H., Ding, Z.: DualRing: generic construction of ring signatures with efficient instantiations. In: Malkin, T., Peikert, C. (eds.) CRYPTO 2021. LNCS, vol. 12825, pp. 251–281. Springer, Cham (2021). https://doi.org/10.1007/978-3-030-84242-0_10
39. Yuen, T.H., et al.: RingCT 3.0 for blockchain confidential transaction: shorter size and stronger security. In: Bonneau, J., Heninger, N. (eds.) FC 2020. LNCS, vol. 12059, pp. 464–483. Springer, Cham (2020). https://doi.org/10.1007/978-3-030-51280-4_25

"We Must Protect the Transformers": Understanding Efficacy of Backdoor Attack Mitigation on Transformer Models

Rohit Raj[(⊠)] [iD], Biplab Roy [iD], Abir Das [iD], and Mainack Mondal [iD]

Department of Computer Science and Engineering, IIT Kharagpur, Kharagpur, India
rrohit2901@gmail.com, biplabroy@kgpian.iitkgp.ac.in,
{abir,mainack}@cse.iitkgp.ac.in

Abstract. Recently, Neural Network based Deep Learning (DL) back-door attacks have prompted the development of mitigation mechanisms for such attacks. Out of them a key mitigation mechanism is *Neural Cleanse*, which helps in the identification and mitigation of DL backdoor attacks. It identifies the presence of backdoors in Neural Networks and constructs a reverse-engineered trigger, which is later used to mitigate the backdoor present in the infected model. However, since the publication of Neural Cleanse, newer DL architectures (e.g., Transformer models) have emerged and are widely used. Unfortunately, it is not clear if Neural Cleanse is effective to mitigate backdoor attacks in these newer models—in fact a negative answer will prompt researchers to rethink backdoor attack mitigation. To that end, in this work, we take the first step to explore this question. We considered models ranging from pure convolution-based models like ResNet-18 to pure Self-Attention based models like ConVit and understand the efficacy of Neural Cleanse after launching backdoor attacks on these models. Our experiments uncover a wide variation in the efficacy of Neural Cleanse. Even if Neural Cleanse effectively counters backdoor attacks in some models, its performance falls short when dealing with models incorporating self-attention layers (i.e., Transformers), especially in accurately identifying target classes and learning reverse-engineered triggers. Our results further hint that, for modern models, mitigation of backdoor attacks by constructing reverse engineering triggers should consider *patches* (instead of pixels).

Keywords: Backdoor Attack · Neural Cleanse · convolution-based models · Self-Attention based models

1 Introduction

With the development of the computational capabilities of modern computers, Artificial Intelligence has acquired a spot as an integral part of our daily lives. In fact, Deep Neural Networks (DNNs) have become the core of many critical tasks like facial recognition, guiding self-driving cars and creating voice interfaces for

---

R. Raj and B. Roy—Both authors contributed equally to the project.

F. Regazzoni et al. (Eds.): SPACE 2023, LNCS 14412, pp. 242–260, 2024.
https://doi.org/10.1007/978-3-031-51583-5_14

home assistants in our day-to-day lives. Deep learning has also been applied to security space for malware [13] and network intrusion detection [14] tasks. Further advancements in the field of Deep learning (e.g., designing new architectures) are continuously improving the performance of different tasks every day. However, still, Neural networks are considered black-boxes in most context because studying the structure of those models give no insights about the structure of the function being approximated by that model [15,16].

In spite of this lack of explainability of output, it is impossible to test deep learning models exhaustively for all possible input values due to the versatility of the application scenarios (e.g., object recognition). Thus even if some models work fine on one input then they might work incorrectly on other input. In fact, the situation might worsen if an attacker can control the inaccuracy of the model output and misdirect an end user. This poses a great challenge of how secure these models are for application on critical real work applications. Thus a large amount of work in the community focused on how deep learning systems are very vulnerable to attacks [12]—e.g., how adding perturbations to inputs of AI systems used in self-driving cars can sometimes force them to make wrong decisions for a particular input. These vulnerabilities enable the possibility of *backdoors* or "Trojans" in DNNs [4]. Backdoors are hidden patterns in the data that have been trained into a DNN model (e.g., by perturbing training data) that result in unexpected behaviour but are undetectable unless activated by some "trigger" input. A "trigger" refers to a small, carefully designed and imperceptible pattern or modification that is added to an input image with the intention of causing a misclassification or some other unintended behaviour when the model makes predictions.

Given the severity of the problem of backdoor attacks, many countermeasures have been developed to identify and mitigate the presence of backdoors in DNNs, but in past works, we found that these countermeasures were tested only on smaller (and simpler) DNN and purely Convolutional Neural Network (CNN) based models [1]. However, with the introduction of transformers [17], many computer vision models, now, work with self-attention layers instead of convolution layers only [18,19]. This created a large gap between models on which countermeasures against backdoor attacks were being tested and DNNs that were being actually deployed in real-world scenarios. In this work, we take a step to bridge this gap.

Specifically, in this work, we consider Neural Cleanse [2] (described in Sect. 3). Neural Cleanse is a popular and representative backdoor attack mitigation algorithm, aimed towards identifying and mitigating backdoor attacks in DNNs. Neural cleanse provides a mechanism to detect backdoor attacks and then provide heuristics (based on *unlearning*) to update the DNN and undo the effect of a trigger. In previous work, Neural Cleanse has been tested on CNN models like VGG-16 and Resnet-101 [1], but there is no work on experimenting with the robustness of Neural Cleanse on self-attention-based networks or a hybrid of the two. These newer models are the state of the art models and created revolution in terms of inference accuracy in practical tasks. Thus, pertaining to the huge popularity of these models, it is necessary to understand if these models can be protected against backdoor attacks, e.g., via Neural Cleanse—we focus on DNN models used in computer visions or vision models. To that end, we ask the following questions in this work in progress:

1. Can backdoor attacks be successfully launched against newer self-attention based or hybrid architectures?
2. Does mitigation strategy like Neural Cleanse works on self-attention-based and hybrid vision models? Why or why not?

We address these two questions using extensive experimentation. We re-implemented Neural Cleanse into pytorch and launched the attacks on a number of models ranging from pure convolution-based models like ResNet-18 to pure Self-Attention based models like ConVit, trained on two popular datasets, wiz. GTSRB (German Traffic Signal Recognition Benchmark) [20] and CIFAR-10[1]. Our results show that backdoor attacks indeed work on both older CNN models as well as newer self-attention based or hybrid architectures. However, Neural Cleanse is significantly less effective on mitigating backdoor attack on newer models. Our analysis further reveal potential reasons behind this discrepancy and identify a path forward. Next, we will start with describing related works for our study.

2 Related Work

Attacks on Deep Learning Models: A large amount of research has been conducted on different types of attacks on Machine Learning models. These attacks can be broadly classified into three categories Integrity attacks [21–23, 28,30], Availability attacks [24,25], and Privacy attacks [26]. There are also class of attacks like model-reuse attacks which exploits the fact that deep learning models can be reused to perform tasks they were not trained for [6]. Backdoor attacks are a type of integrity attack in which training data is poisoned with triggers and changing their label to a particular target class. There is a vast literature on how backdoor attacks can be conducted on DNNs. Some different types of backdoor attacks on DNNs are Outsourcing attacks, and Pretrained attacks [3]. Outsourcing attacks are older forms of backdoor attack, where the attacker has access to the training of models [5,27]. The model can efficiently learn the attacker-chosen backdoor sub-task and its main task at the same. Many variants of outsourcing attacks have been identified by the community in the past. Other examples of outsourcing attacks include dynamic trigger attacks and backdoor reinforcement learning attacks [3]. Pretrained attack is usually mounted via a transfer learning scenario, where the user is limited with few data or/and computational resources to train an accurate model. Therefore, the user will use a public or third-party pretrained model to extract general features. Examples of such backdoors are Trojan attacks and badnets [5,29].

---

[1] https://www.cs.toronto.edu/~kriz/cifar.html.

Mitigation of Backdoor Attack on Deep Learning Models: Counter-measures against backdoors can be largely classified into four categories wiz Blind Backdoor removal, Offline Data Inspection, Offline Model Inspection and Online Input Inspection. Blind backdoor removal methods can be differentiated from other methods based on fact that it does not differentiate backdoored model from a clean model, or clean input from input with trigger. Some methods falling under this class of countermeasures are Fine Pruning [7], Suppression [9], Februus [8], ConFoc [10] and RAB [11]. These methods prove to be effective for backdoored models but when applied on clean models, performance of models tend to decrease. Offline Data Inspection works on strong assumption that defenders have access to the poisoned data. A few methods falling under this class include Spectral Signature, Gradient Clustering, Activation Clustering, Deep k-NN, SCAn and differential privacy [31,32]. These countermeasures are mostly based on clustering algorithms and fail to work effectively in case of special scaling-based backdoor attacks. Offline Model inspections tend to avoid assumptions made by data inspection methods; hence these are more suitable for countering attacks resulting from various attacking surfaces. Methods falling under these classes are Trigger Reverse Engineer, NeuronInspect, DeepInspect, AEGIS, Meta Classifier and Neural Cleanse [2]. These methods generally require high computational overhead and can't deal with large triggers, especially those aiming to reverse engineer the trigger. Online inspection methods can also be applied to monitor the behaviour of either the model or input during run-time.

Research Gap: We found very less amount of literature on the evaluation of the robustness of the Neural Cleanse algorithm [2], especially on modern-day models like ConVit, ViT and DeiT. Work which most closely resembles our work is [1], in which authors compared the performance of various countermeasures mainly on convolution-based models like Resnet-18 and VGG19. To the best of our knowledge, we could not find any work analysing whether self-attention-based computer vision models can be backdoored. In this work, we tried to perform backdoor attacks on self-attention-based and hybrid models, followed by testing the performance of Neural cleanse on such models. Model architectures considered in our study include Resnet-18, ConVit, ViT, DeiT and compact transformer. Our exploration identify that Neural Cleanse does not work well on self-attention based models and hint at a potential reason. For these newer architectures, a mitigation strategy should consider *patches* instead of neurons. Next section describes the methodology of our exploration.

3   Methodology

In this work, we examined the potential of backdoor attack and efficacy of the defense (Neural Cleanse). To that end, we experimented with a variety of models on the GTSRB (German Traffic Signal Recognition) and CIFAR-10 datasets. The models considered in the experimentation phase can be broadly classified into three categories completely convolution-based visual models, completely Self-Attention based visual models and hybrid Models. We start first with a description of these models and then provide an overview of Neural Cleanse along with the attack model, that we followed in this work.

3.1 Computer Vision Models - Preliminaries

Convolution Neural Network: A Convolutional neural network (CNN) is a neural network that has one or more convolutional layers. In our experiments, we primarily focused on a 6-layer CNN network and Resnet-18 to carry out our experiments. ResNet-18 is a convolutional neural network that is 18 layers deep. Skip connections or shortcuts are used to jump over some layers.

Self-attention Based Models: The increasing popularity of transformers in NLP has led to the development of visual models based only on the attention mechanism, completely removing convolution layers. In these Self-Attention based models at first, input images are divided into nonoverlapping patches before embedding them into a multidimensional space. In the context of attention-based models like the Vision Transformer (ViT) [18] and Data-efficient Image Transformer (DeiT) [19], the image patches are also referred to as "tokens". These patches are then treated as individual elements, allowing the model to process them separately and perform attention mechanisms over them.

ViT stands for Vision Transformer. The standard Transformer receives as input a 1D sequence of token embeddings. To handle 2D images, image $x \in R^{H \times W \times C}$ is reshaped into a sequence of flattened 2D patches $x_p \in R^{N \times (P^2 C)}$, where (H, W) is the resolution of the original image, C is the number of channels, (P, P) is the resolution of each image patch, and $N = HW/P^2$ is the resulting number of patches, which also serves as the effective input sequence length for the Transformer. The output of this patch projection is referred to as embeddings.

DeiT stands for Data-efficient Image Transformer. A Data-Efficient Image Transformer is a type of Vision Transformer for image classification tasks. The model is trained using a teacher-student strategy specific to transformers. It relies on a distillation token, ensuring that the student learns from the teacher through attention. The architecture is similar to that of ViT, but it can be trained in much less time than compared to ViT.

Hybrid Models: While pure self-attention-based models provide high accuracy, their data-hungry nature while training puts a bottleneck to their usability. To eliminate such constraints, hybrid models are developed, which have convolution and self-attention layers. In past studies, it has been identified that the first few convolution layers, followed by self-attention layers, enhance the performance of visual models on classification tasks and also reduce the amount of data required to train the model. One such hybrid model is the Compact transformer [34]. Initially, features in the image are identified using convolution layers which are later processed using a transformer encoder. Another hybrid model considered in our study is ConVit [35], which stands for Convolution-like Vision Transformer.

3.2 Setting up Neural Cleanse

Attack Model: Attack models considered by the algorithm are BadNets [5] and Trojan Attack [36]. BadNets is a backdoor attack methodology in which the adversary has access to the training data, and the same trigger is added to the input data points irrespective of the input. In contrast, in Trojan attacks, the trigger is engineered based on the infected model. Both attack models poison the model during its training phase. Neural cleanse assume that the defender has access to trained DNNs, a set of clean samples to test the performance of the model, and access to computational resources to test or modify DNNs.

Backdoor Detection Phase: The fundamental premise of backdoor detection is that, compared to other uninfected labels, the target label might be incorrectly classified as an infected model with considerably smaller adjustments. Therefore, we repeatedly go through all of the model's labels to see whether any may be misclassified with a lower amount of alteration. The three stages below make up our whole method.

- **Step 1:** For a given label, it treats it as a potential target label of a targeted backdoor attack. An optimization scheme is designed to find the "minimal" trigger required to misclassify all samples from other labels into this target label. In the vision domain, this trigger defines the smallest collection of pixels and its associated colour intensities to cause misclassification.
- **Step 2:** Step 1 is repeated for each output label in the model. For a model with $N = |L|$ labels, this produces N potential "triggers".
- **Step 3:** After coming up with N potential triggers, the size of each trigger is measured by the number of pixels each trigger candidate has, i.e. how many pixels the trigger is replacing. Finally, it runs an outlier detection algorithm to detect if any trigger candidate is significantly smaller than other candidates.

Mitigation of Backdoor Attack Phase: After the detection of a backdoor in the model, multiple approaches are proposed to mitigate the backdoor. The first approach involves filtering inputs with a trigger by analysing neural activations. The second approach involves updating DNN via neuron pruning, i.e. removing those neurons that produce strong activations in the presence of triggers. We primarily focus on a third approach which involves updating DNN via unlearning.

Updating DNN via unlearning involves retraining the poisoned model with reversed engineered trigger assisting in unlearning the backdoor present in the model. The methodology involves adding triggers to randomly picked images but keeping their labels intact and then training the model on the modified dataset. For this methodology, two variants are considered, one in which retraining is done on a dataset prepared with reverse engineered trigger and another one in which the dataset is prepared with the original trigger.

Our Implementation of Neural Cleanse: We used the implementation of the Neural cleanse provided in the actual paper[2] and re-implemented it in the Pytorch framework. To ease the understandability of the code, we created a module for the injection of the model (one illustration of trigger injection is shown in Fig. 1), which first trains the model on the clean dataset and then performs *pretrained backdoor attack* by finetuning the model with poisoned input. This is followed by the module for the detection of a backdoor in the model, which also constructs the reverse-engineered trigger.

  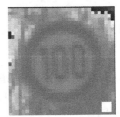

Fig. 1. Image on left shows the original image from the dataset, the image in the middle shows the trigger added to the image, and rightmost image shows poisoned input image

After constructing the reverse-engineered trigger, we updated the DNN by unlearning the model, which uses both the original trigger and reverse-engineered trigger. Both of the triggers are used in the process because it provides us with a heuristic to measure the quality of reverse engineered trigger.

4   Efficacy of Backdoor Attack and Attack Mitigation on Newer Models

We experimented with Neural Cleanse on different types of models. To test the performance of neural cleanse in the identification of a backdoor in the model, we logged the results in Table 2 and Table 4. Finally, to check the quality of reverse engineering, we applied the neural updating method by unlearning introduced in the paper. The results have been presented in Tables 3 and 5.

4.1   Backdoor Attack Success on Newer Architectures

In our experiments, we found that the backdoor attack injection was successful. This can be inferred from Table 3 where the drop of accuracy on clean samples was very low, but the accuracy for inputs with trigger was very high. This trend is consistent across all models, with slightly low accuracy for compact transformers.

---

[2] https://github.com/bolunwang/backdoor.

Table 1. AI (Anomaly Index) and norm of mask for target class found in case of different models

Models	GTSRB		CIFAR-10	
	AI	TargetNorm	AI	TargetNorm
6 layer CNN	2.89	0.51	2.17	0.67
Resnet - 18	2.18	0.78	3.09	0.73
DeiT	Classified wrong	0.73/0.79	1.31	0.67
ViT	Classified wrong	0.81/0.819	1.71	0.85
Convit	2.21	0.68	2.21	0.73
Compact Transformer	2.45	0.76	2.75	0.71

The confidence of Neural Cleanse about the presence of a backdoor in a model is conveyed by the value of AI (Anomaly Index), which represents the amount by which minimum mask size varies from the median value. The AI obtained in experiments has been presented in Table 1. Neural Cleanse detected wrong class in self attention based models like DeiT and ViT.

4.2 Efficacy of Neural Cleanse for Identifying Backdoors

In our experiments, we found that neural cleanse worked well in the case of pure convolution-based models like CNN and Resnet-18.

Table 2. Table showing performance of neural cleanse for backdoor identification; Accuracy of different models on GTSRB dataset, in different scenarios; Accuracy1 - Accuracy of infected models on clean samples; Accuracy2 - Accuracy of the clean model on clean samples; Accuracy3 - Accuracy of the infected model on poisoned samples

Models	Accuracy 1	Accuracy 2	Accuracy 3
6 layer CNN	0.927	0.964	0.983
Resnet - 18	0.97	0.981	0.991
VIT (Finetuned)	0.973	0.979	0.993
DeiT (Finetuned)	0.977	0.983	0.987
Compact Transformer	0.961	0.981	**0.965**
Convit (Finetuned)	0.961	0.98	0.991

Table 3. Table showing performance of neural cleanse for backdoor identification; Accuracy of different models on CIFAR-10 dataset, in different scenarios; Accuracy1 - Accuracy of infected models on clean samples; Accuracy2 - Accuracy of the clean model on clean samples; Accuracy3 - Accuracy of the infected model on poisoned samples

Models	Accuracy 1	Accuracy 2	Accuracy 3
6 layer CNN	0.934	0.965	0.987
Resnet - 18	0.974	0.984	0.991
VIT	0.973	0.984	0.983
DeiT	0.977	0.987	0.984
Compact Transformer	0.972	0.99	0.975
Convit (Finetuned)	0.961	0.98	0.991

Tables 2 and 3 show the quality of backdoor injection in models. We can see that there is a slight drop in the accuracy of models when tested on clean samples, but for poisoned samples, a significant proportion of inputs are classified as the target class. This tends to be in line with results presented in past literature. The accuracy of the infected model on poisoned inputs is slightly less, showing the attack's smaller success in the GTSRB dataset.

One interesting observation in our experiment was that on GTSRB dataset, neural cleanse failed to identify the correct target class for both self-attention models. This was due to a minor size difference obtained between the norm of the mask with the target class and some other classes. Also, in the case of using CIFAR-10 dataset, these two models have low Anomaly Index (AI).

4.3   Quality of Reverse Engineered Trigger Created by Neural Cleanse

The reversed engineered trigger has been shown in Fig. 2. The trigger for ResNet-18 is more visually similar to the original trigger than the trigger for ViT. To test

Table 4. Table showing performance of neural cleanse for backdoor identification; Accuracy of different models on GTSRB dataset, in different scenarios; Accuracy1 - Accuracy of model cleaned using reverse engineered trigger; Accuracy2 - Accuracy of model cleaned using original trigger; Accuracy3 - clean model on clean samples

Models	Accuracy 1	Accuracy 2	Accuracy 3
6 layer CNN	0.935	0.89	0.964
Resnet - 18	0.946	0.94	0.981
Deit	**0.853**	0.94	0.987
ViT	**0.871**	0.96	0.993
Convit	0.913	0.972	0.991
Compact Transformer	**0.74**	0.95	0.981

Table 5. Table showing performance of neural cleanse for backdoor identification; Accuracy of different models on CIFAR-10 dataset, in different scenarios; Accuracy1 - Accuracy of model cleaned using reverse engineered trigger; Accuracy2 - Accuracy of model cleaned using original trigger; Accuracy3 - clean model on clean samples

Models	Accuracy 1	Accuracy 2	Accuracy 3
6 layer CNN	0.947	0.941	0.965
Resnet - 18	0.951	0.956	0.984
DeiT	**0.893**	0.961	0.984
ViT	**0.875**	0.954	0.987
Convit	0.923	0.948	0.990
Compact Transformer	**0.871**	0.962	0.980

Fig. 2. Image on the left shows the original trigger used to infect the model; Image in centre shows reversed engineer for ResNet-18; Rightmost image shows reversed engineered trigger for ViT

further the quality of reverse-engineered triggers, we used neural updating via the unlearning method, which mitigates the backdoor in the model by retraining the poisoned model with reverse-engineered and original triggers.

Table 5 and Table 4 show the accuracy of models after unlearning using the original trigger and reverse engineered trigger. The accuracy of the clean model on clean sample is as expected. While performing the neural updating by unlearning, we observed that accuracy after retraining with reverse engineered trigger was significantly low compared to retraining with the original trigger in the case of Pure self attention-based models showing lower quality reverse engineered trigger. The image generated by Neural Cleanse showed a similar drop in the case of the compact transformer, but the drop in the case of ConVit was not that significant. This behaviour was consistent across both datasets, showing consistency of the pattern observed. From these observations, we hypothesized that the performance of Neural cleanse declines with an increase in the self-attention behavior of the model on which it is being employed.

Finally, we investigate the reason behing these observations—why Neural Cleanse can not devise good quality reverse engineered triggers for pure self-attention networks.

5   Understanding Quality of Mitigation by Neural Cleanse

We first aim to open the black box—specifically we aim to understand the impact of the reverse engineered triggers offered by Neural Cleanse for both older CNN models as well as newer transformer model. We focus on four dimensions—amount of neurons activated by reverse trigger, type of neurons activated by reverse trigger, pace of learning across models and impact of trigger on discrete patches in images (rather than pixels).

5.1   Comparing Fraction of Activated Neurons Across Models

Network Dissection [33] from Bau et al. is a method for quantifying the interpretability of deep visual representations learned by neural networks. This work argued that while neural networks have achieved impressive performance on a variety of visual recognition tasks, the representations learned by these networks are often difficult to interpret or understand. This lack of interpretability can limit the usefulness of neural networks in real-world applications where transparency and explainability are important.

To address this problem, Bau et al. proposed a method to interpret the visual representations learned by neural networks. The method involves using semantic segmentation to identify objects in images and then measuring the activation of individual units in the neural network in response to those objects. They introduce a new metric called the "dissected unit", which measures the activation of a unit in response to a specific object. This metric can be used to quantify the degree to which a unit in the neural network is interpretable, i.e. how well it corresponds to a semantically meaningful visual concept.

The paper demonstrates the usefulness of the proposed method by applying it to several state-of-the-art neural networks trained on object recognition and scene classification tasks. The authors show that the method can be used to compare different layers in a network and to identify which layers contain more interpretable visual features. They also demonstrate that networks with higher interpretability tend to perform better on recognition tasks.

We built on network dissection to fit our purpose of studying the fraction of neurons which get activated in presence of a trigger. Since, we are using different types of models so defining neurons which we consider during this experiment becomes important for the comparison. Therefore, to maintain consistency in the comparisons, we considered outputs of all Linear and Conv2D layer neurons.

Steps of the Algorithm: The existing implementations of Network Dissection [33] are not able to handle self-attention based vision transformers and thus we step into modifying the algorithm as follows:

1. Attach forward hooks to each neuron of each convolutional layer and linear layer of the model: This step involves adding a forward hook to each neuron in every convolutional and linear layer of the neural network model. A forward hook is a function that is executed every time the output of a neuron is computed during a forward pass through the network. By attaching forward hooks to each neuron, we can log the activation of each neuron during the forward pass.

2. Log activation of all hooked neuron activations in absence of trigger: After attaching the forward hooks, we log the activation of each hooked neuron in the absence of any trigger. This means that we simply run the input data through the network and record the activation of each neuron as it is computed.

3. Log activation of all hooked neuron activations in presence of trigger. Next, we log the activation of each hooked neuron in the presence of a trigger. The trigger selectively activates certain neurons and this step enables us to observe how they respond to the input contaminated with the trigger.

Table 6. Percentage of neurons activated due to the presence of original and reverse engineered trigger in the input.

Presence of poison in model	Type of Trigger	6-layer CNN	Resnet	Compact Transformer	ConVit	ViT	DeiT
Poisoned Model	Reverse Eng	27.56	25.56	23.52	27.45	26.84	24.65
Poisoned Model	Original	31.25	30.14	27.56	29.56	34.25	30.47
Clean Model	Reverse Eng	31.25	30.14	27.56	29.56	34.25	30.47
Clean Model	Original	34.25	32.62	31.52	30.52	35.62	32.52

4. Final result is percentage of neurons whose activation has increased more than a threshold: We compare the activation of each neuron in each model in the absence and presence of the trigger and calculate the percentage of neurons whose activation has increased more than a certain threshold. This threshold is typically set to a small percentage of the maximum possible activation value, such as 1% or 5%.

Neurons that meet this criterion are considered to be "triggered" by the trigger pattern. By measuring the percentage of triggered neurons, we can estimate the susceptibility of the network to adversarial attacks. The percentage of neurons activated in each model have been summarized in Table 6. These results showed no significant difference in these models.

5.2 Comparing Importance of Activated Neurons Across Models

With no discerning pattern in the above experiment, we went ahead to see if the same set of neurons as in the previous experiment are getting activated across the models in the presence of *reverse engineered* trigger as well.

Neuron Importance: In this case, following Neural Cleanse, we defined neuron importance. Neuron importance refers to ranking of neurons based on activation due to presence of a trigger in the input to the poisoned model. The higher the activation, lower the rank and hence, the neuron has higher importance.

Steps in the Algorithm: The steps involved in the experiment include:

1. **Attach forward hooks to each neuron of each layer:** Similar to the previous experiment, this step involves adding a forward hook to each neuron in every layer of the neural network model.
2. **Rank neurons according to activation due to presence of original trigger:** After attaching the forward hooks, we first inject original trigger

pattern to the input data and record the activation of each neuron in the presence of the trigger. We then rank the neurons according to their activation levels in response to the trigger. Neurons that exhibit high activation levels in response to the trigger are considered to be important for the network's response to the input.

3. Rank neurons according to activation due to presence of reverse engineered trigger: Next, we inject the reverse engineered trigger pattern to the input data and record the activation of each neuron in the presence of the trigger. We then rank the neurons according to their activation levels in response to the trigger. This step helps us understand how the network responds to reverse engineered trigger and which neurons are identified by Neural Cleanse as being poisoned.

Having identified the neurons most activated by original and reverse engineered trigger, we used precision@k metric to compare the two ranked lists. Precision@k is a commonly used metric for evaluating the performance of recommendation systems and information retrieval systems. It measures the proportion of relevant items that are included in the top k results recommended or retrieved by the system. The metric is particularly useful when the number of recommended or retrieved items is large, as it allows for a finer-grained evaluation of the system's performance.

Finally, to have a better understanding of the results, we divided the training period of Neural Cleanse into three phases. If the model takes 30 epochs to learn reverse engineered trigger, we define phase-1 as the first 10 epochs by which one-third of the training is roughly completed. Phase-2 comprises of the period till two-third of training is complete (20 epochs). Finally, phase-3 lasts till the training is complete. Also, since the models used differ largely in terms of number of neurons we chose a range of values of k instead of fixing to a single value of k.

Table 7. Precision@K for the phase-1 of training period.

Model	K = 10	K = 100	K = 1000	K = 10,000	K = 50,000	K = 100,000
6-Layer CNN	0.3	0.54	0.57	0.53	0.61	**0.62**
Resnet	0.1	0.39	0.42	0.52	0.54	0.51
Compact Transformer	0.0	0.05	0.13	0.19	0.15	0.15
ConVit	**0.0**	**0.14**	**0.12**	**0.21**	**0.26**	**0.21**
ViT	**0.1**	**0.11**	**0.17**	**0.24**	**0.21**	**0.27**
DeiT	0.0	0.09	0.19	0.15	0.25	0.23

The results of this experiment are shown in Tables 7, 8 and 9. CNN achieved very high precision for the first phase of training only, and it improved further.

Table 8. Precision@K for the phase-2 of training period.

Model	K = 10	K = 100	K = 1000	K = 10,000	K = 50,000	K = 100,000
6-Layer CNN	0.3	**0.52**	0.51	0.57	**0.63**	**0.59**
Resnet	0.1	0.41	0.47	0.51	0.58	0.51
Compact Transformer	**0.1**	**0.07**	**0.14**	**0.17**	**0.21**	**0.24**
ConVit	0.0	0.19	0.16	0.24	0.27	0.31
ViT	**0.0**	**0.15**	**0.17**	**0.14**	**0.24**	**0.26**
DeiT	0.0	0.12	0.16	0.24	0.31	0.27

Table 9. Precision@K for the phase-3 of training period.

Model	K = 10	K = 100	K = 1000	K = 10,000	K = 50,000	K = 100,000
6-Layer CNN	0.6	**0.59**	0.61	0.53	**0.57**	**0.59**
Resnet	0.2	0.45	0.42	0.41	0.53	**0.56**
Compact Transformer	**0.0**	**0.14**	**0.19**	**0.24**	**0.28**	**0.34**
ConVit	0.1	0.17	0.24	0.21	0.27	0.29
ViT	**0.0**	**0.15**	**0.19**	**0.21**	**0.29**	**0.31**
DeiT	0.2	0.24	0.21	0.31	0.27	0.34

Also, the important thing to note is that it has a very high precision value for smaller values of k, meaning that neural cleanse successfully identifies poisoned neurons in the case of the CNN model. Resnet model depicted similar nature to 6-layer CNN, but it had slightly lower precision values compared to the CNN model. Compact transformer and ConVit showed very low precision values in the first two training phases, and eventually, they covered up in the last phase. Also, both of these models have very small precision values for small values of k, and they increase eventually, showing that the Neural cleanse failed to correctly identify the right neurons, which are affected most by the backdoor injection. Self-Attention based models show similar nature to the hybrid models, but they show an interesting trend in that they have lower precision during initial phases of model training, but they eventually get higher value compared to the hybrid model. From this, we inferred that learning the most affected neurons in newer models is a slower process compared to older models. Also, they have low precision values for smaller values of k, just like hybrid models.

5.3 Comparing Pace of Learning Across Models

Finally, we quantitatively check if self-attention-based models learn the reverse-engineered trigger. Through this experiment, we wanted to see if all the models learned the reverse-engineered trigger at the same pace.

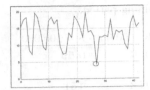 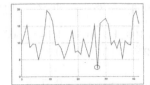 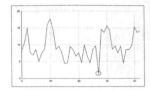

Fig. 3. Figure on left shows minimum norm(y-axis) vs Class label(x-axis) plot at the end of first phase of training for 6-layer CNN. Figure on middle shows minimum norm(y-axis) vs Class label(x-axis) plot at the end of second phase of training for 6-layer CNN. Figure right shows minimum norm(y-axis) vs Class label(x-axis) at the end of training process for 6-layer CNN.

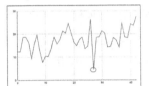 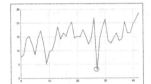 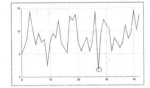

Fig. 4. Figure on left shows minimum norm(y-axis) vs Class label(x-axis) plot at the end of first phase of training for ConVit. Figure on middle shows minimum norm(y-axis) vs Class label(x-axis) plot at the end of second phase of training for ConVit. Figure right shows minimum norm(y-axis) vs Class label(x-axis) at the end of training process for ConVit.

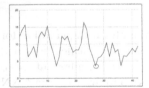 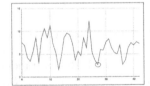 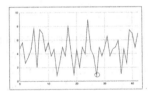

Fig. 5. Figure on left shows minimum norm(y-axis) vs Class label(x-axis) plot at the end of first phase of training for ViT. Figure on middle shows minimum norm(y-axis) vs Class label(x-axis) plot at the end of second phase of training for ViT. Figure below shows minimum norm(y-axis) vs Class label(x-axis) at the end of training process for ViT.

We divided the period of running of Neural Cleanse, i.e., the number of epochs required by Neural Cleanse to learn the reverse-engineered trigger, into multiple phases. Dividing the running period into multiple phases helps monitor the optimisation's progress. We log the minimum norm of activations for each class at the end of each phase. The norm refers to the magnitude of the weight vector of the reverse-engineered trigger for each class. The minimum norm represents the minimum value of the norm achieved during the optimization process for a particular class. By logging the minimum norm at the end of each phase, we can track the progress of the optimization and determine whether the algorithm is converging to a good solution. This logging helped us also to quantify the pace at which the model is learning the reverse-engineered trigger. Also, to study the pace, we have divided the training phase into 3 phases similar to the previous experiment.

To understand the generated results visually, we plotted the minimum norm for each class in all three phases (Figs. 3, 4 and 5). Through this, we concluded the following points:

- CNNs learn the reverse-engineered trigger very early in the training process, and the target class trigger has a significantly lower norm than other classes at all phases of training.
- Hybrid models have a relatively slower learning process than CNNs. For our set of hyperparameters for ConVit, we also noticed that eventually, another class which is not visually similar to the target class gains a very small norm which is still more than the norm of the target class.
- Self-attention-based models have an even slower pace of learning than hybrid models. In both ViT and DeiT, we also noticed that there are multiple classes with very low minimum norms, and some even have lower norms than the target class, leading to misclassification of the target class by Neural Cleanse.

5.4 A Way Forward for Protecting Transformer Models: Focussing on Patches Instead of Pixels

Since the defenses which were applicable for earlier models is not quite effective for self-attention based models, we finally, check what is the key difference between how the self-attention based and old models work. Self-attention based image models revolutionize the way we process visual data by breaking images into discrete patches. This approach is notably different from traditional DNNs, which operate seamlessly on pixel-level data. The implications of this difference are profound. In traditional DNNs, backdoor triggers are often discernible at the pixel level, enabling Neural Cleanse to identify and mitigate them effectively. However, in self-attention models, the patching system introduces a layer of abstraction. This abstraction can effectively camouflage backdoor triggers within the patches, rendering them far less conspicuous to conventional detection methods. Moreover, the non-overlapping nature of patches means that a backdoor trigger can be distributed across multiple patches, making it challenging for Neural Cleanse to identify coherent patterns that indicate a backdoor's presence. This patch-based processing obscures the direct relationship between trigger and output, further complicating the detection process.

Neural Cleanse heavily relied on the reverse engineering of backdoor triggers which are identifiable at pixel level. In the context of self-attention-based image models, this step becomes a formidable challenge due to the unique characteristics of the triggers, Triggers generated in these models tend to be highly nuanced and subtle, often resembling legitimate features of the data.

A Proof of Concept for Potential Effectiveness of Patch-Centric Approach: As a very preliminary test, we compared the Euclidean distances between the original trigger and the CNN-reverse-engineered trigger (0.014) versus the original trigger and the VIT-reverse-engineered trigger (0.023). the former exhibited a more pronounced resemblance, potentially resulting in better performing reverse triggers. This observation leads us to hypothesize that triggers may be generated on a patchwise basis within self-attention based models. Thus, our results hint that, Neural Cleanse's reliance on reverse engineering based on identification of specific, distinguishable trigger patterns resulted in its ineffectiveness to protect self-attention models. In self-attention models, these patterns become intricately intertwined with the natural structure of the data, making it arduous to isolate and categorize them accurately.

6 Concluding Discussion

In this work in progress, we aimed to study the robustness of Neural Cleanse on different models when they face backdoor attacks. We experimented by attacking CNN, ResNet-18, ConVit, Compact Transformer, ViT and DeiT on GTSRB and CIFAR-10 dataset. We further used Neural Cleanse to detect and mitigate attacks on all cases. Through the set of models, we aimed to cover pure convolution-based models, pure self-attention-based vision models and hybrid models. To test the quality of reverse engineered trigger, we used Neural Patching using unlearning, which involves retraining of model with reverse engineered trigger and original trigger to mitigate the backdoor present in the model.

Through our experiments, we found that while backdoor attacks could be successfully applied on newer self-attention based models, the neural cleanse method failed to correctly identify the target class in the case of pure self-attention-based models like ViT and DeiT for the GTSRB dataset. In fact, in the case of CIFAR-10 dataset, the AI index (which shows the confidence of algorithm about the presence of backdoor) was very low compared to other models. The performance drop of the model in the case of retraining with reverse engineered trigger was found to be significantly higher in the case of ViT, DeiT and compact transformer.

Finally, we designed experiments to understand the varying efficacy of Neural Cleanse on observed anomalies. Specifically, we studied neural activation due to the presence of original and reverse-engineered triggers in different models. We also studied the pace of learning of reverse-engineered triggers for different models. Our experiments found that even though there was no significant difference in overall neural activations in all models by either the original or reverse-engineered trigger, the reverse-engineered trigger identified the most poisoned neurons in the case of CNNs but failed drastically for models with self-attention layers. We also noticed that the presence of a self-attention layer slowed down the process of learning reverse-engineered triggers. Our results finally hint that the patching mechanism in the Self-attention model can be the potential reason for this phenomenon. Our results pave the way to more robust and principled backdoor attack mitigation for self-attention based newer vision models.

References

1. Qiu, H., et al.: Towards a critical evaluation of robustness for deep learning backdoor countermeasures (2022). arXiv:abs/2204.06273
2. Wang, B., et al.: Neural cleanse: identifying and mitigating backdoor attacks in neural networks. In: 2019 IEEE Symposium on Security and Privacy (SP), pp. 707–723 (2019)
3. Gao, Y., et al.: Backdoor attacks and countermeasures on deep learning: a comprehensive review (2020). arXiv:abs/2007.10760
4. Liu, Y., Xie, Y., Srivastava, A.: Neural trojans. In: 2017 IEEE International Conference on Computer Design (ICCD), pp. 45–48 (2017)
5. Gu, T., Dolan-Gavitt, B., Garg, S.: BadNets: identifying vulnerabilities in the machine learning model supply chain. arXiv preprint: arXiv:1708.06733 (2017)
6. Ji, Y., Zhang, X., Ji, S., Luo, X., Wang, T.: Model-reuse attacks on deep learning systems. In: Proceedings of the 2018 ACM SIGSAC Conference on Computer and Communications Security (2018)
7. Liu, K., Dolan-Gavitt, B., Garg, S.: Fine-Pruning: defending against backdooring attacks on deep neural networks. RAID (2018)
8. Doan, B.G., Abbasnejad, E., Ranasinghe, D.C.: Februus: input purification defense against trojan attacks on deep neural network systems. In: Annual Computer Security Applications Conference (2020)
9. Sarkar, E., Alkindi, Y., Maniatakos, M.: Backdoor suppression in neural networks using input fuzzing and majority voting. IEEE Des. Test **37**, 103–110 (2020)
10. Villarreal-Vasquez, M., Bhargava, B.K.: ConFoc: content-focus protection against trojan attacks on neural networks (2020). arXiv:abs/2007.00711
11. Weber, M., Xu, X., Karlas, B., Zhang, C., Li, B.: RAB: provable robustness against backdoor attacks (2020). arXiv:abs/2003.08904
12. Chernikova, A., Oprea, A., Nita-Rotaru, C., Kim, B.: Are self-driving cars secure? Evasion attacks against deep neural networks for steering angle prediction. In: 2019 IEEE Security and Privacy Workshops (SPW), pp. 132–137 (2019)
13. Wang, Q., et al.: Adversary resistant deep neural networks with an application to malware detection. In: Proceedings of the 23rd ACM SIGKDD International Conference on Knowledge Discovery and Data Mining (2017)
14. Debar, H., Becker, M., Siboni, D.: A neural network component for an intrusion detection system. In: Proceedings 1992 IEEE Computer Society Symposium on Research in Security and Privacy, pp. 240–250 (1992)
15. Wierzynski, C.: The challenges and opportunities of explainable AI (2018). https://ai.intel.com/the-challenges-and-opportunities-of-explainable-ai
16. FICO's explainable machine learning challenge (2018). https://community.fico.com/s/explainable-machine-learning-challenge
17. Vaswani, A., et al.: Attention is all you need (2017). arXiv:abs/1706.03762
18. Dosovitskiy, A., et al.: An image is worth 16x16 words: transformers for image recognition at scale (2021). arXiv:abs/2010.11929
19. Touvron, H., Cord, M., Douze, M., Massa, F., Sablayrolles, A., J'egou, H.: Training data-efficient image transformers & distillation through attention. ICML (2021)
20. Stallkamp, J., Schlipsing, M., Salmen, J., Igel, C.: The German traffic sign recognition benchmark: a multi-class classification competition. In: Proceedings of the International Joint Conference on Neural Networks, pp. 1453–1460 (2011). https://doi.org/10.1109/IJCNN.2011.6033395

21. Saha, A., Subramanya, A., Pirsiavash, H.: Hidden trigger backdoor attacks (2020). arXiv:abs/1910.00033
22. Ayub, M.A., Johnson, W.A., Talbert, D.A., Siraj, A.: Model evasion attack on intrusion detection systems using adversarial machine learning. In: 2020 54th Annual Conference on Information Sciences and Systems (CISS), pp. 1–6 (2020)
23. Jagielski, M., Severi, G., Harger, N.P., Oprea, A.: Subpopulation data poisoning attacks. In: Proceedings of the 2021 ACM SIGSAC Conference on Computer and Communications Security (2021)
24. Zhou, X., Xu, M., Wu, Y., Zheng, N.: Deep model poisoning attack on federated learning. Future Internet 13, 73 (2021)
25. Shapira, A., Zolfi, A., Demetrio, L., Biggio, B., Shabtai, A.: Denial-of-service attack on object detection model using universal adversarial perturbation (2022). arXiv:abs/2205.13618
26. Shokri, R., Stronati, M., Song, C., Shmatikov, V.: Membership inference attacks against machine learning models. In: 2017 IEEE Symposium on Security and Privacy (SP), pp. 3–18 (2017)
27. Chen, X., Liu, C., Li, B., Lu, K., Song, D.: Targeted backdoor attacks on deep learning systems using data poisoning. arXiv preprint: arXiv:1712.05526 (2017)
28. Li, Y., Li, Y., Wu, B., Li, L., He, R., Lyu, S.: Invisible backdoor attack with sample-specific triggers. In: 2021 IEEE/CVF International Conference on Computer Vision (ICCV), pp. 16443–16452 (2021)
29. Guo, W., Wang, L., Xu, Y., Xing, X., Du, M., Song, D.: Towards inspecting and eliminating trojan backdoors in deep neural networks. In: 2020 IEEE International Conference on Data Mining (ICDM), pp. 162–171. IEEE (2020)
30. Chan, A., Ong, Y.S.: Poison as a cure: detecting & neutralizing variable-sized backdoor attacks in deep neural networks. arXiv preprint: arXiv:1911.08040 (2019)
31. Xiang, Z., Miller, D.J., Kesidis, G.: A benchmark study of backdoor data poisoning defenses for deep neural network classifiers and a novel defense. In: 2019 IEEE 29th International Workshop on Machine Learning for Signal Processing (MLSP). IEEE, pp. 1–6 (2019)
32. Tran, B., Li, J., Madry, A.: Spectral signatures in backdoor attacks. In: Advances in Neural Information Processing Systems (NIPS), pp. 8000–8010 (2018). https://github.com/MadryLab/backdoordatapoisoning
33. Bau, D., Zhou, B., Khosla, A., Oliva, A., Torralba, A.: Network dissection: quantifying interpretability of deep visual representations. In Proceedings of the IEEE Conference on Computer Vision and Pattern Recognition, pp. 6541–6549 (2017)
34. Hassani, A., Walton, S., Shah, N., Abuduweili, A., Li, J., Shi, H.: Escaping the big data paradigm with compact transformers. arXiv preprint: arXiv:2104.05704
35. d'Ascoli, S., Touvron, H., Leavitt, M.L., Morcos, A.S., Biroli, G., Sagun, L.: ConViT: improving vision transformers with soft convolutional inductive biases. In: International Conference on Machine Learning, pp. 2286–2296. PMLR (2021)
36. Tang, R., Du, M., Liu, N., Yang, F., Hu, X.: An embarrassingly simple approach for trojan attack in deep neural networks. In: Proceedings of the 26th ACM SIGKDD International Conference on Knowledge Discovery & data mining, pp. 218–228 (2020)

Author Index

© The Editor(s) (if applicable) and The Author(s), under exclusive license
to Springer Nature Switzerland AG 2024
F. Regazzoni et al. (Eds.): SPACE 2023, LNCS 14412, p. 261, 2024.
https://doi.org/10.1007/978-3-031-51583-5

Printed in the United States
by Baker & Taylor Publisher Services